Stress Testing: Approaches, Methods and Applications

Stress Testing: Approaches, Methods and Applications

Edited by Akhtar Siddique and Iftekhar Hasan

Published by Risk Books, a Division of Incisive Media Investments Ltd

Incisive Media
32–34 Broadwick Street
London W1A 2HG
Tel: +44(0) 20 7316 9000
E-mail: books@incisivemedia.com
Sites: www.riskbooks.com
　　　www.incisivemedia.com

© 2013 Incisive Media
1007347614
ISBN 978-1-78272-008-9
British Library Cataloguing in Publication Data
A catalogue record for this book is available from the British Library

Publisher: Nick Carver
Editorial Development: Amy Jordan
Commissioning Editor: Sarah Hastings
Managing Editor: Lewis O'Sullivan
Designer: Lisa Ling

Copy-edited by Laurie Donaldson
Typeset by Tricolour Design

Printed and bound in the UK by Berforts Group

Contents

Acknowledgements from the Editors   vii

Foreword   xi

About the Editors   xv

About the Authors   xvii

Introduction   xxv
Akhtar Siddique; Iftekhar Hasan
Office of the Comptroller of Currency; Fordham University

1 Governance over Stress Testing   1
David E. Palmer
Federal Reserve Board

2 Stress Testing and Other Risk-Management Tools   15
Akhtar Siddique; Iftekhar Hasan
Office of the Comptroller of Currency; Fordham University

3 Stress Testing for Market Risk   25
Dilip K. Patro, Akhtar Siddique; Xian Sun
Office of the Comptroller of the Currency; Johns Hopkins University

4 The Evolution of Stress Testing Counterparty Exposures   37
David Lynch
Federal Reserve Board

5 Operational Risk: An Overview of Stress-Testing Methodologies   57
Brian Clark; Bakhodir Ergashev
Office of the Comptroller of Currency; Federal Reserve Bank of Richmond

6 Stress Testing of Bank Loan Portfolios as a Diagnostic Tool   71
Paul Calem, Arden Hall
Federal Reserve Bank of Philadelphia

7 Stress-Test Modelling for Loan Losses and Reserves   89
Michael Carhill, Jonathan Jones
Office of the Comptroller of the Currency

8 A Framework for Stress Testing Banks' Corporate Credit Portfolio   109
Olivier de Bandt, Nicolas Dumontaux, Vincent Martin, Denys Médée
Autorité de Contrôle Prudentiel (French Prudential Supervision Authority)

9 EU-Wide Stress Test: The Experience of the EBA   127
Paolo Bisio, Demelza Jurcevic and Mario Quagliariello
European Banking Authority

10 Stress Testing Across International Exposures and Activities   143
Robert Scavotto, Robert H. Skinkle
Office of the Comptroller of the Currency

11 Liquidity Risk: The Case of the Brazilian Banking System   161
Benjamin M. Tabak, Solange M. Guerra, Sergio R. S. Souza,
Rodrigo C. C. Miranda
Banco Central do Brasil

12 Determining the Severity of Macroeconomic Stress Scenarios   193
Kapo Yuen
Federal Reserve Bank of New York

Index   225

Acknowledgements from the Editors

We would like to acknowledge advice from and discussions with colleagues in various settings. Akhtar would like to acknowledge discussions with colleagues from the OCC, Federal Reserve Banks and the FDIC during examinations as well as in policy settings. Encouragement from Mark Levonian and Mike Carhill are particularly acknowledged. We would also like to thank Clayton Lamar for research assistance and help.

To the people in our lives. For Akhtar, the children in his life, Ayaan, Aahil and his nieces Babu and Putul but above all, his parents, wife: Deepa, sister: Moon, and his in-laws. For Iftekhar, his parents, parents in-law, siblings, nephews, nieces, and his spouse.

Foreword

Stress testing is a tool. It is a tool used in many fields, particularly where failure of some component of a complex system can have seriously adverse consequences and high costs: aircraft wings, highway bridges, coronary arteries.

And financial institutions.

Financial firms have long used stress testing as a tool in various aspects of financial management. Firms use stress tests to assess the impact of adverse events on various elements of the organisation, or on the organisation as a whole, to gauge their ability to absorb those stresses and carry on with core activities. Stress testing can reveal vulnerabilities and point the way to actions that reduce those vulnerabilities.

But disruptions in financial markets and continuing economic weakness around the world have focused greater attention on stress testing and its potential value. A widely acknowledged lesson of the global financial crisis was that unusually stressful events or combinations of events can and do occur, and that stress testing can help assess the potential impact of those events and guide appropriate preparation and response. Apart from its role as a tool for management, stress testing fosters a culture of conscientious attention to risk. A common theme in post-crisis discussions with senior management has been that stress testing helps create a robust dialogue around risks and risk management inside any firm.

"Stress testing" really describes a class of tools rather than a single tool. Variations in stress-testing tools – the methods – roughly match the variation in the specific ways stress testing is used – the applications. Chapters of this book highlight distinct but related aspects of stress testing in both methods and applications. Some of the chapters emphasise risk management in the areas of credit risk, market risk, operational risk, liquidity risk and others; other chapters address the role of stress testing within the broader management environment of financial firms, as well as how to ensure that stress testing remains a relevant and effective tool.

With such variety in methods and applications, it is perhaps no surprise that overall approaches to stress testing vary as well. Responsibilities for the many different aspects of stress testing may be centralised or distributed; specific management uses of the results may make sense in certain environments but not in others. There is no secret formula – many different approaches can succeed. Indeed, approaches to stress testing should be expected to vary, because stress tests add their greatest value when they are organised, executed and used in ways that take into account the unique characteristics, operating environment and management style of the firms or institutions using them.

Several chapters also address the increasingly prominent use of stress testing in the supervision and regulation of financial firms. This has been one of the most notable developments in international financial supervision over the last few years, as the renewed focus on stress testing within financial firms has been matched by a simultaneous increase in attention from the supervisory community. Financial authorities around the world have gravitated towards stress testing as a powerful way to promote the health of the firms they regulate. Institutional supervisors tend to focus on effective use of stress testing for institutional risk management, consistent with the ongoing use of stress testing as a risk-management tool. Macroprudential regulators also have recognised the potential value of stress testing, with an emphasis on financial stability applications. Several highly visible system-wide stress-testing exercises – some of which are discussed in this book – were key elements of the public-sector response to the financial crisis; they were used to assess the scope of the problems, evaluate the resiliency of large financial firms and provide transparency and assurance to financial market participants and others.

Effective stress testing relies on three major elements. First comes the selection of meaningful stresses, either hypothetical or actual scenarios, or more abstract approaches based on simulation of risk factors. Second is the translation of those stresses into the impact on the firm, or on the part of the firm subject to stress testing. And third is the assessment of the stress-testing results, the evaluation of the impact of the stress. Relevant measures of impact vary depending on the focus of a specific stress test – liquidity, earnings, credit losses, capital, financial stability – but ideally point the way towards meaningful response and action.

In scenario development, stress translation or impact assessment, stress testing remains a tool in evolution. In particular, while stress-testing practices may converge over time towards a somewhat more standard set of methods and applications, the end state is unlikely ever to evolve to a single, uniform design. This is one of those cases in which details must be tailored to the specific use; no single stress-testing methodology will be appropriate for all applications at all times.

The combination of rapid change in stress-testing methods and increased supervisory focus makes this volume especially relevant, timely and useful. The book rewards readers with comprehensive and thoughtful discussions of stress testing in its many forms, covering a broad range of real-world applications and real-world concerns, and drawing on the knowledge of an impressive set of contributors. Its emphasis on both methods and applications, combined with a consideration of multiple approaches, sets it apart from other offerings with narrower focus.

Many of the contributors are quantitative experts from across the global regulatory community. Readers anxious for insight into supervisory perspectives and expectations can find much to consider in these chapters. A window into the thinking of the supervisory community is always valuable for regulated firms. But supervisory authorship has additional value in this case. Individual financial practitioners know a great deal about practices at their own firms, but less about current approaches, methods and applications elsewhere. In such a rapidly changing field, a narrow focus on practices at any single firm can be misleading. Best practices diffuse across the industry over time, but supervisors have a unique and explicitly horizontal perspective on stress testing, combining insights from the many variations in stress-testing practices they are able to observe across the regulated financial spectrum, and speeding the recognition and adoption of best practices.

As readers consider the chapters of this book, they should not be blind to the fact that, as valuable as the stress-testing tool may be, it is still only one of many tools that can and should be used. There are other valid ways to measure or assess risk. There are also many ways to control that risk. Any tool requires the hand of a skilled user to make it effective. Ultimately, tools, even good ones, are no substitute for sound judgement based on experience. Stress testing must be intelligently applied, with expertise and insight.

With this book as a guide, both financial regulators and financial practitioners can gain insights that will help them do their jobs more effectively. If broader and more thoughtful use of stress testing reduces the impact of future stress events, then time spent with this volume will be time well spent indeed.

Mark Levonian

Senior Deputy Comptroller, US Office of the
Comptroller of the Currency
March 2013

About the Editors

Iftekhar Hasan is the E. Gerald Corrigan Chair in International Business and Finance at the Schools of Business of Fordham University, New York and concurrently serves as a scientific advisor to the Bank of Finland in Helsinki. His research focus is primarily in the areas of financial intermediation, capital market and corporate finance. He is also affiliated as a research associate at the Berkley Center of the Stern School of New York University. Hasan has held visiting positions at universities and organisations in several countries. He is the managing editor of the Journal of Financial Stability and an associate editor in several other journals. Hasan is currently the president of the Eurasia Business and Economics Society. A Fulbright Specialist Scholar, Hasan has over 250 publications in print, including 12 books and edited volumes and over 160 peer-reviewed journal articles in reputed finance, economics, management, operation research, accounting, and management information system journals. He received his PhD from the University of Houston and also received a "Doctor Honoris Causa" from the Romanian American University in Bucharest.

Akhtar Siddique is the deputy director of the Enterprise Risk Analysis Division of the US Office of the Comptroller of the Currency (OCC), where he has worked from 2003. He manages a staff of financial economists who provide technical assistance for examinations of national banks in Pillar II, operational risk, ALLL, economic capital and enterprise-wide stress testing; participate in policy initiatives; and conduct independent research. He directly participates in examinations and intra- and interagency supervisory and policy initiatives, particularly related to counterparty credit risk, economic capital, valuation issues, ALLL, stress testing and Pillar II. He has represented the OCC on the Risk Measurement Group and Interaction of Market and Credit Risk Group of the Basel Committee on Banking Supervision. He has also represented the OCC on the drafting of US interagency rules and guidance relating to stress testing, Pillar II, etc. His research has spanned financial econometrics, asset pricing, corporate finance and numerical methods. Siddique has authored numerous papers published in peer-reviewed journals including the Journal of Finance, the Review of Financial Studies, Management Science and the Journal of Accounting Research. He holds a PhD in Finance from Duke University and taught finance at Georgetown University prior to joining the OCC.

About the Authors

Paolo Bisio is a principal banks expert at the European Banking Authority. He previously served in the Secretariat of the Committee of the European Banking Supervisors and as an analyst in the Banking Supervision Department of Banca d'Italia, the Italian central bank. He has been deeply involved in the supervisory review process of the largest Italian banking groups, the validation of internal models, Pillar II topics and stress testing. In 2010, he coordinated the CEBS task forces on market and credit risks that developed the methodology for the EU-wide stress tests, and played a pivotal role in the different editions of the exercises. He holds a Master's degree in economics from the University of Rome.

Paul Calem is assistant vice president and chief of the Retail Risk Analysis section in the Supervision, Regulation, and Credit Department at the Federal Reserve Bank of Philadelphia. Previously, he was a senior economist in the Division of Banking Supervision and Regulation at the Federal Reserve Board. Calem moved into banking supervision after several years in the private sector at Freddie Mac and the mortgage data and analytics company LoanPerformance, and a prior position in the Division of Research and Statistics at the Federal Reserve Board. He has a PhD in economics from Brown University and a BA in mathematics from Duke University. His current responsibilities include implementing annual supervisory stress testing of large banks' retail portfolios; quantitative support of bank examinations; and policy analysis and research.

Mike Carhill has, since 2003, served as a director in the Risk Analysis Division (RAD) of the US Office of the Comptroller of the Currency (OCC). RAD employs quantitative modelling experts who specialise in one or another of about a dozen lines of business to advise bank examiners, bankers and policymakers on the state-of-the-art in risk-management-information systems, asset-pricing models and statistical modelling of fair-lending compliance. Carhill joined the OCC as a staff economist in 1991, and was deputy director for market risk modelling from 1995 to 2003. Before joining the OCC, he was a staff economist with the Federal Home Loan Bank of Atlanta, engaged in researching the role that interest-rate risk plays in thrift profitability and as a consultant on risk-management issues. He received a PhD in economics in May 1988 from Washington University.

Brian Clark is a senior financial economist in the Enterprise Risk Analysis Division of the US Office of the Comptroller of the Currency. His current research focuses on areas of operational risk and topics in corporate finance and banking. Clark received his PhD in finance from Rensselaer Polytechnic Institute in 2010.

Olivier de Bandt is head of the Research Directorate at the ACP, the French Prudential Supervision Authority, in charge of the supervision of banks and insurance companies. He was previously director of macroeconomic forecasting at the Banque de France. He is also an associate professor at the University of Paris Ouest. De Bandt earned a PhD from the Economics Department of the University of Chicago. His research interests include notably the economics of banking and insurance, stress-testing methods and the analysis of systemic risk.

Nicolas Dumontaux works for the French Prudential Supervision Authority (ACP), as an onsite banking supervisor. He graduated from l'École Nationale de la Statistique et de l'Administration Economique and holds a Master in Economics degree from the Paris School of Economics. Since joining the ACP in 2008, he has been involved in several stress-testing exercises coordinated by the European Banking Authority and has worked on several impact studies such as corporate credit risk and countercyclical capital buffer. Dumontaux began his career as a statistician at the French Ministry of Health.

Bakhodir Ergashev is a lead financial economist in the Supervision, Regulation and Credit Department of the Federal Reserve Bank of Richmond. He heads a team of financial economists responsible for supervisory research and the supervision of risk models at large banking institutions. Ergashev's research has focused on stress-testing risk models, modelling operational risk in the presence of censored losses, incorporating scenarios into operational risk models, and the role of asset commonality in systemic risk. Ergashev joined the Federal Reserve Bank of Richmond in 2006 after earning his PhD in Economics from Washington University. He also has a PhD in Mathematical Statistics from Steklov Institute of Mathematics, Moscow.

Solange M. Guerra works in the Financial Stability Group of the Economic Research Department at the Central Bank of Brazil. She is involved in developing indicators to assess the soundness of the Brazilian banking system, such as default probabilities, governance, concentration and efficiency indexes, and stress tests. Guerra holds an MA in Mathematics and an MA and a PhD in Economics, both from the Brasilia University.

Arden Hall is a special advisory at the Federal Reserve Bank of Philadelphia, specialising in the modelling and risk management of retail credit products. Before this, he held positions in risk management at the Federal Home Loan Bank of San Francisco, Bank of America and Wells Fargo. He holds a MA in Statistics and a PhD in Economics from the University of California, Berkeley.

Jonathan Jones is a senior financial economist in the Risk Analysis Division at the US Office of the Comptroller of the Currency (OCC). He received his PhD in Economics from the University of Colorado. Before joining the OCC, he worked as a senior economist at the Office of Thrift Supervision, the Securities and Exchange Commission and the Office of Tax Analysis at the US Treasury Department, and taught at Vassar College and the Catholic University of America. He has articles in journals such as Applied Financial Economics, the Journal of Corporate Finance, the Journal of Empirical Finance, the Journal of Finance and the Journal of Financial Research.

Demelza Jurcevic is a policy adviser at De Nederlandsche Bank, where she is working in the Financial Risk Management Banking department. She was on secondment for a year (2011–12) at the European Banking Authority. Her main fields of expertise are financial risk management, stress testing, asset-quality review and the supervisory review and evaluation process. In particular, Jurcevic has been intimately involved in developing the CEBS guidelines for stress testing, which were published in summer 2010, and in the EU-wide stress-test exercise of CEBS/EBA and the IMF Financial Sector Assessment Programme for the Netherlands. She is a member of the EBA Stress Test Taskforce as well as the BCBS Pillar II network. Jurcevic received a BA in Economics and an MSc in Financial Economics from Erasmus University of Rotterdam. She is also a certified financial risk manager (GARP).

David Lynch is assistant director for quantitative risk management in banking supervision and regulation at the Board of Governors of the Federal Reserve. He joined the Board in 2005. His areas of responsibility include oversight of models for market-risk capital and counterparty-risk capital. Lynch is a representative of the Risk Measurement Group of the Basel Committee on Banking Supervision. He has worked at the US Securities and Exchange Commission in broker-dealer finance. He holds a PhD in Economics from the University of Maryland.

Vincent Martin works as a senior economist in the macroprudential division of the Research Directorate of the French Prudential Supervision Authority (ACP), and is in charge of solvency and liquidity stress-testing exercises for the French banking sector. He has been involved in stress-testing exercises led by the European Banking Authority and the IMF. Martin joined ACP in 2011, and previously worked for Credit Agricole Corporate and Investment Bank (CACIB) as a quantitative credit risk analyst. He graduated from l'École Nationale de la Statistique et de l'Analyse de l'Information (ENSAI).

Denys Médée works for the French Prudential Supervision Authority (ACP), within the Research Directorate. He graduated from l'École Polytechnique and holds a Master's degree in Economics from Paris University. He previously worked as a modelling expert for the Risk Division of a French bank. Since joining ACP in 2009, he has been involved in onsite supervision, participating in model-validation missions (such as credit risk, VaR, ALM). He has also participated in coordinated top-down/bottom-up stress-testing exercises, and has been appointed as an expert for several IMF technical assistance missions, where he helped to implement and enhance stress-testing frameworks for emerging countries' banking supervisors.

Rodrigo C. C. Miranda works in the Financial Stability Group of the Economic Research Department at the Central Bank of Brazil. He joined the Economic Research Department in 2010 after four years in the Central Bank's IT department. He holds an MSc degree in Computer Science from the University of Brasília.

David Palmer is a senior supervisory financial analyst in the Risk Section of the Division of Banking Supervision and Regulation at the Federal Reserve Board. He focuses on several primary topic areas, including banks' and supervisors' stress-testing activities, banks' model-risk-management practices, banks' internal processes to assess capital adequacy, and banks' credit-risk capital models. He engages in both policy-related projects and onsite examinations. Palmer was a primary author of US supervisory guidance on stress-testing for large banking organisations issued in May 2012. He was also a key contributor to the development of the Federal Reserve's final rules to implement Dodd–Frank capital stress-testing requirements, issued in October 2012. In addition, he was a primary author of the Federal Reserve's supervisory guidance on model risk management issued in April 2011 jointly with the Office of the Comptroller of the Currency. He also serves in a leadership position in the Federal Reserve for evaluating firms' capital-adequacy processes for Pillar II and for the CCAR. Palmer has a Bachelor's degree from Oberlin College and a Master's from Georgetown University.

Dilip K. Patro is the deputy director of the Market Risk Analysis Division of the US Office of the Comptroller of the Currency (OCC). He was an assistant professor of finance before joining the OCC, where he serves as a modelling and model-risk management expert, reviewing and evaluating models used for derivatives pricing, market risk, counterparty credit risk, stress testing and regulatory capital calculations at large national banks. He also represents the

OCC in various policy initiatives of the Basel Committee, including the Macroprudential Supervision Group. Patro is a graduate of IIT, Delhi and a CFA charter holder, and he has a PhD from the University of Maryland at College Park.

Mario Quagliariello is the head of the Risk Analysis Unit at the European Banking Authority. He previously served as a senior economist in the Regulation and Supervisory Policies Department of Banca d'Italia, the Italian central bank. His interests concern macroprudential analysis and stress tests, Basel II and procyclicality, and the economics of financial regulation. Quagliariello has published several articles in Italian and international journals, including the Journal of Banking and Finance, the Journal of Financial Services Research and the and Risk. He edited Stress Testing the Banking System: Methodologies and Applications, published by Cambridge University Press, and co-edited Basel III and Beyond: A Guide to Banking Regulation after the Crisis published by Risk Books. He holds a PhD in Economics from the University of York in the UK.

Robert Scavotto is the lead international expert in the Economics Department of the US Office of the Comptroller of the Currency (OCC). He has over 15 years of experience in country risk analysis, including developing stress-test applications. He has worked on stress-testing policy, including guidance on implementing the Basel stress-testing principles as well as writing the OCC's Annual Stress Test rule. He received his PhD and MA in Economics from Pennsylvania State University and a BA in Economics and Government/International Relations from Clark University

Robert H. Skinkle is a senior international advisory in the Economics Department of the US Office of the Comptroller of the Currency (OCC). He covers the Emerging Markets portfolio, with an emphasis on Asia. Special projects include developing early-warning identification systems, assessing country-risk-management techniques and stress-testing bank portfolios. Prior to this, Skinkle specialised in commercial real estate and systemic risk analysis of the US economy. Before joining the OCC in 1991, he was the regional economist for Wells Fargo Bank in San Francisco. His undergraduate degree in Economics is from the University of California, Berkeley, and he has a Master's in Economics from the University of California, San Diego.

Sergio R. S. Souza works as a researcher in the Financial Stability team in the Research Department at Central Bank of Brazil. He received his BE degree in Mechanical Engineering at the University of São Paulo and MSc and PhD degrees in Economics at the University of Brasília. He joined the Central Bank in January 1998, having initially worked several years developing and implementing systems forming the IT infrastructure for the International Reserves operations conducted by the bank. As a researcher, he has been working with financial systems models, mainly network models and agent-based models, with a focus on financial stability.

Xian Sun is an assistant professor of Finance at Carey Business School at Johns Hopkins University. Before joining Carey Business School, she worked for the US Office of the Comptroller of the Currency (OCC) for three years as a senior financial economist in the Market Risk Division. Her research interests include emerging markets, political institutions and creditor rights. Her papers have been published in prestigious journals such as the Journal of Financial and Quantitative Analysis, the Journal of Banking and Finance and the Journal of International Money and Finance.

Benjamin M. Tabak holds a PhD in Economics from University of Brasília. He works at the Central Bank of Brazil and is a professor at Catholic University of Brasília. His research interests concern banking, financial stability, law and economics, and behavioural modelling.

Kapo Yuen is a supervising bank examiner in the Financial Institution Supervision Group at the Federal Reserve Bank of New York, where he leads a team of quantitative analysts and modellers to support the supervision of systemically important financial institutions. His supervision responsibilities include evaluating the appropriateness of firms' stress-testing models. He has participated in many of the Federal Reserve's Comprehensive Capital Analysis and Review (CCAR) exercises and was one of the authors of the Basel Committee on Banking Supervision's article "Principles for sound stress testing practices and supervision", published in May 2009. Before joining the Federal Reserve Bank of New York in 2006, Yuen worked in several large financial institutions in the US and overseas. He has more than 20 years of financial industry experience, mostly in credit risk management, predictive modelling, credit-scoring and decision strategy. He holds an MS degree in Statistics from the State University of New York at Stony Brook.

Introduction

Akhtar Siddique; Iftekhar Hasan

Office of the Comptroller of Currency; Fordham University

Banks across the globe faced significant challenges during the 2007–9 financial crisis. Declining capital ratios, equity prices, government takeovers and subsidies by the public sector have been norms rather than special cases in many healthy "free-market" economies. The crisis caused the confidence of investors, market makers and lenders to plummet. Local and international regulators attempted to restore confidence across the banking system in general, but particularly with the goal of boosting lending and capital structure. Among other initiatives, regulators are trying to implement stress testing of banks in order to lower or even prevent the possibility of a future banking crisis. The exact details of these tests vary according to specific economies and regulators, but all are intended to examine how banks perform under an adverse or unexpected economic environment, with regard to both macroeconomic uncertainty or bank-specific asset-liability and off-balance-sheet activities. These tests are designed not only to understand the vulnerability of banks, but also to make sure that banks are prepared to face adverse situations with the capital to mitigate potential losses or non-performing assets.

This book considers the stress testing of financial institutions. In the wake of the crisis, stress testing has received prominent media coverage. Many research papers and several books have been published on stress testing. The primary goal of all these initiatives, including the efforts undertaken by this book, is to better understand effective stress testing. As per the subtitle, this book focuses on stress-testing approaches and methods, as well as applications. This book takes a comprehensive approach and covers a wide array of stress-testing methods and scenarios. It makes a significant contribution, as the authors are primarily drawn from regulatory bodies around the world. The authors have considerable experience in the field, as they have been studying and engaged in stress testing at financial institutions for years, and many have been involved in the policy consequences and development that stem from effective stress testing.

Regulators maintain an external view, albeit an external view that is very often closely focused on the financial institutions. In comparison, "quants" at a bank can focus more on the implementation details. Nevertheless, the regulatory view has the advantage of being exposed to different approaches, methods and applications at different institutions. Regulators can therefore weigh in on the relative strengths and weaknesses of different banks. This comparative ability has become particularly important, as smaller institutions that did not typically engage in significant stress testing are now expected to do so. Moreover, stress testing has been evolving very rapidly, and, given that the contributors to this book have been a part of this evolution, they can provide insight into the development and situation of stress testing.

Stress testing has many approaches. For example, at many institutions, finance and treasury have had ownership of the budgeting process. Hence, centralised stress testing could be housed in such a central function. Other institutions have taken a more decentralised approach, wherein the central function has only acted as an aggregator. Effective stress testing does not need a given organisational form or approach. However, a given organisational form will require certain aspects to ensure effectiveness. For example, in a decentralised approach towards stress testing, consistency across the organisation becomes important, and the institution will need to find ways of ensuring that consistency.

An important element to stress testing is that the processes in it need to be effective. That generally has required a build-out of processes and functions. Stress testing includes not only the enterprise-wide stress tests that look at the bank's projected capital with scenarios based on macroeconomic variables, but also other types of stress testing, such as portfolio and transaction-level stress tests.

Given that stress testing is generally conducted for distinct risks, such as credit, counterparty credit, market, liquidity and so forth, the contributions to the book start with governance and controls, and the bulk of the book is devoted to separate chapters on the different risks.

In Chapter 1, David Palmer considers governance and controls for the stress testing of financial institutions. Stress testing is highly technical, makes many assumptions and entails much uncertainty, and so appropriate governance and controls are crucial. Proper stress-testing governance and controls not only confirm that stress tests are conducted in a rigorous manner, but also help ensure that stress tests and their outcomes are subject to oversight.

Differentiation between the roles of the senior management and the board of directors is considered in this chapter. The role of an internal audit should not be forgotten in concerns about governance. The role of validation is also discussed, both in terms of how validation needs to examine data and inputs and how to ensure the integrity of the process. What differentiates validation of stress-testing from validation of models is the emphasis on the process, as well as the need to validate the framework. Very usefully, the chapter provides pointers on the policies, procedures, and documentation for stress testing. Given the recent implementation of enterprise-wide stress testing at most financial institutions, such policies, procedures and documentation are often less developed.

Chapter 2 examines the relationship between the various risk-management tools used by financial institutions and stress testing, particularly the value-at-risk-type, enterprise-wide risk measures. Akhtar Siddique and Iftekhar Hasan discuss consistency between the other risk metrics and stress tests. They then discuss how stress-testing has begun to impact other risk measures.

It is important to note that stress testing has played two distinct roles in the regulatory responses to the financial crisis. The first is the stress tests conducted by the regulators, for example the SCAP in the US and the EBA's stress tests in Europe. Another role has been to increase the amount of capital required of financial institutions by incorporating stressed inputs into the capital calculations. This has happened for market risk in Basel 2.5, as well as for counterparty credit risk in Basel III. This chapter discusses both variants of the interaction that stress testing has had with capital regulation.

Dilip Patro, Akhtar Siddique and Sun Xian discuss stress testing for market risk in Chapter 3. Given the very large number of positions as well as the large number of inputs required, market risk poses challenges for stress testing. The authors discuss the differences between stress testing for market and credit risk (equivalently between trading book and banking book) The difficulty in utilising macroeconomic scenarios into market risk stress tests is another point they focus on. Horizon, and the difficulty in incorporating the aftershock from market events as well as the impact of hedging, are then discussed. The last section focuses on revaluation of the values and / or computation of P&L under the stressed scenarios. This discusses the challenges that banks face in the revaluation as well as what to be concerned about in these areas.

David Lynch, in Chapter 4, discusses stress testing for counterparty credit risk. Counterparty credit risk (CCR) was one of the key avenues through which the financial crisis manifested itself. The measurement and management of counterparty credit risk has become greatly sophisticated over the past 20 or so years. However, stress testing of counterparty credit risk has not kept pace with the evolution of counterparty credit risk measurement and management.

An important aspect of counterparty credit risk that needs to be recognised is that it may be approached by either a credit or market risk perspective. The duality of CCR has led to the adoption of measures that manage to capture some facet of CCR. In terms of credit risk: current exposure, peak exposure and expected exposure are all important measures. In terms of market risk: credit valuation adjustment's (CVA), valuation and the risk generated by changes in CVA are important. Although treating CCR either way is a valid method for portfolio management, failing to consider both opens an institution to risks from the unconsidered perspective, and a single-view approach is better for trading activities and risk-management discipline. Furthermore, there is an unusual problem associated with CCR: wrong-way risk. Wrong-way risk is a type of risk that occurs when exposure is correlated with a counterparty's credit quality, so that exposure increases as the counterparty becomes likelier to default. This does not happen when exposure is fixed, as with a loan, so the application of banking-book risk metrics to CCR can cause considerable difficulties.

Given such a large amount of information, understanding and interpreting stress tests at a portfolio and a counterparty level becomes difficult. The sheer variety of risk measures ensures that stress testing for CCR is a complicated task, but financial institutions are beginning to address these complications and are finally conducting stress tests that go beyond simple tests of current exposure. This is an exciting moment for CCR stress testing, as the best-practice methodologies are only just now being developed.

In Chapter 5, Bakhodir Ergashev and Brian Clark provide background on the current state of operational risk modelling and consider the challenges in the field today. Although data limitations are one of these challenges, there are several areas where merely increasing the quality and quantity of operational loss data is not enough. Significant research is required to address these challenges and to further the field.

Stress testing operational risk increases these challenges even more. Most of these challenges are a consequence of the fact that operational risk exposure is driven by infrequent large events. To model the aggregate loss distribution, for instance, we need additional loss data. Stress testing insufficiently accurate static models only amplifies the model's risk, and modelling dependence with the macroeconomic environment is even more challenging, due to the lack of strong supportive evidence.

Despite the many challenges and limitations associated with operational risk modelling, the authors have offered a variety of fruitful possibilities for institutions to test operational risk exposure. We are currently in a nascent moment for the development of methodology, and, although some methods may appear more useful than others, additional research will be required to determine the utility of any particular one. The authors currently recommend that banks employ an array of models, thereby both providing a variety of perspectives and contributing to possible future research.

Paul Calem and Arden Hall offer an overview of the current regulatory stress-testing environment in Chapter 6. They provide a particularly useful perspective on the limitations of stress testing. The authors focus specifically on the stress testing of balance-sheet loan losses, but much of their work is applicable to bank capital stress tests generally. Given that a balance-sheet loan-loss stress test is based on predictions of borrower repayment under extreme conditions that are generally outside the scope of historical precedents, such testing presents major modelling challenges. Yet, despite such challenges, balance-sheet stress testing can offer a useful view of a financial institution's sensitivity to adverse shocks, and Calem and Hall propose a framework for such testing. A careful and controlled balance-sheet loan-loss stress test can pinpoint sources of risk, order institutions according to risk, indicate the quality of a bank's risk position over time and provide benchmarks for understanding an institution's risk-management processes and capital adequacy. Stress testing can also evaluate the risk sensitivity or risk composition of an institution's loan portfolio.

In Chapter 7, Michael Carhill and Jonathan Jones examine stress-test modelling for loan losses and reserves. Their contribution is driven by their experience of looking at the stress-testing practices of institutions. They observed the decision-making processes at large financial institutions as executives decided that models capable of estimating credit losses conditional on economic scenarios were required for enterprise-wide capital planning and stress testing. A number of supervisory and regulatory developments account for this interest in deploying economic factors in stress testing. Such developments include: the Advanced Internal Ratings Based (AIRB) approach of Basel II; the recommendations of the Basel Committee on Banking Supervision; the Federal Reserve's Supervisory Capital Analysis Program (SCAP) exercise and the following Comprehensive Capital Analysis and Review (CCAR) bank stress tests; and the Dodd–Frank Wall Street Reform and Consumer Protection Act of 2010.

Carhill and Jones present their first-hand observations in this chapter, including their evaluation of the strengths and weaknesses of the approaches they witnessed. They also identify potential challenges and pitfalls that need to be addressed when developing macroeconomic-based credit risk stress-testing models. However, given that this field is rapidly evolving and no best practices have yet been established, the reliability of these models is still questionable. Nonetheless, the financial crisis has made clear the need for banks to include economic and market factors in credit risk models in order to produce accurate stress loan-loss estimates.

Olivier de Bandt, Nicolas Dumontaux, Vincent Martin, and Denys Médée examine in Chapter 8 stress testing for credit risk and focus on risks arising from corporate loans and other credit exposures. Corporate credit risk – known also as wholesale credit risk – is highly important when stress testing global firms. Credit risk is a huge source of risk for banks and is very relevant to an institution's financial solvency. The crisis has underscored the need for stress-testing banks' portfolios, as institutions have incurred significant losses from structured US subprime-related assets. This chapter develops the foundations of a Basel II-type modelling effort to perform credit stress-test scenarios through credit-migration matrices (or transition matrices), which have already been implemented in France and are currently used for top-down stress-test exercises.

Credit risk stems from either actual defaults or migrations of credit ratings, and several model approaches are available to quantify this type of risk. These models may be structural, in which a firm's value and capital structure are modelled, or reduced, in which credit events are exogenous to a firm. The authors use a reduced form in which events are triggered by macroeconomic shock. The authors also focus on credit migrations. The model rests on the premise that the evolution of rating transitions can be linked to a synthetic credit indicator.

In Chapter 9, Paolo Bisio, Demelza Jurcevic, and Mario Quagliariello examine and evaluate the 2011 EU-wide stress tests conducted by the European Banking Authority (EBA) among 91 banks. The objective of the stress tests was to evaluate the EU banking system and the solvency of institutions under scenarios imposed by supervisors. After describing the sample selection, macro scenario and methodology, the authors note that the EBA is satisfied with the progress made by banks in fulfilling the recommendations to ensure appropriate mitigating actions based on the exercise's results.

Needless to say, the overall assessment was not without its criticisms – the EBA received negative feedback on some of its assumptions – but the 2011 exercise was a partial success when assessed against the benchmarks of analytical rigour, communication and resulting actions. The development of a stress-test methodology and its early publication was received positively. The presence of an organised quality-assurance and robust peer review was perceived as helpful as regarding interpretation of the methodology and the development of micro parameters from the macro scenario. The coordinated and extensive disclosure of results was seen as a significant victory for proponents of transparency and was welcomed by market participants and the public.

Robert Scavotto and Robert Skinkle argue in Chapter 10 that, during stress testing of internationally active financial institutions, individual-country characteristics can produce great variation in the stress-test results. Therefore, to perform reliable stress testing we must first approach the estimation of regional or global regressions with caution. Many challenges emerge in cross-country testing, including very basic factors, such as the development of datasets and the acquisition of an understanding of qualitative factors that may be relevant to certain countries. Drawing upon their own experiences in cross-county stress testing, the authors determine that a best-practice methodology entails pursuing an individual-country approach with specific stratifications. The authors' examination of the Korean consumer market as a case study is a well-reasoned approach and provides a novel methodology for any researchers interested in performing cross-country systemic stress tests.

In Chapter 11, Benjamin M. Tabak, Solange M. Guerra, Sergio Rubens Stancato de Souza and Rodrigo Cesar de Castro Miranda discuss the effects of the financial crisis on the Brazilian banking system and liquidity risk. Liquidity risks have risen in the wake of the financial crisis, and there is a need for measures to restore confidence and increase liquidity to enable financial institutions to handle additional risks. Liquidity crises are less frequent than other types, but their impacts can be very significant. Such low-frequency, high-impact events are troubling, insofar as they are not often easily planned for, yet can have as comparably devastating results as more common crises. As expected, liquidity stress tests are not currently as well developed as credit and market risk stress tests, although there is now increased interest in the threats posed by liquidity risks as a result of the financial crisis

Most central banks do not publish the results from their liquidity stress tests, a fact that is indicative of liquidity-modelling complexity and lack of data. The Central Bank of Brazil, however, has published its results since 2009, and provides a useful case study for discussing liquidity stress testing in general. The authors examine the liquidity stress-testing approach that is under use in the Central Bank of Brazil and their methodology and results provide a crucial foray into a field that is in dire need of quality research.

Kapo Yuen discusses in Chapter 12 the question of the severity of supervisory adverse scenarios and provides a methodology to compare the severity of different adverse macroeconomic scenarios. Since 2009, the Federal Reserve System has conducted an annual stress test on the US banking system, called the Comprehensive Capital Analysis and Review (CCAR). During this annual exercise, the Federal Reserve Board provides a supervisory macro scenario for stress testing, but also requires that each financial institution submit an individualised scenario that is particularly relevant to that institution's specific features. The instructions for that individualised scenario are somewhat abstract: they indicate that the scenario must reflect "a severely adverse economic and financial market environment", but the question of what constitutes "appropriate severity" is left unclear. Yuen poses several questions in attempting to determine the severity of a stress scenario: How can we measure severity? How severe is an individualised scenario versus the supervisory macro scenario? Are the individualised scenarios credibly severe? The financial crisis may be a useful starting point to measure severity, but Yuen wonders whether banks have actually changed; severe stress scenarios must be developed that will result in estimates of losses that demonstrate vulnerabilities. In posing these questions, Yuen demonstrates a methodology that can be used to assess the severity of a particular scenario and offers some possible alternate methodologies, as well.

The editors hope readers will learn about both the practical elements of stress testing and stress-testing principles from this book. More practically, they will also learn the pitfalls to avoid while conducting stress testing. The authors have been involved in matters relating to stress testing for many years and have also seen many other good books on stress testing. However, what those books appeared to lack was the discussion of the comparative merits and demerits of various approaches. The regulatory community (at least those members engaged in active conduct or examinations of stress testing) is uniquely suited to this role given its view of stress-testing practices across different institutions. This insight motivated the editors to bring these chapters together.

The views expressed in this chapter are those of the authors alone and do not necessarily represent those of the Comptroller of the Currency or Bank of Finland.

1

Governance over Stress Testing

David E. Palmer
Federal Reserve Board

Governance and controls are a very important aspect of stress testing, yet are sometimes overlooked or given insufficient attention by financial institutions.[1] Proper governance and controls over stress-testing not only confirm that stress tests are conducted in a rigorous manner, but also help ensure that stress tests and their outcomes are subject to an appropriately critical eye. Governance and controls are particularly needed in the area of stress testing given the highly technical nature of many stress-testing activities, the generally large number of assumptions in stress-testing exercises and the inherent uncertainty in estimating the nature, likelihood and impact of stressful events and conditions.

While the exact form of governance and controls over stress-testing activities can and should vary across countries and financial institutions, there are some general principles, expectations and recommendations that financial institutions can follow. The manner in which the principles, expectations and recommendations outlined in this chapter are applied at any given financial institution should involve a "tailored" approach that is specifically tied to the size, complexity, risk profile, culture and individual characteristics of that institution.

This chapter discusses key elements of effective governance over stress testing, including: governance structure; policies, procedures and documentation; validation and independent review; and internal audit. It also discusses other aspects of stress-testing activities that should be considered and reviewed as part of the stress testing governance process.

GOVERNANCE STRUCTURE

Governance structure is one of the primary elements for sound governance over stress testing. While institutions may have different structures based on the legal, regulatory or cultural norms in their countries, it is generally expected that every institution has separation of duties between a board of directors and senior management. This separation of duties is equally important for stress-testing activities, as it helps ensure there is proper oversight and action taken on an ongoing basis. The board and senior management should share some responsibilities – albeit to varying degrees of detail – but also have distinct responsibilities in other cases. Together, an institution's board and senior management should establish comprehensive, integrated and effective stress testing that fits into the broader risk management of the institution.

Board of directors

In general, the board of directors has ultimate oversight responsibility and accountability for the entire organisation. It should be responsible for key strategies and decisions, define the culture of the organisation and set the "tone at the top". This applies to stress-testing as well, as the board is ultimately responsible for the institution's stress-testing activities, even if the board is not intimately involved in the details. Board members should be sufficiently knowledgeable about stress-testing activities to ask informed questions, even if they are not experts in the technical details. The board should actively evaluate and discuss information received from senior management about stress testing, ensuring that the stress-testing activities are in line with the institution's risk appetite, overall strategies and business plans, and contingency plans – directing changes where appropriate.[2] Board members should also ensure they review that information with an appropriately critical eye, challenging key assumptions, ensuring that there is sufficient information with appropriate detail and supplementing the information with their own views and perspectives.

Stress-testing results should be used, along with other information, to inform the board about alignment of the institution's risk profile with the board's chosen risk appetite, as well as inform operating and strategic decisions. Stress-testing results should be considered directly for decisions relating to capital and liquidity adequacy, including capital contingency plans and contingency funding plans. While stress-testing exercises can be very helpful in providing a forward-looking assessment of the potential impact of adverse outcomes, board members should ensure they use the results of the stress tests with an appropriate degree of scepticism, given the assumptions, limitations and uncertainties inherent in any type of stress testing. In general, the board should not rely on just one stress-test exercise in making key decisions, but should aim to have it supplemented with other tests and other quantitative and qualitative information. The board should be able to take action based on its review of stress-test results and accompanying information, which could include changing capital levels, bolstering liquidity, reducing risk, adjusting exposures, altering strategies or withdrawing from certain activities. In many cases, stress-testing activities can serve as a useful "early-warning" mechanism for the board, especially during benign times (ie, non-stress periods), and thus can be useful in guiding the overall direction and strategy for the institution.

Senior management

Senior management has the responsibility of ensuring that stress-testing activities authorised by the board are implemented in a satisfactory manner, and is accountable to the board for the effectiveness of those activities. That is, senior management should execute on the overall stress-testing strategy determined by the board. Senior management duties should include establishing adequate policies and procedures and ensuring compliance with them, allocating appropriate resources and assigning competent staff, overseeing stress-test development and implementation, evaluating stress-test results, reviewing any findings related to the functioning of stress-test processes and taking prompt remedial action where necessary.

In addition, whether directly or through relevant committees, senior management should be responsible for regularly reporting to the board on stress-testing developments (including the process to design tests and develop scenarios) and on stress-testing results (including those from individual tests, where material), as well as on compliance with stress-testing policies. Senior management should ensure there is appropriate buy-in at different levels of the institution, and that stress-testing activities are appropriately coordinated. Such coordination does not have to mean that all stress-testing exercises are built on the same assumptions or use the same information. Indeed, it can be very useful to conduct different types of stress tests to achieve a wide perspective. But senior management should be mindful of potential inconsistencies, contradictions or gaps among its stress tests and assess what actions should be taken as a result. At a minimum, this means that assumptions are transparent and that results are not used in a contradictory manner.

Senior management, in consultation with the board, should ensure that stress-testing activities include a sufficient range of stress-testing activities applied at the appropriate levels of the institution (ie, not just one single stress test). Another key task is to ensure that stress-test results are appropriately aggregated, particularly for enterprise-wide tests. Senior management should maintain an internal summary of test results to document at a high level the range of its stress-testing activities and outcomes, as well as proposed follow-up actions. Sound governance at this level also includes using stress testing to consider the effectiveness of an institution's risk-mitigation techniques for various risk types over their respective time horizons, such as to explore what could occur if expected mitigation techniques break down during stressful periods.

Stress-test results should inform management's analysis and decision-making related to business strategies, limits, capital and liquidity, risk profile and other aspects of risk management, consistent with the institution's established risk appetite. Wherever possible, benchmarking or other comparative analysis should be used to evaluate the stress-testing results relative to other tools and measures – both internal and external to the institution – to provide proper context and a check on results. Just as at the board level, senior management should challenge the results and workings of stress-testing exercises. In fact, senior management should be much more well versed in the details of stress testing and be able to drill down in many cases to discuss technical issues and challenge results on a granular level.

Senior management can and should use stress testing to supplement other information it develops and provides to the board, such as other risk metrics or measures of capital and liquidity adequacy. When reporting stress-testing information to the board, senior management should be able to explain the key elements of stress-testing activities, including assumptions, limitations and uncertainties. Reports from senior management to the board should be clear, comprehensive and current, providing a good balance of succinctness and detail. Those reports should include information about the extent to which stress test models are appropriately governed, including the extent to which they have been subject to validation or other type of independent review (see below). Senior management, as part of its overall efforts to ensure proper governance and controls, is also responsible for ensuring that staff involved in stress testing operate under the proper incentives. Finally, senior management should ensure that there is a regular assessment of stress-testing activities across the institution by an independent, unbiased party (such as internal audit – see below).

Senior management should ensure that stress-testing activities are updated in light of new risks, better understanding of the institution's exposures and activities, new stress-testing techniques, updated data sources and any changes in its operating structure and its internal and external environment. An institution's stress-testing development should be iterative, with ongoing adjustments and refinements to better calibrate the tests to provide current and relevant information. In addition, management should review stress-testing activities on a regular basis to confirm the general appropriateness of, among other things, the validity of the assumptions, the severity of tests, the robustness of the estimates, the performance of any underlying models and the stability and reasonableness of the results. In addition to conducting formal, routine stress tests, management should ensure the institution has the flexibility to conduct new or ad hoc stress tests in a timely manner to address rapidly emerging risks and vulnerabilities.

POLICIES, PROCEDURES AND DOCUMENTATION

Having clear and comprehensive policies, procedures and documentation is integral to sound stress-testing governance. These areas provide the important codification of an institution's practices and allow the institution as a whole to follow the same general principles and standards for its stress-testing activities. Thus, in order to promote a sound control environment and allow for consistency and repeatability in stress-testing activities across the entity, the institution should have written policies that direct and govern the implementation of stress-testing activities in a clear and comprehensive manner. It is generally expected that these policies would be approved and annually reassessed by the board. Stress-testing policies, along with procedures to implement them, should:

❏ describe the overall purpose of stress-testing activities;
❏ articulate consistent and sufficiently rigorous stress-testing practices across the entire institution;
❏ indicate stress-testing roles and responsibilities, including controls over external resources used for any part of stress testing (such as vendors and data providers);
❏ describe the frequency and priority with which stress-testing activities should be conducted;
❏ outline the process for choosing appropriately stressful conditions for tests, including the manner in which scenarios are designed and selected;
❏ include information about validation and independent review of stress tests;
❏ provide transparency to third parties for their understanding of an institution's stress-testing activities;
❏ indicate how stress-test results are used and by whom, and outline instances in which remedial actions should be taken; and
❏ be reviewed and updated as necessary to ensure that stress-testing practices remain appropriate and keep up to date with changes in market conditions, the institution's products and strategies, its risks, exposures and activities, its established risk appetite and industry stress-testing practices.

In addition to having clear and comprehensive policies and procedures, an institution should ensure that its stress tests are documented appropriately, including a description of the types of stress tests and methodologies used, test results, key assumptions, limitations and uncertainties, and suggested actions. Among other things, documentation:

❏ allows management to track results and analyse differences over time, including changes due to methodologies and assumptions as well as changes due to market conditions or other external factors;

❏ is a vital aspect of stress-testing governance as it allows third parties to evaluate stress tests and their components, including for validation and internal audit review;

❏ provides for continuity of operations, makes compliance with policy transparent and helps track recommendations, responses and exceptions; and

❏ is a useful tool for stress-test developers, as it forces them to think clearly about their stress tests, categorise the components of the tests and describe choices made and assumptions used.

Documenting stress tests takes time and effort, so institutions should therefore provide incentives to produce effective and complete documentation. Developers of stress tests should be given explicit responsibility during development for thorough documentation, which should be kept up to date as stress testing and application environment change. In addition, the institution should ensure that other participants document their work related to stress-testing activities, including validators, reviewers and senior management. For cases in which a bank uses stress tests from a vendor or other third party, it should ensure that appropriate documentation of the third-party approach is available so that the stress test can be appropriately understood, validated, reviewed, approved and used.

VALIDATION AND INDEPENDENT REVIEW

Another key element of governance over stress testing is validation and independent review. Stress-testing governance should incorporate validation or other type of independent review to ensure the integrity of stress-testing processes and results. Such unbiased, critical review of stress-testing activities gives additional assurance that the stress tests are functioning as intended. In general, validation and independent review of stress-testing activities should be conducted on an ongoing basis, not just as a single event. In addition, validation and review work for stress testing should be integrated with an institution's general approach to validation and independent review of its quantitative estimation tools – although stress tests may need to be validated and reviewed in a particular manner. Specifically, because stress tests by definition aim to estimate the potential impact of rare events and circumstances, conducting more traditional outcomes analysis used in a more data-rich environment may not be possible. For instance, statistical backtesting of stress-test estimates against realised outcomes may not be feasible.

To address challenges associated with validating stress tests, some institutions may try to test their models using data from non-stress periods, ie, during "good times" or in a "baseline" setting. Such testing can be beneficial to determine whether the stress test generally functions as a predictive model under those conditions. If the stress test does not perform well in a more data-rich environment, that would certainly raise questions about its usefulness. However, while "baseline" outcomes showing good test performance can provide some additional confidence in the stress test, those outcomes should not be interpreted as sufficient for the designated task of estimating stress outcomes. For instance, markets and market actors can behave quite differently in stress environments, and assumed interactions among variables can change markedly (such as higher incidence of nonlinearities). Thus, the model used in a baseline situation may actually require a different specification to properly estimate stress outcomes (or an entirely new model may be needed for stress periods). There can be additional challenges when upgrades or enhancements are made to stress tests, because it may not be immediately clear that the upgraded or enhanced model actually performs better. Here, too, assessing the baseline outcomes can provide some assurance about such changes, but cannot offer full confirmation. In sum, even with rigorous quantitative analytics, there can remain very real limitations in the extent to which stress tests can be formally validated or otherwise fully assessed in terms of quantitative performance.

As an additional response to these validation issues, given the limitations of relying on outcomes analysis, an institution may need to rely on other aspects of validation and independent review of stress tests – such as a greater emphasis on conceptual sound-ness of the stress test, additional sensitivity testing, and simulation techniques. Or an institution may choose to create holdout sam-ple portfolios and run them through its stress-test model. Bench-marking to internal or external models, tools or results can also be beneficial, but institutions should be careful that the benchmarks appropriately fit the institution's risks, exposures and activities. Fi-nally, expert-based judgement should be applied to ensure that test results are intuitive and logical, and to add additional perspective on stress-test performance.

Despite these additional efforts, institutions may continue to be challenged in trying to fully validate their stress tests to the same extent as other models, given the limitations in conducting perfor-mance testing. Such limitations do not mean that those stress tests cannot be used, but there should be transparency about validation status, and information about the lack of full validation should be communicated to users of stress-test results. For cases in which validation and independent review have identified material defi-ciencies or limitations in a stress test, there should be a remediation plan to explain how the stress test will be enhanced or its use lim-ited, or both. Identified deficiencies in stress tests should be com-municated to all stress-test users.

Additional areas of validation and independent review for stress tests that require attention from a governance perspective include:

❏ ensuring that there is appropriate independence and effective challenge in the validation and review process;
❏ including validation and independent review of the qualitative or judgemental aspects of a stress test – such aspects can be an integral component of a stress test and thus should be reviewed in some manner, even if they cannot be tested in a quantitative/ statistical sense;
❏ ensuring that stress tests are subject to appropriate development standards, including a clear statement of purpose, proper theory and design, sound methodologies and processing components, and developmental testing (including testing of assumptions);
❏ acknowledging limitations in stress-testing methodologies, even if they represent best practices;

❏ recognising any data limitations or weaknesses in data quality;

❏ ensuring that stress tests are implemented in a rigorous manner that is appropriate for the stated use, and accounting for any changes to the developed stress test that occur during implementation;

❏ monitoring performance on an ongoing basis and assessing any degradation in performance (where possible);

❏ expressing stress-test uncertainty and inaccuracy, including in the form of confidence bands around estimates and/or factors not observable or not fully incorporated; and

❏ ensuring that vendor or other third-party models are sufficiently validated, including their implementation, to ensure they function as intended and are appropriate for the institution's use.

INTERNAL AUDIT

An additional aspect of governance and controls is the role of internal audit. An institution's internal audit function evaluates practices in a range of risk-management areas, and stress-testing activities should be among them. Internal audit should provide independent evaluation of the ongoing performance, integrity and reliability of stress-testing activities. It is not expected that internal audit will have full knowledge of all stress-test details, or will have to independently assess each stress test used. Rather, internal audit should look across the firm's stress-testing activities and ensure that, as a whole, they are being conducted in a sound manner, are appropriate for the intended purpose and remain current. There should also be an assessment of the staff involved in stress-testing activities regarding their expertise and roles and responsibilities.

Internal audit should also check that the manner in which all material changes to stress tests and their components are appropriately documented, reviewed and approved. In addition, it should evaluate the validation and independent review conducted for stress tests, including all the items listed above relating to validation. In order to conduct such evaluations, internal audit staff should possess sufficient technical expertise to understand the stress tests and challenge their processes and results. It is also important to review the manner in which stress-testing deficiencies are identified, tracked and remediated. On the whole, internal audit serves the valuable task of assessing the full suite of stress-testing activities across the institution on a regular basis to evaluate whether, as a whole, such activities are functioning as intended, in adherence with policies and procedures and serving the institution properly.

OTHER KEY ASPECTS OF STRESS-TESTING GOVERNANCE

This final section outlines some key aspects of stress-testing governance that should also receive attention, and areas in which governance should be exercised. These include stress-testing coverage, stress-testing types and approaches and capital/liquidity stress-testing. The manner in which these areas are addressed can and should vary across institutions. But, at a minimum, these are areas of stress testing that should be addressed in some way by senior management, evaluated as part of the internal control framework and summarised for review by the board.

Stress-testing coverage

❏ Appropriate coverage in stress-testing activities is important, as stress-testing results could give a false sense of comfort if certain portfolios, exposures, liabilities or business-line activities are not included; this underscores the need to document clearly what is included in each stress test and what is not being covered.
❏ Effective stress testing should be applied at various levels in the institution, such as business line, portfolio and risk type, as well as on an enterprise-wide basis; in some cases, stress testing can also be applied to individual exposures or instruments (eg, structured products).
❏ Stress testing should capture the interplay among different exposures, activities and risks and their combined effects; while stress testing several types of risks or business lines simultaneously may prove operationally challenging, an institution should aim to identify concentrations and common risk drivers across risk types and business lines that can adversely affect its financial condition – including those not readily apparent during more benign periods.
❏ Stress testing should be conducted over various relevant time horizons to adequately capture both conditions that may materialise in the near term and adverse situations that take longer to develop.

Stress-testing types and approaches

❏ For any scenario analysis conducted, the scenarios used should be relevant to the direction and strategy set by its board of directors, as well as sufficiently severe to be credible to internal and external stakeholders; at least some scenarios should be of sufficient severity to challenge the viability of the institution.

❏ Scenarios should consider the impact of both firm-specific and systemic stress events and circumstances that are based on historical experience as well as on hypothetical occurrences that could have an adverse impact on an institution's operations and financial condition.

❏ An institution should carefully consider the incremental and cumulative effects of stress conditions, particularly with respect to potential interactions among exposures, activities, and risks and possible second-order or "knock-on" effects.

❏ For an enterprise-wide stress test, institutions should take care in aggregating results across the firm, and business lines and risk areas should use the same assumptions for the chosen scenario, since the objective is to see how the institution as a whole will be affected by a common scenario.

❏ Consideration should be given to reverse stress tests that "break the bank" to help an institution consider scenarios beyond its normal business expectations and see what kinds of events could threaten its viability (even if it is difficult to estimate their likelihood).

Capital and liquidity stress testing

❏ Stress testing for capital and liquidity adequacy should be conducted in coordination with an institution's overall strategy and annual planning cycles; results should be refreshed in the event of major strategic decisions, or other decisions that can materially impact capital or liquidity.

❏ An institution's capital and liquidity stress testing should consider how losses, earnings, cashflows, capital and liquidity would be affected in an environment in which multiple risks manifest themselves at the same time – for example, an increase in credit losses during an adverse interest-rate environment.

❏ Stress testing can aid contingency planning by helping management identify exposures or risks in advance that would need to
be reduced and actions that could be taken to bolster capital and
liquidity positions or otherwise maintain capital and liquidity
adequacy, as well as actions that in times of stress might not be
possible – such as raising capital or accessing debt markets.

❏ Capital and liquidity stress testing should assess the potential
impact of an institution's material subsidiaries suffering capital
and liquidity problems on their own, even if the consolidated
institution is not encountering problems.

❏ Effective stress testing should explore the potential for capital
and liquidity problems to arise at the same time or exacerbate
one another; for example, an institution in a stressed liquidity
position is often required to take actions that have a negative direct or indirect capital impact (eg, selling assets at a loss or incur-
ring funding costs at above market rates to meet funding needs),
which can then further exacerbate liquidity problems.

❏ For capital and liquidity stress tests, it is beneficial for an institution to articulate clearly its objectives for a post-stress outcome,
for instance to remain a viable financial market participant that
is able to meet its existing and prospective obligations and commitments.

CONCLUSION

Similar to other aspects of risk management, an institution's stress-
testing will be effective only if it is subject to strong governance
and effective internal controls to ensure the stress-testing activities
are functioning as intended. Strong governance and effective internal controls help ensure that stress-testing activities contain core
elements, from clearly defined stress-testing objectives to recommended actions. There are many elements that contribute to effective stress-testing governance, foremost being the role of the board
and senior management. Stress testing can be a very powerful risk-
management tool, but the board and senior management should
challenge stress-testing processes and results, demonstrating a
solid understanding of their assumptions, limitations and uncertainties. Additionally, strong governance helps ensure that stress
testing is not isolated within its risk-management function, but

is firmly integrated into business lines, capital and asset–liability committees and other decision-making bodies. Finally, strong governance can help institutions continue to recognise the difficulty in estimating the impact of stressful events and circumstances, thereby acknowledging that stress-test results should be used only with sound judgement and a healthy degree of scepticism.

The views expressed in this chapter do not necessarily represent the views of the Federal Reserve Board or the Federal Reserve System.

1   For the purposes of this chapter, the term "stress testing" is defined as exercises used to conduct a forward-looking assessment of the potential impact of various adverse events and circumstances on a banking institution.
2   Risk appetite is defined as the level and type of risk an institution is able and willing to assume in its exposures and business activities, given its business objectives and obligations to stakeholders.

2

Stress Testing and Other Risk-Management Tools

Akhtar Siddique; Iftekhar Hasan

Office of the Comptroller of Currency; Fordham University

The later chapters in this book are focused on various elements and aspects of stress testing. Stress tests have gained in prominence since the financial crisis of 2007-9. However, stress testing existed in the arsenal of risk managers well before the financial crisis. But it has not existed in isolation: along with stress tests, risk managers have always used other tools.

In our experience, quite sophisticated stress testing existed in many banks' management of market risk before the 2007–9 crisis, and it often focused on the trading book. This included both transaction and portfolio-level stress testing. In contrast, stress testing of credit risk was more likely to be at a transaction level. Portfolio-level stress testing was often rudimentary, if it existed all. Enterprise-wide stress tests tended to be rudimentary (with one or two notable exceptions), as well, especially for institutions that had large banking books.

Risk management in financial institutions has always relied on a panoply of tools and measures. Textbooks on risk management at financial institutions describe various other tools such as position limits and exposure limits, as well as limits on the Greeks, such as on delta or vega.[1]

In this chapter, we discuss the relationship between those other tools and stress testing. We first focus on similarities, differences and consistencies between them. We then discuss the ongoing evolution whereby stress testing has affected other risk-management tools. We also discuss how other risk-management tools are affecting stress testing.

Of the other risk measures, we focus on the value-at-risk (VaR) measures. These include the economic capital (EC) measures. This choice is motivated by the fact that such metrics are designed to capture risk across different types (such as market, credit, interest rate, etc.) in a manner similar to stress testing. Additionally, regulatory capital models as used in Basel II/III can also be viewed as akin to EC models. Enterprise-wide risk limits have often been based on value at risk or its variants. More concretely, many institutions have expressed their risk appetite in terms of a very high percentile such as 99.97% EC.

ENTERPRISE-WIDE STRESS TESTING

As is well known, an important use of stress testing has been to acquire enterprise-wide views of risk, especially in the supervisory stress tests run by regulators around the world. These are the enterprise-wide stress tests.

At a basic level, different risk-management tools can produce different results because of differences in the inputs. For both VaR measures and stress tests, the inputs are data and scenarios.

A stress test may be viewed as translation of a scenario into a loss estimate. In a similar vein, EC or VaR methods also involve translation of scenarios into loss estimates. The distribution of the loss estimates are then used to derive the VaR at a high percentile such as 99% or 99.9%. In practice, stress tests usually focus on a few scenarios, whereas VaR measures commonly utilise a very large number of scenarios.

Hence, as long as identical inputs and similar definitions of loss estimates are used between stress tests and EC/VaR methods, there can be consistency between stress tests and EC/VaR methods, at least when identical scenarios are used.

However, in practice, the loss estimates are often defined quite differently between stress tests and EC methods. In particular, a significant difference is that losses in stress tests have more often than not taken an accounting view rather than a "market" view commonly attempted in EC methods.

The second significant difference has been the horizon. Enterprise-wide stress tests have often examined a long period such as losses over nine quarters in the Dodd–Frank stress tests in the US. In contrast, EC models have focused on losses at a point in time, such as the loss in value at the end of a year.

The final significant difference is the role of probabilities. Scenarios for stress tests can sometimes be generated using distributions of the macroeconomic variables. Therefore, the results of a scenario in a stress test can be assigned a probability, ie, the probability of that scenario. However, probabilities have not played a prominent role in stress tests. For many stress tests conducted around the world, ordinal rank assignments such as "base", "adverse" and "severely adverse" have been done, but with little discussion of the cardinal probabilities attached to them. In contrast, cardinal probabilities generally play a large role in the VaR-type models. For the VaR/EC models using Monte Carlo simulation, there exist complex statistical models underneath. For the VaR models using historical simulation, the history has been viewed as the distribution to draw from. More importantly, in the interpretation and use of the VaR/EC model results, probabilities have played a very large role. A 99.9% VaR loss has often been viewed as a 1-in-1,000 event, albeit with uncertainty (or standard errors) around it.

The last difference has been the approach to scenarios. Stress-test scenarios are often *ad hoc* and conditional, rather than the unconditional scenarios typically generated in VaR-type metrics. Especially, for the regulatory stress tests, the scenario-generation process has looked at the present period as the starting point and then generated two or three hypothetical scenarios from that starting point.

A simple example: stress test

A concrete example can be given for a wholesale portfolio. It is a very simplified example designed to get the idea across rather than provide a guideline to follow. Let us assume the bank is using a two-year scenario that consists of GDP growth and unemployment (see Table 2.1).

Table 2.1 Hypothetical scenarios for two macro variables

Macro variable	1st-year change from base	2nd-year change from base
GDP	−1%	−0.5%
Unemployment	+1%	0%

For wholesale exposures, let us assume that the bank has chosen to model at a portfolio (top-down) level rather than a loan level. At a basic level, the bank needs to estimate the sensitivities of losses in this portfolio to the changes in the two macro variables: GDP growth and unemployment.

Let us assume the following information on the bank's wholesale portfolio (see Table 2.2).

Table 2.2 Portfolio composition for the hypothetical bank

Rating bucket	Balance	1-year default rate (%)	2-year default rate (%)
1	200	0.00	0.00
2	350	0.01	0.02
3	400	0.02	0.10
4	500	0.18	0.53
5	100	1.23	3.31
6	10	5.65	12.35
7	0	21.12	33.53

Let us assume that the bank chooses to use a PD LGD approach. Therefore, the bank needs to compute what the PD is in the stress scenario for each of the two years. Additionally, the bank needs to model which of the exposures transition to a lower rating. Finally, the bank needs to understand what new wholesale loans the bank will generate in the two years and what rating buckets (and PD) the new loans will be in.[2] Based on historical experience, the bank establishes the following first-year and second-year stressed PDs. This may be based on the bank's own historical experience or on industry data. The exposures (EAD) are not expected to change. However, the LGD does change. Using the experience of 2008, the bank finds that, according to Moody's URD data, the LGD for senior unsecured increases from 53% to 63%. The bank chooses to increase its LGD by 10% for all rating buckets. Table 2.3 presents the balances and the stressed parameters for the bank's wholesale portfolio. We are assuming no new business and are not taking into account migration between the two years.

Table 2.3 Projected stressed parameters for the bank's portfolio

Rating bucket	Balance	Stressed LGD	1st-year stressed PD (%)	2nd-year stressed PD (%)
1	100	60%	0.02	0.00
2	200	60%	0.03	0.02
3	400	70%	0.04	0.03
4	500	70%	0.25	0.20
5	100	80%	1.85	1.50
6	200	80%	8.00	8.50
7	500	90%	25.00	20.00

The two-year cumulative loss rate comes out to be 7.44% with these assumptions.

A simple example, continued: EC/VaR.
In the implementation of EC models, banks commonly use a Merton model framework to simulate the defaults and credit quality. In this framework, asset returns are simulated using a factor model framework, and default occurs when the simulated asset value is below a threshold (generally tied to the leverage of the borrower) at the one-year horizon.

In a multifactor setup, for a borrower i with default probability PD

$$Z_i < N^{-1}(PD_i)) \quad \text{where}$$

$$Z_i = \beta_{i1}GDP + \beta_{i2}Unemployment + (\sqrt{1 - \beta_{i1}^2 - \beta_{i2}^2})\eta_i$$

where Z_i is a unit normal variable and GDP and unemployment are simulated values for the two macroeconomic factors. For credit quality, the simulated asset value (and by extension the simulated leverage) is used to impute a spread. It is common for the shock to the spreads to be modelled as a function of Z_i as well. Banks generally generate the asset values using a correlation matrix using correlations between industries and countries.

Banks run these simulations a number of times, sort the losses from the draws, and arrive at the 99th or 99.9th percentile of the loss distribution as the 99th or 99.9th percentile VaR.

The loss for the stress test may correspond to one of the losses and can allow the user to roughly gauge the severity of the stress test.

USE OF VAR MODELS IN STRESS TESTS

Since the VaR models provide a mechanism for computing loss via

$$Loss = PD \times LGD \times EAD$$

One approach that some institutions have taken is to assess where the losses based on stress tests lie in the loss distribution used in the VaR/EC estimation. This process has been one mechanism to associate probability with a given hypothetical or historical stress scenario. Going one step further, some institutions have also used such mechanisms to tie together scenarios across disparate lines of business.

As an example, if a scenario's loss magnitude translates into a 90th percentile loss on the loss distribution for VaR, the bank may take the 90th percentile loss in the EC model as an approximation to the stressed loss for market risk.

No financial institution can be run with zero risk tolerance, nor can all sources of risk be eliminated. However, clearly, some losses are unacceptable because of their magnitudes, irrespective of the scenarios. For such losses, the likelihood (or probability) of the scenario is not that material. However, for most scenarios, the output tends to be used as the loss in that scenario and the likelihood of that scenario.

The assignment of probability via "matching" the stressed loss to a point on the loss distribution serves the useful purpose of coming up with the probability of that scenario. Since, for the practical implementation of stress tests in risk management, assignment of probabilities to the outcomes is important, the probability arrived via the loss distribution can help make the stress tests more actionable.[3]

STRESSED CALIBRATION OF VALUE AT RISK MEASURES

Another approach to incorporating stress into risk measurement methodologies has been the use of stressed inputs. There have been quite a few variants. This has been particularly useful in the market risk area. The incorporation of stress into the risk measurement as well as capital metrics has occurred in both the supervisory approaches and the many banks' internal approaches.

On the supervisory approaches, the new market risk rule requires banks to use stressed inputs, ie, the revisions to the market risk capital framework (BCBS 2011a) states,

> In addition, a bank must calculate a "stressed value-at-risk" measure. This measure is intended to replicate a value-at-risk calculation that would be generated on the bank's current portfolio if the relevant market factors were experiencing a period of stress; and should therefore be based on the 10-day, 99th percentile, one-tailed confidence interval value-at-risk measure of the current portfolio, with model inputs calibrated to historical data from a continuous 12-month period of significant financial stress relevant to the bank's portfolio.

The revisions to the market risk capital framework also explicitly require the use of stress tests: "Banks that use the internal models approach for meeting market risk capital requirements must have in place a rigorous and comprehensive stress-testing program."

Similarly, in the revisions to Basel III (BCBS 2011b), stressed parameters are required: "To determine the default risk capital charge for counterparty credit risk as defined in paragraph 105, banks must use the greater of the portfolio-level capital charge (not including the CVA charge in paragraphs 97–104) based on Effective EPE using current market data and the portfolio-level capital charge based on Effective EPE using a stress calibration. The stress calibration should be a single consistent stress calibration for the whole portfolio of counterparties."

As an illustration, we present some results from Siddique (2010), with six risk factors to simulate the exposures. These are: (1) Three month LIBOR (LIBOR3M); (2) the yield on BAA-rated bonds (BAA); (3) the spread between yields on BAA- and AAA-rated bonds (BAA–AAA); (4) the return on the S&P 500 index (SPX); (5) the change in the volatility option index (VIX); and (6) contract interest rates on commitments for fixed-rate first mortgages (from the Freddie Mac survey) (MORTG). MORTG is in a weekly frequency that is converted to daily data through imputation using a Markov chain Monte Carlo. There are a total of 2,103 daily observations over the period January 2, 2002, through May 10, 2010.

With Monte Carlo, the stressed VaR as 99.9th percentile of a distribution of P&Ls generated using stressed parameters can be constructed. Two separate sets of moments, (1) using the previous 180 days or 750 days' history of the risk factors and (2) the stress period (180 days or 750 days ending in 30.06.09), are used to simulate the risk factors. The 99.9th percentile of the portfolio value is then the 99.9th regular VaR or stressed VaR based on which sets of moments are used. Figure 2.1 illustrates VaR and stressed VaR with a balanced portfolio.

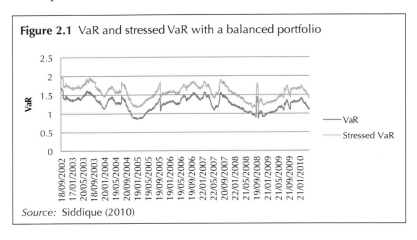

Figure 2.1 VaR and stressed VaR with a balanced portfolio

Source: Siddique (2010)

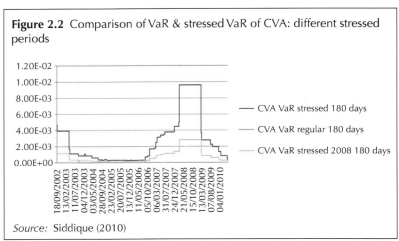

Figure 2.2 Comparison of VaR & stressed VaR of CVA: different stressed periods

Source: Siddique (2010)

Stressed inputs are also used in the capital charge for credit valuation adjustment (CVA) as mentioned above. To assess the impact of the use of stressed inputs for those metrics, Siddique (2010) carries out some other simulations whose results are presented in Figure 2.2.

Two separate periods are used to compute the stressed calibration: (1) 180 days ending 30.09.08; and (2) 180 days ending 30.06.09. The impact of a stressed calibration appears in the early period in the data, where the CVA VaR is substantially higher than the unstressed (regular) CVA VaR. However, in the latter period the unstressed and stressed VaR are identical. It is important to note that an incorrect stress period (ie, ending 30.09.08) can actually produce VaR lower than an unstressed CVA VaR.

There are both advantages and disadvantage of such stressed risk metrics. An obvious advantage is that, with capital for unexpected losses taking into account stressed environments, capital should be adequate when the next stress or shock occurs. That is, a risk metric with a stressed input is usually going to be more conservative.

However, given that the inputs are always stressed, the risk metric will no longer be responsive to the current market conditions, but primarily depend on the portfolio composition.

Only time will tell what the final impact of the incorporation of stress-testing elements into risk management and capital adequacy metrics will be.

CONCLUSION

Stress testing has played a very large role in the assessment of capital adequacy. It has always played a role in risk management as well, which has become much larger as a result of the 2007–9 financial crisis. However, banks have continued to use other risk-management tools such as VaR as well. Nevertheless, stress testing has influenced those tools and those tools have also been used in stress testing.

The views expressed in this chapter are those of the authors alone and do not necessarily represent those of the Comptroller of the Currency or the Bank of Finland.

REFERENCES

Basel Committee on Banking Supervision, 2011a, "Revisions to the Basel II market risk framework", available at http://www.bis.org/publ/bcbs193.pdf.

Basel Committee on Banking Supervision, 2011b, "Basel III: A global regulatory framework for more resilient banks and banking system", available at http://www.bis.org/publ/bcbs189.pdf.

Hull, John, 2012, *Risk Management and Financial Institutions*, 3rd edn (New York: Wiley Books).

Siddique, Akhtar, 2010, "Stressed versus unstressed calibration", Unpublished Manuscript,, Office of the Comptroller of the Currency

1   See, for example, Hull (2012).

2   For the purposes of this simplified example, we are aware that we are making very strong assumptions and simplifications in this example and are ignoring many elements that banks take into account. For example, banks can find that the underwriting of new loans can actually be stricter in a recession, resulting in a lower PD for new business compared with the existing book.

3   Action triggers (when actions need to be taken) for stress tests can be tied to either the output – for example, if the losses exceed a certain level. Alternatively, they can be tied to the input, ie, if the realised input into a test is below/above a threshold. As an example, a stress test can involve a scenario for GDP growth. If GDP growth in a quarter is below a trigger such as −2%, actions can be taken.

3

Stress Testing for Market Risk

Dilip K. Patro, Akhtar Siddique; Xian Sun

Office of the Comptroller of the Currency; Johns Hopkins University

Stress testing has received increased attention from both financial institutions and regulators since the 2007–9 financial crisis. What constitutes reliable and relevant stress tests, however, still stirs a lot of debate among practitioners, stakeholders and researchers. The development and evolving practices of stress testing in the area of market risk management are reviewed in this chapter. In addition, the ways in which stress-testing methodology can be improved for risk management is presented.

Generally speaking, market risk refers to changes in a financial institution's portfolio values due to unanticipated changes in market risk factors such as the price and volatility of equities, interest rates, credit spreads, the price of commodities and foreign-exchange rates. Stress testing for market risk has been an important component of stress tests, both in the internal stress tests run by banking organisations and in the stress tests run by financial regulators. During the financial crisis of 2007–9, the largest losses were often in portfolios sensitive to market risk. Traditionally, stress tests for market risk have been conducted for portfolios in banks' trading books, by using scenarios of possible states for market risk factors. In order to do so, severe but plausible scenarios are often chosen. The choice of scenarios, therefore, is crucial but sometimes inevitably subjective as well. The traditional approaches for scenarios utilise one of the three methods: standard scenarios, historical scenarios and worst-case scenarios.

In the analysis using standard scenarios, the values of portfolios are estimated by stressing the market risk factors by pre-specified shocks, such as changing equity prices by some standard deviations or increasing oil prices to a certain level. These are also referred to as hypothetical scenarios. In the historical-scenarios analysis, market states for a particular historical time period relevant for the bank's portfolio are used. This may include, for example, the 1987 equity crash, the 2007–9 credit crisis, etc. In the worst-case scenario analysis, an automated search over prospective changes in market states is conducted in order to evaluate profits and losses under that scenario.

The traditional stress tests are easy to conduct but have important limitations. For example, the historical scenarios offer reliable but likely less relevant information for risk management in the future; the standard analysis may not be based on the changes in the market states that are close to a stress event; and the worst-case analysis looks at the impacts of changes that are unlikely to occur. Given the drawbacks of traditional stress tests, risk managers have been compelled to use expert judgement along with the results of the stress analyses before taking actions based on results.

The literature on stress testing has grown rapidly, incorporating many suggestions for improvements in stress-testing methods. For example, to integrate stress testing into formal risk modelling, Berkowitz (1999) proposed a solution that includes assigning probabilities to stress-test scenarios; Artzner *et al* (1999) suggested estimating the expected tail loss to address the drawbacks of market value-at-risk (VaR); and Kupiec (1998) discussed the importance of allowing changes in the market states to be correlated. However, it was the financial crisis of 2007–9 that highlighted the importance of stress testing as an important risk-management and regulatory tool, and, as a result, many large banks have incorporated such practices as part of their enterprise-wide risk management. Furthermore, there have been many statutory and regulatory reforms that have required such practices. There has also been an increasing consensus among practitioners, regulators and researchers that stress tests are important because they help banking organisations to understand market risk exposures that methods such as VaR may miss, depending on how VaR models are developed and implemented. The hope is that such information can be used by executive management for strategic planning, capital adequacy and capital allocation, and other major decisions. Stress tests can also help regulators identify risk concentrations and systemic risk, and take mitigating actions.

This chapter discusses several important aspects of stress testing for market risk. First, we focus on the distinction between stress testing for market risk and the more common stress testing for credit risk. After that, we discuss the role of scenarios in market risk and how they may differ from other types of stress tests. A discussion of the horizon for the stress tests follows. The last section focuses on revaluation of the values and computation of profits and losses under the stressed scenarios followed by concluding remarks.

DISTINGUISHING BETWEEN STRESS TESTING FOR MARKET RISK AND CREDIT RISK

Stress testing for market risk and that for credit risk have the common ultimate goal of estimating the impacts on portfolio values of given plausible and severe events. Stress testing for market risk has become almost synonymous with stress testing of the trading book. The trading book, in contrast with the banking book, is characterised by a large number of instruments as well as a larger number of positions and risk factors. Further, mark-to-market losses for trading books are usually measured at a point in time. In particular, derivative positions that are the result of off-balance-sheet activities by financial institutions are often a major focus of market risk stress tests. Probabilistic risk measures, such as VaR, are the primary tool for measuring risk capital as well as computing regulatory capital for such activities. Basel 2.5 has also introduced a "stressed VaR".

On the other hand, stress testing for credit risk is mostly conducted for portfolios in banking books, which primarily consist of portfolios of loans, securities or positions held as investments as well as direct equity investments. The output for stress testing for credit risk could be accounting losses over a period of time due to the impacts on rating changes, probability of default (PD), and loss-given default (LGD). The selection of scenarios could also be more nuanced for the stress testing of credit risks because different segments (such as utility, banking, real estate) in a portfolio may be exposed to different market states. However, trading-book positions are also subject to credit risk if the risk factors include credit spreads. Furthermore, both trading-book and banking-book positions are subject to default of the counterparty for derivatives or securities financing transactions, which is referred to as counterparty credit risk and is discussed in Chapter 4.

Another source of difference between these two types of risk comes from liquidity risk. The impact of changes in liquidity may have an immediate and severe impact on the value of a trading book position. The 2007–9 financial crisis highlighted the severe impacts of extreme illiquidity, which had received little attention in stress testing before the crisis. While banks, regulators and researchers alike have realised the importance of liquidity risk management, incorporating it in the formal stress testing is less straightforward. Liquidity and stress testing are discussed in more detail in Chapter 11.

Aggregation of results from stress tests

Although researchers have proposed sophisticated approaches in aggregating the results of stress tests from various risk sources, concerns remain in bottom-up approaches because it may significantly underestimate the true total risk (Breuer *et al* 2010). For example, Rosenberg and Schuermann (2006) used an approach to aggregate different risk types such as market, credit and operational. They used a bottom-up approach in which various risks (market, credit and operational) are separately analysed and estimated, and then aggregated to produce the total risk. This aggregation relied on the assumption that risk types are subadditive. For example, as Rosenberg and Schuermann (2006) showed, risks can aggregate with perfect correlation ("add-VaR"), which placed an upper bound on the economic capital a bank would need at a given risk-tolerance or confidence level. Risks could also be aggregated using a copula-VaR approach, in which a joint distribution of loss can be estimated by using the shape and location of each of the risk distributions and a dependence function. In general, the aggregated risk estimated by copula-VaR models has tended to be lower than risk estimated by add-VaR. Regardless of whether researchers/practitioners have used an add-VaR or a copula-VaR method to aggregate risk, each of the risk distributions has been separately estimated. The location and shape of the loss distribution for each risk type remain unchanged under summing (with a correlation coefficient of one, or with some "diversification" discount). However, bank losses associated with different risk types may not be additive. In other words, when the worst-case scenario for market risk has occurred, the chance of the worst-case scenario for credit risk may also have increased. This is plausible because financial markets/instruments have become so developed that credit risk is now borne opaquely by capital markets.

STRESS TESTING MARKET RISK AND CHOICE OF SCENARIOS

As in the stress tests for other risks, market risk stress tests have also relied on hypothetical and historical scenarios. There have been other approaches used in the selection of scenarios, such as via mechanically driven searching. Scenarios used in enterprise-wide stress tests have tended to be focused on macroeconomic and financial variables. The scenarios are often specified as vectors of macroeconomic variables such as GDP, unemployment, inflation, house prices and interest rates. The losses resulting from market risk in such scenarios are often difficult to estimate directly. Financial institutions have generally needed to translate the macroeconomic scenarios into changes in market risk factors such as changes in credit spreads, commodity prices and volatilities of the other factors that are used to compute the losses for the market shocks.

As an example, the valuation of a credit default swap depends on the recovery rate and the default probability of the reference asset. If a macroeconomic scenario has been specified in terms of GDP, the unemployment rate and HPI (House Price Index), the bank has created an auxiliary model that translated the macroeconomic variables into default probabilities and recovery rates. Similarly, for financial products such as securitisations, banks generally use systems such as Intex to value the securities.[1] The inputs for Intex are computed from the macroeconomic scenarios using auxiliary models. For a large proportion, if not all, of the exposures subject to market risk, the necessary variables are the inputs for the pricing models used for the trading-book positions. These inputs are prices, volatilities and other parameters such as correlations. Generally, the stress is modelled as very large movements in these inputs.

Given the fairly large flexibility in how the macroeconomic variables are translated into the variables more commonly used in market risk stress testing, comparability and consistency within and across institutions can be a challenge in market risk stress testing as compared with credit risk stress testing. Therefore, in many of the regulatory stress tests based on the Dodd–Frank Act or the Federal Reserve's CCAR (Comprehensive Capital Analysis and Review) in the United States and the supervisory stress tests run by the European Banking Authority (EBA) in Europe, regulators have specified the values for many of the variables that would constitute the inputs for the market risk valuations systems. However, even in those cases, institutions frequently had to come up with inputs for risk factors that the regulators had not specified.

An additional consideration has been that, unlike with the banking book, where a bank is naturally "long credit", for trading-book portfolios a bank may actually have positions that have gains in an adverse scenario. That imposes additional pressures on how (and how well) the results of a market risk stress test are verified. Given that the scenarios provided by regulators may have failed to encompass all possible risk factors that an institution uses, a greater degree of inconsistency in the market risk stress tests compared with credit risk stress tests occurs. This highlights the importance of effective monitoring by the regulator. Although the regulator's goal of specifying the values for the inputs of the market risk valuations is to enhance consistency and comparability within and across the banks, it encounters problems such as "one size does not fit all" and "catch up with the changes". In order to ensure the market risk stress tests correctly reflect an individual bank's riskiness, the regulator needs to subject the inputs, especially those generated by the institutions, to greater scrutiny to validate their representativeness and comprehensiveness.

TIME HORIZON IN MARKET RISK STRESS TESTS

Stress tests for other risk areas such as credit risk have generally focused on the losses over a long horizon such as the nine quarters used for the Dodd–Frank Act and CCAR stress tests in the United States. An important element of these stress tests has been how the portfolio may have changed in the stressed period, such as new business or changes in the value of the existing portfolio even if they do not default. Historically, stress tests for market risk, such as the stress tests focused on trading portfolios, have had very short horizons, such as ten days or even instantaneous, depending on the nature of the trading frequency of the products in the portfolios. The shorter horizon was motivated by more frequent trading and a shorter holding period that has characterised the trading book.

The choice of horizon not only had a direct impact on the valuation of the portfolios under stress tests, but also had significant implications for how banks took actions (such as reducing exposures) based on the outputs of the stress tests. For example, an important aspect of the choice of horizon is what happens after the initial shock, that is to say the aftershock. Alexander and Sheedy (2008) pointed out that the consequences of a shock event can include some or all of the following: further large moves in the same market (as predicted by volatility clustering); large moves in other markets and higher correlations between markets; and increased implied volatility in option markets and reduced market liquidity. In a portfolio-level stress test of market risk, the horizon used may be the same as the horizon for the VaR, such as ten days. In such a scenario, the aftershock may not materialise.

However, for enterprise-wide stress tests the market risk stress tests generally need to be the same horizon as the stress tests for the other risks, such as credit risk, because a common horizon is needed to put the various risks on a common footing. Two features then can become important. The first is that the aforementioned aftershock is then relevant. Simply, taking the 10-day loss and expanding it to a one-year horizon via a method such as multiplying by the square root of time may misstate the losses, since that ignores the aftershocks.[2] The second is the impact of hedging, other management actions and what assumptions are made regarding hedging. Whether hedging is taken into account and how the hedging is accommodated has varied among institutions. Banks have traditionally argued that they can implement dynamic hedging strategies that can end up reducing the unexpected losses of a portfolio in a significant way. However, in a severely stressed environment it is not clear if the hedging instruments remain available with enough liquidity. The experiences with the 1987 crisis showed that dynamic hedging strategies that worked in normal environments failed to take into account the positive feed-back of hedging demand in a stressed environment especially where there very large discontinuities.[3] When lengthening the horizon for the market stress tests while conducting enterprise-wide stress tests, it may be problematic to assume that dynamic hedging is still as ef-fective as in normal markets when everything else is also stressed.

REVALUATIONS AND COMPUTATION OF P&L UNDER THE STRESSED SCENARIOS

Once market stress scenarios are specified, the next step is to re-value the positions in the portfolio under the stressed scenarios. The difference in the value of the positions under the stressed sce-nario and the current value is the profit or loss (generally referred to as P&L). There are several steps in this process of estimation of stressed P&L that may involve approximations and calibrations. These steps are discussed below.

Mark-to-market versus market-to-model valuations

Valuations for routine risk management and reporting purposes rely on either mark-to-market valuations that use closing market prices from exchanges/market consensus prices from a pricing ven-dor, or mark-to-model valuations based on analytical or numerical models. These models often have input parameters that are calibrat-ed using current market prices. These pricing models, or "pricers", form the backbone of revaluations or repricing of positions under stressed scenarios. Whether the positions are marked to market or marked to model, the pricing models are used to generate risk sen-sitivities to risk factors. For example, changes in prices to spot prices are often referred to as delta, while changes in prices to changes in volatility are referred to as vega etc. These risk sensitivities, such as delta, gamma and vega, are based on Taylor-series representation of changes in valuations for changes in risk factors. Banks often use a "bump-and-reprice" approach to estimate these sensitivities.[4] These risk sensitivities are aggregated by product, business unit, legal en-tity and so forth, based on the granularity of desired risk measure-ment and risk reporting. Once we have the pricers and/or the risk sensitivities for the positions in the portfolio, the market shocks un-der stress are applied to reprice those positions.

While in many cases the market shocks may be applied directly to the risk factors, in many other cases it is necessary to apply them as a relative or absolute percentage of the current level of the risk factors. Further, based on how the pricing model takes market inputs, there may be a need for transformation of the stressed scenario risk factor inputs to inputs that can be used in the pricing models. This may also be necessitated by the need to avoid hitting boundary conditions, negative rates or negative forward volatilities.

Revaluations: sensitivity-based, grid-based or full revaluations

When repricing positions under specified scenarios, banks may use risk sensitivities that are usually generated in front-office pricing systems to revalue the positions. Such approximations are reasonable when the risk factor shocks are small. For linear instruments such as cash equity, use of risk sensitivities can be exact. However when revaluing positions for which there is a non-linear relationship between prices and risk factor moves, use of full revaluations using the front-office pricers is recommended, since the Taylor-series approximation using risk sensitivities will not perform well for large moves in risk factors. Apart from use of risk sensitivities using Taylor-series approximations or use of full revaluations where all relevant risk factors are shocked simultaneously, banks may also use what are called valuation grids. These are pre-estimated full revaluations for specified moves in risk factors, and can be for one risk factor or for joint moves in risk factors (two or multidimensional grids). If the stress scenario is in between or outside what are the prespecified grid points (say 1%, 5%, 10% and so forth), interpolation and extrapolation are used to estimate P&L for those scenarios. Although not as reliable as full revaluations using front office systems, grid-based approximation has the advantage of computational speed, especially when dealing with large numbers of positions and/or scenarios.

Revaluations in practice

Banks may use a mix of full revaluation or revaluations using approximations for the various positions. For positions and products that have a non-linear relationship between the prices and the risk factors, full revaluation using front-office systems is the best option. In some cases banks may use middle-office versions of the front-office systems. As long as these are calibrated as frequently as the front-office systems and have the exact implementation, that may be sufficient. Banks may sometimes also have pricers in risk systems that are different from front-office pricers. In such cases it is important to ensure that the valuations from the two systems are consistent and that these models have gone through the model-validation process that is expected of other pricing and risk models.

Model failures, cross-effects, approximations, specific risk and use of proxies

Sometimes valuation models that are designed for normal market conditions may fail to calibrate or price under extreme scenarios. This could be due to things such as negative interest rates or forward rates or approximations such as moment-matching conditions that do not perform well under higher volatilities. Further, the practice of revaluating positions using risk sensitivities or grids may fail to capture the cross effect of shocks across different asset classes (for example, equities and currencies prices and volatilities). A full revaluation by design may capture such effects while use of risk sensitivities and grids may not. In such cases the banks must estimate the impact of such omissions separately and, if found material, make a conservative adjustment to the loss estimates. Similarly, shocks designed for broad market risk factors will not be sufficient for issuer-specific risk, especially if the bank has a concentration in such positions. In such cases, use of name-specific shocks may be necessary. Furthermore, when proxies are used, it must be noted that there will be a basis between the risk factor and the proxy, and the basis may get exacerbated during periods of stress. There do not exist standard fixes for such issues, and management needs to monitor for such failures and deal with them on a case-by-case basis and apply conservative adjustments as necessary. These issues highlight the need for an effective model risk management process at the institution, which should also scope in use of models for stress testing.[5]

CONCLUSION

Stress testing for market risk is an important tool for risk management, capital adequacy and bank supervision. This chapter summarises the important elements of stress testing for market risk at financial institutions, where different scenarios of market risk factors are developed and portfolios sensitive to market risk are revalued under those scenarios to estimate potential losses. This chapter distinguished stress testing for market risk from stress testing for credit risk, discussed development of stress-test scenarios, importance of time horizons in stress testing and challenges with aggregation of results for various types of risks. Finally, this chapter discussed methods for revaluation of the portfolios under stress scenarios and some things to consider as part of an effective model risk management for stress testing.

The views expressed in this chapter are those of the authors alone and do not necessarily represent those of the Comptroller of the Currency. The authors would like to thank Jonathan Jones and Wenling Lin for helpful comments.

REFERENCES

Alexander, Carol, and Elisabeth Sheedy, 2008, "Developing a stress-testing framework based on market risk models", *Journal of Banking & Finance* 32, pp. 2220–36.

Artzner, Philippe, *et al*, 1999, "Coherent Measures of Risk." *Mathematical Finance* 9, pp. 203–28.

Berkowitz, Jeremy, 1999, "A Coherent Framework for Stress-Testing", manuscript, Board of Governors of the Federal Reserve.

Breuer, T., *et al*, 2010, "Does adding up of economic capital for market- and credit risk amount to conservative risk measurement?", *Journal of Banking and Finance* 34, pp. 703–712.

Kambhu, John, 1997, "The size of hedge adjustments of derivatives dealers' US dollar interest rate options", manuscript, Federal Reserve Bank of New York.

Kupiec, Paul, 1998, "Stress-testing in a Value at Risk Framework." *Journal of Derivatives* 6, pp. 7–24.

Rosenberg, J. V., and T. Schuermann, 2006, "A general approach to integrated risk management with skewed, fat-tailed risks", *Journal of Financial Economics* 79, pp. 569–614.

1   Intex is software widely used by many banks. It has provided deal cashflow models, analytics and structuring software for RMBSs, ABSs, CMBSs, CDOs, CLNs and covered bond securities.

2   Whether applying a simple square-root-of-time rule understates or overstates the losses in such a situation is unclear in the authors' experience, and depends on the assumptions and the markets. In some cases, mean reversion over a one-year period means that a straight square root of time overstates losses.

3   Kambhu (1997) assesses the magnitude of hedging demand from dealers in fixed-income markets.

4   A Taylor series is a series expansion of a function from the values of the function's derivatives at single point.

5   See OCC bulletin 2011–12 for principles of effective model risk management.

4

The Evolution of Stress Testing Counterparty Exposures

David Lynch
Federal Reserve Board

The call for better stress testing of counterparty credit risk exposures has been a common occurrence from both regulators and industry in response to financial crises (CRMPG I 1999; CRMPG II 2005; FRB 2011). Despite this call, statistical measures have progressed more rapidly than stress testing. In this chapter we examine how stress testing may be improved by building off the development of the statistical measures. We begin by describing how the measurement of counterparty risk has developed by viewing the risk as a credit risk and as a market risk. The problems this creates for a risk manager who is developing a stress-testing framework for counterparty risk are then identified. Methods to stress-test counterparty risk are described from both a credit risk perspective and from a market risk perspective, starting with the simple case of stressing current exposures to a counterparty. These stress tests are considered from both a portfolio perspective and individual counterparty perspective. Last, some common pitfalls in stress testing counterparty exposures are identified.

THE EVOLUTION OF COUNTERPARTY CREDIT RISK MANAGEMENT

The measurement and management of counterparty credit risk (CCR) has evolved rapidly since the late 1990s. CCR may well be the fastest-changing part of financial risk management over the time period. This is especially true of the statistical measures used in CCR. Despite this quick progress in the evolution of statistical measures of CCR, stress testing of CCR has not evolved nearly as quickly.

In the 1990s a large part of counterparty credit management involved evaluation of the creditworthiness of an institution's derivatives counterparties and tracking the current exposure of the counterparty. In the wake of the Long-Term Capital Management crisis, the Counterparty Risk Management Policy Group cited deficiencies in these areas and also called for use of better measures of CCR. Regulatory capital for CCR consisted of add-ons to current exposure measures (BCBS 1988.) The add-ons were a percentage of the gross notional of derivative transactions with a counterparty. As computer technology has advanced, the ability to model CCR developed quickly and allowed assessments of how the risk would change in the future.

The fast pace of change in CCR modelling can be seen in the progression of statistical measures used to gauge counterparty credit risk. First, potential-exposure models were developed to measure and limit counterparty risk. Second, the potential-exposure models were adapted to expected positive-exposure models that allowed derivatives to be placed in portfolio credit risk models similar to loans (Canabarro, Picoult and Wilde 2003). These two types of models are the hallmark of treating CCR as a credit risk. Pykhtin and Zhu (2007) provide an introduction to these models. The treatment of CCR as credit risk was the predominant framework for measuring and managing CCR from 2000 to 2006 and was established as the basis for regulatory capital as part of Basel II (BCBS 2005). During this time, risk mitigants such as netting agreements and margining were incorporated into the modelling of CCR. The definitions of these exposure measures used in this chapter follow those in BCBS (2005).

❏ Current exposure is the larger of zero and the market value of a transaction or portfolio of transactions within a netting set, with a counterparty that would be lost upon the default of the counterparty, assuming no recovery on the value of those transactions in bankruptcy. Current exposure is often also called replacement cost.

❏ Peak exposure is a high-percentile (typically 95% or 99%) of the distribution of exposures at any particular future date before the maturity date of the longest transaction in the netting set. A peak exposure value is typically generated for many future dates up until the longest maturity date of transactions in the netting set.

❏ Expected exposure is the mean (average) of the distribution of exposures at any particular future date before the longest-maturity transaction in the netting set matures. An expected exposure value is typically generated for many future dates up until the longest maturity date of transactions in the netting set.

❏ Expected positive exposure (EPE) is the weighted average over time of expected exposures where the weights are the proportion that an individual expected exposure represents of the entire time interval. When calculating the minimum capital requirement, the average is taken over the first year or over the time period of the longest-maturity contract in the netting set.

Furthermore, an unusual problem associated with CCR, that of wrong-way risk, has been identified (Levin and Levy 1999; Finger 2000). Wrong-way risk occurs when the credit quality of the counterparty is correlated with the exposure, so that exposure grows when the counterparty is most likely to default. When exposure is fixed, as is the case for a loan, this does not occur, so adaptation of techniques used in other areas of risk management is more difficult.

At the same time, the treatment of CCR as a market risk was developing, but was largely relegated to pricing in a credit valuation adjustment (CVA), prior to the financial crisis of 2007–9. This was first described for Swaps (Sorensen and Bollier 1994; Duffie and Huang 1996) and has since become widespread due to the accounting requirement of FAS 157 (FASB 2006). The complexities of risk-managing this price aspect of a derivatives portfolio did not become apparent until the crisis. Prior to the crisis, credit spreads for financial institutions were relatively stable and the CVA was a small portion of the valuation of banks' derivatives portfolios. During the crisis, both credit spreads and exposure amounts for derivative transactions experienced wide swings, and the combined effect resulted in both large losses and large, unusual gains. Financial institutions are just now beginning to develop their frameworks to risk-manage CVA. The regulatory capital framework has adopted a CVA charge to account for this source of risk (BCBS 2011).

The treatment of CCR as a credit risk or CCR as a market risk has implications for the organisation of a financial institution's trading activities and the risk-management disciplines (Picoult 2005; Canabarro 2009). Both treatments are valid ways to manage the portfolio, but adoption of one view alone leaves a financial institution blind to the risk from the other view. If CCR is treated as a credit risk, a bank can still be exposed to changes in CVA. A financial institution may establish PFE limits and manage its default risk through collateral and netting, but it still must include CVA in the valuation of its derivatives portfolio. Inattention to this could lead to balance-sheet surprises. If CCR is treated as a market risk, dynamically hedging its CVA to limit its market risk losses, it remains exposed to large drops in creditworthiness or the sudden default of one of its counterparties. A derivatives dealer is forced to consider both aspects.

The view of CCR has implications for how the risk is managed as well. The traditional credit risk view is that the credit risk of the counterparty can be managed at inception or through collateral arrangements set up in advance, but there is little that can be done once the trades are in place. At default the financial institution must replace the trades of the defaulting counterparty in the market all at once in order to rebalance its book. A large emphasis is placed on risk mitigants and credit evaluation as a result.

The view of CCR as a market risk allows that its counterparty credit risk can be hedged. Instead of waiting until the counterparty defaults to replace the contracts, the financial institution will replace the trades with a counterparty in the market before it defaults by buying the positions in proportion to the counterparty's probability of default. Thus a counterparty with a low probability of default will have little of its trades replaced in advance by the financial institution, but, as its credit quality deteriorates, a larger proportion of those trades will be replaced by moving them to other counterparties. At default, the financial institution will have already replaced the trades and the default itself would be a non-event.

IMPLICATIONS FOR STRESS TESTING

The dual nature of CCR leads to many measures that capture some important aspect of CCR. On the credit risk side, there are the important measures of exposure: current exposure, peak exposure and expected exposure. On the market risk side there is the valuation aspect coming from CVA, and there is the risk generated by changes in the CVA, as measured by VaR of CVA, for example. This creates a dazzling array of information that can be difficult to interpret and understand at both portfolio and counterparty levels. The search for a concise answer to the question "What is my counterparty credit risk?" is difficult enough, but an equally difficult question is "What CCR measures should I stress?"

When confronted with the question of stress testing for CCR, the multiplicity of risk measures means that stress testing is a complicated endeavour. To illustrate this complexity we can compare the number of stresses that a bank may run on its market risk portfolio with the number of similar stresses a bank would run on its counterparty credit risk portfolio. In market risk, running an equity crash stress test may result in one or two stress numbers: an instantaneous loss on the current portfolio and potentially a stress VaR loss. A risk manager can easily consider the implications of this stress.

In contrast, the CCR manager would have to run this stress at the portfolio level and at the counterparty level, and would have to consider CCR as both a credit risk and a market risk. The number of stress-test results would be at least twice the number of counterparties plus one.[1] The number of stress-test results would at least double again if the risk manager stressed risk measures in addition to considering instantaneous shocks.[2] The number of stress values that can be produced can bewilder even the most diligent risk manager, and overwhelm IT resources.

Despite this array of potential stress results, a risk manager must stress-test counterparty exposures to arrive at a comprehensive view of the risk of the financial institution's portfolio.[3] This chapter provides a description of the types of stress tests that can be run to get a picture of the CCR in a financial institution's derivative portfolio.

STRESS TESTING CURRENT EXPOSURE

The most common stress tests used in counterparty credit are stresses of current exposure. To create a stressed current value, the bank assumes a scenario of underlying risk-factor changes and reprices the portfolio under that scenario. Generally speaking, a financial institution applies these stresses to each counterparty. It is common practice for banks to report their top counterparties with the largest current exposure to senior management in one table, and then follow that table with their top counterparties, with the largest stressed current exposure placed under each scenario in separate tables.

For example, Table 4.1 shows an example of what a financial institution's report on its equity crash stress test for current exposure might look like. The table lists the top 10 counterparties by their exposure to an equity market crash of 25%. It shows the following categories: the counterparty rating, market value of the trades with the counterparty, collateral, current exposure, and stressed current exposure after the stress is applied but before any collateral is collected. This provides a snapshot of which counterparties a CCR manager should be concerned about in the event of a large drop in equity markets. A financial institution would construct similar tables for other stresses representing credit events or interest-rate shocks. These tables would likely list different counterparties as being exposed to the stress scenario, since it is unlikely that the counterparty with the most exposure to an equity crash is the same as the counterparty with the most exposure to a shock in interest rates.

Table 4.1 Current exposure stress test: equity crash

($MM)					
Scenario: Equity market down 25%					
($MM)	**Rating**	**MtM**	**Collateral**	**Current Exposure**	**Stressed Current Exposure**
Counterparty A	A	0.5	0	0.5	303
Counterparty B	AA	100	0	100	220
Counterparty C	AA	35	0	35	119
Counterparty D	BBB	20	20	0	76
Counterparty E	BBB	600	600	0	75
Counterparty F	A	-5	0	0	68
Counterparty G	A	-10	0	0	50
Counterparty H	BB	-50	0	0	24
Counterparty I	A	35	20	15	17
Counterparty J	BB	24	24	0	11

This type of stress testing is quite useful, and financial institutions have been conducting it for some time. It allows the bank to identify which counterparties would be of concern in such a stress event, and also how much the counterparty would owe the financial institution under the scenario. However, stress tests of current exposure has a few problems. First, aggregation of the results is problematic, and, second, it does not account for the credit quality of the counterparties. Also, it provides no information on wrong-way risk.

While the individual counterparty results are meaningful, there is no meaningful way to aggregate these stress exposures without incorporating further information. If we were to sum the exposures to arrive at an aggregate stress exposure, this would represent the loss that would occur if every counterparty defaulted in the stress scenario. Unless the scenario were the Apocalypse, this would clearly be an exaggeration of the losses. Other attempts to aggregate these results are also flawed. For example, running the stressed current exposure through a portfolio credit risk model would also be incorrect, since expected exposures, not current exposures, should go through a portfolio credit risk model (Canabarro, Picoult, Wilde 2003). Table 4.1 does not provide an aggregate stressed amount as a result.

The stressed current exposures also do not take into account the credit quality of the counterparty. This should be clear from the outset, since it accounts only for the value of the trades with the counterparty and not the counterparty's willingness or ability to pay. This is an important deficiency since a US$200 million exposure to a start-up hedge fund is very different from a US$200 million exposure to an AAA corporate. While we could imagine a limit structure for stressed current exposure that takes into account the credit quality of the counterparty, most financial institutions have not gone down this path for stressed current exposure. The degree of difficulty involved in doing this for each scenario and each rating category is daunting, mostly because the statistical measures such peak exposure provide a more consistent way to limit exposure by counterparties who may be exposed to different scenarios. From Table 4.1, it is unclear whether the CCR manager should be more concerned about Counterparty C or Counterparty D in the stress event. While Counterparty C has a larger stressed current exposure than Counterparty D, Counterparty C has a better credit quality.

Last, stress tests of current exposure provide little insight into wrong-way risk. As a measure of exposure that omits the credit quality of the counterparty, these stress tests without additional information cannot provide any insight into the correlation of exposure with credit quality. Stresses of current exposure are useful for monitoring exposures to individual counterparties, but do not provide either a portfolio outlook or incorporate a credit quality.

STRESS TESTING THE LOAN EQUIVALENT

To stress-test in the credit framework for CCR, we first have to describe a typical stress test that would be performed on a loan portfolio. The typical framework for loans is to analyse how expected losses would change under a stress.

For credit provisioning, we might look at an unconditional expected loss across a pool of loan counterparties. Expected loss for any one counterparty is the product of the probability of default, p_i, where this may depend on other variables, exposure at default, ead_i, and loss-given default, lgd_i. The expected loss for the pool of loan counterparties is:

$$EL = \sum_{i=1}^{N} p_i \cdot ead_i \cdot lgd_i$$

A stress test could take exposure at default and loss-given default as deterministic and focus on stresses where the probability of default is subject to a stress. In this case, the probability of default is taken to be a function of other variables; these variables may represent an important exchange rate or an unemployment rate, for example. In this case, the stressed expected loss is calculated conditional on some of the variables affecting the probability of default being set to their stressed values; the stressed probability of default is denoted p_i^s; and the stressed expected loss is:

$$EL_s = \sum_{i=1}^{N} p_i^s \cdot ead_i \cdot lgd_i$$

The stress loss for the loan portfolio is EL_s-EL. A financial institution can generate stress tests in this framework rather easily. It can simply increase the probability of defaults, or it can stress the variables that these probabilities of defaults depend on. These variables are typically macroeconomic variables or balance-sheet items for the counterparty. The stress losses can be generated for individual loan counterparties as well as at an aggregate level.

This framework can be adapted for CCR treated as a credit risk. In this case the probability of default and loss-given default of the counterparty are treated the same, but now exposure at default is stochastic and depends on the levels of market variables. EPE multiplied by an alpha factor (Picoult 2005; Wilde 2005) is the value that allows CCR exposures to be placed in a portfolio credit model along with loans and arrive at a high-percentile loss for the portfolio of exposures (both loan and derivatives).[4] The same procedure is applied here and EPE is used in an expected-loss model. In this case expected loss and expected loss conditional on a stress for derivatives counterparties are:

$$EL = \sum_{i=1}^{N} p_i \cdot \alpha \cdot epe_i \cdot lgd_i$$

$$EL_s = \sum_{i=1}^{N} p_i^s \cdot \alpha \cdot epe_i^s \cdot lgd_i$$

Stress losses on the derivatives portfolio can be calculated similarly to the loan portfolio case. A financial institution can stress the probability of default similarly to the loan case by stressing probability of default or the variables that affect probability of default, including company balance-sheet values, macroeconomic indicators and values of financial instruments. It can also combine the stress losses on the loan portfolio and the stress losses on its derivatives portfolio by adding these stress losses together.

Table 4.2 shows the results of a typical stress test that could be run that would shock the probability of default of counterparties in a derivatives portfolio. The stress test might parallel the increase in PD by industry after the dotcom crash in 2001–2. The expected loss, stressed expected loss and the stress loss may all be aggregated and even combined with similar values from the loan portfolio.

In addition, a financial institution has a new set of variables to stress. Exposure, as measured by EPE, depends on market variables such as equity prices and swap rates. A financial institution can stress these market variables and see their impact. It should be noted that it is not clear whether a stress will, in aggregate, increase or decrease expected losses. This will depend on a whole host of factors, including the directional bias of the bank's portfolio, which counterparties are margined and which have excess margin. This is in marked contrast to the case where stresses of the probabilities of default are considered. Stresses to the variables affecting the probability of default generally have similar effects and the effects are in the same direction across counterparties. When conducting stresses to EPE, a bank need not consider aggregation with its loan portfolio.[5] Loans are insensitive to the market variables and thus will not have any change in exposure due to changes in market variables.

There are a whole host of stresses that can be considered. Typically a financial institution will use an instantaneous shock of market variables, these are often the same current exposure shocks from the previous section. In principle, we could shock these variables at some future point in their evolution or create a series of shocks over time. This is not common, however, and shocks to current exposure are the norm. In the performance of these instantaneous shocks, the initial market value of the derivatives is shocked prior to running the simulation to calculate EPE. How this shock affects EPE depends on the degree of collateralisation and the "moneyness" of the portfolio, among other things.

Table 4.3 shows how a financial institution might reconsider its stress test of current exposure in an expected-loss framework. Now, in addition to considering just current exposure, the financial institution must consider including the probability of default over the time horizon and the expected positive exposure in its stress-test framework. In this case we are looking at changes to current exposures and thus EPE. We hold the PD constant here. The expected loss, even under stress, is small and measured in thousands. This is due to the rather small probabilities of default that we are considering. We are able to aggregate expected losses and stress losses by simply adding them up.

A financial institution can consider joint stresses of credit quality and market variables as well. Conceptually, this is a straightforward exercise, but, in practice, deciding how changes in macroeconomic variables or balance-sheet variables are consistent with changes in market variables can be daunting. There is very little that necessarily connects these variables. Equity-based approaches (Merton 1974; Kealhofer 2003) come close to providing a link; however, it remains unclear how to link an instantaneous shock of exposure to the equity-based probability of default. While exposure can and should react immediately, it is unclear whether equity-based probabilities of default should react so quickly.

Table 4.2 PD stress: dotcom crash

	PD (%)	EPE (US$m)	LGD (%)	EL (US$m)	Stressed PD (%)	Stressed EL (US$m)	Stress loss (US$m)
Counterparty AA	0.05	213.00	0.70	0.08	0.50	0.77	0.69
Counterparty BB	0.03	202.50	0.60	0.04	0.30	0.38	0.34
Counterparty CC	0.45	75.00	0.70	0.24	0.62	0.34	0.09
Counterparty DD	0.90	30.00	0.65	0.18	1.20	0.24	0.06
Counterparty EE	1.05	10.00	0.75	0.08	1.40	0.11	0.03
Counterparty FF	0.09	157.00	0.50	0.07	0.12	0.10	0.02
Counterparty GG	0.98	68.00	0.70	0.48	1.02	0.50	0.02
Counterparty HH	2.17	3.00	0.34	0.02	3.00	0.03	0.01
Counterparty II	0.03	150.00	0.20	0.01	0.05	0.02	0.01
Counterparty JJ	0.50	50.00	0.60	0.15	0.50	0.15	0.00
Aggregate				1.36		2.63	1.27

Table 4.3 Expected-loss stress test in a credit framework

				Scenario: Equity market down 25%					
	PD (%)	MtM (US$m)	Collateral (US$m)	CE (US$m)	EPE (US$m)	EL (US$000)	stress EPE (US$m)	stress EL (US$000)	stress loss (US$000)
Counterparty A	0.03	0.5	0	0.5	4.37	0.09	303.00	6.09	6.00
Counterparty B	0.02	100	0	100	100.00	1.34	220.00	2.95	1.61
Counterparty C	0.02	35	0	35	35.16	0.47	119.00	1.59	1.12
Counterparty D	0.18	20	20	0	3.99	0.48	76.00	9.16	8.68
Counterparty E	0.18	600	600	0	3.99	0.48	75.00	9.04	8.56
Counterparty F	0.03	-5	0	0	2.86	0.06	68.00	1.37	1.31
Counterparty G	0.03	-10	0	0	1.98	0.04	50.04	1.00	0.96
Counterparty H	1.2	-50	0	0	0.02	0.02	25.12	19.73	19.72
Counterparty I	0.03	35	20	15	16.31	0.33	19.20	0.36	0.04
Counterparty J	0.12	24	24	0	3.99	0.32	14.66	1.03	0.71
aggregate						3.62		52.32	48.70

This leads to another drawback: the difficulty of capturing the connection between the probability of default and exposure that is often of concern in CCR. There are many attempts to capture the wrong-way risk, but most are ad hoc. At present the best approach to identifying wrong-way risk in the credit framework is to stress the current exposure, identify those counterparties that are most exposed to the stress and then carefully consider whether the counterparty is also subject to wrong-way risk.

Stress tests of CCR as a credit risk allow a financial institution to advance beyond simple stresses of current exposure. They allow aggregation of losses with loan portfolios, and also allow consideration of the quality of the counterparty. These are important improvements that allow a financial institution to better manage its portfolio of derivatives. Treating CCR as a market risk allows further improvements (notably, the probability of default will be inferred from market variables), and it will be easier to consider joint stresses of credit quality and exposure.

STRESS TESTING CVA

When stress testing CCR in a market risk context, we are usually concerned with the market value of the counterparty credit risk and the losses that could result due to changes in market variables, including the credit spread of the counterparty. In many cases a financial institution will consider its unilateral CVA for stress testing. Here, the financial institution is concerned with the fact that its counterparties could default under various market scenarios. In addition, we might consider not only that a financial institution's counterparty could default, but also that the financial institution in question could default to its counterparty. In this case, the financial institution is considering its bilateral CVA. Initially we just consider stress testing the unilateral CVA.

First we use a common simplified formula for CVA to a counterparty that omits wrong-way risk (Gregory 2010).

$$CVA_n = LGD_n^* \cdot \sum_{j=1}^{T} EE_n^*(t_j) \cdot q_n^*(t_{j-1}, t_j)$$

Where:

$EE_n^*(t_j)$ is the discounted expected exposure during the jth time period calculated under a risk-neutral measure for counterparty n.

$q_n^*(t_{j-1}, t_j)$ is the risk-neutral marginal default probability for counterparty n in the time interval from t_{j-1} to t_j and T is the final maturity.

LGD_n^* is the risk-neutral loss-given default for counterparty n.

Aggregating across N counterparties:

$$CVA = \sum_{n=1}^{N} LGD_n^* \cdot \sum_{j=1}^{T} EE_n^*(t_j) \cdot q_n^*(t_{j-1}, t_j)$$

Implicit in this description is that the key components all depend on values of market variables. $q_n^*(t_{j-1}, t_j)$ is derived from credit spreads of the counterparty, LGD_n^* is generally set by convention or from market spreads and $EE_n^*(t_j)$ depends on the values of derivative transactions with the counterparty. To calculate a stressed CVA we would apply an instantaneous shock to some of these market variables. The stresses could affect $EE_n^*(t_j)$ or $q_n^*(t_{j-1}, t_j)$.

Stressed CVA is given by:

$$CVA^S = \sum_{n=1}^{N} LGD_n^* \cdot \sum_{j=1}^{T} EE_n^S(t_j) \cdot q_n^S(t_{j-1}, t_j)$$

And the stress loss is CVA^s-CVA.

Stressing current exposure, as described previously, has similar effects. An instantaneous shock will have some impact on the expected exposure calculated in later time periods, so all of the expected exposures will have to be recalculated. Stresses to the marginal probability of default are usually derived from credit spread shocks.

Similarities can be seen between stress testing CCR in a credit risk framework and doing so in market risk framework. There is a reliance in both cases on expected losses being the product of loss-given default, exposure and the probability of default. However, these values will be quite different, depending on the view of CCR as a market risk or credit risk. The reasons for the differences are many, and the use of risk-neutral values for CVA as opposed to physical values for expected losses is the most prominent. In addition, CVA uses expected losses over the life of the transactions, whereas expected losses use a specified time horizon, and the model for determining the probability of default is market-based in CVA.

Using a market-based measure for the probability of default provides some benefits. It is possible in these circumstances to incorporate a correlation between the probability of default and the exposure. Hull and White (2012) describe methods to do this. They also demonstrate an important stress test that is available, a stress of the correlation between exposure and the probability of default. They show that the correlation can have an important effect on the measured CVA. Since there is likely to be a high degree of uncertainty around the correlation, a financial institution should run stress tests to determine the impact on profit and loss if the correlation is wrong.

To capture the full impact of various scenarios on CVA profit and loss, a financial institution should include the liability side effects in the stress as well. This part of the bilateral CVA (BCVA), often called DVA, captures the value of the financial institution's option to default on its counterparties. The formula for DVA is similar to the formula for CVA except for two changes. First, instead of expected exposure, we have to calculate the negative expected exposure (NEE). This is expected exposure calculated from the point of view of the counterparty. Second, the value of the option to default for the financial institution is dependent on the survival of the counterparty, so the probability that the counterparty has survived must enter into the calculation as S_I. A similar change must be made to the CVA portion, since the loss due to the counterparty defaulting now depends on the financial institution not defaulting first. The bilateral CVA formula is (Gregory 2010):

$$BCVA = \sum_{n=1}^{N} LGD_n^* \cdot \sum_{j=1}^{T} EE_n^*(t_j) \cdot q_n^*(t_{j-1}, t_j) \cdot S_I^*(t_{j-1})$$

$$- \sum_{n=1}^{N} LGD_I^* \cdot \sum_{j=1}^{T} EE_n^*(t_j) \cdot q_I^*(t_{j-1}, t_j) \cdot S_n^*(t_{j-1})$$

The subscript I refers to the financial institution. Notable in this formulation is that the survival probabilities also depend on CDS spreads and now the losses depend on the firm's own credit spread. This may lead to counterintuitive results such as losses occurring because the firm's own credit quality improves. When looking at stress tests from a bilateral perspective, the financial institution will also have to consider how its own credit spread is correlated with its counterparties' credit spread. Stress losses can be calculated in a similar way as for CVA losses by calculating a stress BCVA and subtracting the current BCVA.

BCVA allows CCR to be treated as a market risk. This means CCR can be incorporated into market risk stress testing in a coherent manner. The gains or losses from the BCVA stress loss can be added to the firm's stress tests from market risk. As long as the same shocks to market variables are applied to the trading portfolio and to the BCVA results, they can be aggregated by simple addition.

COMMON PITFALLS IN STRESS TESTING CCR

Financial institutions are only beginning to conduct a level of stress-testing beyond stressing current exposure. The methodologies to conduct these tests are only just being developed. It is also rare for CCR to be aggregated with either stress tests of the loan portfolio or with trading-position stress testing results in a consistent framework. With better modelling of CCR exposures and CVA, it is possible to begin aggregating stress tests of CCR with either the loan portfolio or trading positions.

Since most financial institutions will do some form of stressing current exposure, it is tempting to use those stresses of current exposure when combining the losses with loans or trading positions. The analysis above shows that expected exposure or expected positive exposure should be used as the exposure amount, and that using current exposure instead would be a mistake.

In fact, the use of current exposure instead of expected exposure can lead to substantial errors. This can be shown using a normal approximation (Gregory 2010) to expected exposures, which is accurate for linear derivatives with no intermediate payments. Figure 4.1 plots current exposure and expected exposure after a million-dollar shock to the market value of the derivative. For at-the-money exposures, the difference between current exposure and expected exposure is almost half the value of the shock.

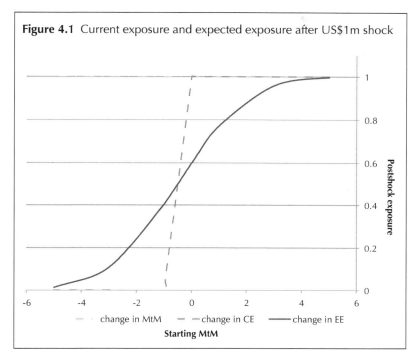

Figure 4.1 Current exposure and expected exposure after US$1m shock

Use of delta sensitivities to calculate changes in exposures is also especially problematic for CCR, since it is highly nonlinear. While this can save on computational resources, the errors introduced are not obvious and the linearisation can be highly misleading. At-the-money portfolios with large price moves applied to the portfolio are especially prone to errors from using delta approximations.

CONCLUSION

A counterparty credit risk manager now has a multiplicity of stress tests to consider. Too many stress tests can hide the risk of a portfolio, but a fair number of stresses is important to develop a comprehensive view of the risks in the portfolio. Both the credit risk and market risk views are important since both fair-value losses and default losses can occur no matter how a financial institution manages its CCR. More integrated stress tests can be generated by combining the credit risk view with the loan portfolio, or the market risk view of CCR can be combined with the trading book. The true difficulty remains combining the default stresses and the fair-value stresses to get a single comprehensive stress test. This difficulty aside, counterparty credit risk managers now have more tools at their disposal to measure and manage CCR. The irony is that regulators have begun to move derivative transactions to central clearing to reduce the counterparty credit risk problem just as the ability to manage counterparty credit risk is making major advances.

The views expressed in this article are the author's own and do not represent the views of the Board of Governors of the Federal Reserve System or its staff.

REFERENCES

Basel Committee on Banking Supervision, 1988, "The International Convergence of Capital Measurement and Capital Standards" July.

Basel Committee on Banking Supervision, 2005, "The Application of Basel II to Trading Activities and the Treatment of Double Default Effects" July.

Basel Committee on Banking Supervision, 2011, "Basel III: A Global Regulatory Framework for More Resilient Banks and Banking Systems" June.

Canabarro, E., 2009, "Pricing and Hedging Counterparty Risk: Lessons Relearned?", in Canabarro, E., *Counterparty Credit Risk Measurement, Pricing and Hedging* (London: Risk Books).

Canabarro, E., E. Picoult and T. Wilde, 2003, "Analyzing Counterparty Risk", *Risk* 16(9), pp. 117–22.

Counterparty Risk Management Policy Group I, 1999, "Improving Counterparty Risk Management Practices", June.

Counterparty Risk Management Policy Group II, 2005, "Toward Greater Financial Stability: A Private Sector Perspective", July.

Duffie, D., and M. Huang, 1996, "Swap Rates and Credit Quality", *Journal of Finance* 51, pp. 921–49.

Federal Reserve Board, 2011, "Interagency Counterparty Credit Risk Management Guidance", SR 11-10, July.

Financial Accounting Standards Board, 2006, "Statement of Financial Accounting Standards No. 157 – Fair Value Measurements", September.

Finger, C., 2000, "Toward a Better Estimation of Wrong-Way Credit Exposure", *Journal of Risk Finance* 1(3), pp. 43–51.

Gregory, J., 2010, *Counterparty Credit Risk: The New Challenge for Global Financial Markets* (London: John Wiley and Sons).

Hull, J., and A. White, 2012, "CVA and Wrong Way Risk", *Financial Analysts Journal* 68(5), September–October, pp. 38–56.

Kealhofer, S., 2003, "Quantifying Credit Risk I: Default Prediction", *Financial Analysts Journal*, January–February, pp. 30-=44.

Levin, R., and A. Levy, 1999, "Wrong Way Exposure – Are Firms Underestimating Their Credit Risk?", *Risk*, July, pp. 52–5.

Merton, R. C., 1974, "On the Pricing of Corporate Debt: The Risk Structure of Interest Rates", *Journal of Finance* 29, pp. 449–70.

Picoult, E., 2005, "Calculating and Hedging Exposure, Credit Valuation Adjustment, and Economic Capital for Counterparty Credit Risk", in Pykhtin, M., *Counterparty Credit Risk Modelling: Risk Management, Pricing and Regulation* (London: Risk Books).

Pykhtin, M., and S. Zhu, 2007 "A Guide to modelling counterparty Credit Risk", *GARP Risk Review*, July–August.

Sorensen, E., and T. Bollier, 1994, "Pricing Swap Default Risk", *Financial Analysts Journal* 50, May–June, pp. 23–33.

Wilde, T., 2005, "Analytic Methods for Portfolio Counterparty Credit Risk", in Pykhtin, M., *Counterparty Credit Risk Modelling: Risk Management, Pricing and Regulation* (London: Risk Books).

1   The stresses are run for each counterparty and at the aggregate portfolio level. The stress may also be run for various subportfolios, divided by region or industry, for example. These would have to be run in both a credit and market risk context.

2   It might increase even more since there are multiple risk measures of importance in CCR.

3   This is included in regulatory guidance on stress testing for counterparty credit risk, for example in SR 11-10 (Federal Reserve Board 2011).

4   Alpha typically depends on the quantile at which we measure economic capital. In this case it would be the alpha calculated at the expected loss. For this reason it may differ from the alpha used for economic or regulatory capital calculations.

5   Although exposure for loans is insensitive to market variables for the most part, there can still be some increase in expected losses if probabilities of default are correlated with market variables. Furthermore, loan commitments and some other loan products can have a stochastic exposure.

5

Operational Risk: An Overview of Stress-Testing Methodologies

Brian Clark; Bakhodir Ergashev

Office of the Comptroller of Currency; Federal Reserve Bank of Richmond

Numerous international regulatory standards require the implementation of stress testing as a risk-management tool. The Basel Committee on Banking Supervision (2009) (henceforth BCBS), a key international regulatory guidance on stress testing, recommends including stress tests in a bank's overall risk-management toolkit. The document broadly refers to stress tests as "the evaluation of a bank's financial position under a severe but plausible scenario". It provides general principles for stress testing practices, while allowing banks ample discretion in choosing stress-test methodologies. However, the document refrains from prescribing any particular stress-testing approach, thereby leaving banking institutions with broad discretion in choosing stress-testing methodologies.

The purpose of stress testing is often viewed by regulatory bodies and financial institutions as a means to determine how a financial institution's capital or financial position would be impacted on by an adverse scenario. In most applications, this requires modelling a link between a macroeconomic event or series of macroeconomic events and the performance of a bank's portfolio of assets. In the context of credit and market portfolios, this is often an extension of the models banks already have in place to model and manage the risk of these portfolios because they often have factor models in place.

The state-of-the-art operational risk models, however, do not readily lend themselves to similar stress-testing applications because they tend to be less risk-sensitive compared with most other types of risk models. In other words, correlations between operational risk losses and the macroeconomic or internal business environment variables are generally not explicitly modelled. This poses obvious challenges for stress testing operational risk. As we expand on below, the primary reasons for this include the relatively short history of operational risk modelling, limited historical loss data and the fact that most operational risk models have been developed with the explicit purpose of capital modelling.[1]

In this chapter, we begin with a brief description of the evolution of operational risk models to provide the reader with a better understanding of the unique challenges inherent to modelling and thus stress testing operational risk. We then describe the implications of these unique challenges to stress testing and provide several potential solutions.

MODELLING OPERATIONAL RISK

Although modelling operational risk is a relatively new discipline for banks, it is an important part of the Basel Final Rule (2007). The Final Rule allows banks to use internally developed, risk-based approaches to measure credit and operational risk. For operational risk, the Rule allows banks to follow an Advanced Measurement Approach (AMA) and states the following (Final Rule 2007, p. 69294):

> Given the complexities involved in measuring operational risk, the AMA provides banks with substantial flexibility and, therefore, does not require a bank to use specific methodologies or distributional assumptions. Nevertheless, a bank using the AMA must demonstrate to the satisfaction of its primary Federal supervisor that its systems for managing and measuring operational risk meet established standards, including producing an estimate of operational risk exposure that meets a one-year, 99.9th percentile soundness standard.

The Rule also specifies that banks incorporate four elements into the capital quantification model: (1) internal loss data, (2) external loss data, (3) scenario analysis and (4) business environment and internal control factors (BEICFs). Despite the fact that the Final Rule effectively does not specify how banks must measure or model exposure to operational risk, most large US banks have settled on the loss-distributional approach (LDA) as the primary quantification methodology. Given this widespread use of the LDA across the industry, we now describe the basic approach.

The loss-distribution approach

The goal of the LDA is to model an aggregate loss distribution in a value-at-risk (VaR) framework. The aggregate loss distribution is defined as the total dollar amount of operational risk losses over a given time horizon. Banks typically use historical loss data to separately model severity and frequency distributions and then calculate the aggregate loss distribution through a convolution of these two distributions. In a VaR application, the bank would define a capital charge as a high percentile of this distribution. As an example, the Final Rule (2007) defines the 99.9th percentile of the aggregate loss distribution over a one-year horizon as the minimum regulatory capital requirement.

Because of the complexity of operational risk and the various types of loss events that are defined as operational losses, banks tend to use the LDA to model operational risk for various risk cells, which are commonly referred to as units of measure. Each unit of measure is meant to capture the operational risk losses stemming from a homogeneous data-generating process. Although the specific unit-of-measure definitions vary across banks, most define units of measure along business lines and event types. In the Final Rule, BCBS (pages 69314–15) explicitly defines seven event types:

1. INTERNAL FRAUD: Operational losses resulting from an act involving at least one internal party of a type intended to defraud, misappropriate property or circumvent regulations, the law or company policy, excluding diversity and discrimination.
2. EXTERNAL FRAUD: Operational losses resulting from an act by a third party of a type intended to defraud, misappropriate property or circumvent the law.
3. EMPLOYMENT PRACTICES AND WORKPLACE SAFETY: Operational losses resulting from an act inconsistent with employment, health or safety laws or agreements, payment of personal injury claims or payment arising from diversity or discrimination events.

4. CLIENTS, PRODUCTS, AND BUSINESS PRACTICES: Operational losses resulting from the nature or design of a product or from an unintentional or negligent failure to meet a professional obligation to specific clients (including fiduciary and suitability requirements).

5. DAMAGE TO PHYSICAL ASSETS: Operational losses resulting from the loss of or damage to physical assets from natural disasters or other events.

6. BUSINESS DISRUPTION AND SYSTEM FAILURES: Operational losses resulting from disruption of business or system failures.

7. EXECUTION, DELIVER AND PROCESS MANAGEMENT: Operational losses resulting from failed transaction processing or process management or losses arising from relationships with trade parties or vendors.

In practice, banks have anywhere from a handful to the order of several dozen units of measure. Even with a careful choice of units of measure, a bank may not be able to fully achieve the homogeneity within each unit. The main reasons for the remaining heterogeneity include data limitations and the size and scope of the bank. Regardless of the number of units of measure, banks are adopting the LDA approach independently to model each risk cell.

Because it is a common belief that losses of different units of measure might exhibit certain levels of dependence, a bank's overall capital charge should be aggregated from individual capital charges of its units of measure through, for example, the use of a copula. Copulas are designed to capture various dependence structures within marginal distributions (ie, the aggregate loss distributions of individual units of measure) of a continuous multivariate distribution (ie, the overall aggregate loss distribution at the bank level). Once an appropriate dependence structure is established with the use of copulas, the operational risk capital charge would then be equivalent to the 99.9th percentile of the overall aggregated loss distribution in the case of the Basel Final Rule.

While the LDA may be an appropriate framework for modelling operational risk capital, especially at the high percentile the Final Rule requires, it is often criticised for its lack of sensitivity to risk factors. Furthermore, since the standard LDA framework does not explicitly model the link between macroeconomic variables and operational risk losses, it poses obvious challenges for macro stress-testing operational risk. Without going into the details of these criticisms, suffice it to say at this point that the general framework poses several challenges for stress testing operational risk, which we expand on below.

Challenges to modelling operational risk

Regardless of the methodology used, practitioners are faced with significant challenges when modelling operational risk. Several of these challenges are unique to operational risk because of the nature of operational losses, and many are due to the relatively short history of modelling operational risk. In any case, each of the following challenges impacts on how we can stress-test operational risk.

The prevailing majority of risk models employed in measuring operational risk are statistical models that are static in nature. Dynamic factor models that are supposed to link operational risk with its drivers are still, at the time of writing, under development. Since static statistical models are extreme simplifications of real-world relationships, they are not capable of capturing the true nature of risk. Below, we list several reasons why dynamic models are still in the development phase and, in doing so, outline the challenges of modelling operational risk in general.

First, banks have a limited amount of operational risk data, especially large-tail events that tend to drive operational risk capital. This creates challenges, as even the largest US institutions have been collecting reliable and comprehensive operational risk data only since about 2000. Adding even more complexity is the fact that most banks collect detailed operational loss data only above a certain collection threshold and thus are left with censored data, which makes fitting severity distributions all the more challenging.

Second, because the LDA approach originated in the insurance and actuarial industries, it was developed with the explicit intent of modelling maximum exposure or worst-case scenarios. Similarly, in operational risk applications, the LDA approach is commonly used for capital-modelling purposes and thus the goal is to fit the tail of the distribution. Therefore, modellers tend to focus on higher moments of the distributions. In terms of stress testing, the implication is that there is less focus on fitting the mean of the distribution. Therefore, estimating the base case, or expected loss, is not the primary goal. The implication is that even if operational losses could be linked to risk factors in an LDA framework, it is not clear what would be gained by stressing the expected loss.

Third, the nature of operational risk loss events makes it especially challenging to establish a clear link between macroeconomic events and loss severity. In particular, operational risk exposure tends to be driven by low-frequency, high-severity events generated by fat-tailed, sub-exponential distributions, and, unlike with a portfolio of loans or equity securities, the maximum exposure is essentially unbounded. For example, single events such as rogue trades, class-action lawsuits and natural disasters that cost banks billions of dollars each year are very difficult to model, especially with the relatively small sample sizes available. And it is these large, infrequent losses that tend to drive operational risk exposure. This creates obvious challenges for stress testing because the stress distribution should be realistic enough to assign plausible likelihoods to such losses to ensure a sufficient capital buffer. On the one hand, the stress distribution should ensure a bank has sufficient capital to cover any severe but plausible stress event or a set of events. On the other hand, if not careful, we might end up with a stress distribution assigning unrealistically high probabilities to single events, each individually capable of putting a bank out of business.

Finally, the timing of operational risk events and operational risk losses can be complex. This further complicates estimation of dependence between operational losses and macroeconomic events. Most notably, large losses tend to be legal suits where the control failure that caused the event precedes the legal reserve and settlement or fine by several years. One implication is that it is not clear what date to use in the estimation of the relationship between the macroeconomic events and the operational loss events. On one hand, from a risk-management perspective, it may be best to know the correlation between the timing of control failures and the macroeconomic environment, so managers can prevent future control breakdowns. On the other hand, from a capital-impact perspective, we would wish to model the relationship between the macroeconomic environment and the loss-realisation date.

All of these factors combine to pose significant challenges for stress-testing operational risk. In particular, the LDA approach is not easily amenable to a stress-testing framework. However, despite these challenges, there are several methodologies banks can use to stress-test operational risk, including several within the basic LDA framework. In the remainder of the chapter, we discuss these approaches.

APPROACHES TO STRESS TESTING OPERATIONAL RISK

In this section, we outline several methodologies for stress testing operational risk. We also note that a bank need not use any one methodology in isolation and would likely benefit from implementing a combination of the approaches to better understand its exposure to operational risk.

Stress testing frequency distribution within the LDA

Banks tend to use Poisson or negative binomial distributions to model frequency and some have had success using factor models. If a link between risk factors and operational risk-loss frequency could be established, then stress testing via the frequency distribution would be relatively straightforward. For example, Chernobai, Jorion and Yu (2011) use publicly reported loss data for a large set of financial institutions and develop a Poisson panel regression model for the mean annual frequency of loss arrival. In their model, the Poisson frequency parameter is regressed against a set of firm-specific and macroeconomic variables.

Such a model could be used to stress-test operational risk. Namely, by supplying the model with stressed values of the macroeconomic and firm-specific variables we could extrapolate stressed frequency values and use them to calculate estimated stress values of capital. Stressed values of macroeconomic and firm-specific variables could be generated in an integrated framework under different historic or hypothetical scenarios affecting both sets of variables simultaneously. One caveat to this approach is that it assumes that estimated relationships between the frequency and the explanatory variables of the model as well as the loss severity distribution are not affected by stressed conditions.

An important downside to this approach is that operational risk exposure tends to be driven by low-frequency, high-severity losses.

Consequently, the impact of stressing the frequency distribution on the overall operational risk exposure is small compared with stressing severity.

Stress testing severity distribution within the LDA

Stress testing via the severity distributions in the LDA approach is challenging for the opposite reasons to stressing the frequency distribution. While the shape of the severity distribution is extremely important for measuring operational risk exposure, it is all the more difficult to establish a link between operational risk and macroeconomic risk factors.

In addition to the heavy-tailed nature of the losses, the timing between the events and realisation of losses also makes this challenging. More research needs to be done in this direction. We do not foresee that stress testing severity distributions without bringing any additional information about the tail behaviour (ie, information going beyond what is contained in historically observed losses) is the most fruitful way of approaching stress testing of operational risk exposure.

Stress testing using scenarios

The Final Supervisory Guidance (2012), which was developed to provide a guidance on stress testing for large banks in the US, recommends that the banks consider using several stress-testing approaches, one of which is scenario analysis. In addition to this regulatory document, there are several risk-specific regulatory documents related to stress-testing requirements. For example, the Final Rule (2007) requires Basel II financial institutions to incorporate scenario analysis into their operational risk assessment and quantification systems. Scenario analysis refers to the application of a broad range of historical and/or hypothetical scenarios to various levels of the banking organisations, in order to assess their vulnerability to adverse circumstances.

Perhaps Kupiec (1998) is among the earliest papers focusing on stress testing VaR models through the use of scenarios. While Kupiec uses historical scenarios to stress-test risk models, we could also use hypothetical expert-generated scenarios. In the context of stress testing market risk models, Berkowitz (2000) proposes a mixture approach to stress testing VaR models in which a probability distribution and a probability of occurrence are assigned to each scenario. The stressed VaR model is derived as a probability mixture of the original VaR model and the set of identified scenarios. Taking into account well-known drawbacks of VaR as a risk measure, Aragones, Blanco and Dowd (2001) propose to complement Bertkowitz's framework by estimating expected tail loss (ETL), an alternative to VaR. Although ETL possess superior properties relative to VaR (Artzner *et al* 1999), one important drawback of ETL is that it does not exist if the loss distribution does not have finite first moment. VaR can still be calculated for such distributions. In addition, quantifying the ETL involves integration, which makes it more difficult to estimate than the VaR. Also, regulatory rules require the use of the VaR measure to quantify risk. For these reasons, we focus on VaR in this chapter.

Incorporating scenarios in a mixture framework for the purpose of stress testing an operational risk model is difficult, at least for the following reason. In operational risk, capital is determined by the VaR risk measure as a fixed and prespecified level of VaR (ie, the 99.9th percentile), which is in the far tail of the loss distribution. Therefore, the effect of each scenario on the original VaR is not always obvious under the mixture framework. Scenario realisations exceeding the original VaR might lead to a higher stress VaR measure conforming with the main purpose of stress testing, while those falling short of the original VaR may even reduce the stress VaR. The net effect is not clear. If line-of-business managers are responsible for generating operational loss scenarios, they might avoid generating a reasonable number of scenario losses from the far tail if doing so will negatively affect their performance. If, as a result, too few scenarios have been generated from the far tail relative to the rest of the severity distribution's domain, then this situation might lead to a reduction in capital. Furthermore, whether the reduction in capital happened due to expert opinions or simply because of a disproportionately lower number of far-tail scenarios is not clear. In other words, the mixture approach, in its original form, does not possess a built-in protection against producing stress risk VaR measures that fall short of the original risk measures.

To address the above-described shortcoming of the mixture approach, Ergashev (2012) proposes an alternative theoretical framework for incorporating scenario losses into operational risk modelling. The basis of this framework is the idea that we need to focus on worst-case scenarios, because only those scenarios contain valuable information about the tail behaviour of operational losses. A simple rule for identifying the worst-case scenarios from the pool of all scenarios is proposed. Only the information contained in the worst-case scenarios enters the quantification process in the form of lower bound constraints on the specific quantile levels of the severity distribution. Therefore, the stress VaR values never fall below the original VaR values. This framework could be used to stress-test the original severity distribution without any need for re-estimating the stress severity distribution, because the last distribution is explicitly derived during the process of incorporating the worst-case scenarios.

Converting the macroeconomic scenario into a 1-in-N-year event
As discussed above, the most significant challenge in terms of stress testing operational risk is that, to date, the relationship between operational losses and macroeconomic factors has not been clearly modelled. Regardless of the reason for this, it poses challenges for managers trying to use macroeconomic scenarios to stress operational risk exposure. Ideally, we could resolve these issues and develop risk-sensitive operational risk models. We also need to consider the possibility that the industry and academic literature have not had much success in modelling these relationships because they might not exist.

Since it is difficult to establish a modelled relationship between macroeconomic factors and operational risk losses, in this section we simply assume that there is a one-to-one correspondence between quantiles of both distributions. To the extent that this assumption is true, we could convert the macroeconomic scenario to a 1-in-N-year event and simply compute the $1 - 1/N$ quantile of the aggregate operational loss distribution as the corresponding stress event. More specifically, we assume that, if a specific macroeconomic scenario corresponds to 1-in-N-year event in the historically observed distribution of the macroeconomic variable(s), then this scenario would trigger 1-in-N-year loss event in the operational loss distribution as well.

This is an appealing approach to stressing operational risk capital for banks that already have an established AMA model based on the LDA approach simply because it would not require any additional model development.

One downside of this approach, however, is that the link between operational risk exposure and the specific scenario is established only through the likelihood of the scenario occurring. The implication is that stress testing operational risk in this setting does not allow us to distinguish between banks with different characteristics.[2] Therefore, it is essentially equivalent to the BCBS Final Rule (although the percentiles and time horizon may be different). Another potential drawback relates to our above discussion regarding the challenges associated with using LDA to estimate expected losses, and specifically the fact that LDA is designed to model the tail of the loss distribution. Of course, this concern could be mitigated to a certain extent by estimating the LDA model with a focus on the percentile of interest.

Stress testing the dependence structure

Another potential way of stress testing in the LDA framework is to stress the dependence structure. The idea is that, during stressed periods, internal controls may be more prone to breakdown and the link between losses across units of measure may intensify. As discussed above, banks generally model the aggregate loss distribution for each unit of measure and then combine the units of measure using a copula-based approach.

There are two basic parts to the dependence model which could be stressed: (1) the choice of copula and (2) the dependence structure embedded in a particular copula modelling the dependence between units of measure. Either, or both simultaneously, could be stressed.

The appealing aspect of stress testing the dependence model is that most experts agree that dependency structures across financial assets tend to change in periods of stress. The financial crisis of 2007–9 also highlighted the importance of taking into account possible changes in dependence structure. However, we should also emphasise that stress-testing dependence is among the most difficult approaches to stress testing. First, justifying the copula choice is not an easy task with a limited number of observed losses. Second, the embedded dependence structure is difficult to estimate. Copulas involve a substantial number of parameters to estimate, which is difficult to accomplish given the fact that the sample sizes of observed losses are not large in practical applications. Third, as per the above discussion regarding the timing of operational loss event dates, the calibration of even a simple correlation between events is not straightforward.

Stress testing and model risk

Model risk is present in all financial models. In the case of operational risk, it is especially relevant for reasons including those discussed above and the fact that the field is still in its infancy.[3] This makes stress testing even more important in operational risk than in the other risk area. However, stress testing a model with a potentially substantial model risk is not an easy task. Here, sensitivity analysis, as a special case of stress testing, can be used in conjunction with the above approaches to demonstrate that a model is not overly sensitive to certain reasonable changes to the parameter values or the assumptions of the model.

CONCLUSION

We began this chapter by providing the reader with a high-level background to state-of-the-art operational risk modelling. Within this discussion, we have made explicit reference to the challenges inherent in modelling operational risk. While data limitations are at or near the top of the list of challenges, there are several areas where simply increasing the quality and quantity of operational loss data alone will likely not be sufficient. In other words, these challenges are not going away any time soon, and further research is needed to advance the field.

In terms of stress testing operational risk, the challenges are magnified. Most of them arise from the fact that operational risk exposure tends to be driven by infrequent large events. For example, modelling the aggregate loss distribution accurately requires additional loss data, especially in the tail of the distribution. Stress testing insufficiently accurate static models could amplify the model risk. Modelling dependence with the macroeconomic environment is equally challenging due to the lack of strong supportive evidence.

Despite these challenges and limitations associated with operational risk modelling, we have laid out several potentially fruitful methodologies for banks to stress-test their operational risk exposure. While some appear more promising than others, each of the methodologies is still in its infancy and more research is needed to decide on the appropriateness of any one method. Therefore, we recommend a bank to use a variety of alternative models to estimate the impact of a stress scenario on operational risk capital.

The views expressed in this chapter are those of the authors and do not necessarily reflect the position of the Federal Reserve Bank of Richmond, the Office of the Comptroller of Currency, the US Department of the Treasury or the Federal Reserve System. Bakhodir Ergashev is at the Federal Reserve Bank of Richmond, Charlotte Office, 530 East Trade Street, Charlotte, NC 28202; email: Bakhodir.Ergashev@rich.frb.org. Brian Clark is at the Enterprise Risk Analysis Division of the Office of the Comptroller of Currency, 400 7th Street SW, Washington, DC 20219; email: Brian.Clark@occ.treas.gov.

REFERENCES

Aragones, J. R., C. Blanco and D. Dowd, 2001, "Incorporating stress tests into market risk models," *Derivatives Quarterly*, issue 7, pp. 44–9.

Artzner, P., et al, 1999, "Coherent Measures of Risk", *Mathematical Finance* 9(3), pp. 203–28.

Basel Committee on Banking Supervision, 2009, "Principles for sound stress testing practices and supervision".

Berkowitz, J., 2000, "A coherent framework for stress testing," Journal of Risk, 2(2), 1-11.

Chernobai, A., P. Jorion and F. Yu, 2011, "The determinants of operational risk in U.S. financial institutions", *Journal of Financial and Quantitative Analysis* 46(6), pp. 1683–725.

Ergashev, B., 2012, "A theoretical framework for incorporating scenario analysis into operational risk modeling", *Journal of Financial Services Research* 41(3), pp. 145–161.

Final Rule, 2007, "Federal Register, Vol. 72, No. 235, Rules and Regulations Modelling operational risk", US Department of Treasury, Federal Reserve System, and Federal Deposit Insurance Corporation.

Final Supervisory Guidance, 2012, "Supervisory Guidance on Stress Testing for Banking Organizations with More Than $10 Billion In Total Consolidated Assets", US Department of Treasury, Federal Reserve System, and Federal Deposit Insurance Corporation.

Kupiec, P., 1998, "Stress Testing in a Value at Risk Framework", *Journal of Derivatives* 6, pp. 7–24.

Model Risk Management Guidance, 2011, "Supervisory Guidance on Model Risk Management", Board of Governors of the Federal Reserve System and Office of the Comptroller of the Currency.

1   Hence, the focus is on the tail of the loss distributions as opposed to credit and market risk models that have been developed with the purpose of modelling expected losses.

2   For example, consider the case of a housing price shock as the stress scenario. In this case, a bank with no exposure to mortgages would be subject to the same level of stressing its operational risk capital as a bank with a significant amount of exposure to mortgages.

3   Model Risk Management Guidance (2011) defines model risk as "the potential for adverse consequences from decisions based on incorrect or misused model outputs and reports".

6

Stress Testing of Bank Loan Portfolios as a Diagnostic Tool

Paul Calem, Arden Hall

Federal Reserve Bank of Philadelphia

In the aftermath of the financial crisis and its attendant government interventions to stabilise financial markets, stress testing of bank capital adequacy has taken on a prominent role in monitoring risk and capital adequacy at large banking organisations.[1] The stress tests are designed to provide a comprehensive view of bank risk exposure, including exposure to balance-sheet loan losses; revenue declines; counterparty credit risk; trading and market risk; and operational risk.

In February 2009, the federal banking agencies – led by the Federal Reserve – created a stress test and required the nation's 19 largest bank holding companies to apply it as part of the Supervisory Capital Assessment Program (SCAP).[2] The immediate motivation for the 2009 stress test was to determine how much additional capital a bank holding company would need to ensure that it would remain a viable financial intermediary even in the adverse scenario, with the Treasury Department prepared to provide capital to any bank that could not raise the required amount from private sources.[3] The SCAP experience demonstrated the value of a simultaneous, forward-looking projection of potential losses and revenue effects based on each bank's own portfolio and circumstances.

In November 2011, the Federal Reserve issued a new regulation requiring banking organisations with consolidated assets of US$50 billion or more to submit an annual capital plan. Under the rule, the Federal Reserve annually evaluates each institution's capital adequacy, internal capital adequacy assessment processes and their plans to make capital distributions such as dividend payments or stock repurchases. This annual exercise, named the Comprehensive Capital Analysis and Review (CCAR), is designed to ensure that institutions have robust, forward-looking capital planning processes that account for their unique risks, and sufficient capital to continue operations throughout times of economic and financial stress. Company-run and supervisory stress tests are a critical part of this annual capital review. They are used to determine whether a firm's capital distribution plans are consistent with remaining a viable financial intermediary even in an adverse scenario.[4]

Congress drew on the lessons of the 2009 exercise by including a requirement for stress testing in the 2010 Dodd–Frank Wall Street Reform and Consumer Protection Act. Bank holding companies with total consolidated assets of US$50 billion or more and non-bank financial companies that the Financial Stability Oversight Council has designated for supervision by the Federal Reserve began annual supervisory stress testing and semi-annual company-run stress testing under DFA rules in 2012; these also serve the purpose of CCAR stress testing.[5] Bank holding companies with total consolidated assets between US$10 billion and US$50 billion and savings and loan holding companies and state member banks with total consolidated assets of more than US$10 billion will also undergo annual company-run stress tests. Stress tests for these firms were slated to begin in 2013.

In May 2012, the regulatory agencies published a "Supervisory Guidance on Stress Testing for Banking Organizations with More Than $10 Billion in Total Consolidated Assets". As defined by the guidance, stress testing consists of "exercises to conduct a forward-looking assessment of the potential impact of various adverse events and circumstances". This guidance covers a much wider application of stress testing than those conducted for CCAR and DFA.

An important component of the CCAR and DFA stress tests is exposure to credit losses from commercial and consumer loans held on balance sheet, particularly losses from high-risk residential and commercial mortgage lending. These have figured prominently in overall stress projections due to the lingering impacts of high-risk mortgage lending and to the positing of stress scenarios involving a further steep decline in house prices and rise in unemployment. Discussion in this chapter is two-tiered. It includes high-level discussion of principles applicable to bank capital stress tests generally, concerning objectives and limitations of stress testing, design of appropriate scenarios, and the role of models. Where the discussion turns to particular issues related to model estimation, however, we narrow the discussion to modelling of balance sheet loan loss, which is our particular area of experience.

A balance-sheet loan-loss stress projection is distinguished by quantification of losses arising directly from a borrower's failure to repay a loan held on the bank's books. Generally, banks have access to historical data on the repayment performance of commercial and retail credits from which statistical inferences can be obtained regarding borrower performance under varying economic conditions. A loan-loss stress test, however, is based on modelling of borrower repayment performance under conditions at the extremes, generally outside the scope of historical experience. As such, it entails major modelling challenges.

In this chapter we propose a framework for bank capital stress-testing based on recognising inherent limitations of the process; setting objectives appropriate to these limitations; designing appropriate scenarios; and applying credible models. The discussion emphasises that, despite the challenges and limitations, bank capital stress testing in 2012 provides a useful diagnostic analysis of a banking institution's sensitivity to adverse shocks impacting on the loan portfolio. Stress testing can help pinpoint sources of risk; rank order institutions according to risk; indicate improvement or deterioration in a bank's risk position over time; and provide benchmarks for evaluating an institution's risk-management processes and capital adequacy.

The chapter is organised as follows. The next section discusses the purposes and limitations of stress testing and suggests a set of suitable objectives. The following section describes appropriate scenario design and the elements of a credible model estimation process. We then conclude.

DEFINING AND ACHIEVING STRESS-TEST GOALS

Ideally, the goal of bank capital sheet stress tests is to alert the bank or bank regulator to an unacceptable level of insolvency risk. Of course, the level of risk that is unacceptable is subjective, and judgements about it are likely to differ among investors, bank management and the regulators. But, even with a specified a level of risk, this goal, while simple to state, is difficult to operationalise for several reasons.

First, the connection to stress scenarios is not straightforward. Risk is multidimensional. The translation of a particular type of risk into a scenario seems feasible, but risks are correlated, so isolating a single type of risk may simplify the scenario unrealistically. However, designing a scenario based on correlations among types of risk poses implementation challenges and complicates the interpretation of stress-test results. If risks are best represented by a multivariate probability distribution, this seems to imply that no single scenario or small number of scenarios can adequately represent the tails of the distribution. And, if correlations are not accurately known, there can be little assurance that selected scenarios adequately represent tail risks.

Second, stress tests rely on models or constructs that may generate erroneous predictions. In other words, they are subject to substantial model risk and statistical uncertainty. Stress-test models of necessity are simplified representations of reality. They are generally based on past experience as embodied in historical data, which may not be relevant to the next stress event. Moreover, historical data typically covers relatively short periods and are often incomplete, lacking information on important predictors of loss. Even with a correctly specified model and adequate data, estimation of model parameters is subject to statistical error. Finally, because bank balance sheets, financial activities and operational structures are complex, stress-loss predictions depend on combinations of models, making it exceedingly difficult to measure the estimation error for aggregate losses.

Despite these problems, we maintain the view that bank capital stress tests can provide valuable information to bank managers and regulators. We also believe, however, that, while the information obtainable from stress tests is useful, it is inherently limited. The practical value of stress tests depends first and foremost on recognising their limitations and defining appropriate objectives.

Limitations of stress tests

As described above, stress testing is fraught with limitations if approached with the goal of accurately forecasting losses or precisely quantifying risk. To succeed at this level, analysts would need to work out the underlying causes of default as applicable to unprecedented or evolving conditions, rather than just find historical correlations. Statistical techniques and even economic theory may provide little guidance here.

Precision is unattainable with respect to both assignment of probabilities to any particular scenario and estimation of credit losses conditional on assigned scenarios. The question of scenario design is addressed in some detail below; for now, suffice it to say that scenario selection is critical to the information content of a stress test. Scenarios that are too mild could lead to failure to identify at-risk banks; those that are too harsh may generate excessive concerns and will not differentiate risk levels among banks.

Model risk and statistical uncertainty impede predictive accuracy of stress-test models. Model risk arises when the circumstances or scenarios of the stress test diverge from the historical experience on which the model is based, or when data limitations preclude consideration of relevant predictors of credit loss. Statistical uncertainty arises even in the extraordinary case of a fully and correctly specified empirical model, because model coefficient estimates will have a range of uncertainty (confidence interval) around them.

Balance-sheet loan-loss models being built for stress testing surely benefit from the availability of data from the credit crisis and subsequent recession and housing-value decline in 2007 through 2009. Models built with data covering a narrower range of economic conditions cannot be expected to extrapolate as well. Models built with data from the much wider range of economic conditions should do better in deriving estimates based on past experience. However, they remain vulnerable to error when extrapolated beyond their range of economic conditions, to unprecedented situations such as a "double-dip" housing recession.

The CCAR exercise conducted at the end of 2011 to evaluate banks' ability to absorb stress losses during 2012 through 2013 illustrates this aspect of model risk. The unemployment scenario selected for this exercise has the national unemployment rate rising above 13%, well outside the realm of recent historical experience regarding both level and one-year change. Thus, determining the impact of the unemployment scenario on retail and wholesale balance-sheet losses requires a significant degree of extrapolation of fitted historical relationships. Moreover, the CCAR loan-loss models are based on previously observed relationships between borrower repayment performance and macroeconomic variables, which may not generalise to the next downturn.

Future relationships may diverge from those implied by a balance-sheet loan-loss model due to inadequacies of historical data or limits to our understanding of behavioural aspects of repayment. Borrower behaviour around "turning points" in the economic environment or in response to adverse economic events is particularly difficult to accurately predict. For example, credit performance on first-lien mortgages as reflected in first-time delinquency has been improving somewhat faster than models generally predict; see, for instance, Goodman *et al* 2012. The moderating delinquency is partly explained by macroeconomic variables and observable dimensions of borrower credit quality. However, given the large percentage of borrowers who continue to have little or no equity in their homes, and the modest pace of economic recovery, models have tended to predict somewhat slower improvement in mortgage repayment performance. Thus, unobservable factors appear to be at play.[6] The impact of reversion to an adverse housing market and unemployment situation, as would be posited for a stress test, similarly could depend on such unobservable factors, implying substantial uncertainty around predictions of mortgage credit performance for the stress test.

When statistical models are estimated using large datasets, the amount of uncertainty around coefficient estimates generally is small, so that statistical uncertainty tends to be less of a concern than model risk. Even within large datasets, however, statistical uncertainty is aggravated when the number of observations available for inferring the impact of a key risk driver of the stress test is small, or when important variables are measured with error. For example, within the population of mortgage borrowers with negative equity in 2012, the number of observations thins out at higher levels of negative equity, leading to uncertainty around the impact of a further, large decline in home values on this population of borrowers.

An additional, potential limitation of bank capital stress tests pertains to the context in which they are implemented, as distinct from any inherent statistical or methodological weaknesses. Stress-test implementation carries a potential for excessive focus on model-building and model application, at the expense of gathering and analysing other relevant information or of recognising risks that lie outside the bounds of the model. A related problem is the potential for excessive focus on process and methodology, whereby the stress test becomes a mechanical or rigid process of risk assessment, displacing relevant qualitative analysis and impeding modeller creativity. Indeed, there may be circumstances where, due to the available data or the nature of the emerging risk, back-of-the-envelope-type calculations based on plausible assumptions may provide better insight than a statistical model.[7]

Practical objectives for stress tests

Given the major limitations around predictive accuracy of stress-test models, what constitutes reasonable objectives for a stress-test exercise? We believe that the following are practical and effective uses of bank capital stress testing:

❏ establishing a standard for an acceptable level of post-loss capital;
❏ differentiating banks by relative risk to identify and remediate banks that lie outside of an acceptable range;
❏ providing benchmarks for evaluating other quantitative loss models;
❏ probing the risk-sensitivity of the loan portfolio or other bank portfolios to relevant economic variables;
❏ probing the risk composition of the loan portfolio or other bank portfolios; and
❏ delineating the bounds of statistical modelling – highlighting risks outside the realm of historical data.

In establishing a standard for capital adequacy, the stress test would be applied on a pass/not pass basis. In this context, the stress test would be based on a single stress scenario or a small set of scenarios that represent an appropriate level of risk.

This use of the stress test may seem somewhat arbitrary, given the limitations of stress-test models, although no less arbitrary than other regulatory capital standards and offering the advantage of a relatively strong empirical basis for quantifying risk. The decision rule can be made less arbitrary by combining the stress-test results with other relevant information by experienced managers or regulators to reach conclusions about the level of risk and the actions that may be needed to reduce risk.

Using stress tests to rank banks according to risk potentially allows greater flexibility around scenario design, because this does not involve identifying the single, specific stress threshold that corresponds to an appropriate capital standard. While scenarios would need to be plausible, the range of admissible scenarios is determined by what would be informative about relative risk exposures across banks.

This use of stress tests clearly would be confined to bank regulators. However, an analogous, internal use of bank stress tests would be to evaluate relative risk across exposure categories or credit products.

Benchmarking is a natural application of stress tests. For instance, supervisory stress tests can be used as benchmarks for assessing banks' internal loss estimates, while banks' models can provide benchmarks for assessing the reasonableness of loss reserving or economic capital models.

Probing the risk sensitivity and risk composition of bank loan, investment, trading or other portfolios is also a very natural application. Analysis of bank performance under a variety of stresses can reveal weaknesses and anticipate developments likely to raise the bank's level of risk. The goal of probing risk composition is to identify at-risk portfolios or exposure categories.

These objectives pertain to use of a stress-test model to directly quantify risk. Stress-testing exercises can also be informative to the extent that they focus attention on the distinction between risks that are modelled and those not amenable to modelling. Thus, indirectly, the stress-testing process can help identify emerging risks, such as those arising from product innovation or loan origination channels or technologies, outside the bounds of the historical data and current stress-test models.

For the sake of brevity, we forgo more extended discussion of these objectives. It should be self-evident that they are consistent with effective risk management or supervision of banking institutions and that model risk is not an impediment to their implementation. They depend only on the design of appropriate scenarios and the development of logically and statistically sound and reasonably robust loss models, topics we address next.

SCENARIO DESIGN AND MODEL ESTIMATION

After specifying an appropriate objective, the next step is to design stress scenarios that are consistent with the objective. The ability to achieve the objective additionally depends on adequacy and credibility of the models and the model-estimation process.

Scenario design

The choice of stress scenarios potentially introduces error distinct from model risk or statistical uncertainty: it may illuminate the wrong region of the risk distribution, leaving the region that should be the focus of bank supervision unobserved. One step towards a better process should be to describe explicitly the goal of the stress-testing exercise, and the way in which stress-test results will be used.

At its most basic, stress-test design depends on the type of stress it aims to measure. For instance, the Supervisory Capital Assessment Program (SCAP) and Comprehensive Capital Analysis and Review (CCAR) exercises aimed at measuring classic financial stress for systemically important banks – are there sets of plausible if unlikely events that would produce credit losses on a bank's assets, and suppress its future income to the extent that its capital level would fall to a dangerous level? Such a focus on individual bank risk ignores network effects – the risk that one bank's capital will fall to an inadequate level because of the failure of another systemically important bank. It also ignores risk of adverse liquidity events such as depositor runs or collapse of a loan sale or securitisation market.

The scenarios that the Federal Reserve employed for SCAP and CCAR represent one way that financial stress can be created: through a serious recession. These scenarios take the existing economic conditions as a starting point and then hypothesise an immediate sharp global decline in economic activity, represented through forecast time series on a few fundamental domestic and international macroeconomic drivers. These include GDP and disposable-income growth, unemployment, inflation and interest rates, and stock, commercial real-estate and house prices for the US, plus a more limited set of drivers for major international trading partners.

The Federal Reserve scenarios from the latest round of CCAR certainly represent a stressful episode for banks, but does forecast performance under these scenarios provide all the information needed to asses banks' systemic risk? In particular, are there important dimensions of risk that are being overlooked? Are there plausible scenarios along other dimensions that would produce a different pattern of capital impacts across banks than the dimensions included in the Federal Reserve scenarios?

Certainly if Bank A were well capitalised in Scenario 1, and Bank B were undercapitalised, but in equally likely Scenario 2 the results were reversed, then regulators should be aware of both results. Finding whether other plausible scenarios besides a sharp recession would produce distinctly different patterns of outcomes would require loss forecasts under a large number of scenarios, a potentially daunting task.

If stresses that are different in kind represent one source of additional information, then what about stresses of varying severity? The answer to this question would seem to depend on the objective of the stress test. If the objective is a single pass/fail rule, then a single, specific severity threshold is necessary. However, if banks will be ranked, with decisions about capital adequacy made based not only on stress-test results but also on additional factors such as quality of risk management, then a wide range of scenario severities could provide additional information and a more nuanced view of capital adequacy. For instance, an institution viewed as particularly well managed might be subjected to less severe scenarios for determining capital adequacy.

The Dodd–Frank Act requires banks to model at least three scenarios, including baseline and adverse scenarios as well as a severely adverse scenario all provided by the Federal Reserve. The severely adverse scenario is used to assess the adequacy of bank capital. The baseline and adverse scenarios provide additional information about the sensitivity of bank performance to stress and may be useful for more general risk assessment, but are not used to assess capital adequacy at the time of writing.

Creating and forecasting an even more severe version of the Federal Reserve's severely adverse scenario would be relatively straightforward, but would it provide additional useful information? Is there something to be learned from a scenario in which many or all banks become undercapitalised? Potentially, the answer is yes. If increasing the severity of the scenario substantially lowered a bank's ranking among its peers, it could indicate a risk exposure not indicated in less severe scenarios. However, the scope for more adverse scenarios should be limited to those with a non-negligible likelihood of occurring.

If stress testing is to be used as a tool to explore the risk structure of the systemically important banks, then stress scenarios focused on specific types of exposures could be useful. For example, if the regulator wants to identify banks particularly exposed to losses in commercial real estate, then a scenario simulating distress in that particular market will more precisely identify at-risk banks than a general recession scenario that includes a downturn in commercial real estate among several stressors.

Careful exploration of targeted stress scenarios is likely to give the regulator a useful picture of the sources and distribution of risk, but, again, carrying out such an analysis would be a large task. It would also generate multiple views of the riskiness of individual banks, which then must be synthesised into an overall view of the adequacy of the bank's capital plan. Too great a proliferation of stress-test results could just make that task harder, rather than increase its accuracy.

In the discussion to this point, scenarios appear as completely exogenous events. However, the entire rationale for stress testing systemically important banks is that they have the capacity to feed the stress they receive back into the economy. So scenario analysis as described above implicitly assumes either that there are no feedbacks or that the scenario in some sense represents the impact of both the initial economic stress and the net effect of all the feedbacks from systemically important banks. If, as a result of regulation based on the stress test, systemically important banks remain well capitalised through the stress scenario, then an assumption of no feedbacks may be reasonable. However, if feedbacks are expected, then the stress scenario must become dynamic. Initial economic stress impacts the large banks, is distributed within their network, and then feeds back to the economy as a whole, which then determines the economic stress for the next period. A structure like this, incorporating all potential feedbacks, is much more complex than anything so far attempted.

A final issue relating to stress scenarios relates to their variability through time. As with any type of capital regulation, the use of stress testing implicitly assigns capital weights to asset classes and off-balance-sheet exposures. These can reasonably be expected to affect future bank asset choices. Assuming that loss modelling will never become an exact science, bank optimisation with respect to implicit stress test risk weights could increase risk in ways difficult to detect *a priori*. With this concern in mind a case might be made for some variation in stress scenarios over time simply to avoid over reliance on a single view of bank risk, and thereby reduce un-measured risk in the banking system.

Model estimation

Models are the means of translating economic scenarios into loss forecasts. The goals of stress testing articulated above require that the model provide an accurate representation of historical variation of losses in relation to economic conditions (dynamic relationships). The model also should provide credible projections of future losses under severely adverse economic conditions. In addition, the model should accurately capture relevant (cross-sectional) relationships across different types of exposures within a portfolio, such as between loan and borrower characteristics and credit risk in the case of balance-sheet loan-loss models. Finally, the model should incorporate conservatism in choice of model structure and variable specification as a counter-weight to the inevitable data limitations and model risk.

At the same time, practical considerations dictate that the models be as simple and transparent as possible. For instance, in the case of supervisory models, the models must be amenable to relatively quick application to the portfolios of multiple institutions during the annual stress-testing cycle. They must also be conducive to annual updating and validation and submission to some level of public scrutiny.

Accuracy in capturing historical variation requires testing alternative model specifications with the aim of improving the model's fit over the economic cycle. Similarly, accuracy in capturing cross-sectional relationships requires investigating alternative model specifications. Specification testing, of course, is limited by the set of variables within the historical, development database and by the set of economic variables for which scenarios are obtainable.

In building balance-sheet loan-loss models for stress tests, there tend to be more rapidly diminishing returns to specification testing compared with other activities, for two reasons. First, the objectives of stress testing are relatively broad. Assessing the bank's ability to withstand a severe economic downturn generally requires less granular attention to individual borrower characteristics than other applications such as credit scoring, for example, where the focus is on each borrower's marginal contribution to credit risk. Second, the marginal improvements in a model's fit that might be achieved through extensive specification testing will do little to offset the substantial model risk inherent in a stress-testing exercise.

In stress testing, as in modelling generally, improving a model's fit historically does not necessarily improve the accuracy of predictions. One potential complication is "overfitting" of historical relationships, whereby a model produces estimates based on temporary or spurious correlations rather than stable causal relationships. An overfitted model may match historical variation but at the expense of eroding the model's predictive accuracy, reducing its transparency or weakening its theoretical or intuitive foundation.

In stress testing, this concern is exacerbated by the possibility that improving the model's accuracy in capturing historical variation may involve weakening estimated relationships to economic variables. This could lead to less conservative stress-loss predictions, diminishing the credibility of the stress test. For example, in a time series or dynamic panel-type loan loss model, inclusion of a lagged loss rate may substantially improve the historical fit of the model as well as the accuracy of short-term forecasts. However the autoregressive term might partly capture the impact of economic conditions, causing weaker estimated economic relationships and less conservative stress-loss forecasts.

One way to limit the potential for overfitting is to apply economic theory to guide the selection of variables for the model. A second is to be guided by the dictum "less can be more": improvements to historical fit accorded by increasing the complexity of a model or number of included variables should be balanced against the increased potential for overfitting. Particular caution should be applied with respect to inclusion of potentially endogenous variables that improve the fit to historical data but weaken the estimated relationship between default and macroeconomic variables.

Another potential problem is that a model may be robust in-sample but not with respect to loss prediction under stress scenarios. In other words, minor alterations may have little impact on model goodness of fit but imply substantially different losses under stress scenarios. The preferred specification should be robust not only with respect to in-sample fit but also robust or at least conservative (in the sense of providing an upper bound on loss estimates) with respect to stress-loss prediction.

Even out-of-sample testing or backfitting is of more limited value in the stress testing arena compared with other modelling contexts, and should be interpreted with caution. A model may predict well out-of-sample under non-stress conditions, but have limited credibility for stress-loss prediction. Thus, for example, a balance-sheet loan-loss model that is predicting higher-than-observed delinquency rates during a favourable or improving economic environment may be preferable to one that has been re-estimated to provide a better fit. While it is important to monitor the performance of a statistical prediction model, including a stress-test model, through backtesting missing the mark is not necessarily an indication of a need to re-estimate. Rather, especially in the context of a stress test, off-the-mark prediction is an issue to investigate and seek to understand, with the goal of improving the model as needed.

In the realm of stress testing, the goal for the development and validation of balance-sheet loan-loss models is not forecast accuracy *per se*. Rather, the goal is to provide credible loss forecasts under the assumption that borrowers' responses to the stress scenarios will resemble historical performance under broadly comparable conditions. There can be no assurance either that future behaviour under stress conditions will resemble past performance, or that the historical data incorporate a sufficiently diverse range of economic conditions to guarantee accuracy of the prediction. Moreover, the stress scenarios are unlikely to actually materialise (hopefully they will not), ruling out a true backtest of the model. Hence, robustness of stress-loss predictions and appropriate conservatism of model assumptions are equal if not more important considerations than model performance in backtesting.

CONCLUSIONS

Bank capital sheet stress testing is a potentially useful tool for bank risk management and supervisory risk assessment. However, loss predictions under stress scenarios necessarily represent extrapolations of experience and knowledge and should be considered as such. Model risk and statistical uncertainty impede predictive accuracy of stress-test models. Thus, a bank capital stress test can provide a benchmark, but not a forecast.

As such, stress testing can be used to establish a standard for capital adequacy; to identify and remediate banks that lie outside of an acceptable range of exposure to credit loss; and to provide benchmarks for evaluating other quantitative loss models. Stress testing is also potentially useful as an analytical tool to probe the risk sensitivity or risk composition of the loan portfolio. Somewhat paradoxically, it is also useful for illuminating the limits of statistical modelling; that is, for highlighting risks outside the realm of historical data.

While using stress-test results in a pass/not-pass mode is straightforward, well-executed stress tests should be able to support a more nuanced view of bank risk. For example, stress tests could highlight specific activities that make a disproportionate contribution to overall risk for the institution and deserve deeper review. However, stress testing can potentially produce very large amounts of information. To be used effectively, stress-test results must be conveyed in a form that can be effectively understood and acted on by bank managements and regulators.

The design of both individual stress scenarios and an effective set of scenarios for a stress test are problems that are ripe for further research and development. For example, the Federal Reserve scenarios from the 2011 CCAR represent a stressful episode for banks, yet it is still important to consider whether the forecast performance under these scenarios provides all the information needed to assess banks' systemic risk.

To achieve effective stress tests, institutions must recognise the specific demands of forecasting for stress scenarios, and design their model development process appropriately. Loss modelling for stress testing puts a premium on ability to extrapolate reasonably. The preferred modelling approach or model specification should be robust not only with respect to in-sample fit but also robust or at least conservative with respect to stress-loss prediction.

With respect to balance-sheet loan-loss models in particular, there tend to be more rapidly diminishing returns to specification testing and out-of-sample validation efforts in stress testing compared with other modelling contexts. Pursuing marginal gains in model fit will do little to offset the substantial model risk inherent in the stress-testing exercise, but may lead to overfitting, which will reduce a model's reliability.

Likewise, a loan-loss model may predict well out-of-sample under non-stress conditions, but have limited credibility for stress-loss prediction. Robustness of stress-loss predictions and appropriate conservatism of model assumptions are equally important to consider along with model performance in backtesting

When implementing a bank capital stress-test process, it is important to be mindful of the potential for the process to promote inefficient use of resources and impede creativity in assessing risk. Excessive focus on methodological issues in model-building and model application can divert attention from gathering and analysing other relevant information. Likewise, excessive focus on process and methodology may cause the stress test to become a mechanical risk assessment exercise, impeding creativity and hampering recognition of emerging risks.

If undertaken without a clear sense of the limitations, and without clear objectives or a context for judging model effectiveness, bank capital stress testing can end up becoming an open-ended activity and drain on resources with no satisfactory conclusion. Effective and efficient application of bank capital stress tests requires acknowledging the limitations of the exercise; setting feasible objectives; designing scenarios consistent with the articulated goals; and developing loss models subject to sensible and cost-effective robustness criteria.

The views expressed in this chapter are those of the authors and do not reflect the views of the Federal Reserve Bank of Philadelphia, Federal Reserve System or Office of the Comptroller of the Currency. We thank William Lang and Amy Jordan for many helpful comments.

REFERENCES
Goodman, Laurie S., *et al*, 2010, "Negative Equity Trumps Unemployment in Predicting Defaults", *Journal of Fixed Income* 19(4), Spring, pp. 67–72.

1 For additional historical perspective, see the speech "Developing Tools for Dynamic Capital Supervision" by Federal Reserve Governor Daniel K. Tarullo at the Federal Reserve Bank of Chicago Annual Risk Conference, April 10, 2012.

2 The test involved two scenarios – one based on the consensus forecast of professional forecasters and the other based on a severe, but plausible, economic situation – with specified macroeconomic variables such as GDP growth, employment and house prices. Each participating institution was asked to supply, in a standardised format, detailed information on portfolio risk factors and revenue drivers that supervisors could use to estimate losses and revenues over a two-year period conditional on these scenarios.

3 The Federal Reserve's decision to disclose the results of the test on a firm-specific basis served a second purpose: to provide investors, and markets more generally, with information that would help them form their own judgements on the condition of US banking institutions.

4 In the first quarter of 2011, the Federal Reserve had conducted a similar review of the 19 firms that had participated in the SCAP. As part of the CCAR, the Federal Reserve evaluates institutions' capital adequacy, internal capital adequacy assessment processes, and their plans to make capital distributions, such as dividend payments or stock repurchases. The stress test is only one of several essential components of the capital review. The Federal Reserve may object to a capital plan because of significant deficiencies in the capital planning process, as well as because one or more relevant capital ratios would fall below required levels under the assumptions of stress and planned capital distributions.

5 There are two sets of instructions: one for the 19 firms that participated in the CCAR in 2011, the other for 12 additional firms with at least US$50 billion in assets that have not previously participated in a supervisory stress-test exercise. The level of detail and analysis expected in each institution's capital plan will vary based on the company's size, complexity, risk profile and scope of operations. The instructions include a supervisory stress scenario that will be used by all of the firms and the Federal Reserve to analyse firms' capital needs to withstand such a scenario while continuing to act as a financial intermediary. For the 19 firms that participated in the CCAR in 2011, the Federal Reserve will also conduct a supervisory stress test using internally developed models to generate loss estimates and post-stress capital ratios.

6 In short, several years of high default rates on mortgages may have filtered out higher-risk borrowers, including along unmeasured dimensions of credit quality. Unobserved heterogeneity may be tied to the household's overall balance-sheet composition and vulnerability to income or wealth shocks.

7 For an example of such a rough calculation or scenario-based analysis that provided warning as early as 2006 of the potential impact of payment shocks from hybrid ARM resets, see http://www.loanperformance.com/infocenter/whitepaper/FARES_resets_whitepaper_021406.pdf

7

Stress-Test Modelling for Loan Losses and Reserves

Michael Carhill, Jonathan Jones
Office of the Comptroller of the Currency

The widespread use of macroeconomic and financial factors in the quantitative models that banks use to forecast their credit losses has been an important development. The financial crisis of 2007–9, and the associated severe recession, underscored the need for banks to incorporate economic and market conditions into their retail and wholesale credit risk models in order to produce credible stress loan-loss estimates. Prior to the crisis, banks were unable to estimate, and apparently uninterested in estimating, the credit losses that would result from a recession, probably because a generation of bank executives had never experienced a severe recession. This left banks unprepared for the severe loan losses that occurred between 2008 and 2010. In onsite supervision of national banks' credit-risk management systems during the past several years, the authors have observed that bank executives at the larger banks, in response to the 2007–9 crisis, have determined that models capable of estimating credit losses conditional on stress economic scenarios were necessary for enterprise-wide capital planning and stress testing, and so directed their staffs to begin model-development efforts.

Several recent supervisory and regulatory developments probably also have accentuated this trend. First, the largest US banks that are subject to the Advanced Internal Ratings Based (AIRB) approach of Basel II (and Basel III) are required to conduct a cyclicality stress test in Pillar I and a forward-looking stress test of credit risk as part of the Internal Capital Adequacy Assessment

Process in Pillar II. Second, the Basel Committee on Banking Supervision issued a consultative paper in January 2009 that recommended that banks use enterprise-wide stress tests to provide a forward-looking assessment of their risk profile and capital adequacy (Basel Committee 2009). Third, in an attempt to quell rapidly escalating fears about the solvency of the US banking system during the 2007-9 crisis, the Federal Reserve conducted its Supervisory Capital Analysis Program (SCAP) in spring 2009. The SCAP, a macroprudential supervisory bank stress test, used a stressful macroeconomic scenario to assess the capital adequacy of the 19 largest US bank holding companies.[1] Building on the success of the SCAP exercise, the Federal Reserve conducted its Comprehensive Capital Analysis and Review (CCAR) bank stress tests in 2011, 2012 and 2013 using macroeconomic stress scenarios that involved a much larger number of macroeconomic and financial factors than were used in the SCAP.[2]

Finally, the Dodd–Frank Wall Street Reform and Consumer Protection Act of 2010 required certain financial companies with total consolidated assets of more than US$10 billion to conduct annual stress tests using a minimum of three macroeconomic scenarios (baseline, adverse and severely adverse) provided by the company's primary federal regulator. As a result, enterprise-wide stress testing (and an associated formal capital-planning process) has become a regulatory requirement for all banks and federal savings associations with more than US$10 billion in total assets.

Since 2008, substantial work has been conducted to develop macro-forecasting models for retail and wholesale credit risk, especially at the largest banks. In this chapter, some of the internal modelling practices that the authors have observed at national banks, where macroeconomic and financial risk drivers have been incorporated into the quantitative models used to generate retail and wholesale credit loss forecasts and loan-loss reserve estimates, are discussed. Some of the strengths and weaknesses of the various modelling approaches are also presented. Finally, several econometric specification and estimation issues the authors have observed that need to be addressed by banks in developing their macroeconomic-based credit risk stress-testing models are discussed.

BANK MODELS FOR LOAN LOSSES AND RESERVES

Most of the risk-assessment models needed for enterprise-wide stress tests (eg, trading risk and banking-book interest-rate risk models) have been in place at banks for quite some time. Therefore, the major modelling challenge has involved the development of credit-risk models that incorporate macroeconomic and financial variables. Prior to the crisis of 2007–9, banks had relied on a variety of quantitative and expert-judgement approaches in their credit-risk modelling. For retail credit risk, banks relied on credit and behavioural scoring models, matrix models, roll-rate and Markovian-chain models, and vintage models.[3] With very few exceptions, none of these models incorporated macroeconomic conditions, but instead rank-ordered credit applicants by their unconditional probability of default (PD). While most of the models can be used to generate a borrower-specific PD, the relationship between macroeconomic factors and defaults rates was, for the most part, not taken into account.

For wholesale credit risk, loan officers' expert judgement was used in credit-grading systems to assign each borrower a risk grade. Similar to retail credit risk, historical data can be used to provide estimates of the PD for each risk grade. However, macroeconomic factors were not used prior to the financial crisis of 2007–9, except perhaps indirectly, since economic conditions were viewed by banks as tending to unduly influence the loan officers' credit-risk judgement.

ALLOWANCE FOR LOAN AND LEASE LOSS MODELS

All banks subject to credit risk must establish an adequate allowance for loan and lease losses (ALLL), which is intended to cover expected credit losses (measured in the form of charge-offs) over a given horizon.[4] The ALLL is a stock and recorded as a contra-asset (ie, an asset with a negative balance) on the bank's balance sheet. In the financial reports banks issue each quarter, changes in the ALLL are referred to as loan-loss provisions, and included in non-interest expense and deducted from net income. When banks take charge-offs, the amount is subtracted from the ALLL. Although net loan-loss provisions and net charge-offs (ie, gross charge-offs less recoveries) can be negative, this typically happens infrequently. Under the uniform capital standards of US federal banking regulators, loan-loss reserves up to a value of 1.25% of risk-weighted assets are included in Tier 2 regulatory capital.

While accounting standards are vague on the issue, the horizon used for charge-off forecasts in setting loan-loss reserves is typically one year for retail loans, and one or two years for wholesale loans. At smaller banks, the method used for determining the ALLL is typically based on expert judgement. At larger banks, a combination of quantitative models and expert judgement is used in determining reserves.

The total ALLL consists of a quantitative reserve component and a qualitative reserve component. The quantitative component is based on historical charge-offs, while the qualitative component typically has reflected an expert-judgement-based adjustment that captured factors such as changes in lending policies and procedures and changes in international, national and local economic and business conditions that are not reflected in historical charge-offs. Since 2008, however, the ALLL has become more quantitative and forward looking, at least at larger banks, many of which now use statistical and econometric methods to capture the sensitivity of charge-offs to changes in macroeconomic and financial variables. For example, ALLL qualitative models may have a macroeconomic modelling component with two or three macroeconomic variables lagged several quarters up to a year. Moreover, many banks have begun to conduct stress tests of the qualitative component of their loan-loss reserves using multiple macroeconomic scenarios (Pocock 2012).

The overall aggregate predictive accuracy of banks' ALLL models can be evaluated by comparing the ratio of the subsequent year's charge-offs to the beginning-of-year loan-loss reserves. Table 7.1 presents data taken from the December 31 financial statements over the period 2005–11.

Table 7.1 Charge-offs as a percentage of beginning of year ALLL, commercial banks, 2005–11 (unweighted means)

Year	2005	2006	2007	2008	2009	2010	2011
15 largest banks	22%	36%	48%	108%	103%	79%	56%
All banks	19%	18%	25%	48%	73%	58%	50%

As shown in Table 7.1, assuming the typical one-year charge-off coverage target for reserves, banks dramatically overstated their reserves in the boom years that ended in 2007. This result shows the near-total lack of a relation between ALLL and charge-offs during the good years, suggesting banks perhaps had motives other than credit losses in setting their loan-loss reserves such as income smoothing, regulatory capital management and private information signalling.[5] In sharp contrast, the largest 15 banks understated their reserves in 2008 and 2009, a period that covered the height of the 2007–9 crisis, and the associated recession, which was the worst since the Great Depression.

The authors' loan-loss reserve results for the 15 largest banks reported in Table 7.1 are consistent with those of Furlong and Knight (2010), who have argued that the unusually low levels of reserves compared with eventual loan losses in 2008 and 2009 reflected two underlying causes. First, accounting standards limit banks' ability to set aside provisions for loans that are performing, but that might become delinquent in the future, without evidence that charge-offs would increase. Second, banks' forecasts of the severity of recessions and subsequent future loan losses are characterised by large errors. Given the extreme severity of the 2007–9 crisis, and the unprecedented decline in real-estate values, it was not surprising that the largest banks substantially underreserved in 2008 and 2009. As such, then, banks that forecast losses and set provisions based on past experience would have severely underestimated the credit losses that eventually occurred during the crisis of 2007–9.

POOL-LEVEL LOSS MODELS

Pool-level models are top-down models used by banks to forecast charge-off rates by retail and wholesale loan type as a function of macroeconomic and financial variables. The typical pool-level model has defined the loan type broadly. For example, all commercial real-estate (CRE) loans may be defined as the pool, or, alternatively, CRE loans may be divided into their major subtypes, eg, industrial, hospitality, retail. For the large banks subject to the CCAR stress test, the level of granularity for the portfolios has reflected the granularity requested in the CCAR reporting templates. At some banks, the charge-off time series might extend back five years, while at other banks the charge-off history might extend back twenty years – a period that would capture the past three US recessions. Even at the pool level, however, many banks have found it difficult to create internal datasets for charge-offs that are long enough for credible estimation. Those banks that cannot create sufficiently long time series usually resort to having an external vendor create the charge-off time-series datasets.

The charge-off rates used by banks in their top-down regression models are measured quarterly, which means that a five-year time series contains only 20 observations, and a 20-year time series has only 80 observations. This paucity of data creates a premium on parsimony in model development. Therefore, most banks use only from one to four macroeconomic and financial risk drivers as explanatory variables, to preserve degrees of freedom in their regression-based forecasting models. At most banks, the macroeconomic and financial variables that are considered for use in the charge-off regressions are usually determined by an executive-level committee that has been assigned to specify the various economic scenarios. Banks' modellers then use a combination of statistical significance tests and management's expert judgement to arrive at the final set of macroeconomic and financial variables that are used in the regressions for each loan type. Some banks have decided to use the same set of variables for each loan type, sometimes sacrificing predictive accuracy for the sake of consistency.

The primary advantage of pool-level models has been the focus on the charge-off rate instead of loan-loss reserves.[6] While still an estimate, charge-offs are taken by banks at a time that more closely aligns with the actual realised losses, and thus are much more accurate and closer to the specific quantity of interest than are reserves. The primary disadvantage of pool-level models is that borrower-specific characteristics are generally not used as explanatory variables, except at the aggregate level using pool averages. For example, for first-lien residential mortgage loans, defaults are extremely rare on loans for which the loan-to-value (LTV) ratio is less than 100%, but rise at an increasing rate as the current LTV ratio goes above 100% (Goodman *et al* 2010; UBS 2005). This asymmetry means that the pool average LTV ratio generally has not helped to predict mortgage defaults. To illustrate, assume a mortgage pool for which half of the mortgages have an LTV ratio of 50% and the other half have an LTV ratio of 130%. Given such a mortgage pool, the average LTV ratio would be 90%, and a zero default rate would probably be predicted, even though borrowers whose loans have an LTV ratio of 130% would default at a high rate.

Banks typically have used single-equation, reduced-form regression models to forecast the annualised net charge-off rate quarterly for each loan-type portfolio. For the most part, these regression models are dynamic and specified as autoregressive models of order p, where p lags of the charge-off rate (the dependent variable in these regressions) are used as explanatory variables to account for the substantial autocorrelation displayed by charge-off rates. Besides the reduced-form autoregressive econometric models, a small number of banks have been developing and using simple error-correction models to forecast annualised net charge-off rates (Crook and Banasik 2012; Assouan 2012). For all top-down models, quarterly net charge-offs are derived by multiplying the net charge-off rate forecasts by balance forecasts provided by the banks' corporate treasuries.

A potential concern associated with banks' use of autoregressive forecasting models is the significant correlation between the macroeconomic and financial risk drivers. This multicollinearity can serve to mute the effect of shocks to the macroeconomic and financial variables on the charge-off forecasts. This is an important issue in conducting effective and meaningful stress tests, since it may not be possible to quantify the full impact of macrofinancial shocks on credit losses when there is significant correlation among the macroeconomic and financial variables, as well as between these variables and lagged values of the charge-off rate. Also, the use of an autoregressive model may prevent the charge-off rate (the dependent variable) from responding quickly to a shock in the macroeconomic and financial variables due to including lags of the charge-off rate as explanatory variables.

As far as the development of the top-down charge-off models is concerned, smaller mid-size banks (those close to the $10 billion asset threshold for banks required to conduct enterprise-wide stress testing under the Dodd–Frank Act) may not have the financial resources necessary to attract skilled statisticians and econometricians. For these banks, then, an attraction of the pool-level models is that ordinary least squares (OLS) estimation typically can be used.

LOAN-LEVEL LOSS MODELS

Loan-level models are bottom-up models used by banks to forecast the expected loss by retail and wholesale loan type for each loan. The expected loss is calculated for each loan. In these loan-level models, the sum of expected losses across all loans provides an estimate of portfolio losses.

The large US banks that are subject to the AIRB approach typically have used the Pillar I definition of default in calculating PD, loss-given default (LGD), and exposure at default (EAD) in the bottom-up models. For the most part, account-level PDs are estimated using logistic regressions that include both internal borrower-specific characteristics and macroeconomic and financial variables as predictors. In contrast, LGDs are usually estimated using a regression model at the portfolio level that includes macroeconomic and financial risk drivers. Finally, EAD for term loans equals the principal balance at default, including currently undrawn commitments. In order to capture the larger positive correlation between PD and LGD during periods of stress, many banks use the same macroeconomic risk drivers in their PD and LGD regression models. (Technically, AIRB models use pools of loans, but Basel II specifies that the loans in each pool must be essentially identical to each other in terms of credit risk, so the AIRB models are defined as loan-level here.)

In contrast to the relative simplicity of top-down charge-off models, there are a variety of loan-level methodologies that can be used, but these models are much more complex to specify and estimate. Loan-level methodologies generally require more sophisticated econometric and simulation techniques. Also, the macroeconomic and financial risk drivers are often correlated with borrower-specific characteristics, and similar to the pool-level autoregressive models discussed above, the multicollinearity among the regressors serves to mute the effect of shocks to the macroeconomic and financial variables on expected losses. This is an important issue in conducting effective and meaningful stress tests, since it may not be possible to quantify the full impact of macrofinancial shocks on credit losses.

For many banks, loan-level models require data that are not available, particularly as long historical time series. US banks that are subject to the AIRB approach of Basel II have been maintaining detailed data on borrower-specific characteristics since the early 2000s. However, other banks generally find it to be a big challenge to create historical data on borrower-specific characteristics. As noted above, some banks have resorted to using vendors to provide pool-level charge-off data. However, vendors may not be able to provide borrower-specific data at a reasonable cost for these banks. As a result, apart from the Basel II AIRB banks, the authors generally have observed historical loan-level data at other banks of at most five years in length.

In principle, loan-level models would appear to be superior to pool-level models in terms of forecast accuracy, since they use both macroeconomic factors and loan-specific characteristics as predictors of expected losses. However, the forecasting superiority of loan-level models remains to be adequately demonstrated by out-of-sample backtesting. Hughes and Stewart (2008) empirically addressed the issue of whether aggregate models of credit risk yielded better forecasts of portfolio aggregates than loan-level models. Using simulation techniques, they found that pool-level models performed better than loan-level models.

Credit and behavioural scoring models with macroeconomic factors

A simple model used by banks combines credit scores, such as the Vantage or FICO score, and macroeconomic factors to predict defaults or severe delinquencies, and then produces default probabilities at the loan level. These loan-level estimates are then aggregated to produce a pool-level default rate. An example of this approach was provided by Hughes (2009), who showed that macroeconomic factors had predictive power for defaults and delinquencies. Other work also has documented the importance of macroeconomic factors as predictors of loan-level defaults, deliquencies and credit scores (Hughes 2008; Thomas 2000; Bellotti and Crook 2009).

Credit migration analyses

Many banks' stress-testing models use credit-migration or roll-rate analysis. Migration in this context refers to the movement of a loan through a transition matrix of some kind, where the rows indicate some measure of current credit quality, and the columns indicate the next period's credit quality.

Retail migration matrices are usually based on delinquency status. For each loan type, the bank defines the number of days delinquent, at which point the loan is deemed to be in default. The matrix is typically terminated at that point, although it can include a column that shows the loan to have been converted to collateral. A stylised migration matrix for first-lien residential mortgages is shown in Table 7.2.

The transition of a loan from current to 1–30 days past due is probably the most important metric for measuring the sensitivity to macroeconomic factors. However, at least for retail credit, 1–30-day delinquencies are very volatile. They display a significant seasonal component, and consist of payments that are missed accidentally, but then quickly cured, and so-called "rolling 30s", where the borrower has missed one payment that is never made up. As a result, few, if any, banks use this delinquency bucket in their retail credit modelling.

Table 7.2 A stylised retail transition matrix

To From	Current	30–60 days past due	60–90 days past due	Default (90+ days past due or real- estate-owned)
Current	98%	2%	0	0
30–60 DPD	40%	20%	40%	0
60–90 DPD	20%	20%	20%	40%
Default	2%	4%	8%	20%

Note: The last row does not add to 100% due to the conversion of REO to cash.

The time-and-state invariant transition probabilities assumed for the typical first-order Markovian transition matrix used by banks are restrictive and not the most realistic default-modelling approach (van Deventer 2009; Kiefer and Larson 2004). However, most banks interpret the conditions loosely and calculate the PD as the product of adverse credit migrations. In Table 7.2, assuming static transition probabilities, the PD of a current loan at the 90-day horizon is (0.02*0.4*0.4), reflecting the probability of transition from "current" (actually 1–30 days past due) to 30–60 days past due multiplied by the probability of transitioning from 30–60 to 60–90 days past due multiplied by the probability of transitioning from that bucket to default. Similarly, the default probability of a 30-day delinquent loan at the 90-day horizon is (0.2*0.4*0.4)+(0.4*0.4), ie, the probability that the borrower makes a payment but then misses the next two payments plus the probability that it misses the next two payments, and so on. There are several ways to convert the 90-day default rate to the 12-month default rate typically used for retail loans.

The transition-matrix approach produces only the probabilities of default, and not the LGD. As a result, modellers must estimate the LGD separately. For most types of retail loans, the LGDs are close to 100%, with the exception of first-lien residential mortgages, where substantial recoveries are typically expected. Prior to the housing bubble of the 2000s, the rule of thumb was an LGD of 20% to 30% for prime residential mortgages (Qi and Yang 2009) and an LGD of 40% to 50% for subprime mortgages.[7] In the aftermath of the crisis of 2007–9, however, that rule of thumb has become too simplistic to apply. The alternative approach has been to calculate the LGD of a loan as a function of the loan-to-value ratio at the time of default plus an add-on for recovery costs. Frequently, the loan-to-value ratio is modelled as a function of a scenario-specific home-price index.

Wholesale credit migration matrices are usually based on the credit ratings assigned to the obligors by the bank. Banks typically have assigned 10 to 20 grades to wholesale debtors, rank-ordering them in terms of their PD. For each rating grade, the PD at any horizon can be calculated as a historical average. Usually, the internal ratings are based on the expert judgement of the loan officers, although quantitative models are increasingly being used to supplement the expert judgements.

Unlike for retail loans, most wholesale loans keep the same grade from month to month. While most of the stability in ratings is probably real, some is undoubtedly due to inertia on the part of the loan officers. Moreover, banks probably vary considerably in the diligence of their loan officers in keeping the internal credit ratings up to date.

For a given relationship between internal loan grade and default rating, the stress-testing challenge for banks has been to estimate how changes in economic conditions correlate with changes in loan grade. In the first years after 2008, the impact of changing economic conditions tended to be based on the expert judgement of the loan officers, but there has been movement towards the use of macroeconomic-based models. Since the macroeconomic models require a history of internal loan-grade migrations, the macroeconomic sensitivities of these migrations can be affected by the loan officers' diligence and ability in maintaining up-to-date loan ratings.

For wholesale LGDs, many banks assign a rating analogous to the PD ratings. Some banks combine the PD and LGD ratings into one rating, which effectively produces an expected-loss rating. Other banks simply assign a historical-average LGD, which could be model-based. Unlike retail LGDs, wholesale LGDs are highly sensitive to macroeconomic and financial factors (Frye and Jacobs 2012).

In order to account for the changing risk profile of both retail and wholesale portfolios at the loan level, the authors have observed some banks using dynamic credit transition matrices that are conditional on stressed economic scenarios (Bangia *et al* 2002). Retail transition matrices are based on delinquency status, while wholesale transition matrices are based on internal risk ratings. These dynamic transition matrices, which are conditional on macroeconomic and financial variables, require nonstationary Markov chains (Grimshaw and Alexander 2011).

There are several different econometric approaches for estimating transition probabilities that the authors have observed. The simplest was to estimate the relationship between macroeconomic and financial variables and the PD using OLS. Technically, this is not a valid approach, since the migration probabilities are bounded by zero and one, while OLS assumes an unbounded distribution. However, for most of the intermediate cells in a transition matrix, probabilities are reasonably close to 50%, so the boundary issue is less of an issue. However, the transition from current to 30-days past due is close to a zero probability, while transitions from the late delinquency buckets to default are close to a probability of one.

There are two possible solutions to this problem. One approach is to find an alternative method for estimating initial and late-stage transitions, but the authors have not seen such an approach implemented by banks. A second method would be to standardise the transition probabilities (ie, characterise observations by the number of standard deviations from the mean), thereby converting the transition probabilities from a bounded to an unbounded distribution. The authors have seen this approach implemented, but, as of late 2012, there has not been sufficient time for banks to compare forecasts with actual results.

The preferred econometric approach is to use a logistic regression to combine borrower-specific characteristics with macroeconomic variables to predict credit migration as a loan-level binary outcome. Chen *et al* (2011) used this approach, and showed that macroeconomic variables appeared to outperform borrower characteristics in predicting credit migrations. They also found that generalised maximum entropy outperformed a multinomial logit model. However, as with the other models discussed here, they did not include a substantial out-of-sample comparison of forecasts with actual results.

A variant on the use of migration matrices

In this approach, the modeller predicts the proportion of loans in each migration bucket as a function of macroeconomic and financial variables, rather than using the transition probabilities as the dependent variable. In other respects, such as estimating LGDs and draws on unfunded commitments, the approach is the same as for migration analyses. An alternative implementation would use a multinomial logit or ordered probit regression model.

Charge-off rates across loan types

Since economic risk factors change at the same time for all banks, it would be convenient for modellers if charge-offs for different loan types responded with the same lag to changes in macroeconomic and financial variables. Table 7.3 shows charge-off rates across loan types, by year.

Table 7.3 shows that CRE charge-off rates tend to lag other lending types, such as C&I, Consumer and HELOC loans, by about one year. Otherwise, charge-off rates for all loan types increased for the most part much in tandem. For example, charge-off rates for both C&I and residential construction loans have peaked at the same time.

Table 7.3 Annual percentage charge-off rates, by loan type, industry aggregates (weighted means)

	C&I	Consumer	Credit card	HELOC	Res. const.	Owner-Occ. CRE	CRE	2nd-lien, closed-end residential	1st-lien residential
2005	0.7	1.8	5.9	0.1	0.0	0.1	0.1	0.3	0.1
2006	0.6	1.5	4.3	0.2	0.1	0.1	0.1	0.4	0.1
2007	0.8	2.0	5.0	0.5	0.5	0.1	0.2	0.7	0.2
2008	1.4	2.7	6.3	1.9	4.2	0.1	0.5	3.1	0.9
2009	3.1	3.6	10.2	3.0	7.6	0.6	1.5	5.8	1.4
2010	2.4	2.7	10.9	2.8	7.8	0.9	2.4	5.2	1.4
2011	1.3	2.4	6.7	2.2	5.2	0.8	1.8	4.5	1.1
2012 (1H)	0.9	2.0	5.2	2.0	2.9	0.6	1.2	4.5	0.9
Qrtly peak	2009 Q4, 4.0	2009 Q2, 3.6+	2010 Q1, 14.5	2009 Q4, 2010 Q1, 3.3	2009 Q4, 9.9	2010 Q4, 1.2	2010 Q4, 2.7	2009 Q4, 6.6	2009 Q4, 1.9

Source: Call Reports. The charge-off rates for 2012 are through June 30. The peak in credit-card charge-off rates was probably artificial, as FAS-167 required banks to put revolving-trust securitisations back onto the balance sheet, with a resulting charge-off surge

ECONOMETRIC MODELLING ISSUES

In conducting onsite supervisory review during the past several years, the authors have observed a common set of econometric issues that arise when model developers incorporate macroeconomic and financial variables into regression-based forecasting models. These issues have generally fallen into those related to regression specification and those related to estimation. Potential remedies for the econometric issues identified below can be found in many econometrics textbooks.

Specification issues

First, in choosing the set of macroeconomic and financial variables to be included as explanatory variables in the regression models, model developers have frequently used pairwise Pearson correlation coefficients between the dependent variable, eg, charge-off rates, and the various macroeconomic and financial explanatory variables to determine the subset of economic variables considered for the final econometric models. Typically, the correlation coefficients are rank-ordered and the three or four economic variables with the largest correlation coefficients are considered for use in the regression specification. This is a rather narrow approach to selecting the final explanatory variables. It is well known, for example, that Pearson correlation coefficients can only detect linear association between variables, and they do not capture significant dynamic nonlinear relationships that could be present. They are also likely to pick up spurious relationships that are driven by a third common variable that is omitted from consideration.

Second, the lag lengths for the macroeconomic and financial variables are typically chosen in an ad hoc manner. Although there are optimal lag-length search procedures that could be used in specifying the lag lengths, these very often are not used. This issue would also apply to the choice of lag length for the dependent variable used in autoregressive models. The choice of lag length for the macroeconomic variables is important, since the use of lags that are too short results in changes to the dependent variable that do not capture the full impact of a macroeconomic shock.

Third, modellers typically have not engaged in a careful and well-documented, empirically-based approach to the choice between levels, log-levels or first differences of the charge-off rate variables and the macroeconomic and financial variables in the top-down regression models. This issue has also been observed for bottom-up loan-level models. Generally, it would be preferable to test the sensitivity of stress-test results to the choice of functional form and variable transformations.

Fourth, there generally has been little or no attention paid to the difference between trend-stationary series and difference-stationary series (ie, those time series with a unit root or stochastic trend). This is considered to be an important specification issue for time-series regression modelling. For most banks, it appeared that only the possibility of difference-stationary data was considered in specifying the regression models. Spurious autocorrelations can easily be induced in a time series showing trend, either by mistakenly removing a deterministic trend from difference-stationary data or by differencing trend-stationary data. Because of this, careful attention should be paid to the type of non-stationarity characterised by the time-series data.

Fifth, the regression models used are for the most part specified as being linear in the macroeconomic and financial variables. The assumption of linearity can impose important restrictions on the responses of the dependent variable for stress-testing analysis. For example, the linearity restriction imposes the following severe properties: symmetry, ie, the magnitude of the responses is the same regardless of whether the macro shock is positive or negative; proportionality, ie, responses are proportional to the change in the macro factor; and history independence, ie, the shape of responses is independent of initial conditions of the macroeconomic variables (Misina and Tessier 2008).

Sixth, the potential for a significant seasonal component in the dependent and predictor variables has been typically ignored. For example, charge-off rates display significant quarterly variation that could be taken into account by including quarterly dummy variables in the top-down regression specifications.

Estimation issues

First, there has been a lack of comprehensive diagnostics to assess the validity of the estimated regression models, including functional form, variable selection and lag-length choice. For example, there has typically been inadequate attention paid to the properties of the regression residuals, such as serial correlation and heteroscedasticity, and the presence of outliers, influential observations and structural breaks. Also problematic has been the use of the Durbin–Watson (DW) statistic to test for serial correlation when lagged dependent variables are used as regressors. The DW test is biased towards accepting the null hypothesis of no serial correlation in such cases, and therefore should not be used.

Second, outlier observations are frequently deleted from the datasets used for estimation. Instead of doing so, robust estimation techniques such as median regression should be explored to address the issue.

Even when model development is sound and robust, the most important test of a model comes when out-of-sample forecasts are compared to actual values in evaluating a model's predictive accuracy.

CONCLUSION

The financial crisis of 2007–9, and the associated severe recession, underscored the need for banks to incorporate economic and market conditions into their retail and wholesale credit risk models in order to produce credible stress loan-loss forecasts. While substantial work has been conducted to develop macro-forecasting models for retail and wholesale credit risk, especially at the largest banks, the industry has not yet established what could be viewed as best modelling practices. In this chapter, some of the internal modelling practices that the authors have observed at national banks, where macroeconomic and financial risk drivers have been incorporated into the quantitative models used to generate retail and wholesale credit loss forecasts and loan-loss reserve estimates, have been discussed. Some of the strengths and weaknesses of the various modelling approaches have also been presented.

The views in this chapter are those of the authors and do not necessarily represent the views of the Office of the Comptroller of the Currency.

REFERENCES

Assouan, Steeve, 2012, "Stress Testing a Retail Loan Portfolio: An Error Correction Model Approach", *Journal of Risk Model Validation* 6(1), pp. 3–25.

Bangia, Anil, Francis Diebold, André Kronimus, Christian Schagen, and Til Schuermann, 2002, "Rating Migration and the Business Cycle, with Application to Credit Protfolio Stress Testing", *Journal of Banking and Finance*, 26, pp. 445-474.

Basel Committee on Banking Supervision, 2009, "Principles for Sound Stress Testing Practices and Supervision", Bank for International Settlements, May.

Basel Committee on Banking Supervision, 2012, "Models and Tools for Macroprudential Analysis", Bank for International Settlements, Working Paper No. 21, May.

Bellotti, Tony, and Jonathan Crook, 2009, "Credit scoring with macroeconomic variables using survival analysis", *Journal of the Operational Research Society* 60, pp. 1699–707.

Chen, Qing Qing, Dennis Glennon and Amos Golan, 2011, "Estimating Conditional Mortgage Delinquency Transition Matrices", working paper, Office of the Comptroller of the Currency, Washington, DC.

Choy, Murphy, and Ma Nang Laik, 2011, "A Markov Chain Approach to Determine the Optimal Performance Period and Bad Definition for Credit Scorecard", *Research Journal of Social Science & Management* 1(6), October, pp. 227–34.

Crook, Jonathan, and John Banasik, 2012, "Forecasting and explaining aggregate consumer credit delinquency behaviour", *International Journal of Forecasting* 28, pp. 145–60.

Floro, Danvee, 2010, "Loan Loss Provisioning and the Business Cycle: Does Capital Matter?: Evidence from Philippine Banks", Bangko Sentral ng Pilinas, working paper, March.

Foglia, Antonella, 2009, "Stress Testing Credit Risk: A Survey of Authorities' Approaches", *International Journal of Central Banking* 5(3) September, pp. 9–42.

Frye, John, and Michael Jacobs Jr., 2012, "Credit Loss and Systematic Loss Given Default", *Journal of Credit Risk* 8(1).

Furlong, Fred, and Zena Knight, 2010, "Loss Provisions and Bank Charge-offs in the Financial Crisis: Lessons Learned", *FRBSF Economic Letter 2010–16*, May.

Goodman, Laurie S., Roger Ashworth, Brian Landy, and Ke Yin, 2010, "Negative Equity Trumps Unemployment in Predicting Defaults", *Journal of Fixed Income* 19(4), Spring, pp. 67–72.

Grant Thornton LLP, 2012, "Allowance for Loan and Lease Losses (ALLL) Adjustment Factors".

Grimshaw, Scott, and William Alexander, 2011, "Markov Chain Models for Delinquency: Transition Matrix Estimation and Forecasting", *DMM Forecasting*.

Henderson, Christopher, 2009, "Retail Credit Risk Models: What Do These Models Look Like and How Did They Fare in the Crisis?", FRB of Philadelphia, June.

Hughes, Tony, and Robert Stewart, 2008, "Forecasting and Stress Testing Using Model Pool Level Data", Moody's Analytics, August.

Hughes, Tony, 2008, "The Macroeconomics of Credit Scores", Moody's Analytics.

Hughes, Tony, 2009, "The Economic Credit Score", Moody's Economy.Com.

Kiefer, Nicholas M., and C. Erik Larson, 2004, "Testing Simple Markov Structures for Credit Rating Transitions", OCC Working Paper Series, 2004-3.

Malik, Madhur, and Lyn Thomas, undated, "Modelling Credit Risk in Portfolios of Consumer Loans: Transition Matrix Model for Consumer Credit Ratings", working paper, University of Southampton, United Kingdom.

Misina, Miroslav, and David Tessier, 2008, "Non-Linearities, Model Uncertainty, and Macro Stress Testing", working paper, Bank of Canada.

Pocock, Mark, 2012, "Perspectives on Recent Allowance for Loan and Lease Loss Modeling Issues", Office of the Comptroller of the Currency, working paper (preliminary), Washington, DC.

Qi, Min, and Xiaolong Yang, 2009, "Loss Given Default of High Loan-to-Value Residential Mortgages", *Journal of Banking and Finance* 33, pp. 788–99.

Qu, Yiping, 2008, "Macro Economic Factors and Probability of Default", *European Journal of Economics, Finance and Administrative Sciences* (13), pp. 192–215.

Schuermann, Til, 2012, "Stress Testing Banks", Wharton Financial Institutions Center, working paper, April.

Tanta, 2007, "Delinquencies and Defaults for UberNerds", CalculatedRiskBBlog.com, July.

Thomas, Lyn, 2000, "Survey of Credit and Behavioural Scoring: Forecasting Financial Risk of Lending to Consumers", *International Journal of Forecasting* 16, pp. 149–72.

UBS, 2005, *Mortgage Strategist*, December 13.

Van Deventer, Donald, 2009, "Reduced Form Macro Factor and Roll Rate Models of Mortgage Default: An Introduction and Application", Kamakura Corporation, October.

1   Macroprudential bank stress tests are used to assess the key vulnerabilities of the banking system as a whole to macroeconomic and financial shocks. See Foglia (2009), BCBS (2012) and Schuermann (2012) for details.

2   The 2009 SCAP used three macroeconomic variables in its state space for the banking-book stress test: GDP growth, unemployment and house price index. The CCAR bank stress tests in 2011, 2012 and 2013 focused on estimates of projected revenues, losses, reserves and pro forma capital levels under a baseline, a severe and an adversely severe stress economic scenarios. See Schuermann (2012) for a more detailed discussion.

3   Henderson (2009) discussed banks' retail credit risk models, their features and how the models performed during the financial crisis of 2007–9.

4   See SFAS 5, SFAS 11, SFAS 112, and SFAS 114. While those in the industry still referred to these as "FAS-5" and "FAS-114", SFAS 5 has become ASC 450 and SFAS 114 has become ASC 310. The primary components of a bank's ALLL consist of loans collectively evaluated for impairment (the FAS 5 part), loans individually evaluated for impairment (the FAS 114 part) and loans acquired by the bank with decreased credit quality (the SOP 03-3 part). See Thornton (2012) for a detailed discussion.

5   The academic literature has distinguished between non-discretionary and discretionary factors used by banks in setting their loan-loss provisions and reserves. Non-discretionary factors refer to those related to changes in loan credit quality and economic conditions, while discretionary factors refer to those related to income smoothing, regulatory capital management and private information signalling. Floro (2010) conducted an empirical study of the two sets of factors used by banks in setting their loan-loss reserves.

6   For nearly all the types of models discussed here, many model developers have used the Pillar I convention of Basel II and have modelled exposure at default, LGD and probability of default separately in estimating expected losses. These models are more complex and less parsimonious than those that forecast charge-offs directly and, therefore, subject to a higher degree of modelling uncertainty. Despite the loss of parsimony, however, there is evidence that the pool-level charge-off models perform no worse than those using a more granular expected loss approach (Frye and Jacobs 2012).

7   The latter is based on the authors' conversations with industry experts in residential-mortgage recoveries.

A Framework for Stress Testing Banks' Corporate Credit Portfolio

Olivier de Bandt, Nicolas Dumontaux, Vincent Martin, Denys Médée

Autorité de Contrôle Prudentiel (French Prudential Supervision Authority)

Since the financial crisis of 2007 and beyond, which drew unprecedented attention to the stress testing of financial institutions, stress-tests exercises have become a central risk-management tool to assess the potential impact of extreme events on banks' P&L and balance-sheet structures.

Stress tests are viewed as complementary to traditional risk-measurement metrics such as value-at-risk (VaR), as they are an important mechanism for detecting weaknesses of both a single financial institution and threats to financial stability. Nowadays, financial institutions are required to perform regular exercises within Pillar II of the regulatory framework of the Basel Accord in order to assess the global impact of adverse events or changes in market conditions on banks' capital adequacy. Supervisory authorities as well are used to leading such exercises: the International Monetary Fund (IMF) with its regular Financial Sector Assessment Program, the European Banking Authority (EBA) with its European "bottom-up" stress tests, including a disclosure step, and national supervisory authorities, which all have built dedicated tools, especially for regular top-down exercises. The scope of stress testing includes traditional credit risks, market risks, operational risks, interest-rate risks and, since the financial crisis, liquidity risks.

Stress testing corporate credit risk, also known as "wholesale credit risk", is a key component of stress testing for global institutions. Credit risk in itself (including retail credit risk) is indeed one of the major sources of risk for banks, judging by the extent of banks' credit risk-weighted assets (RWAs),[1] and, accordingly, may have a major impact on the solvency of financial institutions. The subprime crisis has highlighted the need for stress testing banks' portfolios as numerous credit institutions incurred major losses and write-downs from structured US subprime related assets since mid-2007.

This chapter examines stress testing for credit risk, focusing on risks arising from corporate loans and other credit exposures.[2] It aims at introducing a Basel II-type modelling framework to perform credit stress-test scenarios through credit migration matrices (or transition matrices), which has been implemented by French authorities and is currently used as a tool for top-down stress-test exercises. This approach is still relevant under the Basel III framework, since nothing new has been introduced in the Basel III framework with respect to the assessment of credit risks of banks' corporate portfolios.

The chapter is organised as follows: the first section briefly depicts the model our stress-test framework rests on, which is largely based on the Merton model; then we introduce the way this framework is implemented to conduct top-down stress-test exercises; finally, we comment on a few outputs of the stress tests.

THE MODEL SPECIFICATION

Several models are available for quantifying credit risk, this risk stemming either directly from actual defaults of credit exposures, or indirectly from migrations of credit ratings, taking into account their prudential treatment.[3] These models may be either structural (modelling of firms' value and capital structure) or reduced forms, where credit events are exogenous to the firms. Here we rely on the latter approach, with credit events triggered by macroeconomic shocks, and focus on credit migrations (see ECB, 2007, for alternative industry credit models).

The model we introduce in this section relies on the basic idea that the evolution of rating transitions can easily be linked to a synthetic credit indicator.[4] The main hypothesis is that the underlying asset value of a firm evolves over time, through a simple diffusion process, and that default is triggered by a drop in firm's asset value below the value of its callable liabilities. In the Merton framework, shareholders actually hold a call option on the firm, while debt-holders hold a put option.

General specification

Based on the assumption that changes in the logarithm of the firm's asset value ($\Delta \log A_i$) can be related to both a systemic factor (Z, the credit index) and an idiosyncratic factor (ε_i) via a factor model, the specification is the following for firm i:

$$\Delta log A_{i,t} = -\sqrt{\rho} Z t + \sqrt{1-\rho}\, \varepsilon_{i,t} + c_i$$

where c_i is the long-run growth of firm i's asset value and ρ is the asset correlation between any two firms in the portfolio. All firms are supposed to have identical characteristics (eg, their correlation to Z) with respect to their credit rating, which then leads us to identify i as a credit class rather than an entity.

Assuming, then, that changes in asset value are normally distributed (Z and ε_i are mutually standard normal variables and mutually independent), the default probability may be expressed as the probability of a standard normal variable falling below a critical value, defined as the different ratings (with a total of n classes, with $n=8$). Similarly, thresholds can be set up for rating migrations, as graphically represented in Figure 8.1.

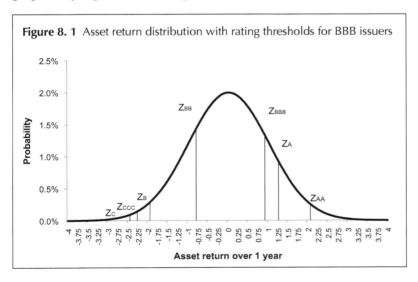

Figure 8. 1 Asset return distribution with rating thresholds for BBB issuers

This framework, on which is also based the Basel II Asymptotic Single Risk Factor (ASRF) model, results in the following relations with respect to default probabilities:

$$PD_i \mid \{Z_t = \Phi^{-1}(\alpha)\} = \Phi \left[\frac{\Phi^{-1}(\overline{p}_i) + \sqrt{\rho}\, \Phi^{-1}(\alpha)}{\sqrt{1-\rho}} \right]$$

where $PD_i \mid \{...\}$ is the (conditional) default probability in state Z, Φ is the Gaussian cumulative distribution function, $\overline{p}_i$ is the long term average probability of default (PD) of class i (i=1,...n) (or unconditional PD) and α is the probability that the value Z (or below) occurs. The closer α is to 0, the less frequent is the crisis and the greater its severity. In the Basel II framework, α is equal to 0.1% (this corresponds to the regulatory confidence level of 99.9%, which is the required confidence level to compute regulatory capital requirements under Basel II & III frameworks). In our application we use n=8 risk classes, where class 8 stands for the default class. Default probabilities along with rating migrations depend on a sole parameter (Z_t, the credit latent index discussed below), meaning that migrations matrices can be modelled through one macro factor (ASRF: Asymptotic Single Risk Factor).

This formula, expanded to every component of the nxn (here 8x8) transition matrix, is:

$$P_{ijt} = \Phi \left[\frac{\Phi^{-1}(\overline{P}_{i8} + ... + \overline{P}_{ij} + \sqrt{\rho}\, Z_t)}{\sqrt{1-\rho}} \right] - P_{i8t} - ... - P_{i,j+1,t}$$

This approach, which aims at representing transition matrices by a single parameter, was studied by Belkin, B., Forest, L. R. Jr and Suchower, S. J. (1998). They follow the CreditMetrics framework proposed by Gupton, Finger and Bhatia (1997).

Estimation of the correlation factor

The correlation factor ρ between the obligor i and the general state of the economy (in the ASRF model, all obligors are linked to each other by this single risk factor Z, which reflects the general state of the economy) has been estimated in order to obtain the best possible fit of historical data by the model, under the hypothesis that the correlation is the same for all obligors (and thus rating classes).

THE STRESS-TESTING FRAMEWORK

The following framework is based on a relationship between the latent credit index and the macroeconomic situation. This link is indeed fundamental, since most stress-test exercises start with the choice of a set of macroeconomic stress scenarios. Those stress scenarios are then linked to risk parameters – default rates (DRs), loss rates, regulatory PDs, regulatory LGDs, transition matrices – which will, in the end, affect banks' solvency.

Our approach is based on an intermediary variable, namely the aggregate DR. First, we measure the link between GDP (or the macroeconomic scenario) and the DR, then between the DR and the latent credit index, in order to compute the stressed transition matrix.

The different steps described here are based on relationships uncovered for France, in particular regarding the link between credit risk and the macroeconomy, but we explain how they may be replicated for other institutions/countries.

The data

Adequate data is of course necessary for calibrating the model. While specific information on the loan portfolios of institutions are essential, we show how to rely on S&P transition matrices,[5] a method that can be to some extent transferable to other institutions/countries as long as they have a similar global portfolio of corporate loans.

Prudential Common Reporting

Our framework basically requires information on the structure of banks' portfolios by types of rating. They are available from banks' Prudential Common Reporting (COREP).[6] COREP is a set of European harmonised data on solvency issues (own-funds adequacy, credit RWAs, market RWAs, operational RWAs) handled by the EBA. It intends to enhance the level of harmonisation of the supervisory reporting. A specific COREP template is dedicated to the credit risk of IRB corporate portfolios, in which the regulatory PDs for each class of risk are reported to the French authorities by banks in the quarterly prudential COREP templates.

This information is actually combined with mappings (provided by the onsite-inspections division) that convert the internal rating system of each bank into the S&P rating scale. This step is facilitated by the fact that most banks use such a conversion scale to compute, when possible, a distance between their internal rating and agency ratings, as an indicator for assessing the performance of their internal models. This is a necessary step in order to stress banks' portfolios by using S&P transition matrices.

The S&P transition matrices

Our framework takes advantage of the S&P CreditPro database, which contains issuer ratings history for 15,726 obligors over the 1981–2011 period, of which 2,127 ended in default. The obligors are mainly large corporate institutions – sovereigns and municipals are excluded – and pools include both US and non-US industrials, utilities, insurance companies, banks and other financial institutions, and real-estate companies.[7]

Over the past two decades from 1990 to 2011, three major business cycles can be distinguished: (i) the recession that took place in the wake of the First Gulf war at the beginning of the 1990s (GDP growth dropped to −0.3% in 1991 in the US and to −0,7% in 1993 in France); (ii) the burst of the Internet bubble (GDP growth dropped in the US to 1.1% in 2001 from over 4% from 1998 to 2000, while in France GDP growth declined to 0,9% in 2002 and 2003 from over 3.5% in 2000); and (iii) the 2007-and-beyond subprime crisis (both American and French GDP growth dropped to less than −3% in 2009).

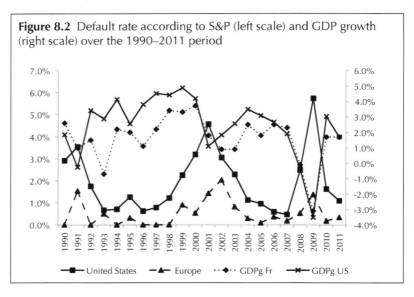

Figure 8.2 Default rate according to S&P (left scale) and GDP growth (right scale) over the 1990–2011 period

During each of these periods, DRs surged both in Europe and the US (see Figure 8.2). It is especially striking after the burst of the Internet bubble, during which (i) the DR of American corporates reached the level of 4.5% (2% in Europe) and (ii) the total amount of debt-defaulting was historically high due to failures of major companies (Enron, WorldCom, Parmalat and so on). DRs during the subprime crisis surged even higher in the US (5.70% in 2009).

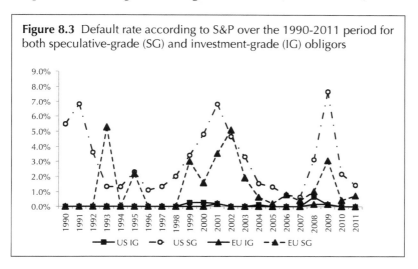

Figure 8.3 Default rate according to S&P over the 1990-2011 period for both speculative-grade (SG) and investment-grade (IG) obligors

If DRs, and, more globally, credit migrations, are therefore clearly linked to the economic context, it turns out that default events mainly involve speculative-grade obligors (rated BBB and below). Investment-grade obligors are much less sensitive to the business cycle, underlining two different dynamics for investment-grade corporates on the one hand, and for speculative-grade (which is actually the main driver of the global DR) on the other hand (see figure 8.3).

In Table 8.1, annual S&P transition matrices displaying probabilities to migrate from one rating to another are based on a "static pool approach". Credit-migration rates are computed by comparing ratings on the first and last days of the year to construct the migration rates. Rating movements within the year are accordingly not counted. This estimation approach, based on average behaviour, does not actually capture rare events such as back-and-forth transitions or series of consecutive downgrades within the year. Default is considered to be an absorbing risk class: if a recovery from default may be observed, it is extremely rare. Usually, firms having defaulted are excluded from the pool the following year, which prevents the recovery trajectory to ever be caught in a one year transition matrix.

Table 8.1 S&P average credit rating transition matrix (1990–2011)

	AAA	AA	A	BBB	BB	B	CCC, CC, C	D
AAA	90.2%	8.9%	0.5%	0.2%	0.0%	0.0%	0.2%	0.0%
AA	0.3%	89.3%	9.8%	0.6%	0.0%	0.0%	0.0%	0.0%
A	0.0%	2.1%	92.3%	5.1%	0.2%	0.1%	0.0%	0.0%
BBB	0.0%	0.1%	4.2%	91.2%	3.4%	0.7%	0.1%	0.2%
BB	0.0%	0.1%	0.4%	5.1%	86.9%	6.4%	0.5%	0.6%
B	0.0%	0.0%	0.2%	0.5%	7.1%	82.7%	4.8%	4.7%
CCC, CC, C	0.0%	0.0%	0.3%	0.6%	1.1%	13.0%	58.1%	27.1%
D	0.0%	0.0%	0.0%	0.0%	0.0%	0.0%	0.0%	100.0%

As we have seen, migration matrices may be driven by a standard normal distribution – (almost) without losing any information. Migrations are then not depicted by migration rates but through a set of thresholds that depend on the latent variable Z.

As an example, we suppose that an issuer is currently rated A. Table 8.2 and Figure 8.4 show the migration probability from the current A rating to any of the other eight ratings, together with the corresponding threshold from a standard normal distribution.

Table 8.2 Migration rates and scores for an A-rated issuer (1990–2011)

	AAA	AA	A	BBB	BB	B	CCC, CC, C	D
Migration rates	0.0%	2.1%	92.3%	5.1%	0.2%	0.1%	10.0%	0.0%
Score bins	]3.61 ; +∞[	]2.03 ; 3.61]	]-1.60 ; 2.03]	]-2.64 ; -1.60]	]-2.88 ; -2.64]	]-3.25 ; -2.88]	]-3.30 ; -3.25]	]-∞ ; -3.30]

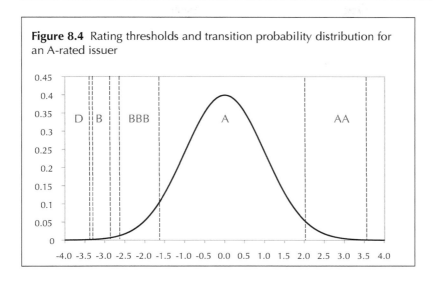

Figure 8.4 Rating thresholds and transition probability distribution for an A-rated issuer

Under adverse economic conditions, the normal distribution of rating migration would shift to the left, implying worse ratings levels (see figure 8.5), meaning that the probability of downgrade and default increases. As the whole credit-migration matrices are driven by a single-parameter Z, which depicts the average financial health of corporate institutions (credit index), this shift corresponds to a simple change in the value of Z.

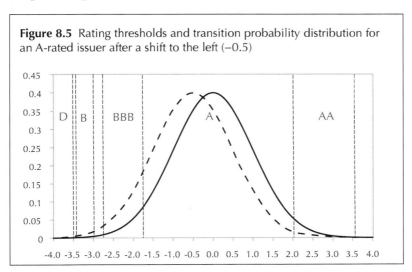

Figure 8.5 Rating thresholds and transition probability distribution for an A-rated issuer after a shift to the left (−0.5)

The economic situation: linking GDP to the aggregate default rate

In order to calibrate the model, we need to measure the link between the macroeconomic environment and defaults. The results presented here are specific to the French situation, hence would need to be re-estimated to implement it inn other countries. However, the method is quite general and can be replicated, following the same steps. This implies:

❏ defining an economic situation scale, as a percentage deviation from maximum defaults;
❏ linking defaults to (national) macroeconomic determinants; and
❏ mapping the aggregate DR into the latent credit index, and we offer a numerical method for doing that.

The model we present is mainly designed to compute RWAs, through PDs linked to the macroeconomic environment. The impact of stressed scenarios on P&Ls, including credit losses, is computed through another model (Coffinet, Lin, Martin, 2009; Coffinet and Lin, 2010).

The economic situation scale

Our economic situation index is the DR since this is both highly correlated to macro-variables like the GDP and directly linked to the situation of corporate institutions.

In our stress-test framework, the state of the economy is accordingly measured on the following scale:

$$\lambda_t = \frac{\widehat{DR_t} - \overline{DR}}{DR_{crisis} - \overline{DR}}$$

where $\widehat{DR_t}$ is the DR forecast at t and $\overline{DR}$ is the average DR over the sample period and DR_{crisis} is the DR reached during the worst crisis observed over the period under observation (in our example, this is computed as a mean of yearly DR for the years 1991, 2001, 2002, 2009). λ_t equals 0 on average over the business cycle, 1 when the reference crisis is reached. If λ_t equals 0.33 for example, the economic situation would be one-third of the maximum historical deviation from the average DR.[8] This scale is unbounded so as to suit stress scenarios which never occurred previously.

Forecasting the default rate in a stress-testing exercise

The link between the DR and the macroeconomic environment may obviously be subjected to more discussions than those presented below. We aim through this couple of equations to provide some alternative specifications for the link between the DR and the economic situation, using different macroeconomic variables. These equation can be used in order to project the DR over the simulation horizon of the stress tests (each scenario would consist of time series of GDP, inflation, interest rates and so forth) that would be fed into the equation to get a DR scenario. The equations are estimated by Ordinary Least Squares. These equations should be re-estimated for implementing our model to other countries.

$$\begin{cases} DR_t = \underset{(0.0003)}{2.565}^{***} + \underset{(0.0038)}{0.579}^{***} DR_{t-1} - \underset{(0.0010)}{0.379}^{***} GDPg_t - \underset{(0.0021)}{0.887}^{***} INFL_{t-1} \\ R^2 = 0.67, DW = 2.17 \end{cases}$$

(8.1)

Where DR is the default rate, GDPg is GDP growth, INFL is the inflation

$$\begin{cases} DR_t = \underset{(0.0019)}{2.673}^{***} - \underset{(0.0077)}{0.372}^{***} GDPg_t - \underset{(0.0345)}{0.705}^{**} INFL_{t-1} \\ R^2 = 0.39, DW = 1.05 \end{cases}$$

(8.2)

$$\begin{cases} DR_t = \underset{(0.0077)}{3.584}^{***} + \underset{(0.0286)}{0.478}^{**} DR_{t-1} - \underset{(0.0032)}{0.348}^{***} GDPg_t - \underset{(0.0074)}{0.798}^{***} INFL_{t-1} - \underset{(0.3278)}{0.125} UR_t \\ R^2 = 0.70, DW = 2.15 \end{cases}$$

(8.3)

Where URt stand for the unemployment rate at t.

$$\begin{cases} DR_t = \underset{(0.0012)}{2.4512}^{***} + \underset{(0.0055)}{0.5718}^{***} DR_{t-1} - \underset{(0.0017)}{0.3744}^{***} GDPg_t - \underset{(0.0050)}{0.8508}^{***} INFL_{t-1} + \underset{(0.6097)}{0.0507} SPREAD \\ R^2 = 0.68, DW = 2.12 \end{cases}$$

(8.4)

Where SPREAD is the spread between the interest rates on the ten-year French Treasury note and the three-month Euribor.

Among the prominent points highlighted by these equations are as follows.

❏ THE INERTIA OF THE DR: The DR inertia, ie, the autoregressive coefficient in equations (1), (3) and (4), is both strong and significant: past values of the DR provide good forecasting results.

❑ THE INDICATORS OF THE STATE OF THE ECONOMY: According to the range of econometric tests, led by the ACP, the most relevant economic variables with respect to DR forecasting are GDP growth and the unemployment rate.

❑ THE FINANCIAL ENVIRONMENT. The spread between long-term interest rates (10y) and short-term ones (3m) used in equation (4) is both classical and relevant. However, its impact is often mild and positive.[9]

In addition, it might be interesting to integrate feedback effects between defaults and the business cycle (Bruneau, de Bandt and El Amri 2012).

The "conversion" function: mapping the aggregate default rate into the latent credit index to generate the stressed transition matrix

The final step is to map our time series of defaults (more precisely of our economic situation scale, which is a simple transformation of defaults, as indicated earlier) into our latent macroeconomic systemic factor on which the transition matrices are based. We provide here a numerical method for doing that, which could be easily replicated. We thus define a second conversion scale in order to convert the crisis percentage into the corresponding stressed transition matrix.

For that purpose, we consider the actual transition matrix observed when the economy enters into the recession periods mentioned above (namely in 1991, 2001–2 and 2009).[10] We compare that matrix to the unconditional transition matrix over the sample period. The latter matrix can be viewed as a through-the-cycle transition matrix.

More precisely, we define a scale based on the couple $Z_{0\%crisis}$ and $Z_{100\%crisis}$, which are the two credit indexes that respectively best fit (i) the through-the-cycle transition matrix (TM_{TTC}) as the average of transition matrices observed over the period and (ii) the "crisis" transition matrix (TM_{crisis}) as an average of the transition matrices observed in 1991, 2001, 2002 and 2009. Note that we chose a simple average transition matrix conditional on exceeding the probability of 82% (which would be equivalent to the 4 worst observations in a 22-year sample). However, we could have used variable weights over time to compute an average transition matrix highlighting different crisis episodes (banking- or industry-related crisis).

From the comparison of the observed and asymptotic single-risk-factor (ASRF) transition matrices we derive the value of the latent macroeconomic systemic factor corresponding, respectively, to "normal times" and "crisis":

$$\begin{cases} \hat{Z}_{0\%crisis} = \arg\min_{Z_t} |TM_{TTC} - TM(Z_t)| \\ \hat{Z}_{100\%crisis} = \arg\min_{Z_t} |TM_{crisis} - TM(Z_t)| \end{cases}$$

Several kinds of matricial norms can be used: we chose the Euclidian norm, typically used in linear optimisation problems. Assuming the relationships $Z_t = Z_{0\%} \Leftrightarrow \lambda_t = 0$ and $Z_t = Z_{100\%} \Leftrightarrow \lambda_t = 1$ between the state of the economy and the credit index, the final step is to compute the value of the macroeconomic systemic risk, which comes from the following "conversion" function:

$$Z_t = [(Z_{100\%crisis} - Z_{0\%crisis}) \times \lambda_t + Z_{0\%crisis}]$$

where λ_t depends on the spread between the long-term average DR and the one forecast over the stress horizon. The stressed transition matrix is then used to compute the level of RWAs (under the large corporate parameters of the Basel II formula, using regulatory PDs).

We should mention that, in our stress-test framework, the transition matrices do not depend on one parameter Z but on two parameters ($Z_{investment\ grade}$; $Z_{speculative\ grade}$) in order (i) to stick to a simple approach – we could have as many credit indexes as notches within S&P transition matrices – and (ii) to reflect the two distinct regimes followed by investment-grade and speculative-grade obligors. Indeed, as depicted earlier in this chapter, global DRs are largely driven by the credit quality of speculative-grade counterparties, so that the identified crisis periods are periods of crisis for speculative-grade obligors, rather than for investment-grade ones. Practically, this means that two sets of parameters ($Z_{0\%crisis}$, $Z_{100\%crisis}$) have been estimated, one on the investment sub-part of the TTC and crisis matrices, and one on the speculative sub-part.

NUMERICAL APPLICATION

We present now a few outputs of the model for stress testing. First, we provide more detailed information on necessary inputs, namely banks' exposures. We then use the model presented in the section "The stress-testing framework" above to compute ratings migration on banks' portfolios, hence to compute the level of RWAs under stress. We present the aggregate results for our sample of five of the largest French banks in a baseline and a stressed scenario.

Composition of French large banks' corporate credit portfolio and evolution over time of exposures at default

An initial portfolio is made up of corporate credit exposures of the five largest French banks. Information on exposures and risk profile[11] is available in COREP reports. Banks' portfolios are relatively diversified in terms of sectors. Most exposures are investment-grade and are mainly located in Europe and North America.

Based on this information, we need to compute the evolution over time of exposures at default (EAD).

Let us assume that the horizon of the following exercise is two years, so, starting from end-year 0, the stress test ends Year 2.

Starting with a portfolio of assets in different rating categories, we compute how the portfolio changes over time following a shock. This implies computing a stressed transition (or migration) matrix with the probability of moving from one rating category to another. Technically, this is a Markov chain matrix, assuming that all information at time t+1 is contained at time t.

Furthermore, banks' balance sheets are supposed to be static (as opposed to dynamic), meaning that the total non-defaulted exposures remain stable over the stress period. The assumptions made in our example could very well be modified.

Calculation of risk-weighted assets and capital requirements for credit risk.

Formally, considering an initial portfolio with a given risk structure $EAD0,i$ at time 0 with $i=AAA, AA,...,D$, the dynamic behaviour of the portfolio has the following form:

$$EAD_{t,i}=EAD_{t-1,i}[TM_t^{stress}(Z_{IG};Z_{SG})+\Delta EAD_t]$$

The portfolio risk structure depends on the credit migration matrix, which is a function of macroeconomic and financial factors. $\Delta EADt$ is the growth of new loans; it is adjusted so as to comply with the static balance-sheet constraint. Regulatory capital requirements are then calculated according to the Basel II formula.

We consider the two hypothetical following scenarios:

❏ a baseline scenario based on GDP growth projections from the IMF's World Economic Outlook (WEO); and
❏ an adverse scenario that is supposed to lead to a maximum cumulated deviation from baseline of two standard deviations of GDP growth for 2012–13.

Table 8.3 shows the main key macroeconomic factors that drive our two scenarios.

Table 8.3 Macroeconomic variables' forecast used for a stress-test simulation

	Baseline		Adverse	
	2012	2013	2012	2013
Inflation (%)	1.7	1.5	1.3	0.2
GDP real growth (%)	0.5	1.0	−1.9	0.0

The main outcomes under these two scenarios, in terms of risk parameters (regulatory PDs) and capital requirements (RWA levels), which are the main final output of our stress-testing framework, are displayed in Table 8.4. Changes in RWAs in the table are computed as the sum of changes in RWAs over five of the largest French banks.

Table 8.4 Main outcomes under the baseline and adverse scenarios

	Baseline		Adverse	
	2012	2013	2012	2013
Stressed regulatory PDs (annual rate of change)	+2%	+12%	+15%	+11%
RWAs (annual rate of change)	+2.6%	+5.3%	+12.9%	+5.9%

Table 8.4 shows the outcome of this sensitivity analysis in which regulatory PDs[12] and migration rates were stressed over the 2012–13 period. It is worth noticing that other regulatory parameters, such as LGD and correlations, have not been stressed in this particular exercise. The results in Table 8.4 illustrate the existence of a smoothing effect of the stressed scenario on RWAs, due to the negative relationship between regulatory PDs and the correlation with the credit index (ρ), as assumed in the internal-ratings-based (IRB) model.

The outcome of this simulation shows that the sensitivity of IRB minimum capital requirements to increases in regulatory PDs and credit migrations is significant. Indeed, an increase of PD by 15% in 2012 (resp. 13% in 2013) in the adverse scenario raises capital requirements by about 11% (resp. 5.9% in 2013). Moreover, the initial shock, a deep recession in 2012, raises both risk parameters and capital requirements at least up to 2013. This is consistent with our expectations, since Basel II formulas rely on through-the-cycle PDs, which tend to smooth the impact of the shock at the very beginning of the stress but makes it last longer.

CONCLUSION

Credit risk remains one of the most important risks faced by commercial banks. This chapter provides a stress-testing framework for banks' corporate credit portfolios, a framework that is currently used by French authorities to perform biannual top-down exercises.

This framework is therefore appropriate for data available at a supervisory authority level and aims to achieve the best trade-off between simplicity and robustness. Our stress-test framework takes advantage of the quarterly prudential COREP templates and of the S&P CreditPro database, which provides statistics over the previous two decades regarding credit migration of more than 10,000 American and European companies.

The calibrations proposed – namely AR models for observed DRs, which assume stationary explanatory variables as well as mean reversion dynamics – are consistent with the Basel II framework, which relies on through-the-cycle risk parameters (PDs). This framework is therefore fully relevant for benchmarking bottom-up exercises. Furthermore, from a regulatory point of view, this framework is a realistic approach to how banks compute their RWAs: regulatory parameters, such as PDs and LGDs, are estimated as through-the-cycle parameters, possibly with an add-on coefficient for prudence (taking into account downturn economic conditions for LGD). As a consequence, they tend to become less and less sensitive to a given stress period, given that they are based on ever-increasing historical datasets. It is indeed important in our view that the stress-testing framework be as close as possible to the actual regulation governing the computation of RWAs.

Views expressed do not necessarily correspond to those of the Autorité de Contrôle Prudentiel.

REFERENCES

Belkin, B., Forest, L. R. Jr and S. J. Suchower, 1998, "A one-parameter representation of credit risk and transition matrixes", *CreditMetrics Monitor* (3rd Quarter.

Bruneau, C., O. de Bandt and W. El Amri, 2012, "Macroeconomic fluctuations and corporate financial fragility", *Journal of Financial Stability*, 8, pp. 219–35.

Coffinet, J., and S. Lin, 2010, "Stress-testing banks' profitability", Banque de France Working Paper 306.

Coffinet, J., S. Lin and C. Martin, 2009, "Stress-testing French banks' subcomponents", Banque de France Working Paper 242.

Dumontaux, N., and D. Médée, 2009, "Prévision de matrixes de transition en fonction d'un scénario macroéconomique", Autorité de Contrôle Prudentiel, mimeo.

Gupton, G., C. Finger and M. Bhatia, 1997, "CreditMetrics-Technical Document", Morgan Guaranty Trust Co.

Merton, R., 1974, "On the Pricing of Corporate Debt: the Risk Structure of Interest Rates", *Journal of Finance*, 29, 449-470

Standard & Poor's, 2012, "Annual 2011 Global Corporate Default Study and Rating Transitions", *Global Fixed Income Research*.

Standard & Poor's, 2008, "Annual 2007 Global Corporate Default Study and Rating Transitions", *Global Fixed Income Research*.

Vasicek, O., 1991, "Limiting Loan Loss Probability Distribution", KMV Corporation.

1   In the case of France, credit-risk RWAs represents more than 75% of total RWAs.

2   Exposures from structured credit products or from over-the-counter (OTC) derivatives exposures are not covered here.

3   Prudential filters may sometimes dampen the effect of marked-to-market gains or losses.

4   See Dumontaux and Médée, 2009.

5   See Standard and Poor's (2012) and Standard and Poor's (2007).

6   For any further information, see http://www.eba.europa.eu/Supervisory-Reporting/COREP.aspx

7   The structure of the corporate portfolio of French banks, dominated by international groups, allows the use of such a reference sample to calibrate their stress-testing framework. It could therefore be extended to other global banks, once we are ready to assume that all global banks tap the same markets, in terms of risk characteristics, but differ in terms of portfolio composition.

8   Actually, it is one-third of the deviation between the average default rate and DRcrisis (the mean of yearly DRs for the years 1991, 2001, 2002, 2009).

9   There is a vast literature on the forecasting properties of the slope of the yield curve.

10 Notice that we consider the recession dates in the US since the database we used is based on a sample of US and European firms, also assuming that large corporates are global companies significantly affected by the US business cycle. In the practical implementation of stress tests, however, we assume that this calibration also holds for the portfolio of corporate assets held by French banking groups. Such an assumption is imposed by the data constraints (ratings on corporate assets as provided in the Banque de France FIBEN database are available only with a lag, preventing their use in real-time stress testing).

11 The breakdown by rating is given by the S&P equivalent of internal rating.

12 Regulatory PDs, consistent with Basel II regulations, are estimated as a long-term moving average of observed default rates; a stressed default rate, which is produced by our model, is therefore included in the new time window at the end of each year, thus yielding a stressed regulatory PD.

9

EU-Wide Stress Test: The Experience of the EBA

Paolo Bisio, Demelza Jurcevic and Mario Quagliariello

European Banking Authority

In the midst of the financial crisis, the European Banking Authority (EBA) was established on January 1, 2011, with a broad remit that included safeguarding the stability of the EU financial system.[1] According to its founding regulation,[2] the EBA is required, in cooperation with the European Systemic Risk Board (ESRB), to initiate and coordinate EU-wide stress tests to assess the resilience of financial institutions to adverse market developments. While the stress test is a key component of the EBA's toolkit, it is only one of a range of supervisory tools used by the EBA for assessing the resilience of individual institutions as well as the overall resilience of the European banking system.

The first EU-wide stress test of 22 banks was performed by the Committee of European Banking Supervisors (CEBS), the EBA's predecessor, in 2009. The individual results of the stress test were kept confidential. Only a press release was published with the key results. Some details of the macroeconomic scenario were published (GDP, unemployment and property prices). Furthermore, the results were published in a very concise manner:

> Under such adverse scenario, the potential credit and trading losses over the years 2009–2010 could amount to almost €400 bn. However, the financial position and expected results of banks are sufficient to maintain an adequate level of capital also under such negative circumstances. Notably, the aggregate Tier 1 ratio for the banks in the sample would remain above 8% and no bank would see its Tier 1 ratio falling under 6% as a result of the adverse scenario.[3]

In 2010, CEBS performed another EU-wide stress test among 91 banks; an aggregate report was published as well as individual bank results. The individual bank results consisted of a single page with the level of Tier 1 capital, risk-weighted assets (RWAs), losses and loss rates for both scenarios (baseline and adverse).

Building on the experience of two previous EU-wide stress tests undertaken by CEBS, the EBA conducted a stress test among 91 banks in 2011. This exercise was undertaken in coordination with National Supervisory Authorities (NSAs), the ESRB, the European Central Bank (ECB) and the European Commission (EC).

The exercise was conducted on a bank-by-bank basis, on the highest level of consolidation of the banking group. The objective of the stress test was to assess the resilience of the EU banking system, and the specific solvency of individual institutions, to hypothetical stress events under certain severe scenarios decided on by supervisors in conjunction with the ESRB/ECB. It was a microprudential stress test focused primarily on assessing banks in a bottom-up manner in a way that is conservative and consistent across the EU.

In this chapter we describe the EBA's experience in carrying out the EU-wide stress test, with a focus on 2011, and provide some insights into the design, organisation and management of such a complex exercise. After a first, introductory section, we move to the summary of the main findings of the stress test and conclude with our views on the lessons learnt from the 2011 exercise.

KEY CHARACTERISTICS OF THE EBA 2011 STRESS-TEST EXERCISE[4]

The 2011 EU-wide stress-test exercise was characterised as a constrained bottom-up stress test. While banks are required to use their internal models for estimating possible losses in a stress scenario, the EBA identified common minimum methodological assumptions, imposed a single adverse scenario and carried out an in-depth quality-assurance process. This is probably the most important feature of the EBA's stress test, a precondition for ensuring comparability of the results across institutions from different countries and a level playing field in the implementation of supervisory measures following the stress test.

Therefore, the organisation of an EU-wide stress test requires complex preparatory work, involving both methodological and procedural aspects. For the 2011 exercise, the preparatory phase started in September 2010, and 10 months later the bank-by-bank results were published.

The first step in running an EU-wide stress-test exercise was to define the sample of banks to be involved and objective of the exercise. As for the former, the 2011 exercise was carried out among 91 banks at consolidated bank group level. The selection of the sample was based on representativeness (50% of national banking sector and 65% of the European banking sector), with the possibility for NSAs to add additional banks when deemed relevant from a financial stability perspective. The objective was to assess the overall resilience of the EU banking system and to identify possible capital needs at specific institutions.

In fact, the EU stress test has been – like similar exercises carried out in other countries during the financial crisis – a pass/fail test: banks that proved to be not able to maintain enough capital in the adverse scenario have been requested to raise new capital or to activate mitigating measures, if available.

The second step in the process is developing the macro scenario. The baseline scenario was based on the European Commission forecasts, while the adverse scenario has been developed by the ECB in cooperation with the ESRB. The stress-test horizon was set at two years, as in many regulatory stress tests. The adverse scenario was composed of three elements: (1) a set of EU-shocks mostly tied to the persistence of the sovereign debt crisis, (2) a global negative demand shock originating in the US and (3) a USD depreciation vis-à-vis all currencies. In the adverse scenario the cumulative GDP drop in the EU was 4%, with a fall of the residential house price by 15% at EU level. Besides the macro scenario for positions in the banking book, market-risk shocks were designed for stress testing the positions in the trading book as well. The market-risk shocks were aligned with the macro scenario. For example, share prices within Europe decreased by 15% instantaneously in the adverse scenario. Furthermore, a specific stress scenario was applied for securitisation positions in the banking and trading book. To that end, predefined migration matrices for the baseline and adverse scenario were used, based on historical experience.

The third step in the process is designing the stress-test methodology. As mentioned above, the EBA 2011 stress-test exercise was carried out by following a constrained bottom-up approach. A bottom-up stress test is a microprudential test that relies on specific idiosyncratic data and approaches (for example, banks used their internal models – where available – to calculate the impact of the stress test on the balance sheets and the profit-and-loss accounts). But the exercise was constrained by a series of EBA-prescribed restrictive assumptions and a common macro scenario. The design of the methodology was a challenging task aimed at striking the right balance between realism and conservatism, respecting the banks' specificities and ensuring consistency of treatment and comparability of the results. While this is common to different system-wide exercises, the EU setting required extra effort in order to ensure consistency across banks belonging to different jurisdictions and subject to not-fully harmonised rules and supervisory practices.

In general, the methodology was designed in respect of the existing and forthcoming prudential and accounting rules applicable in the time horizon of the exercise, notably the International Accounting Standards (IAS) and the Capital Requirement Directive (CRD) and amendments. Two main features were thus the application of the prudential filters and the application of the amortised cost for the assets booked in the held-to-maturity portfolio (EBA 2011a).

Another important element for the credibility of the entire exercise was to define the capital threshold in terms of Core Tier 1 ratio (CT1). Notwithstanding the lack of a consistent definition of CT1 capital in the pre-Basel III regulation, the EBA decided to deduct hybrid capital instruments from the Tier 1 capital, in order to identify a common definition in line with – even though not equal to – the Basel concept of common equity Tier 1. Government support measures were recognised as eligible CT1 capital. By setting a common definition of CT1 capital, comparability across the banks involved in the exercise was ensured. The threshold was set at 5%, which banks were expected to meet after taking into account the impact of the adverse scenario.

A key assumption designed to ensure consistency in the constrained bottom-up approach, and which had a large impact on the results of the stress test, was considering banks' balance sheets as static over the time horizon of the exercise, ie, no management actions were allowed for mitigating the impact of the adverse scenario (static balance-sheet assumption). In practice, this implied a constant business mix, constant funding mix, a zero growth rate, the rollover of maturing assets and liabilities and no workout of defaulted assets. This approach guaranteed comparability of the results across banks and a level playing field, at the cost of reducing the realism of the exercise (see also the last section).

The methodology also imposed some constraints on the stress test's starting point. In particular, banks were requested to subtract the PL-impact of the market risk shocks on the trading book portfolio from the average net trading income of a bank over the last five years. Since estimating net trading income before stress would have been difficult, using a historical average represented a simple and conservative benchmark. Furthermore in order to incorporate funding risk, the EBA prescribed to a certain extent the evolution in the cost of funding. For example, the interest expenses to be paid for wholesale funding had to increase according to the evolution of the interest rate envisaged in the macroeconomic scenario. Another assumption prescribed was that there is a perfect correlation between the evolution in the sovereign credit spread and that in the bank's credit spread. Furthermore, banks have only been allowed to pass up to 50% of the cost of funding increase to the clients through a potential adjustment to the credit spread on the maturing loans.

The reliability of the results and the comparability across banks were then assured through three lines of defence (EBA 2011c): (i) the banks' own internal controls, (ii) the consistency checks carried out by the national supervisors and (iii) a quality assurance process carried out by the EBA.

This last line of defence was a new aspect of the 2011 stress test, with an ad hoc task force in charge of performing a thorough peer review and assessing the proper application of the common methodology. This level of cooperation, with national experts coming to join EBA staff for a prolonged period in assessing results, was a step forward in stress-test cooperation in the EU. Banks' results, in particular in terms of risk parameters for credit risk, have also been compared and outliers identified. The computation of benchmarks has been performed using the granular data collected by the EBA, including exposures at default (EADs), probabilities of default

(PDs) and loss-given defaults (LGDs) with asset-class and counterparty countries' breakdowns. However, it is worth underlining that no asset quality review was undertaken ahead of or during the stress-test exercise. This is in the remit of national supervisors.

In some cases, banks were required to revise their estimates in order to bring them into a more consistent range. Indeed, although the EBA did not request an automatic application of the benchmarks, banks were asked in some cases to revaluate their initial estimations, providing explanations in case of significant deviation and resubmitting the results if explanations were considered inadequate. As the result of peer review, additional guidance was provided to banks for clarification purposes and in order to obtain consistency across banks. In this additional guidance (see, EBA, 2011), the EBA prescribed for example an approach to determining regulatory risk parameters and thus additional provisions to be held by banks for sovereign and institutional exposures (see Panel 9.1).

PANEL 9.1 TREATMENT OF SOVEREIGN AND FINANCIAL INSTITUTIONS' EXPOSURES IN THE BANKING BOOK

Due to discrepancies between the additional provisions for sovereign and financial institutions across banks, the EBA prescribed the additional provisions to be held by banks by setting the additional provisions equal to the increase in expected loss. The EBA developed an approach based on probabilities of default attributed by rating agencies and assuming downgrades depending on the conditions of the specific countries. The first step was to identify the degree of the downgrade (number of notches), which was linked to the initial rating. For exposures with AAA ratings, no downgrade was needed. For AA exposures a two-notch downgraded needed to be applied. At last, for exposures with BBB+ rating, a four-notch downgrade was requested (floor at CCC). After the application of the downgrade to the initial rating, this rating after stress needed to be mapped to a PD. For simplicity and consistency purposes, the EBA used the two years' cumulative default rates observed by the three well-known rating agencies Fitch, Moody's and S&P (see Table 9.1). The LGD to be used for the calculation of the impairments was set by the EBA at 40%. The increased provisions amount is equal to the multiplication of the PD after the downgrade and the LGD of 40%.

Further benchmarks were also identified for the computation of the increase in the cost of funding, the impact caused by the transition to the Basel 2.5 framework for market risk capital requirements.

RESULTS AND DISCLOSURE

One interesting point to note is that, from the announcement of the start of the stress test, banks raced to strengthen their capital base in order to ensure they were deemed strong in anticipation of it. To this end, while the EBA, together with NSAs, ECB, ESRB and EC, were preparing for the launch of the EBA 2011 stress-test exercise in March 2011, some banks that were selected to participate in the exercise were already increasing their capital base. In total, the capital base of the banks participating in the exercise increased by €50 billion between January and April 2011.

The average CT1 ratio of the banks decreased from 8.9% to 7.7% after two years of stress. In total, eight banks had a CT1 ratio below 5%, leading to a total capital deficit of €2.5 billion. Table 9.1, published by the EBA (2011c) provides an overview of the results of the EBA 2011 stress test exercise.

In total, eight banks had a CT1 ratio under the adverse scenario below the set 5% benchmark.

Following the publication of the 2011 EU-wide stress test results in July 2011, the EBA issued a recommendation (EBA 2011e) to national supervisory authorities (NSAs) to ensure that appropriate mitigating actions were put in place with respect to (i) banks with a CT1 ratio below 5% in the adverse scenario and (ii) banks with a CT1 ratio close to 5% in the adverse scenario and with sizeable exposures to sovereigns under stress.

Along with the bank-by-bank stress-test results, the EBA also published detailed information about banks' actual exposures. This was part of an unprecedented effort for increasing transparency and reducing uncertainty over EU banks' financial conditions. In total 3,200 data points were published per bank resulting in an unprecedented level of harmonised disclosure of the results and banks' exposure data. In fact, disclosure has represented a complement to the analysis conducted by the EBA itself, allowing market participants to make their own assumptions and possibly testing further scenarios beyond the EBA baseline and adverse scenarios for the banking book and the trading book.

Table 9.1 Results of the 2011 EU-wide stress test – country data

Adverse scenario												
	2010	2012	< 2%	< 3%	< 4%	< 5%	< 6%	< 7%	< 8%	< 9%	< 10%	> 10%
AT	8.2%	7.6%	0	0	0	1	0	0	0	1	0	0
BE	11.4%	10.2%	0	0	0	0	0	0	0	0	0	2
CY	7.7%	5.7%	0	0	0	0	1	1	0	0	1	0
DE	9.4%	6.8%	0	0	0	0	2	4	2	1	1	2
DK	9.8%	11.9%	0	0	0	0	2	5	2	3	1	3
ES	7.4%	7.3%	0	0	3	2	7	5	1	3	2	2
FI	12.2%	11.6%	0	0	0	0	0	0	1	1	0	1
FR	8.4%	7.5%	0	0	0	0	0	0	0	0	0	0
GB	10.1%	7.6%	0	0	0	0	0	0	0	0	0	0
GR	10.2%	6.1%	1	0	0	1	2	1	2	1	0	0
HU	12.3%	13.6%	0	0	0	0	0	0	2	0	0	1
IE	6.2%	9.8%	0	0	0	0	0	0	0	0	0	2
IT	7.4%	7.3%	0	0	0	0	1	2	1	0	0	0
LU	12.0%	13.3%	0	0	0	0	0	0	0	0	0	1
MT	10.5%	10.4%	0	0	0	0	0	1	0	1	1	1
NL	10.6%	9.4%	0	0	0	0	0	0	0	1	1	1
NO	8.3%	9.0%	0	0	0	0	0	0	0	0	0	0
PL	11.8%	12.2%	0	0	0	0	2	2	0	0	0	1
PT	7.1%	5.7%	0	0	0	0	0	0	0	0	2	0
SE	9.0%	9.5%	0	0	0	0	0	0	0	1	2	1
SI	5.7%	6.0%	0	0	0	0	1	0	0	1	0	0
Total	8.9%	7.7%	1	0	3	4	16	18	11	12	7	18

Source: EBA (2011c)

134

LESSON LEARNED FROM THE EBA 2011 STRESS TEST

The EBA 2011 stress-test exercise has represented an important step towards an EU-wide forward-looking assessment of risks and vulnerabilities in the European banking sector. The development of a common methodology and its early publication was very well commented on by the different stakeholders. This ensured transparency for market participants as regards the assumptions and the mechanics of the exercise as well as consistency across banks in conducting the stress-test exercise. At the same time, the commitment for future exercises is to further anticipate the publication of the methodology, in order to enhance the interaction with the industry ahead of the launch of the exercise and, ideally, testing the templates for data collection.

Furthermore, the decision to set the capital threshold at CT1, and communicating the capital threshold (5% CT1) in advance of publishing the stress-test results, guaranteed a credible and disclosed capital benchmark. Early disclosure also encouraged banks to strengthen their capital positions ahead of the test by raising €50 billion between January and April 2011.

The quality assurance and peer review were also beneficial and added value in terms of ensuring adequacy in the interpretation of the methodology and the mapping of the macroeconomic scenario into micro-parameters. Looking ahead, further work on the early definitions of benchmarks to be used in this process is needed and would lead to even more robust results.

Last, but not least, the unprecedented level of harmonised disclosure of the results and banks' exposure data disclosure was perceived a significant step in the direction of greater transparency. In particular, disclosure on banks' actual exposures and starting points has added value and contributed to reducing uncertainty about the state of health of the EU banking sector. It also allowed analysts to perform their own assessment and complement the EBA's scenarios with further sensitivities.

Along with significant pros, the EBA stress test has been also challenged. Some criticisms relate to the process and the ongoing fine tuning of templates and benchmarks during the exercise itself as more information became available. The process for future stress tests will attempt to overcome this by road-testing templates and gathering information on benchmarks *ex ante*. However, particular criticism was in terms of the outcome of the exercise and of some of its assumptions.

Market concerns about the EU banking system and the financial stability implications thereof were deemed not to be directly addressed by the stress-test exercise. A first problem was probably linked to the design of the macroeconomic scenario. Indeed, the adverse scenario agreed when the exercise was launched was taken over by later events, with a further deterioration of the economic environment (vis-à-vis an expected modest recovery) and the eruption of the sovereign crisis. In addition, funding problems and, more importantly, liquidity squeeze pointed to the lack of a review of banks' liquidity positions. Finally, increasing pressure on asset quality, especially in some jurisdictions and for some asset classes, reduced the credibility of the results. In particular the capital shortfall has been perceived as far too optimistic, also in relation to the lack of severe sovereign stress for exposures in the banking book. This criticism was, however, partly tackled by the EBA by running a capital exercise in Q4 2011 (see Panel 9.2).

It should be noted, however, that this criticism is only partially grounded. In some cases, observers have not been able to read more carefully the published results and correctly interpret the data disclosed by the EBA. It has been partly a communication problem linked to the misperception of what a stress test can (and cannot) deliver.

It is beyond the purpose of this chapter to analyse this issue in depth, but it is interesting to show a different way of presenting the stress-test results in terms of incremental impact instead of overall level of CT1 ratio.

Figures 9.1 to 9.3, based on data published by the EBA, show for instance the impact of the stress scenario on banks' loss rates for the retail and corporate exposures and represent an intuitive way for identifying banks more affected, also in relation to the country-specific change in GDP.

In Table 9.2, also based on public data for a sub-sample of banks, we ranked banks by impact of the adverse scenario on some P&L flows, capital position and RWAs.

Table 9.2 tells us quite a different story with some banks that dealt with significant problems that the stress test had actually identified as more sensitive (or less resilient) to the EBA's adverse scenario. In our view, the message is clear: the mechanics of the stress test have some shortcomings that cannot be easily avoided, but a more in-depth and imaginative analysis of the results would have provided interesting insights.

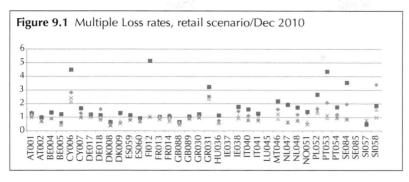

Figure 9.1 Multiple Loss rates, retail scenario/Dec 2010

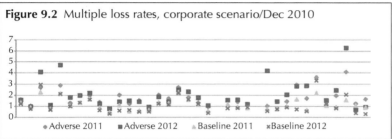

Figure 9.2 Multiple loss rates, corporate scenario/Dec 2010

● Adverse 2011   ■ Adverse 2012   ▲ Baseline 2011   × Baseline 2012

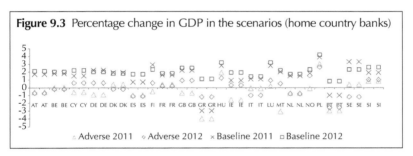

Figure 9.3 Percentage change in GDP in the scenarios (home country banks)

△ Adverse 2011   ◇ Adverse 2012   × Baseline 2011   □ Baseline 2012

A last point is related to the preparation of future EBA stress tests. An important aspect to manage is the expectations from the market. A stress test is not a forecast of the future: it is just the assessment of what would happen should an event, subject to a probability distribution, materialise. A stress scenario needs to be severe but plausible. The sovereign crisis has broadened the perspective with respect to plausibility and severity. The objective of an EU-wide stress-test exercise needs to be clarified in advance. Moreover, it needs to be communicated what stress testing does and does not do. So for the next EU-wide stress-test exercise, which was planned for 2013, the lesson learned from the EBA 2011 stress-test exercise would be incorporated as much as possible.

Table 9.2 Ranking of banks according to the impact of the 2011 EU-wide stress test

Bank code	Bank name	Operative Income	Trading book	Cost funding	Impairments	RWA	CT1	CT1R Adv-Bas
AT001	Erste Bank Group (EBG)	4	3	5	3	5	3	3
AT002	Raiffeisen Bank International (RBI)	5	4	3	2	4	4	2
BE004	Dexia	7	4	6	6	6	5	5
BE005	KBC Bank	7	7	6	3	7	5	5
CY006	Marfin Popular Bank Public Co Ltd	2	7	2	7	3	7	6
CY007	Bank of Cyprus Public Co Ltd	6	5	3	5	2	6	6
DE017	Deutsche Bank AG	3	6	7	2	7	2	4
DE018	Commerzbank AG	5	6	3	4	7	5	5
DK008	Danske Bank	1	6	4	1	1	2	1
DK009	Jyske Bank	2	3	7	1	4	1	7
ES059	Banco Santander S.A.	1	3	1	3	5	1	2
ES060	Banco Bilbao Vizcaya Argentaria S.A. (BBVA)	2	3	6	3	3	1	4

Table 9.2 (continued)

FI012	Op-Pohjola Group	5	5	7	6	5	4	3
FR013	Bnp Paribas	7	2	2	4	6	4	4
FR014	Credit Agricole	6	5	4	4	1	4	2
GB088	Royal Bank of Scotland Group Plc	7	3	7	1	5	6	6
GB089	Hsbc Holdings Plc	6	2	7	2	7	3	5
GR030	Efg Eurobank Ergasias S.A.	4	1	2	5	3	7	7
GR031	National Bank of Greece	1	7	2	7	4	7	7
HU036	Otp Bank Nyrt.	2	4	5	3	3	1	7
IE037	Allied Irish Banks Plc	7	7	1	1	6	7	6
IE038	Bank of Ireland	7	5	2	2	1	7	7
IT040	Intesa Sanpaolo S.P.A	2	1	6	4	4	4	3
IT041	Unicredit S.P.A	3	4	6	4	6	5	2
LU045	Banque et Caisse d'Epargne de l'Etat	4	6	5	7	1	1	1
MT046	Bank of Valletta (Bov)	4	7	7	7	1	5	3

Table 9.2 (continued)

NL047	Ing Bank NV	5	4	1	5	7	2	7
NL048	Rabobank Nederland	3	6	3	5	7	2	6
NO051	Dnb Nor Bank ASA	3	1	5	7	1	2	1
PL052	Powszechna Kasa Oszczednosci Bank Polski S.A. (Pko Bank Polski)	1	1	4	6	3	3	1
PT053	Caixa Geral de Depósitos, SA	6	7	5	6	4	6	5
PT054	Banco Comercial Português, SA (BCP Or Millennium Bcp)	6	1	3	5	6	7	4
SE084	Nordea Bank AB (Publ)	5	2	1	6	1	3	1
SE085	Skandinaviska Enskilda Banken AB (Publ) (Seb)	3	2	7	7	5	3	3
SI057	Nova Ljubljanska Banka D.D. (NLB D.D.)	1	2	1	1	2	6	2
SI058	Nova Kreditna Banka Maribor D.d. (NKBM D.D.)	4	5	4	2	2	6	4

PANEL 9.2 EBA 2011 CAPITAL EXERCISE

In December 2011, the EBA launched a capital exercise in order to reassure market participants on the resilience of EU banks to a sovereign shock. This was part of a more general plan to break the link between banks and sovereigns via (i) direct capital injections into banks from EU bodies, (ii) effective EU-wide bank term debt guarantees, and (iii) higher capital buffers across the entire banking system.

In this context, in December 2011 (EBA 2011d), the EBA issued a recommendation that banks raise their CT1 capital to 9% after accounting for an additional buffer against stressed sovereign risk holdings. The capital exercise was not a stress-test exercise, since no stress scenario was prescribed. In the capital exercise banks were required to evaluate, in a prudent manner, their sovereign exposures.

The recommendation requires banks to strengthen their capital positions by building up an exceptional and temporary capital buffer against sovereign debt exposures to reflect market prices as at the end of September 2011. In addition, banks were required to establish an exceptional and temporary buffer such that the Core Tier 1 capital ratio would reach a level of 9% by the end of June 2012.

The buffer requirement was not designed to cover losses in sovereigns, but to provide a reassurance to markets about the banks' ability to withstand a range of shocks and maintain adequate capital levels. The sovereign capital buffer has been clearly established as a one-off measure and not as a permanent requirement.

CONCLUSION

This chapter described the EBA experience in running the EU-wide stress test, focusing on the 2011 exercise. In particular, we tried to highlight what the challenges were – in terms of methodology, governance of the process and communication – of a stress test covering an ample sample of banks from different jurisdictions which are subject to banking regulations that are not fully harmonised.

There are various peculiarities in handling this kind of exercise, but we would like to conclude with three main messages.

The first is that a choice needs to be made between comparability and realism in designing the stress test. The EBA privileged the former and opted for a static balance-sheet assumption and a constrained bottom-up setting. This may be criticised from a theoretical perspective, but it is the only manageable approach in practice and contributes to ensure a level playing field.

Second, the results of the stress test cannot be interpreted in a mechanistic way, but should be read carefully and subject to further sensitivities. In that respect, the disclosure exercise that accompanied the release of the stress-test results greatly contributed to reduce uncertainty on banks' exposures to different sources of risk.

Finally, communication is key and it is important to increase awareness of what a stress test can and cannot deliver. In that respect, managing expectations is part of the preparation for a stress test, particularly if individual results are disclosed. This avoids the spreading of a false sense of security as well as of complacency.

The opinions expressed in this chapter are those of the authors and do not involve the EBA and its Members. Useful comments and suggestions from Piers Haben are gratefully acknowledged.

REFERENCES
EBA, 2010, "Aggregate outcome of the 2010 EU-wide stress test exercise coordinated by CEBS in cooperation with the ECB", July.

EBA, 2011a, "EU-wide stress test Methodological note", Version 1.1, March.

EBA, 2011b, "EU-wide stress test: Methodological note – Additional guidance", June 9.

EBA, 2011c, "EU-wide stress test aggregate report", July 15.

EBA, 2011d, "Capital buffers for addressing market concerns over sovereign exposures – Methodological Note", December 8.

EBA, 2011e, "Recommendation on the creation and supervisory oversight of temporary capital buffers to restore market confidence" (EBA/REC/2011/1), December 8.

EBA, 2012, "Report on the fulfilment of the EBA Recommendation following the 2011 EU-wide stress test", April 30.

1   High Level Group on Financial Supervision in the EU published a report in February 2009, the so-called De Larosière Report. The aim of the report was to lay out a framework to take the EU further in its process of integration, which includes (i) a new regulatory agenda (Basel III), (ii) stronger coordinated supervision (eg, EBA) and (iii) effective crisis-management procedures.

2   Regulation (EU) No. 1093/2010 of the European Parliament and of the Council of November 24, 2010.

3   CEBS's press release on the results of the EU-wide stress testing exercise (2009).

4   This section analyses the results presented in EBA (2011a and 2011b).

10

Stress Testing Across International Exposures and Activities

Robert Scavotto, Robert H. Skinkle
Office of the Comptroller of the Currency

Stress testing foreign exposures of internationally active financial institutions presents an array of challenges from developing data-sets to understanding and factoring in qualitative factors that may drive loss rates. These factors can be a function of the government or more simply related to developments in lending practices within a given market. Our work to stress test consumer loan portfolios across a group of countries led us to conclude that a stress-test approach for consumer portfolios in Asia is best pursued on an individual-country basis with a stratification of the consumer portfolio by secured and unsecured credits. This chapter describes our work in this area and uses the Korean consumer market as a case study.

CONDUCTING STRESS TESTS OF INTERNATIONAL ACTIVITIES IN AN IDIOSYNCRATIC WORLD

Financial institutions with international business activities, including operations in foreign markets, have a number of questions to consider in designing stress tests that cover these activities, exposures and risks. The first and most important is deciding on the purpose of the stress test, since international risks can overlie a number of different risk types, such as credit, market and operational. International risks can be viewed as an overlay since there are determinants of loss rates to consider that are additional to those in a more standard functional form of a model estimated using data and exposures strictly within a single country. For example, if corporate default rates were simply determined by the economic growth rate within a domestic economy, this function would have to be altered if the corporate obligor was also exposed to risks from government intervention in the provision of foreign exchange.

In foreign markets, banks and borrowers are subject to country risk, which is the risk that economic, social and political conditions and events in a foreign country will affect an institution (OCC 2008). Further, these conditions can manifest themselves in the form of a crisis, such as a sovereign-default, exchange-rate or banking-system crisis. These crises can happen in any combination and in any order and need to be considered in the design of an international stress test. Emerging-market countries have been more prone to these crises, but, as evidenced by Iceland (banking-system and exchange-rate crises), Ireland (banking-system crisis) and Greece (sovereign default, as evidenced by a forced restructuring), developed countries are also vulnerable to these crises. Thus, depending on the purpose and scope of the stress test, factoring the potential for one or more crises into the downside scenario is an important consideration when stress testing international portfolios. Being subject to these types of risks also requires that the stress-testing framework be forward-looking and flexible so that stress tests can be executed should sudden changes in economic, financial, political or social conditions take place.

Given the wide range of risk types and potential crises that a bank is exposed to in foreign markets, the scope of the stress test needs to capture the majority of a bank's foreign exposures, activities and risks. The scope of the stress test can also pre-identify transmission channels for some of the losses, but, as managers and modellers think through the scenario under consideration, additional risk channels may be identified and incorporated into the stress test. For example, a recession scenario may open up a liquidity risk channel if the country is highly indebted, has a low level of international reserves and is reliant on foreign capital inflows to finance its debt. These channels may surface as the scenario, and incorporated shocks in the stress test will be driven by internal or external factors. For example, does the scenario incorporate an internal shock, such as a change in government policies, eg, nationalisation of an industry that triggers a sharp decrease in investment activity, or an external shock where the scenario envisions a sovereign default by a major trading partner? Given the complexities that international activities introduce, there is a much wider range of factors and principles that firms need to account for in the design of the stress test. In particular, firms should check to see if Principles 7–15 of the Basel Committee on Banking Supervision's (BCBS) May 2009 report[1] have been implemented and are guiding the stress test.

One way to consider and track the risks that the firm could be exposed to is through a table, such as Table 10.1.

Table 10.1 Potential risks to factor into stress tests for international activities

Country	Transfer Risk[2]	Nationali- sation	Sovereign default	Operational risk from civil strife	...	Bank holiday	...
Argentina		X	X				
...	X			X		X	X
Zambia					X		

A traditional recession-based scenario should be considered a minimum stress test for most foreign-country exposures and activities. The level of complexity of the stress test would vary substantially for a firm with limited exposures in a few countries compared with a firm operating in more than 100 countries using complex products and risk-mitigation strategies. A firm with more complex operations may at the outset of developing its stress-test platform identify a set of countries of highest priority, eg, through the use of a simple calculation of risk-adjusted exposures, known concentrations, or a contagion scenario set of identified countries. The firm may also be able to group countries with similar economic structures (commodity-based, fixed exchange rate) or risks (highly indebted with both current account and fiscal deficits) until the full stress-testing framework can be built. Proceeding in this manner also may help overcome some of the data challenges that the modellers may face, such as generating or obtaining a consistent set of data elements across all of the countries the firm operates in.

Some of the risks are idiosyncratic to individual countries, such as operational risks to the firm from civil strife or imposition of regulatory controls, which imposes challenges to doing a cross-country systemic stress test. However, in the knowledge that these factors are present, the model can control for those elements using various econometric techniques, such as fixed-effects regressions that introduce country dummy variables. These factors can then be tested separately through sensitivity or country-specific stress tests to determine whether material risks were masked by the modelling technique employed. This is likely to involve considerable expert judgement that senior management should be made aware of during the design, testing and reporting on the stress tests.

The final critical elements of the stress test will be the measurement(s) chosen for its objective – capital, earnings, informing bank strategies – and determining a set of potential action points for monitoring and executing risk-mitigation strategies should the scenario materialise. The governance of the stress-testing framework should provide direction for determining these elements; but, at a minimum, the results should be clear, actionable and well supported, and inform decision-making vertically within the firm as well as horizontally across all business lines and functions that manage international activities or would be exposed to those risks.

DATA CHALLENGES IN ESTIMATING INTERNATIONAL STRESS TESTS

The measurement(s) chosen for assessing the international stress test (in accordance with its purpose) will depend in part on the data available for the model estimation – a significant challenge for some countries and variables. Cross-country data has been facilitated by the Basel Committee's efforts to standardise measures for capital; the international accounting standards for capturing key financial indicators for corporations and financial institutions; and the IMF's standardisation of basic macroeconomic data. However, the availability of comparable, cross-country data can diminish significantly depending on the risk type(s) assessed and model strategy chosen, particularly at more granular levels, and may require the financial institution to start building a dataset. Significant data issues will need to be conveyed to senior management, risk managers and business lines, since the interpretation of stress-test results needs to be pragmatic and viewed in light of data limitations relative to home country stress tests.

There are some common public sources for data, including the IMF's international financial statistics and trade data; the World Bank's external debt and governance indicators; and central bank, supervisory and ministry-of-finance websites. Private-sector firms may collect additional elements. The multilateral organisations have worked to make the measurement of the data consistent across countries; however, this may not be the case when collecting individual country data, so it is critical to understand how variables are defined and measured and not assume that, because the name of the variable is similar to that used in other countries, they are indeed identical or consistently measured. Delinquency rates and non-performing loan ratios are good examples of variables that may be defined differently across countries. In Russia, for example, the non-performing assets ratio includes just the past due portion of the loan. Such definitional variations can distort comparisons of portfolio credit quality across countries. This is true whether the data is obtained directly from in-country sources or from vendors that have collected it and packaged it for end-users. The data limitations can be particularly acute and constrain the ability to implement consistent, granular stress-test analyses across countries. However, using proxies, stress tests on a country-by-country basis may be feasible.

There may be a more basic problem when what would normally be considered a standard variable is simply not collected by one or more countries. For example, the unemployment rate is a significant explanatory variable for retail loan performance across countries. However, in India, the government has not collected monthly or quarterly unemployment-rate data across the country, since the logistical difficulties are enormous and the cost prohibitive, or in some countries the unofficial labour market is so large as to render the official unemployment numbers meaningless. Therefore, when a model is being developed, a starting point is to inventory the available data series for each country the bank is exposed to and then consider possible proxies for those data series that cannot be obtained. Some proxies can be developed from what theoretically should be highly correlated variables, such as the level of industrial production and the level of employment, or there is the possibility of obtaining and using proxies from structurally similar economies and banking systems.

There are also some basic data considerations and challenges for banks' internal datasets, including identifying the country of risk, the location of collateral and the reliability of guarantees.

STRESS TESTING INTERNATIONAL RETAIL PORTFOLIOS

A good stress-testing framework employs multiple conceptually sound stress-testing approaches. This is particularly true with international activities, as data limitations may force some programmes to be basic sensitivity analyses while some more advanced banks could do full-scope, enterprise-wide stress tests with multiple scenarios. In this section we will focus on stress testing international retail portfolios to estimate expected losses on bank exposures to foreign consumers. Retail models are more challenging as, to our knowledge, there are no existing comprehensive, comparable cross-country datasets on which to base models. Further, significant variations in laws and culture can affect retail default rates and, due to differences in creditor rights, the level of loss-given default (LGD). This can cause the relationship of economic variables to loss rates to vary from country to country and from product to product. However, on a country-by-country basis for most developed countries and a number of emerging-market countries, data can be gathered on retail loan performance and basic macroeconomic and governance variables.

The loan performance data can be obtained from a bank's own loss history or from the central bank/supervisors, which report aggregated data on loan-loss rates, even possibly segmented by consumer product type. Portfolio segmentation may be necessary when building models for a bank operating across countries or with multiple loan types. For example, within the portfolio of countries that we have modelled, secured portfolios did not yield significant coefficients or meaningful regression equations, while there was success with unsecured lending. An important lesson from our modelling experience was that international retail models are not necessarily the same as modelling home country portfolios or even across countries within a region, eg, Asia, and that basic portfolio diagnostics and more in-depth examination of the country's consumer market was required to develop a sound model.

Segmenting the portfolios within and across countries has the benefit of isolating potential correlations and eliminating noise and offsetting impacts. With so many moving parts in a multiple-country, multiple-product-type model, results can be watered down or rendered insignificant. Indeed, in our modelling work, the assessment of an aggregated portfolio of secured and unsecured products for individual countries did not yield robust results. For example, a retail portfolio in the Eurozone could include Greece and Germany with both credit cards and first-lien home mortgages. If this were the case, then it would seem that the most logical approach for this retail portfolio would be a segmented portfolio approach, ie, one that isolates, to the extent possible, the retail portfolio's various moving parts on both the left and right sides of the equation:

$$\text{Country X Losses (Mortgages)} = f \text{ (home prices, interest rates, unemployment)}$$

$$\text{Country X Losses (Credit Cards)} = f \text{ (unemployment, inflation, interest rates, credit growth)}$$

It is possible that data diagnostics and evaluation of portfolio characteristics of the retail portfolios reveal that some countries could be grouped into a homogeneous portfolio, barring the presence of idiosyncratic risks as discussed in earlier.

STRUCTURAL AND CYCLICAL ISSUES
For each county, a number of structural and cyclical considerations had to be considered and factored into the models. Structural considerations include the structure of the capital markets and legal framework for the institution's products and services as well as creditor rights, which affect LGD estimates. For emerging markets, there are structural changes occurring to both the economy and banking system (such as financial deepening) that need to be taken into consideration. These structural changes can cause correlations and variable relationships between dependent variables and prospective independent variables to change or break down. The chart in Figure 10.1 showing Brazil's unemployment rate juxtaposed with the percentage of banking system loans to individuals that are past due by 90 days or more highlights this point.

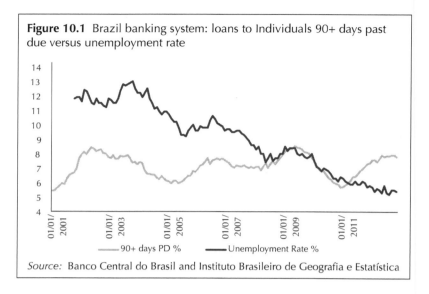

Figure 10.1 Brazil banking system: loans to Individuals 90+ days past due versus unemployment rate

Source: Banco Central do Brasil and Instituto Brasileiro de Geografia e Estatística

As Figure 10.1 indicates, in the years from 2002 to 2012, Brazil has experienced a long-run decline in its unemployment rate, reflecting, in part, a period of structural change and rapid development for the economy. As a result, the predictive power of the unemployment rate for the consumer loan portfolio performance had deteriorated. In fact, the correlation between changes in past due loans and the unemployment rate became negative in 2011, a counterintuitive result. Over this same period, bank lending expanded rapidly with institutions targeting new (and untested) consumers with an array of products from credit cards to payday lending (an example of financial deepening and the evolution of the banking system).

The introduction of new products and other financial innovations is an important consideration when designing stress tests. In such countries as Hungary and Poland during the early 2000s, banks started marketing Swiss-franc-linked mortgage products, which offered interest rates significantly lower than comparable local currency loans. By the summer of 2008, according to the IMF, the foreign-currency share of new house-purchase loans in Hungary hit 70%. The global financial crisis of 2008 and 2009 resulted in a surging value for the Swiss franc, precipitating a repayment crisis for Hungarian homeowners. This underscores the importance of understanding the portfolio characteristics in the design of stress tests.

Not only is segmenting by product type important, but segmenting by classes of borrowers, as well as by loan vintage, could yield meaningful differences in the results of the stress tests. For example, countries with a new generation or economic class of borrowers, loan-loss experience may be difficult to predict, as the loss experience is likely to differ from the loan-loss history for borrowers with longer credit histories. Many countries have established credit bureaus and that can be useful for segmenting different borrower classes (if those registries are made publicly available). The existence and quality of local credit bureaus is a function of the length of their existence, the type of information they collected and the quality controls over the registries. In Australia, the credit bureau contains only negative information. However, "comprehensive credit reporting" will begin in 2014. In 2003, Hong Kong's credit bureau, which was established in the early 1980s, expanded the type of information provided, in the wake of changes to Hong Kong's privacy laws. Modellers need to determine whether there are significant variations in credit registries across countries (eg, some reported only negative information) that can also contribute to bank underwriting decisions and ultimately have a bearing on cross-country loss rates.

Cyclical considerations entail not only debt levels and servicing, but also credit growth relative to the economic cycle, particularly if the real rate of growth for the banking system has been rapid. If the rate of real credit growth is rapid, eg, greater than 10%, then the bank has to consider not only the condition of its own portfolio but the potential condition of the portfolios of its competitors as well, since the possibility of widespread degradation of underwriting standards could lead to regulatory actions if not a full-blown banking crisis. If a crisis is a possibility, then the scenario under consideration may need to be re-scoped or an additional, more severe downside scenario may need to be executed.

FACTORING IN FOREIGN REGULATORY ACTIONS

Regulatory actions complicate the predictive power of past portfolio performance under forward-looking stress tests. Supervisory authorities have implemented a range of macroprudential regulations aimed at controlling loan growth and striving to prevent asset bubbles. Such measures include lowering the maximum loan-to-value (LTV) ratios for mortgage loans as well as implementing requirements on debt service capabilities for consumer loans. Such measures have been widely adopted across Asian consumer lending markets, from Korea to Singapore, though there are significant variations in the stringency of the measures. While largely a positive for loan performance, these measures will potentially affect the performance of loan-loss models.

If the assessment is for possible regulatory actions, then more typical administrative measures such as increasing LTV requirements and lowering debt-to-income measures could affect the revenue stream of the bank, while increased provisioning requirements could affect net income and the market's perception of the bank. As such, not only should these actions be factored into scenarios but models must also account for these actions in bank performance and the wider affect on the macroeconomy.

In addition, regulatory actions can have negative impacts on markets through moral hazard and forbearance. Taiwan's experience in 2004–6 is a case in point. During this period, banks aggressively expanded unsecured consumer loans. As charge-off rates spiked, the government responded with restructuring measures offering easier repayment terms that covered 30% of outstanding credit-card balances, according to IMF estimates (Laeven and Laryea 2009). These restructured loans were for the most part reclassified as performing. Such regulatory moves can have a large effect on model performance, which needs to be accounted for in the evaluation of the results and possibly require modification to and re-estimation of the model.

Quantitative proxies can be developed for these seemingly qualitative factors. For example, the potential for a wider range of regulatory actions should be considered in the scenario if the risk of a political backlash from rising defaults is a possibility. In addition, potential changes in regulatory requirements depend on the quality of the regulator, the maturity of the banking sector and validity of the legal system. Quantitative measures for these elements are available and could be factored into the modelling process. For example, the World Bank publishes numerical estimates for six governance indicators, which could then be incorporated into the model directly or transformed into an index.[3]

ASIAN CONSUMER PORTFOLIOS: STRATIFICATION REQUIRED

Stress testing retail portfolios may require stratification between secured and unsecured lending, due to wide variances in loss rates between these two broad types of lending. An analysis of loss rates across Asian countries underscores the need to differentiate between secured and unsecured retail portfolios. As highlighted in Figure 10.2, mortgages and car loans involve collateral and tend to pose lower risk than unsecured lines of credit, such as credit cards. In Singapore for example, Moody's (2009) has an expected loss for housing loans of 0.05% under their base case, compared with 5.3% for other individual loans. The expected loss under the stress case is 2.5% for housing and 17.0% for other loans to individuals.

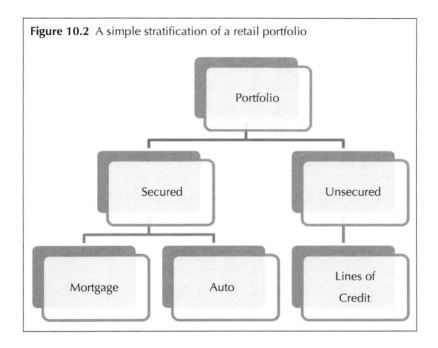

Figure 10.2 A simple stratification of a retail portfolio

In Asia, historical loss rates on mortgages are extremely low primarily due to conservative underwriting standards that are typical in Asia (for example, low LTV ratios, and lenders typically have full recourse). Even in extreme downside scenarios – such as in the Hong Kong home price collapse during the late 1990s – mortgage loss rates typically do not spike in this region. Stress tests of the mortgage portfolios in Asia confirmed this, as the results did not show material loss rates under a basic recession downside scenario. This does not mean that periodic stress tests for mortgage portfolios are not required or stressed using alternative scenarios – such as a disaster-based scenario – just that other portfolios should receive higher priority until the full enterprise-wide stress-testing framework is operational. In contrast, more meaningful and material results were obtained when assessing unsecured and credit-card lending.

Case study: Korea's credit-card crisis and structural changes in the consumer market

Korea was chosen as a case study since we anticipated collecting a relatively rich dataset, given that Korea experienced three crises in 10 years:

1. 1997–8 Asian crisis;
2. 2002–4 credit card crisis; and
3. 2007–9 global credit crisis.

The Korean credit-card crisis of the early 2000s provided a good cycle to stress-test. The crisis was precipitated by a rapid increase in credit growth and surging consumer debt levels. In particular, the surge in Korean credit-card debt relative to GDP was closely followed by a spike in impaired assets (Kang and Ma 2007). This crisis provided a key ingredient for model development: a time series that included a complete credit cycle to evaluate.

But, even with the Korean crisis providing a useful cycle, many changes have occurred in the Korean consumer credit market since 2003, and these changes had to be taken into account when specifying models for the post-credit-card-crisis period. In particular, the tightening of macroprudential regulations, stronger bank risk management and controls (underwriting), better credit infrastructure and a less crowded, more competitive banking system affected the environment.

Another important change in the Korean credit-card market since the crisis was the change in product composition, from higher-risk cash-advance products to less risky instalment products. According to the Korean Financial Supervisory Service, cash advances accounted for 65% of credit-card loans in 2002, compared with less than 20% by 2011. These changes have contributed to the development of a vastly different Korean consumer credit market, and this structural change needed to be accounted for in the model.

STRUCTURAL BREAKS AND DUMMY VARIABLES

Another potential structural break was from industry consolidation, since a merger between a strong and weak institution can introduce a structural break in the time series data for the combined institution. This poses a decision point for the sample size for the analysis – typically, a longer time series is desirable to ensure the largest possible number of observations, but this must be weighed against the need to control for structural breaks in the data series.

In the Korean estimations, a dummy variable for the credit-card crisis was included in the credit-card model. The dates for the dummy variable were chosen based on the Quandt Andrews Breakpoint test for structural breaks. Breaks were identified at December 2002 and April 2005.

Indeed, there is a broader point at work here, particularly when considering emerging-market economies and other banking systems. The emerging-market banking systems can be dynamic, rapidly evolving systems, with new products being introduced routinely and new borrowers with little to no experience with credit. Depending on the magnitude and the size of the concentration the bank has, these elements can introduce sizeable stress losses for the bank. These factors can also introduce noise into time series data and need to be assessed and potentially addressed within the model specifications.

ESTIMATING LOSSES ON KOREAN CREDIT CARDS AND UNSECURED LOANS

A primary goal in the design of these models was to identify how macroeconomic shocks affect portfolio credit quality. There are at least two approaches for imputing a shock: one would be a straightforward application of a historical shock, while a second approach would be to apply a combination of the most extreme performance, to date, in terms of both depth and duration, for key economic variables from each of the crises. To have this stress – a low-probability but high-impact event – Korea would have to experience internal and external economic, financial market shocks simultaneously. It is important to think through and estimate a wide range of scenarios given the potential for contagion. The focus of the discussion below is on identifying the underlying risk factors that could cause a substantive deterioration in the asset quality of the portfolio.

To capture turning or inflection points in asset quality and provide a larger number of observations, monthly data was favoured over quarterly data. For the credit-card market, bank-level data was used, as the Korean supervisors did not start posting monthly performance data until 2005. In many countries, the regressions will have to be estimated using quarterly data, since that is the only publicly available data, or banks may be able to use internal databases that have higher-frequency data.

A decision on whether to estimate the level of losses or the ratio of losses relative to credit-card receivables was also required in laying out the approach. Additionally, the issue of modelling gross or net losses was considered. The choice between the gross and net losses can have dramatic effects on estimation results as recoveries (the difference between gross and net) can be lumpy on a monthly basis. In addition, the pattern and behaviour of recoveries (and therefore net losses) will vary by product type and country. Bankruptcy laws and other local provisions (recourse versus non-recourse lending) and secured versus unsecured lending (as well as the value of collateral) will all have an impact on recovery assumptions. If using internal data, historical experience with recoveries can typically be extrapolated and evaluated to determine the most appropriate dependent variable.

INDEPENDENT VARIABLES: KOREAN CREDIT CARDS AND UNSECURED LOANS
In general, the performance of the consumer credit markets was assumed to be thus:

To determine the drivers of credit-card loss rates, a large number of variables that could cause cashflow problems and drive delinquencies and defaults were considered:

❏ economic growth (GDP) and related measures such as exports, industrial production and the unemployment rate;
❏ monetary indicators such as inflation rates, credit growth and interest rates; and
❏ wealth measures such as home prices and stock indexes.

Not all contemporaneous measures showed clear predictive power for credit card loss rates

DATA DIAGNOSTICS MAY ALTER THE MODEL SPECIFICATION

As part of data diagnostics, the data was reviewed graphically, and statistical tests were conducted to determine the underlying properties for such things as stationarity. Stationarity, whereby statistical parameters do not change with time, is a required property for time series regressions, which is often obtained by first differencing the variable, ie, subtracting the prior period's observation from the current period's observation. We also checked for correlation among the variables.

Table 10.2 Correlation matrix of Korean macroeconomic factors

	unemployment	credit growth	exports index	unemployment (-2)	unemployment (-3)	credit growth (-3)	credit growth (-24)	exports index (-6)
unemployment	1.00							
credit growth	-0.42	1.00						
exports index	0.08	-0.20	1.00					
unemployment (-2)	0.81	-0.50	0.20	1.00				
unemployment (-3)	0.77	-0.51	0.24	0.92	1.00			
credit growth (-3)	-0.29	0.89	-0.09	-0.48	-0.41	1.00		
credit growth (-24)	-0.03	-0.12	-0.48	0.00	0.02	-0.10	1.00	
exports index (-6)	-0.06	-0.19	-0.04	0.00	0.00	-0.21	-0.19	1.00

Numbers in parentheses indicate the lag of that variable

Table 10.2 shows that the unemployment rates are highly correlated with one another (0.81 and 0.77) as is credit growth with the credit growth from three months back (0.89). Any time a variable is highly correlated (0.80 or greater), the model developer should consider dropping one of the two variables.

ESTIMATION RESULTS

Given the likelihood of borrowers drawing on savings to stave off defaulting, different lags of the independent variables were also included in the regressions. Our estimations showed that lag structures can vary dramatically from indicator to indicator across countries. The following variables were important risk factors for Korean credit-card loss rates: the change in the unemployment rate and credit growth with 3-month and 24-month lags. The regressions did incorporate a dummy variable identifying the credit-card crisis and an autoregressive (AR) term. The AR term was used to correct for serial correlation. For unsecured lending, the change in the unemployment rate, credit growth and an export index were significant in the estimation of monthly Korean unsecured loan loss rates over the sample period 2000–10 (using monthly data).

As noted above in the general discussion on structural and cyclical issues, rapid consumer credit growth is frequently a significant factor (with a several-quarter lag) in contributing to future credit losses, particularly if the seasoning of these new credits coincides with an economic event. Various lags for the real credit growth variable were significant but the lag length was purely a function of the data as opposed to a point that would be predicted by theory, ie, 6-, 12-, 18-, 24-month lags were not necessarily significant since the timing of the cycle was not readily apparent. Akaike Information Criterion (AIC) was used to determine the best lags of each independent variable, but this raises the probability that the out-of-sample predictive power of the model will be weak and require further analysis of the model specification.

For example, several consumer credit risk managers have pointed out that, in emerging-market economies, consumer loan performance can be dramatically affected by inflation (food prices, for instance). A key consideration in this regard is the income segment of the institution's portfolio: lower-income borrowers are more vulnerable to rising inflation rates than the more affluent consumers. So the model could possibly be improved if this data were available or could be constructed or proxied.

SUMMARY

Although the modelling of unsecured portfolios proved promising as changes in macroeconomic variables showed a causal relationship in the changes in Korean credit-card loss rates, the truly important element of this work was the required study of the Korean credit cycles, consumer product markets, regulatory actions and economic shocks arising from multiple quarters – both internal and external – and that these factors differed to varying degrees across countries in Asia. This underscored the need to evaluate markets on an individual basis and to proceed with caution when trying to estimate regressions across a region or globally. This is not a small undertaking, but it yields a large benefit by being able to anticipate potential drivers of future portfolio losses.

The views expressed in this chapter are those of the authors and do not necessarily reflect those of the Office of the Comptroller of the Currency or the US Department of the Treasury.

REFERENCES

IMF, 2012, "Macrofinancial Stress Testing – Principles and Practices", working paper, August 22, "Best Practice" principles 1–7, pp. 19–45.

Kang, Taesoo, and Guonan Ma, 2007, "Credit card lending distress in Korea in 2003", Bank for International Settlements.

Laeven, Luc, and Thomas Laryea, 2009, "Principles of Household Debt Restructuring", IMF Staff Position Note, June.

Moody's, 2009, "Approach to Estimating Singaporean Banks' Credit Losses".

OCC, 2008, "Country Risk Management, Comptroller's Handbook", p. 1.

1   See http://www.bis.org/publ/bcbs155.htm. See also IMF 2012, pp. 19–45, for an alternative formulation of principles.

2   "Transfer risk is the possibility that an asset cannot be serviced in the currency of payment because of a lack of, or restraints on the availability of, needed foreign exchange in the country of the obligor" – "Guide to the Interagency Country Exposure Review Committee Process", 2008, p. 1.

3   The six World Bank indicators are: voice and accountability; political stability/absence of violence; government effectiveness; regulatory quality; rule of law; and control of corruption (see http://info.worldbank.org/governance/wgi/sc_country.asp).

11

Liquidity Risk: The Case of the Brazilian Banking System

**Benjamin M. Tabak, Solange M. Guerra,
Sergio R. S. Souza, Rodrigo C. C. Miranda**

Banco Central do Brasil

Stress tests are already a widely used tool for risk management of financial institutions. Central banks and individual banks run these tests for determining potential risk sources that they might encounter in scenarios of severe change in the macroeconomic situation and assessing their resilience to such events. By testing themselves or the financial system as a whole beyond normal operational capacity, they can quantify vulnerabilities, and the stability of the given system or entity may be studied and pursued more easily (Vazquez, Tabak and Souto 2012).

To design and apply a stress test, many important assumptions should be taken. The first step must be identifying the specific risk and vulnerability of concern. In the literature about stress testing of banking risks, the most common type of risks considered are credit, market and liquidity. The majority of papers have focused on assessing credit risk, since this is the bank's most important risk component. However, liquidity stress testing is getting more visibility and importance.

Although liquidity crises are not so frequent, their impacts are high (low-frequency, high-impact events), especially due to their contagious effects and to the consequences of the interaction between the banking risk factors. After the global financial crisis of 2007–9 there is an increasing interest in studying the vulnerabilities provided by liquidity risks. From this important event many lessons can be taken. The De Larosière Group (2009) points out the key lesson that regulators paid little attention to the system as a whole, while too much focus was given to microprudential supervision of individual institutions.

The crisis served to show weakness in the stress-testing exercises performed on financial institutions and systems around the world (Ong and Čihák 2010). It also showed how the vicious dynamics of liquidity risk can undermine the stability of the financial system (Van den End 2010). To Aikman *et al* (2009), the crisis illustrates the importance of modelling the closure of funding markets to financial institutions and accounting for liquidity feedbacks within any model of systemic risk. In sum, the ongoing crisis serves as an alert to the importance of managing liquidity risk and, therefore, it underscores the need to explicitly take into account liquidity risk in stress-testing frameworks (Van den End 2009).

Once they had understood the importance of stress testing liquidity risk, researchers working for different financial institutions around the world started to develop methods to endogenise liquidity risk in a stress-testing framework. This task is quite complex, since a method has to be developed that has the ability to quantify dependences and interactions between the various types of risk. Wong and Hui (2009) suggest that for banking stability it is important to assess the extent to which a banking system is exposed to the interaction of risks. In their paper, the stress-testing framework explicitly captures the link between default risk and deposit outflows. Not only is the interaction of the risks incorporated but also their contagious effects. The framework presented by Aikman *et al* (2009) also attempts to fully integrate funding risks and solvency risk.

In a framework of stress testing for liquidity risk, two components are important: (i) funding liquidity risk (concerning the bank's balance-sheet liability side: there may be a bank run by depositors or the bank may be unable to rollover liabilities) and (ii) market liquidity risk (asset side: illiquidity in the market for the bank's assets, when the bank needs to sell them). An example of a stress-test model that involves both components is the one presented by Van den End (2009). By considering the first and second rounds (feedback) of shocks, the model presented endogenises market and funding liquidity risks and captures, as second-round effects, the collective response of heterogeneous banks and reputational effects. The IMF originally centred its liquidity tests on the paper of Čihák (2007) using bank balance-sheet data to perform bank-run-type stress tests on a bank-by-bank level. Aikman *et al* (2009), on the other hand, focused on the role of asset-side (market liquidity) feedbacks.

Some papers innovate with their stress-testing models. One topic that motivated some interesting material was the establishment of minimum standards for liquidity risk (Liquidity Coverage Ratio, or LCR, and Net Stable Funding Ratio, or NFSR) by Basel III (BCBS 2010). To study the effects of these new minimum standards, Van den End (2010) developed a stress study that linked funding cost liquidity to regulation and central bank operations. The conclusions from its model outcomes support policy initiatives such as the ones proposed by the Basel Committee (BCBS 2010). By testing scenarios of stress, the paper finds that banks that adjust to the Basel III establishments (such as by holding a higher stock of liquid assets) have substantially lower second-round effects and tail risks. These findings highlight the importance of defining a sufficiently high-quality level of liquid assets to limit the idiosyncratic risks to a bank. The outcomes of the tests also evidence the important role of stronger liquidity profiles in reducing the risk of collective reactions by banks and therefore in preventing second-round effects and instability of the financial system as a whole.

Van den End and Kruidhof (2012) simulate the systemic implications of the LCR using a liquidity stress-testing model. The authors model the LCR as a macroprudential instrument that can be used to moderate the adverse side effects that arise due to interactions of bank behaviour with the regulatory liquidity constraint. The authors applied tests with different switching rules and banking sector structures. By testing the reduction of the minimum LCR requirements, the paper finds that a flexible approach of the LCR in stressed times reduces the number of bank reactions and associated negative side effects. Another rule tested was the widening of the buffer definition, and the measure was found to be effective in limiting the interaction between the minimum requirement and bank reactions. At extreme stress levels, the paper finds that the LCR becomes ineffective as a macroprudential instrument and, in order to maintain the stability of the system, a lender of last resort is requested.

The development of the framework that endogenises liquidity risk into stress tests is an essential stage of the stress-testing exercise. Maybe just as important are the stages of data-collecting, information-processing and numerical analysis. The top-down and bottom-up approaches are the two strategies of information processing that can be applied to stress testing bank risks. The advantage of running a test with the bottom-up approach is the use of more detailed data and less complexity in modelling liquidity shocks. The disadvantage is that, unlike the top-down approach, these tests are less consistent. The advantages of the top-down approach include more consistent results and more flexibility to simulate different scenarios of shocks. According to Čihák (2007), the majority of stress tests presented in financial-stability reports are based on bank-by-bank data. Central banks that are not involved in microprudential supervision and do not have access to more detailed data rely on top-down approaches.

The BCBS (2011) published a document on the progress in implementing macroprudential policy frameworks, gathering information on the subject. Although the document discussed macroprudential policy and systemic risk, many of its considerations can be readily applied to liquidity risks, given their systemic nature. According to the document, risk measures should be able to capture the time and cross-sectional dimensions of risk, which define requirements for metrics to be created and monitored. The main measurement approaches that apply, extracted from a survey conducted by the IMF (2011), includes the following: indicators of imbalances (eg, of bank credit, liquidity and maturity mismatch, and currency risk), indicators of liquidity market conditions, metrics of concentration of risk within the system and stress testing. The metrics of concentration of risk within the system (eg, the network-theory-related measurements, like connectivity and centrality, or the results of default cascade simulations) are related to the cross-sectional dimension of risk, focusing on the channels of contagion and amplification, and could be used to determine the systemically important institutions, while the stress testing is used to evaluate the resilience of individual banks and of the banking system as a whole.

Stress tests for liquidity are not so developed as stress tests for credit and market risks. However, important works have been done by central banks researchers, as the already mentioned Van den End (2010), Wong and Hui (2009), and Aikman *et al* (2009). These models are usually integrated with credit or market risk. This feature is the main difference between these models and the approach for liquidity stress testing at the Central Bank of Brazil.

Despite the importance of liquidity risk stress testing, most central banks do not publish results from liquidity stress tests. This reflects the liquidity-modelling complexity and the need of more detailed and high-frequency data. The Central Bank of Brazil has published liquidity stress test results since 2009. From the side of the banks, a survey with Brazilian banks indicates that their risk-management policies have been improved to account for possible liquidity problems. Many banks have started to run liquidity stress tests after the financial crisis. However, it is not usual to disclose the results.

Given the importance of developing liquidity stress-test models we focus on the Brazilian banking system and how it has been impacted on by the financial crisis, focusing on liquidity issues. We then present the Brazilian banking system, before discussing the impacts of the crisis on the system, employing contagion tests to show that banks may have heterogeneous responses to liquidity shocks. The following section presents a discussion on liquidity stress testing performed by the Central Bank of Brazil, as well as results from a survey of banks that operate in the Brazilian banking system. The last section draws our conclusions.

THE BRAZILIAN BANKING SYSTEM

Banks are financial institutions with a major role in a capitalist economy. Their importance is a consequence of their roles as money creators, as managers of the payments system and as financiers of economic activities. At the same time, as rational agents, banks take actions to maximise their profits. Restrictions can come from the macroeconomic environment and from the banking system microstructure. This condition gives a hint on the risks involving the banking system and why they are potentially dangerous. Fragility in banks' individual accounting and management, combined with macroeconomic shocks, can lead to crises in the system. When such crises happen, the consequences can be great and will include impacts on the economies' credit situation, interest rates and investments, and bring about negative changes in the levels of economic activity. To maintain a solid and healthy banking system, it is essential to establish bank regulations supplemented by constant supervision.

The Brazilian banking system began its trajectory at the beginning of the 19th century, when the Banco do Brasil (Bank of Brazil) was founded and later was partially considered a monetary authority (da Costa, 2012). However, it was only between 1930 and 1945 that the most important banks were founded and the Brazilian banking system effectively began to grow, reaching the total of 644 banks in 1944. Since its start, Brazil's banking system went through various transformations, mainly adaptations to the various changes in national and international politics and economic scenarios. These transformations led to a system with solid regulations, supervised by the Central Bank of Brazil (created in 1964). Based on the Federal Constitution of 1988, some of the Central Bank functions as a monetary authority are the issue of money, the determination of the reserves requirements of banks and controlling liquidity with open market operations.

The banking system's condition in the late 20th and early 21st centuries was shaped by important structural transformations that occurred in the early 1990s. These transformations were consequences of the implementation of measures of monetary policy in 1994 and 1995. The 1994 measure is known as "Plano Real", in which the exchange rate between the Brazilian currency (real) and the American dollar was initially set at 1 to 1. This measure was used by the government to stabilise the economy, which had been passing through a long period of high inflation rates initiated in 1964, during the military regime (1964–85). The impact of this plan on the banking system was deep. One of the major changes faced by banks was on their profits' sources. During the high inflation period, banks took advantage of the condition to profit from floating; however, after the currency stabilisation, this kind of revenue vanished. Banks found an alternative source of profit by charging their customers fees for services provided. The demand for credit also increased, given the increase of the predictability horizons allowed by the stabilisation of the economy and the more optimistic associated expectations. The banks' profit with services, which represented only 8% of the GDP in 1990, reached 10.5% in 1993 and 21.5% in 1995.

Important policies were also implemented in 1995. Programmes were created to restructure and fortify the financial system, preventing liquidity crises and stabilising the system. Another relevant measure taken that year were the incentives given to the opening of the Brazilian financial system to foreign capital and banks. The objective of this action was to attract foreign banks to the national system and expand the credit supply. This would increase banks' competition, forcing them to reduce costs by improving their management to become more efficient. To the population and firms, the benefits would be a greater variety of banks and lower interest rates. The measure was indeed effective in attracting more foreign banks, but the concentration increased. This happened because mergers and acquisitions not only involved the new-entrant foreign banks but also were performed by domestic institutions among themselves. During the first four years after the "Plano Real", 104 financial institutions suffered some kind of adjustment. The number of domestic private banks and state-owned banks reduced while the number of foreign-controlled banks increased by less than the reduction in the number of domestic banks. In 1993, foreign-controlled banks owned 7.28% of the total financial system, reaching 25.91% by 1999.

From 1999, Brazilian banks began an innovation process. They developed techniques of fundraising and asset management, increasing their loans-to-reserves ratios. The efficient use of the interbank market can be considered the key innovation (da Costa 2012). The period between 2003 and 2006 was marked by greater access by the population to banks and credit. Between 2001 and 2006, the number of accounts in the banking system increased by 52%. Savings accounts were the most popular service provided and increased 50%, while the growth of current accounts was 37%. The popularisation of banking services became possible due to technological advances, which included the installation of ATMs and credit-card readers in busy areas and retail outlets. These indirect banking facilities increased the supply of banking services without the need for an increase in the number of bank agencies. Popular credit programmes offered by commercial banks also brought about an expansion in the economy's consumption demands.

By 2012, the Brazilian financial system had 2,218 operating financial institutions. In December 2011, the total assets of Brazil's whole financial system exceeded BRL5,135 billion. Its stock of credit operations reached BRL2 trillion, which corresponds to 49% of the country's GDP in the same period. The banking system is a part of the financial system, composed of independent institutions and financial conglomerates, which must contain at least one institution from a commercial bank, a savings bank or a multiple bank, since it is authorised to receive demand deposits. In March 2012, the banking system's assets totalled BRL4,486 billion, a share of 84% of the whole financial system's total assets. These institutions' evolution of total assets is illustrated by Figure 11.1.

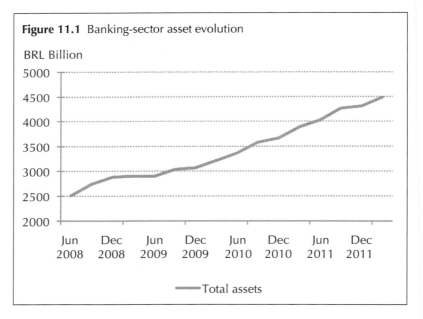

Figure 11.1 Banking-sector asset evolution

The Brazilian banking system's history shows periods of concentration alternating with periods of increase in the number of banks. In the early 1990s, as we have seen, the banking system went through a structural transformation. In that period of banking crisis, privatisations and incentives to the entry of foreign banks, the domestic banking system went through a decrease. In 1994, there were 271 commercial and multiple banks; by 2002, they were 167. In 2012, there were 160 banks.

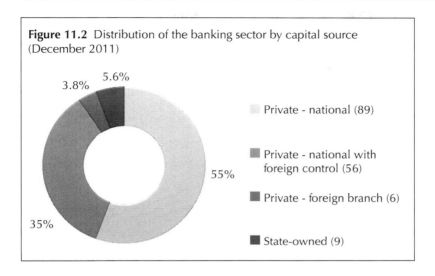

Figure 11.2 Distribution of the banking sector by capital source (December 2011)

Private - national (89)

Private - national with foreign control (56)

Private - foreign branch (6)

State-owned (9)

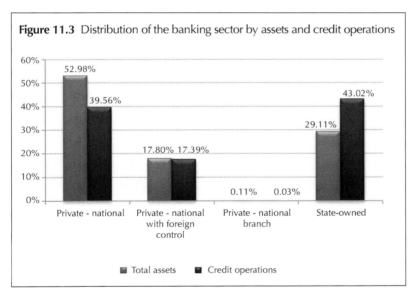

Figure 11.3 Distribution of the banking sector by assets and credit operations

Figure 11.2 shows the division of the Brazilian banking system by type of control (in number of banks and percentages). The participations of each of these categories in the aggregated credit operations and total assets in the same period are shown in Figure 11.3. This figure shows that the state-owned banks increased their participation in credit operations as a result of government measures to maintain the level of economic activity after the crisis. Total credit operations grew between the second half of 2009 and the same half of 2011, as shown in Figure 11.6. Additional indicators of the financial system's concentration are the HHI and CR4 indexes. HHI is the Herfindahl–Hirschman Index. According to the Horizontal Merger Guidelines, published by the Department of Justice and Federal Trade Commission (EUA), HHI of less than 0.15 means that the market is not concentrated; HHI between 0.15 and 0.25 means that the market is moderately concentrated; and HHI above 0.25 indicates that the market is highly concentrated. CR4 stands for four-firm concentration ratio. It measures the market share of the four largest banks in the system. Values between 50% and 80% indicate medium concentration. The levels of concentration in the Brazilian financial system are monitored by the Central Bank of Brazil. These indexes are calculated for asset totals, credit operations and deposit totals. The HHI values of the system for the second half of 2011 indicate that the Brazilian banking system is non-concentrated to moderately concentrated from the point of view of all these three quantities (respectively 0.13, 0.14 and 0.1509). The CR4 readings for the three quantities in the same period were 67.21%, 69.2% and 72.55%, respectively, which show that the four largest banks, in total assets, hold a slightly higher total deposits ratio, with approximately the same total credit ratio. This means these banks, as a group, do not have a special participation in the system: as credit providers or deposit holders, their participation corresponds to their size.

EFFECTS OF THE SUBPRIME CRISIS ON BRAZILIAN BANKING SYSTEM

Since 2007, important events have been taking place in international banking. The American banking crisis of 2008 spilled over into economies around the world. The collapse of large banks in the US had a domino effect that led to the collapse of even entire economies, as occurred in Greece in the late 2000s. The impact on the Brazilian banking system and economy wasn't as catastrophic. Due stricter regulations and controls imposed in 1995, the Brazilian banking system has remained relatively solid when facing the international crises and has been preserved without much loss. Also, the macroeconomic politics of fiscal austerity and the regime of inflation targeting adopted allowed Brazil to stand out among emergent countries and continue to attract foreign interest. The liquidity situation of Brazilian banks can be shown by the evolution of the system-wide liquidity index in Figure 11.4.

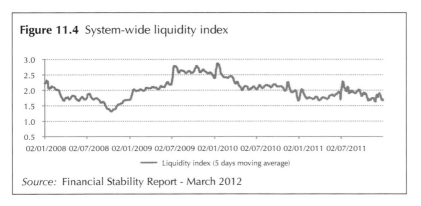

Figure 11.4 System-wide liquidity index

Source: Financial Stability Report - March 2012

The index is calculated by the Central Bank and is the ratio between (a) institutions' total liquid assets available to honour their obligations and (b) the possible losses in liquidity that institutions would be subject to in stress situations. Such situations include unexpected withdrawals and sudden changes in the market scenario. The BCB publishes an aggregated liquidity index for the whole banking sector in the financial-stability report, along with a detailed liquidity analysis of the financial system. More details on calculation of the liquidity index and its use to monitor the financial system liquidity will be presented later.

Volatility in exchange and interest rates usually increases the liquidity required in the case of stress situations (has a negative impact on the index). Figure 11.5 illustrates the behaviour of the volatility of these rates since 2008. The highest volatility occurred, of course, when the crises began. Figure 11.6 shows the finance of credit expansion and liquid assets since 2008.

From the Figures 11.4 and 11.5, it can be observed that the international financial crisis had a greater impact on the Brazilian financial system's liquidity during 2008. During the period, the volatility of the exchange and interest rates was very high and certainly increased the possible losses that the institutions would be subjected to in concrete stress situations. This is related to a decrease in the liquidity index during the period. After 2008, the trajectory of the system's liquidity had a recovery and the trend for the following year was of healthy liquidity conditions. According to the Financial Stability Report (FSR) from the Central Bank in the second half of 2009, the banking system presented an large amount of high-quality liquid assets and had low dependency on foreign resources. These conditions reduced Brazil's vulnerability to liquidity risks and international turbulence. By the first half of 2010, the liquidity of Brazilian financial institutions had returned to the pre-crisis level (BCB 2010).

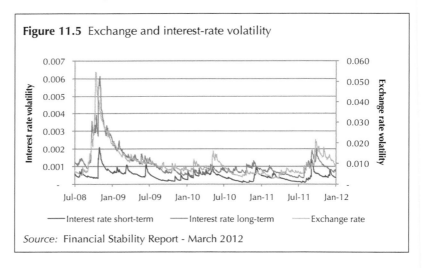

Figure 11.5 Exchange and interest-rate volatility

Source: Financial Stability Report - March 2012

The Financial Stability Report (BCB 2012) concerning the year of 2011 concludes that the banking system's liquidity is in a very favourable situation. The Brazilian banking system had the ability to finance its own operations, mostly with funds raised in the domestic market. In the first half of 2011, the system's funding increased by BRL186.1 billion, representing a 9.1% increase compared with the previous semester. The growth in liquid assets (composed basically of federal government bonds) was remarkable, favoured by the slower growth of the volume of credits (BCB 2011). In the second half of 2011, the system's funding increased by BRL246.9 billion (an 11.2% increase). In this period, the credit expansion was reduced by the available resources from domestic and foreign markets. The liquidity index remained at a good level even after the negative shock caused by the volatility of the interest and exchange rates (BCB 2012).

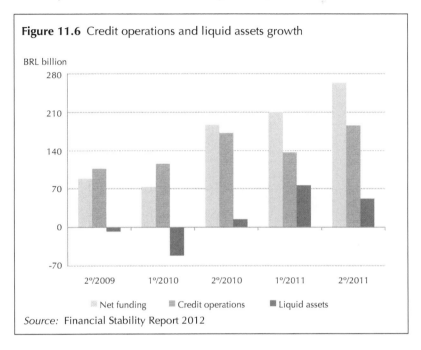

Figure 11.6 Credit operations and liquid assets growth

Source: Financial Stability Report 2012

Deposits (including savings, on-demand and time deposits) have been the major funding source for Brazilian banks. Deposits presented a declining trend in terms of the share of total funding from December 2005 to December 2007. However, in 2008, this trend was reversed due to the crisis's effects on time deposits. Time deposits' interest rate increased to attract funds, which would compensate for the reduction in other sources of liquidity, especially foreign funding. Consequently, the amount of time deposits increased 31.1% in the second half 2008 (BCB 2008 and 2009). Savings deposits have been tracking the funding growth, remaining stable in terms of relative shares. From 2008 to 2011, savings accounted for 17% to about 20% of total funding (see Figure 11.7).[1] Regarding on-demand deposits, we can see in Figure 11.7 that their relative shares declined from 10% in December 2009 to 7.8% in December 2011. On average, these three types of deposits account for more than 60% of total funding between 2008 and 2011. Deposits up to BRL70,000 are guaranteed by the Credit Guarantee Fund (the Fundo Garantidor de Créditos (FGC)). From the total amount of time deposits, the largest holders are households, followed by legal entities (see Figure 11.8).

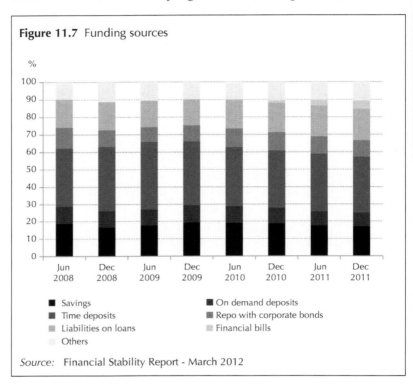

Figure 11.7 Funding sources

%

Savings · Time deposits · Liabilities on loans · Others · On demand deposits · Repo with corporate bonds · Financial bills

Source: Financial Stability Report - March 2012

Financial bills became a more interesting source of funding due to an exemption on reserves requirements for their holders, which became effective in late 2010. Since then, financial bills have presented a growth trend; however, they account for only a small share of the system's total liabilities (BCB 2012). Financial bills are a source of long-term funding and have contributed to the lengthening of the banking system's liabilities profile, as they cannot be redeemed in total or partially before their maturity date (according to the Resolução BCB No. 3.836/2010). This is desirable since the loan's average term has increased due to an increased number of mortgages in the credit portfolios (BCB 2011).

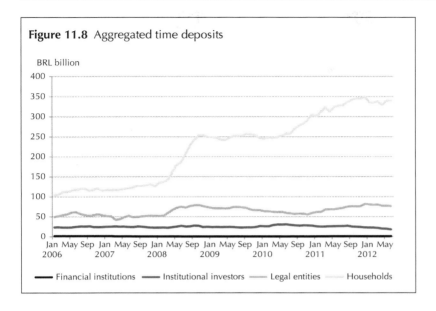

Figure 11.8 Aggregated time deposits

Between 2008 and 2011, liabilities on loans have accounted, on average, for about 16% of total funding. These sources of funding include foreign funding. Most banks that use foreign funding are small foreign banks, whose business model is not related to credit. Nevertheless, only a small part of these banks' funding comes from abroad. The large foreign banks rely mainly on domestic funding. Besides this, liabilities in foreign currency have reduced since the subprime crises (see Figure 11.9). Thus, turbulences in international markets have had a limited impact on the Brazilian banking system (BCB 2012). Liabilities on loans also include loans from the Brazilian Development Bank (BNDES).

A general look at banks' funding structures highlights the existence of institutional differences. Large banks have more diversified sources of funding, and, due to a wide network of branches, these banks have more access to retail deposits. This source of funding is more stable, reducing the liquidity risk. On the other hand, smaller banks rely mainly on time deposits and have a less diversified funding structure. Financial bills provide a more stable source of funding to their issuers, while being more attractive for their holders, especially if they are large banks, due to a reserve requirement exemption associated with it, which is larger than the one related to time deposits. As smaller banks already have an exemption from reserve requirements due to their low amount of funding, holding financial bills is not as interesting for these banks (see Figure 11.10).

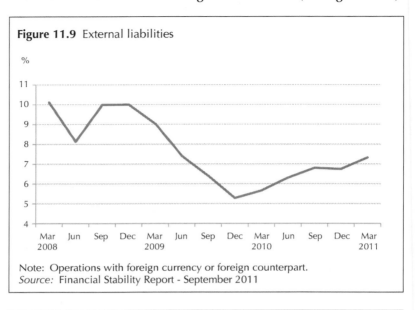

Figure 11.9 External liabilities

Note: Operations with foreign currency or foreign counterpart.
Source: Financial Stability Report - September 2011

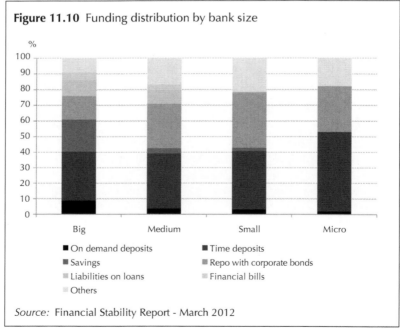

Figure 11.10 Funding distribution by bank size

Source: Financial Stability Report - March 2012

Funding-source patterns also differ sharply among the types of control segments. Foreign banks concentrate their funding on time deposits, while public banks tend to emphasise savings. On the other hand, private banks are more focused on repo operations (BCB 2008).

Altogether, the Brazilian banking system relies mainly on domestic sources of funding and is prepared to cope with an occasional liquidity stress. However, liquidity is not equally distributed among banks. Smaller banks that rely on time deposits from large customers are subject to higher liquidity risks during stress periods. These banks can get funding from credit assignment transactions. In August 2011, the Central Bank of Brazil created the Credit Transfer Bureau, in which banks must register credits' assignments (BCB 2011).

Brazilian banks have a more stable funding source, as the reliance on retail deposits is higher than on wholesale funding. Nonetheless, for some banks, institutional investors may represent an important funding source. Therefore, in moments of stress, these banks may incur in liquidity problems. To overcome these problems during the financial crisis the Central Bank of Brazil created a new type of deposit that is guaranteed by the Credit Guarantee Fund (the Fundo Garantidor de Créditos (FGC).

The FGC has an important role in the security of the national financial system. In March 2009, the FGC's Special Guarantee of Time Deposits (DPGE) was implemented. This measure helped the smaller institutions to recover their funding (the amount in the term deposits of small banks grew by about 24% from March to May of the same year). An improvement in the rediscount regulation was also implemented. The deadlines of the rediscount operations were extended and the central bank was authorised to impose restrictive prudential measures to manage the financial institutions (Mesquita and Torós 2010).

The BCB took measures to address the liquidity constraint both in domestic and foreign currencies: bank reserve requirements were lowered; lines of credit in foreign exchange were provided to the private sector; the central bank offered US dollars in spot market auctions and foreign-exchange swap contracts.[2]

Figure 11.11 shows an increase in time deposits, from BRL270 billion in December 2007 to over BRL500 billion in October 2008. The largest growth in deposits was observed in financial institutions and households, followed by companies with a more modest growth. Institutional investors' deposits were maintained at about the same level. That signals a shift towards seemingly less risky investments (that is, time deposits).

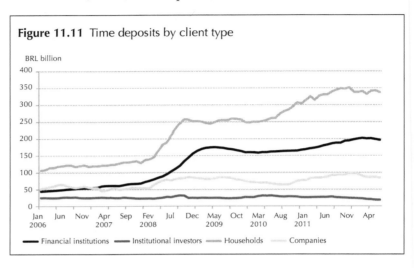

Figure 11.11 Time deposits by client type

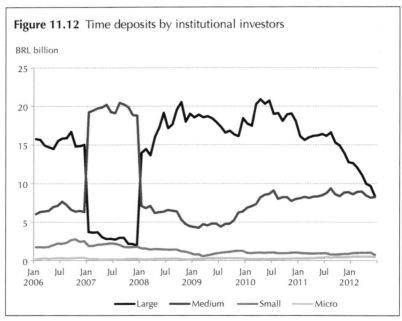

Figure 11.12 Time deposits by institutional investors

Conventional wisdom would expect more informed investors to seek better rates (and therefore riskier investments) in tranquil times, and safer investments in riskier times. That was also evident in time deposits from institutional investors in Brazil. In 2006, large banking institutions and conglomerates had the lion's share of time deposits from institutional investors, about BRL15 billion, whereas the medium-sized banks' share was about BRL6 billion. From January 2007 to December 2007 this was reversed, with about BRL19 billion in time deposits in medium banks and about BRL3 billion in large banks. In January 2008 the situation was once again reversed, as time deposits shifted towards large banks, which are usually regarded as less risky. That movement can be seen quite clearly in Figure 11.12 and signals a flight-to-quality movement in time deposits.

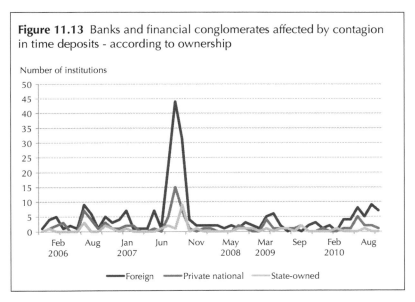

Figure 11.13 Banks and financial conglomerates affected by contagion in time deposits - according to ownership

This flight to quality is also evident in correlation contagion tests. Regarding financial contagion as "a significant increase in correlations after a shock to one institution", a series of correlation-change tests was run based on the Forbes and Rigobon (2002) statistic (FR) devised by Fry, Martin and Tang (2008). In these tests, the log difference of the weekly time deposits' stock was tested for contagion using a vector auto-regressive model and 30-week crisis windows.

The test results indicate how many institutions were affected by contagion within each crisis window, and are summarised in Figures 11.13 and 11.14. The contagion results indicate that most banks affected by contagion were small and medium-sized banks. Regarding ownership, foreign institutions were the most affected by contagion, followed by Brazilian private domestic banks. The peak of contagion was in the windows starting in September to November 2007 and ending in March to May 2008. These time-deposit movements and time-deposit contagions seem to indicate that, during the financial crisis, there was an investor movement towards assets such as guaranteed time deposits or time deposits at large national institutions that were deemed safer at the time. During the crisis, the market perception was that the resilience of small and medium-sized banks reduced, which was translated into the transfer of time deposits from these institutions to large ones, corresponding to a liquidity transfer between them.

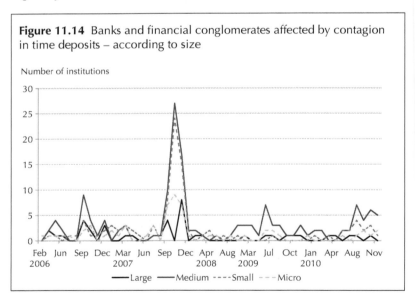

Figure 11.14 Banks and financial conglomerates affected by contagion in time deposits – according to size

LIQUIDITY STRESS TESTS IN BRAZIL
Central bank's approach
In Brazil, liquidity risk monitoring is part of the banking supervisory process and includes a continuous follow-up of the systemi-

cally important financial institutions and a liquidity stress test. The liquidity stress test combines the bottom-up and top-down approaches. It considers, for each individual financial institution, the different classes of assets and raised funds, but does not take into account the linkages among institutions, resulting in a liquidity index for each institution. This index is a short-term liquidity index similar to Basel III's LCR (see Figure 11.4).

The liquidity index is the ratio between the total liquidity and the estimated liquidity needs. The total liquidity is the amount of liquid assets each institution can dispose of to meet its obligations. It is calculated as the sum of active market operations with maturity on the next day (eg, involving federal securities, active interbank deposits and bank deposit certificates maturing the next day), with active interbank deposits and bank deposit certificates maturing after the next day, weighted by coefficients associated with a possible early redemption of these instruments. The calculation of the total liquidity also considers the balance of other accounting assets: cash, shares, foreign currencies and investments in mutual funds, gold and foreign federal securities.

The estimated liquidity needs is the liquidity level an institution needs to keep to withstand funding volatility and losses under market stress. It is calculated from:

❑ deposits' volatility under stress on a two-week horizon;
❑ deposits' concentration index (excluding interbank deposits), taking into account value ranges and client profiles (individuals, firms, financial institutions and institutional investors);
❑ Interbank deposits raised maturing after the next working day, considering, for short-term Interbank deposits, that they will not be renewed, and a possible early redemption for the remaining Interbank deposits;
❑ remaining liabilities on the balance sheet; and
❑ stressed market net positions.

Liquidity stress tests are very useful to assess whether specific banks have liquidity vulnerabilities. In this case, bank supervision can follow up a bank's risks and make accurate interventions. Furthermore, it is useful to design proper public policies to reduce shocks that stem from systemic liquidity problems. The Central Bank of Brazil has performed macroeconomic stress tests and monitored the liquidity of financial institutions to identify possible sources of liquidity stress. Additionally, it has sought to enhance the efficiency and stability of the Brazilian financial system by improvements to the accounting procedures for registering credit assignment operations, by the reduction of the issuance limits of DPGEs by the FGC, by changes on the balance-sheet items subject to reserve requirements and by the gradual introduction of Basel III's recommendations (BCB 2012).

An important measure in the case of Brazil has been the DPGE, which has helped create a liquidity cushion for medium-sized banks, which were suffering from a liquidity shortage immediately after the crisis. These measures have proven to be very successful at relatively low cost, and have increased confidence in the financial system, which is crucial in the middle of a crisis.

The main lesson to be drawn from the financial crisis is that liquidity is crucial. Evaluating it on a continual basis is important and the results from liquidity stress tests can be a very useful monitoring tool and suggest whether liquidity problems are local, specific to certain banks or systemic, in which case public policies can be triggered to help circumvent these problems.

Individual banks' approaches

This section presents some results from the liquidity stress-testing survey carried out by the Central Bank of Brazil on June 2012. The survey aimed to better understand the methods and scenarios that banks used in their liquidity stress tests. It is similar to the survey applied to European banks (ECB 2008).

To mitigate liquidity risks, banks need effective risk management. Fundamental to this task, liquidity stress tests allow banks to assess the possible impact of exceptional but plausible stress scenarios on their liquidity position and can help them to determine the size of liquidity buffers.

The respondent banks say liquidity risk is considered the second most important type of risk in their risk management; the most important is credit risk. Although some banks have been performing liquidity stress tests since about 2002, the majority of them began to perform these tests after 2008.

A total of 46 large banks received the survey and 27 banks provided information about their liquidity stress tests, including the largest Brazilian banks. From these banks, 23 perform internal liquidity stress tests while 4 of them use vendors' models.

All banks but one in the survey quantify liquidity risk tolerance. In the sample, 17 banks affirm they quantify risk tolerance by a system of limit settings. These limits are usually defined based on expert judgement. In eight banks, the quantification of liquidity risk tolerance is based on stress tests. Other forms, less frequently used, to quantify liquidity risk tolerance are: cashflow forecast (6 banks), concentration of the liquidity sources (2) and survival horizon (1). The ECB (2008) affirms that banks focus on risk containment – systems of limits interrelated with liquidity risk tolerance – rather than the quantification of liquidity risk tolerance *per se*. The explanation for this is that the quantification of liquidity risk tolerance is a difficult task. The major problem in the area of liquidity risk management is that liquidity risk events are of low probability but high impact, which implies that is not feasible to assign probabilities to all (reasonably well-defined) possible liquidity shocks. It seems that Brazilian banks have the same focus.

Time horizon
The time horizon of liquidity stress tests indicates the horizon the bank considers necessary to take corrective measures to mitigate liquidity risks occasionally detected. The majority of banks (17) perform liquidity stress tests monthly and some banks (8) perform them daily. Time horizons for stress-test scenarios mainly vary between four weeks and three months, although longer time horizons are also cited (see Figure 11.15). Almost every bank uses short or medium time horizons to perform their stress tests. However, the period considered as short, medium or long is not uniform among banks. A short period may comprise from one to twelve weeks, while a medium period comprises from two to twelve months. The most commonly time horizons considered are four weeks for a short period and three months, for a medium period.

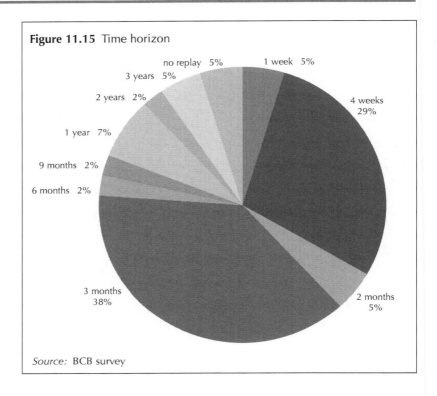

Figure 11.15 Time horizon

Source: BCB survey

Scenarios

The scenarios banks use consider the risk sources and magnitudes they relate to their business. Most banks (15) perform tests under market-wide stress scenarios, but only six banks use idiosyncratic scenarios. A considerable number of the surveyed banks (13) use a combination of adverse market conditions and idiosyncratic shocks to their institutions. Of these banks, only 9 run the combined scenario, while 3 also run both market and idiosyncratic scenarios separately and one bank also runs the market scenario. Of those banks that do not run tests with combined scenarios, the majority (15) rely exclusively on either tests with market stress scenarios (9) or tests with a firm-specific stress scenario (1). Five banks declared that they considered other types of stress test scenarios and one did not respond to the question (Figure 11.16).

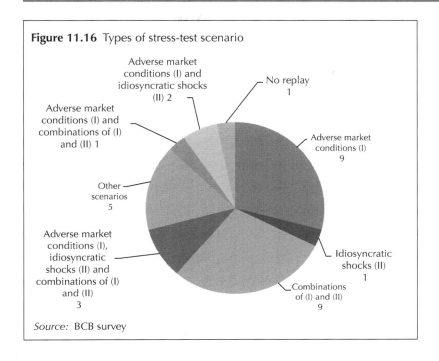

Figure 11.16 Types of stress-test scenario

Adverse market conditions (I) and idiosyncratic shocks (II) 2

No replay 1

Adverse market conditions (I) and combinations of (I) and (II) 1

Adverse market conditions (I) 9

Other scenarios 5

Adverse market conditions (I), idiosyncratic shocks (II) and combinations of (I) and (II) 3

Idiosyncratic shocks (II) 1

Combinations of (I) and (II) 9

Source: BCB survey

The surveyed banks described a multiplicity of scenarios with different sets of assumptions concerning the effect that these scenarios were expected to have on both the assets and liabilities sides of their balance sheets. However, there are some sources of stress that are common in most scenarios:

❑ reduction in asset prices;
❑ increased collateral and margin calls;
❑ increased delinquency;
❑ reduced access to funding markets;
❑ increased deposits withdrawals;
❑ non-rollover of term deposits; and
❑ utilisation of credit lines previously approved.

Although most banks claim they perform a combination of adverse market conditions and idiosyncratic-scenarios tests, it is not defined which shocks they consider as coming from market conditions or from bank-specific situations. Only a few banks consider bank-specific sources of stress, such as downgrade and liquidity problems in the group.

Most banks make assumptions about deposits in their stress scenarios. These assumptions are consistent with the structure of the BBS and the economic outlook. In the BBS, banks rely on domestic funds provided mainly by deposits. Another source of stress, usual for more than one-third of the banks, is an increase in delinquency. Brazil has experienced a fast credit growth, so banks seem to be aware of the effects of credit risk on liquidity.

According to the IMF (2012), the Brazilian financial sector is exposed to international commodities and capital markets' volatility effects, but the risks related to them are significantly mitigated by a flexible exchange rate; strong macro- and microprudential policy frameworks; and financial institutions' sound balance sheets, high capital, profitability and abundant liquid assets. However, banks consider this source of stress by means of assumptions about collateral or margin calls.

The vast majority of banks consider prospective approaches. Most banks forecast their cashflows by means of assumptions about the impact on inflows and outflows. However, it is not clear how these assumptions are made. It seems to be based on expert judgement.

Concerning scenario revisions, all respondents reported that liquidity stress scenarios are revised, with 19 banking conducting revisions regularly. From these banks, eight review their scenarios annually and six do it monthly. The events that trigger adjustments in the stress scenarios include, in no particular order of importance, changes in the macroeconomic scenario; changes in policies, guidelines and practices at the group level; changes in regulations; changes in monetary policy; business developments; changes in the levels of delinquency; changes in markets. From the 27 banks, 23 need either approval from an asset-and-liability committee, a risk committee or a board of directors for significant adjustments to the liquidity stress test scenarios. Regarding the stress-test level, eleven banks perform them at the entity level, while eight perform stress tests at the group level. However, only six banks perform stress tests at both levels. Five banks perform liquidity stress tests at other levels, such as the currency level.

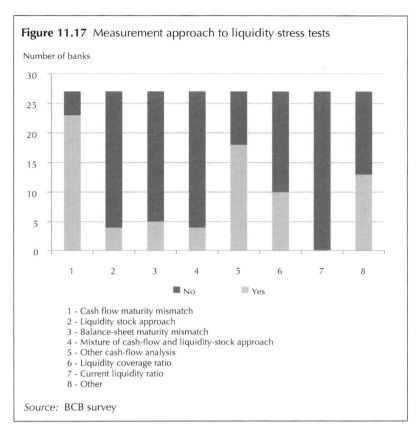

Figure 11.17 Measurement approach to liquidity stress tests

Number of banks

1 - Cash flow maturity mismatch
2 - Liquidity stock approach
3 - Balance-sheet maturity mismatch
4 - Mixture of cash-flow and liquidity-stock approach
5 - Other cash-flow analysis
6 - Liquidity coverage ratio
7 - Current liquidity ratio
8 - Other

Source: BCB survey

Banks use more than one approach to quantify their liquidity risk exposure (see Figure 11.17). According to the survey, the most common type of measurement approach (23 banks) is the cashflow maturity mismatch, followed by other cashflows analyses (18). The main advantages of the cashflow maturity mismatch seem to be that it is transparent, flexible and simple and gives a general overview of risk (ECB 2008). Matz and Neu (2007) argue that measures built on maturity mismatch and cashflow modelling help to reflect the dynamic nature of liquidity. The main disadvantage is that it is considered to be a short-term tool that does not reveal long-term liquidity problems (ECB 2008).

In summary, the respondent banks consider liquidity risk an important source of risk. The importance attributed to it increased after 2008, which can be related to the start of performing liquidity stress tests by the majority of institutions. The time horizon and sources of stress considered reflect the threats against which the individual institutions want to be protected, which depend on the particularities of their business.

Banks are reluctant to disclose the results of their stress tests, doing so, on demand, mainly to rating agencies and supervisors. Only a few banks frequently disclose their stress-test results to auditing firms, committees and boards. What possible reasons do banks give for this reluctance? Although most banks agree that disclosure would enhance market discipline in liquidity risk management and see value added in disclosing the results of liquidity stress tests, all banks agree strongly (19) or agree (8) that the results of liquidity stress tests cannot be interpreted without a detailed understanding of the scenarios and the considerations underlying them (Figure 11.18).

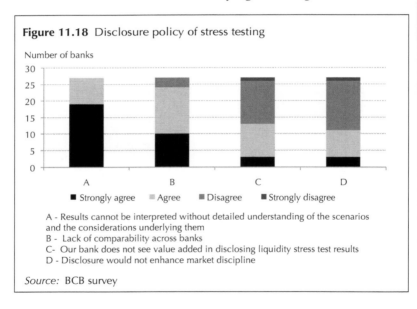

Figure 11.18 Disclosure policy of stress testing

Number of banks

■ Strongly agree   ■ Agree   ■ Disagree   ■ Strongly disagree

A - Results cannot be interpreted without detailed understanding of the scenarios and the considerations underlying them
B - Lack of comparability across banks
C- Our bank does not see value added in disclosing liquidity stress test results
D - Disclosure would not enhance market discipline

Source: BCB survey

CONCLUSIONS

This chapter discusses the effects of the financial crisis on the Brazilian banking system. The financial crisis has had major impacts worldwide, and liquidity risks have risen accordingly. There was an urgent need for macroprudential measures to help banking systems regain confidence and increase their liquidity to cope with additional risks.

We have presented the liquidity stress-testing approach in use in the Central Bank of Brazil and the results of a survey on liquidity stress testing that has been applied to banks that operate in the Brazilian banking system.

Overall, the Brazilian Banking system has experienced a small impact from the financial crisis due to several macroprudential measures and strong bank supervision and regulation. This impact affects banks differently. Medium-sized banks experienced a strong liquidity constraint due to a fly-to-quality movement in time deposits. Regarding ownership, foreign banks were the most affected by contagion. To avoid a confidence crisis, the BCB took measures both in domestic and foreign currencies that helped banks to overcome liquidity problems.

The survey applied to the largest Brazilian banks showed that liquidity risk is the second most important risk in their risk management. It seems that the crisis led to an improvement in the banks' risk management, since most of them started to perform liquidity stress tests after the period of turbulences starting in 2007. There is a considerable diversity in liquidity stress-test scenarios. However, most banks use a combination of adverse market conditions and tests of idiosyncratic-shock scenarios. The findings show that banks do not rely on any single measure of liquidity but they have a preference for measurements related to cashflows.

Benjamin M. Tabak gratefully acknowledges financial support from CNPQ Foundation. The opinions expressed in this chapter are those of the authors and do not necessarily reflect those of the Central Bank of Brazil.

REFERENCES

Aikman, D., *et al*, 2009, "Funding liquidity risk in a quantitative model of systemic stability", Bank of England Working Papers 372, Bank of England.

BCB, 2007, "Financial Stability Report", Banco Central do Brasil 6(2).

BCB, 2008, "Financial Stability Report", Banco Central do Brasil 7(2).

BCB, 2009, "Financial Stability Report", Banco Central do Brasil 8(1).

BCB, 2010, "Financial Stability Report", Banco Central do Brasil 9(2).

BCB, 2011, "Financial Stability Report", Banco Central do Brasil 10(2).

BCB, 2012, "Financial Stability Report", Banco Central do Brasil 11(1).

BCBS, 2010, "Basel III: International framework for liquidity risk measurement, standards and monitoring", Bank for International Settlements, December.

BCBS, 2011, "Macroprudential Policy Tools and Frameworks" Bank for International Settlements, October.

Čihák, Martin, 2007, "Introduction to Applied Stress-testing", IMF Working Papers 07/59, International Monetary Fund.

Da Costa, F. N., 2012, "Brasil dos Bancos", University of São Paulo Press, São Paulo, Brazil.

ECB, 2008, "EU banks' liquidity stress-testing and contingency funding plans" (http://www.ecb.int/pub/pub/prud/html/index.en.html).

Forbes, K. J., and R. Rigobon, 2002, "No contagion, only interdependence: Measuring stock market comovements, *Journal of Finance* 57(5), pp. 2223–61.

Fry, R., V. L. Martin and C. Tang, 2008, "A new class of tests of contagion with applications to real estate markets" CAMA Working Papers 2008-01, Australian National University, Centre for Applied Macroeconomic Analysis.

IMF, 2011, "Macroprudential Policy: An Organizing Framework", background paper, March.

IMF, 2012, "Brazil, Financial System Stability Assessment", June 20.

Matz, L., and P. Neu, 2007, "Liquidity Risk Measurement and Management: *A Practitioner's Guide to Global Best Practices"* (Wiley Finance Series, Wiley & Sons (Asia)).

Mesquita, M., and M. Torós, 2010, "Considerações sobre a Atuação do Banco Central na Crise de 2008", Banco Central do Brasil, Working Paper Series, March.

Ong, Li L., and Martin Čihák, 2010, "Of Runes and Sagas: Perspectives on Liquidity Stress-testing Using an Iceland Example," IMF Working Papers 10/156, International Monetary Fund.

Silva, L. A. P., and R. E. Harris, 2012, "Sailing through the Global Financial Storm: Brazil's recent experience with monetary and macroprudential policies to lean against the financial cycle and deal with systemic risks", Banco Central do Brasil, Working Paper Series, August.

De Larosière Group, 2009, "The de Larosière Report", February.

Van den End, J. W., 2009, "Liquidity Stress-Tester: A Model for Stress-testing Banks' Liquidity Risk," *CESifo Economic Studies* 56(1), pp. 38–69, April.

Van den End, J. W., 2010, "Liquidity Stress-Tester: Do Basel III and Unconventional Monetary Policy Work?", DNB Working Papers 269, Netherlands Central Bank Research Department.

Van den End, J. W., and M. Kruidhof, 2012, "Modelling the liquidity ratio as macroprudential instrument", DNB Working Papers 342, Netherlands Central Bank, Research Department.

Vazquez, F., B. M. Tabak and M. Souto, 2012, "A macro stress test model of credit risk for the Brazilian banking sector", *Journal of Financial Stability*, 8, pp. 69-83.

Wong, E., and C. Hui, 2009, "A Liquidity Risk Stress-Testing Framework with Interaction between Market and Credit Risks," Working Papers 0906, Hong Kong Monetary Authority.

[1] An analysis of the distribution of these deposits among its holders shows that, in 2006, 54.1% of the total amount was concentrated at the level of up to BRL100 per account, with 41,565,238 depositors (BCB 2007).

[2] For more details about the measures taken by Brazilian authorities, see Mesquita and Torós (2010) and Silva and Harris (2012).

[3] Adapted from "a significant increase in cross-market linkages after a shock to one country (or group of countries)", by Forbes and Rigobon (2002).

12

Determining the Severity of Macroeconomic Stress Scenarios

Kapo Yuen

Federal Reserve Bank of New York

In the midst of the 2008 financial panic caused by the collapse of the subprime housing market, the US government responded with unprecedented measures, including liquidity provision through various funding programmes, debt and deposit guarantees and large-scale asset purchases. In February 2009, the US banking supervisors conducted the first-ever system-wide stress test on 19 of the largest US bank holding companies (BHCs), known as the Supervisory Capital Assessment Program (SCAP) (Federal Reserve 2009a). The stress test required these 19 BHCs to undergo simultaneous, forward-looking exercises designed to determine whether they would have adequate capital to sustain lending to the economy in the event of an unexpectedly adverse scenario. By conducting this SCAP exercise, the supervisors hoped that it would reduce uncertainty and restore confidence in the US financial institutions. In their 2010 staff reports, Peristian, Morgan and Savino (2010), of the Federal Reserve Bank of New York, concluded that the SCAP might have helped to quell the financial panic by releasing vital information about the BHCs. They claimed, "While investors did not need supervisors to tell them which banks had capital deficiencies, they were surprised by the size of the capital gaps and they used that information to revalue banks."

Since conducting the SCAP in 2009, the Federal Reserve System has conducted annual stress tests on the US banking system, called the Comprehensive Capital Analysis and Review (CCAR).

Additionally, the Dodd–Frank Wall Street Reform and Consumer Protection Act requires the Federal Reserve Board to conduct annual stress tests of bank holding companies with total consolidated assets of US$50 billion or more. In each CCAR, the Federal Reserve Board generates an adverse macroeconomic scenario (two adverse scenarios in 2013) and requires BHCs to submit at least one adverse scenario that is related to their own specific portfolios and risk profiles. While the 2013 instructions for CCAR indicate that the adverse scenario developed by the BHC must reflect "a severely adverse economic and financial market environment", it does not specify what should be the "appropriate severity" of an adverse scenario used for the capital planning. This chapter will discuss the severity of the supervisory adverse scenarios and provide a simple methodology to compare the severity of different adverse macroeconomic scenarios. In particular, the key questions we aim to answer are:

❏ how to measure the severity of a firm's BHC macro stress scenario;
❏ how severe the BHC stress scenario is when compared with the supervisory stress scenarios; and
❏ what implications can be drawn about the credibility of the BHC's stress scenario.

THE US SUPERVISORY STRESS SCENARIOS
As part of the Federal Reserve System's Comprehensive Capital Analysis and Review (CCAR), US domiciled top-tier bank holding companies (BHCs) are required to submit comprehensive capital plans, including *pro forma* capital analyses, based on at least one BHC defined adverse scenario. The adverse scenario is described by quarterly trajectories for key macroeconomic variables (MVs) over the next nine quarters (or longer, as in 2013). In addition, the Federal Reserve generates its own supervisory stress scenarios so that firms are expected to apply both BHC and supervisory stress scenarios to all exposures to estimate potential losses under stressed operating conditions. Separately, firms with significant trading activity are asked to estimate a one-time potential trading-related market and counterparty credit losses under their own BHC scenarios and market stress scenarios provided by the supervisors.[1]

For the supervisory stress scenarios, the Federal Reserve provides firms with global market shock components that are one-time, hypothetical shocks to a large set of risk factors. For the last two CCAR exercises, these shocks involved large and sudden changes in asset prices, rates and CDS spreads that mirrored the severe market condition in the second half of 2008.

Since CCAR is a comprehensive assessment of a firm's capital plan, the BHCs are asked to conduct an assessment of the expected uses and sources of capital over a planning horizon. In the 2009 SCAP, firms were asked to submit stress losses over the next two years, on a yearly basis. Since then, the planning horizon has changed to nine quarters. For the last three CCAR exercises, a BHC is asked to submit its pro forma, post-stress capital projections in its capital plan beginning with data as of September 30, and spans the nine-quarter planning horizon. The projections begin in the fourth quarter of the current year and conclude at the end of the fourth quarter two years forward. Hence, for defining BHC stress scenarios, firms are asked to project the movements of key macroeconomic variables over the planning horizon of nine quarters. Our analysis on determining the severity of macro stress scenarios is based on the movements of the macroeconomic variables in these nine quarters. As for determining the severity of the global market shock components for trading and counterparty credit losses, it will not be discussed in this chapter because it is a one-time shock and the evaluation will be on the movements of the market risk factors rather the macroeconomic variables. This is examined in Chapter 3.

In the 2011 CCAR, the Federal Reserve defined the stress supervisory scenario using nine macroeconomic variables: Real GDP, Consumer Price Index (CPI), Real Disposable Personal Income, Unemployment Rate, Three-Month Treasury Bill Rate, 10-Year Treasury Bond Rate, BBB Corporate Rate, Dow Jones Index and National House Price Index (Federal Reserve 2011a). In CCAR 2012, the number of macroeconomic variables that defined the supervisory stress scenario increased to 14. Besides the original nine variables, the added variables were Nominal GDP Growth, Nominal Disposable Income Growth, Mortgage Rate, Market Volatility Index and Commercial Real Estate Price Index (Federal

Reserve 2011b) Additionally, there is another set of 12 international macroeconomic variables, three macroeconomic variables and four countries/country blocks, included in the supervisory stress scenario. As for CCAR 2013, the Federal Reserve System uses the same set of variables to define the supervisory adverse scenario (Federal Reserve 2012) as in 2012. Since the BHCs are required to define their own adverse scenarios of "a severely adverse economic environment", one way to determine the "appropriate severity" of the BHCs' stress scenarios is to compare them with the supervisory adverse scenarios. Although it is stated that the BHC stress scenarios should reflect the BHC's unique vulnerabilities to factors that affect its exposures, activities and risks, by comparing the severity of the BHC's and supervisory stress scenarios we can determine whether the estimates of the losses are consistent with the relative severity of the stress scenarios. For example, if the BHC's own stress scenario is determined to be more severe than the supervisory scenario, but the estimated losses from the supervisory scenario are larger, then we would need to examine the details of the stress loss estimation methodology to determine the causes of this inconsistency.

ALIGNING THE US SUPERVISORY STRESS SCENARIOS
Let us consider the two CCAR supervisory stress scenarios in 2011 and 2012 and the supervisory severely adverse scenario in 2013. By comparing the forecast of the macroeconomic variables over the next nine quarters, we will try to determine which scenarios are the most and least severe.

In general, comparing severity of stress scenarios is relative. That is, we can usually deduce with relative confidence that Scenario A is more severe than Scenario B, but it is much more challenging to quantify how much more severe is Scenario A over Scenario B. In other words, it is much more difficult to define a metric to measure the severity of a stress scenario. Later in this chapter, we will attempt to use a historical event as a reference to give some sights on the measurement of severity.

Table 12.1 The Federal Reserve supervisory adverse scenarios with nine quarters of projections

CCAR 2011 Common Variables	Q3 2010	Q4 2010	Q1 2011	Q2 2011	Q3 2011	Q4 2011	Q1 2012	Q2 2012	Q3 2012	Q4 2012
Real GDP	13,261	13,332	13,393	13,255	13,206	13,138	13,178	13,229	13,343	13,453
Real Disposable Personal Income	10,237	10,271	10,299	10,318	10,236	10,179	10,081	10,054	10,047	10,066
Unemployment Rate	9.6	9.6	9.6	10.1	10.6	11.0	11.1	11.0	10.9	10.6
CPI	218.0	219.0	219.9	220.9	221.7	222.3	222.9	223.4	224.0	224.7
3-Month Treasury Yield	0.16	0.16	0.19	0.07	0.13	0.13	0.13	0.13	0.13	0.13
10-Year Treasury Yield	2.90	2.57	2.64	2.66	2.79	2.77	2.71	2.98	3.12	3.35
BBB corporate yield	5.07	4.69	4.86	5.88	6.26	6.46	6.16	6.27	6.22	6.25
Dow Jones Total Stock Market Index	11,947	12,069	11,822	9,116	8,809	8,716	10,682	11,083	11,498	11,930
National House Price Index	142	140	139	137	134	132	130	128	127	126

CCAR 2012 Common Variables	Q3 2011	Q4 2011	Q1 2012	Q2 2012	Q3 2012	Q4 2012	Q1 2013	Q2 2013	Q3 2013	Q4 2013
Real GDP growth	2.46	-4.84	-7.98	-4.23	-3.51	0.00	0.72	2.21	2.32	3.45
Real Disposable Personal Income growth	-1.73	-6.02	-6.81	-4.29	-3.16	-0.57	0.74	1.66	2.69	2.27
Unemployment Rate	9.09	9.68	10.58	11.40	12.16	12.76	13.00	13.05	12.96	12.76
CPI inflation rate	3.09	2.21	1.78	1.02	0.89	0.35	0.23	0.21	0.30	0.32
3-Month Treasury Yield	0.02	0.10	0.10	0.10	0.10	0.10	0.10	0.10	0.10	0.10

Table 12.1 (*continued*)

10-Year Treasury Yield	2.48	2.07	1.94	1.76	1.67	1.76	1.74	1.84	1.98	1.98
BBB corporate yield	4.87	5.65	6.83	6.81	6.75	6.45	6.07	5.83	5.74	5.51
Dow Jones Total Stock Market Index	11,771.86	9,501.48	7,576.38	7,089.87	5,705.55	5,668.34	6,082.47	6,384.32	7,084.65	7,618.89
National House Price Index	136.86	135.13	131.61	127.50	123.12	119.08	115.15	111.92	109.77	108.48

CCAR 2013 Common Variables	Q3 2012	Q4 2012	Q1 2013	Q2 2013	Q3 2013	Q4 2013	Q1 2014	Q2 2014	Q3 2014	Q4 2014
Real GDP growth	2.0	-3.5	-6.1	-4.4	-4.2	-1.2	0.0	2.2	2.6	3.8
Real Disposable Personal Income growth	0.8	-3.8	-6.7	-4.6	-3.2	-1.5	0.8	0.9	2.5	2.8
Unemployment Rate	8.1	8.9	10.0	10.7	11.5	11.9	12.0	12.1	12.0	11.9
CPI inflation rate	2.3	1.8	1.4	1.1	1.0	0.3	1.0	0.9	0.7	0.6
3-Month Treasury Yield	0.1	0.1	0.1	0.1	0.1	0.1	0.1	0.1	0.1	0.1
10-Year Treasury Yield	1.6	1.4	1.2	1.2	1.2	1.2	1.2	1.5	1.7	1.9
BBB corporate yield	4.2	5.6	6.4	6.7	6.8	6.5	6.2	6.2	6.0	5.9
Dow Jones Total Stock Market Index	14997.8	12105.2	9652.6	9032.8	7269.1	7221.7	7749.3	8133.9	9026.1	9706.7
National House Price Index	143.4	141.6	137.9	133.6	129.0	124.7	120.6	117.2	115.0	113.6

Before we begin to examine the three supervisory scenarios, we have to make the following key assumptions.

❑ All scenarios start on the same quarter, Q3 2010, and the projections are over the nine quarters from Q4 2010 to Q4 2012. Hence the scenarios are compared by measuring the change over the nine quarters on the macroeconomic variables.

❑ The scenarios are compared on the set of common macroeconomic variables. For example, in 2012 and 2013, the Market Volatility Index is included in the supervisory stress scenario, but not in 2011, thus this variable is excluded. Therefore, the set of common macroeconomic variables for comparison are all the variables that are defined in the supervisory scenario of 2011 CCAR.

Of the nine macroeconomic variables, Real GDP, CPI, and Real Disposable Personal Income are expressed as growth rates in 2012 and 2013 (see Table 12.1). To convert them back to Real GDP, CPI and Real Disposable Personal Income, we use Equation 12.1 to convert growth rates into actual values, and align all the starting values using the Q3 2010 actual values. For variables such as Unemployment Rate (UR), we first align all the starting values to be Q3 2010, then we use the percentage change over the period (Equation 12.2) to convert the 2012 and 2013 projections to the projections with the same starting values. For example, the Real GDP Growth Rate (Real_GDPGR) is converted to Real GDP (Real_GDP) by the following equation:

$$Real\_GDP_{i+1} = Real\_GDP_i * \left\{ \left(1 + \frac{Real\_GDPGR_{i+1}}{100} \right)^{0.25} \right\} \quad (12.1)$$

For other variables, the alignment is just the percentage change over the period,

$$UR\_2011_{i+1} = UR\_2011_i \left(1 + \frac{(UR_{2012\,i+1} - UR_{2012\,i})}{UR_{2012\,i}} \right) \quad (12.2)$$

Table 12.2 The macroeconomic variables with nine quarters of projections on the four scenarios

Scenario	CCAR Common Variables	Q3 2010	Q4 2010	Q1 2011	Q2 2011	Q3 2011	Q4 2011	Q1 2012	Q2 2012	Q3 2012	Q4 2012
2011	Real GDP	13,261	13,332	13,393	13,255	13,206	13,138	13,178	13,229	13,343	13,453
2012	Real GDP	13,261	13,097	12,828	12,690	12,577	12,577	12,599	12,668	12,741	12,849
2013	Real GDP	13,261	13,143	12,938	12,793	12,657	12,619	12,619	12,687	12,769	12,889
Hypothetical	Real GDP	13,261	12,690	12,690	12,690	12,690	12,690	12,690	12,690	12,690	12,690
2011	Real Disposable Personal Income	10,237	10,271	10,299	10,318	10,236	10,179	10,081	10,054	10,047	10,066
2012	Real Disposable Personal Income	10,237	10,079	9,903	9,795	9,717	9,703	9,721	9,761	9,826	9,881
2013	Real Disposable Personal Income	10,237	10,138	9,964	9,847	9,768	9,731	9,750	9,772	9,832	9,901
Hypothetical	Real Disposable Personal Income	10,237	9,700	9,700	9,700	9,700	9,700	9,700	9,700	9,700	9,700
2011	Unemployment Rate	9.58	9.61	9.62	10.11	10.56	11.02	11.12	11.04	10.87	10.64
2012	Unemployment Rate	9.58	10.20	11.15	12.02	12.82	13.45	13.70	13.75	13.66	13.45
2013	Unemployment Rate	9.58	10.53	11.83	12.66	13.60	14.07	14.19	14.31	14.19	14.07
Hypothetical	Unemployment Rate	9.58	12.66	12.66	12.66	12.66	12.66	12.66	12.66	12.66	12.66
2011	10-Year Treasury Yield	2.90	2.57	2.64	2.66	2.79	2.77	2.71	2.98	3.12	3.35
2012	10-Year Treasury Yield	2.90	2.42	2.27	2.05	1.95	2.05	2.04	2.15	2.31	2.32

Table 12.2 (continued)

2013	10-Year Treasury Yield	2.90	2.54	2.18	2.18	2.18	2.18	2.18	2.72	3.08	3.44
Hypothetical	10-Year Treasury Yield	2.90	2.80	2.80	2.80	2.80	2.80	2.80	2.80	2.80	2.80
2011	3-Month Treasury Yield	0.16	0.16	0.19	0.07	0.13	0.13	0.13	0.13	0.13	0.13
2012	3-Month Treasury Yield	0.16	0.69	0.69	0.69	0.69	0.69	0.69	0.69	0.69	0.69
2013	3-Month Treasury Yield	0.16	0.16	0.16	0.16	0.16	0.16	0.16	0.16	0.16	0.16
Hypothetical	3-month Treasury yield	0.16	0.50	0.50	0.50	0.50	0.50	0.50	0.50	0.50	0.50
2011	BBB corporate yield	5.07	4.69	4.86	5.88	6.26	6.46	6.16	6.27	6.22	6.25
2012	BBB corporate yield	5.07	5.87	7.11	7.09	7.03	6.71	6.31	6.07	5.97	5.73
2013	BBB corporate yield	5.07	6.76	7.73	8.09	8.21	7.85	7.48	7.48	7.24	7.12
Hypothetical	BBB corporate yield	5.07	8.09	8.09	8.09	8.09	8.09	8.09	8.09	8.09	8.09
2011	CPI	218.0	219.0	219.9	220.9	221.7	222.3	222.9	223.4	224.0	224.7
2012	CPI	218.0	219.2	220.2	220.8	221.3	221.4	221.6	221.7	221.9	222.0
2013	CPI	218.0	219.0	219.8	220.4	220.9	221.1	221.6	222.1	222.5	222.9
Hypothetical	CPI	218.0	222.0	222.0	222.0	222.0	222.0	222.0	222.0	222.0	222.0
2011	Dow Jones Total Stock Market Index	11,947	12,069	11,822	9,116	8,809	8,716	10,682	11,083	11,498	11,930
2012	Dow Jones Total Stock Market Index	11,947	9,643	7,689	7,195	5,791	5,753	6,173	6,479	7,190	7,732
2013	Dow Jones Total Stock Market Index	11,947	9,643	7,689	7,195	5,791	5,753	6,173	6,479	7,190	7,732

Table 12.2 (continued)

Hypothetical	Dow Jones Total Stock Market Index	11,947	7,200	7,200	7,200	7,200	7,200	7,200	7,200	7,200	7,200	7,200
2011	National House Price Index	142.4	140.4	139.1	136.8	134.3	131.8	129.6	127.8	126.8	126.4
2012	National House Price Index	142.4	140.6	136.9	132.6	128.1	123.9	119.8	116.4	114.2	112.8
2013	National House Price Index	142.4	140.6	136.9	132.6	128.1	123.8	119.7	116.3	114.2	112.8
Hypothetical	National House Price Index	142.4	120.0	120.0	120.0	120.0	120.0	120.0	120.0	120.0	120.0

After aligning the supervisory stress scenarios from CCAR 2011, 2012 and 2013, we also create an additional hypothetical stress scenario to illustrate how the severity of stress scenarios can be compared between the supervisory scenarios and a "BHC-developed" stress scenario, as part of the BHC's requirements under CCAR. Table 12.2 shows the three supervisory and the hypothetical scenarios as they are all aligned at Q3 2010. All the scenarios have the same set of macroeconomic variables and they are all aligned to the same value as of Q3 2010. Hence, by comparing the changes of the macroeconomic variables over the next nine quarters, we can examine the severity of each scenario relative the others.

HISTORICAL TREND OF THE MACROECONOMIC VARIABLES

In generating the supervisory adverse scenarios, the Federal Reserve emphasises that the scenarios are not economic forecasts, but rather hypothetical scenarios that show significant contraction in economic activities. A contraction in economic activities means macroeconomic indicators such as GDP, employment, stock indexes, investment spending, capacity utilisation, household income, housing prices and inflation fall, while the unemployment rate and personal and corporate bankruptcies rise. Of the nine common macroeconomic variables, the one that is most related to stress economic conditions is a drop in Real GDP. As for the rest of the common variables, most economists would agree that a stress economic condition will associate with a decrease in Real Disposable Personal Income, Dow Jones Index and House Price Index, and an increase in Unemployment Rate. However, for CPI, BBB Corporate Bond Rate, Three-Month Treasury Yield and the 10-Year Treasury Yield, it is not so clear that an increase or decrease in any one of these variables will indicate a stress economic condition.

We will use historical data to examine each of the common variables to understand its relationship with historical recessions. All the historical values are obtained from the Board of Governors' document on Supervisory Scenarios[2].

In the US, from 1980 to 2013, there have been nine periods of negative economic growth over one fiscal quarter or more (see Figure 12.1). According to the National Bureau of Economic Research (NBER), there have been five periods considered recessions:[3]

❑ January 1980–July 1980: 6 months;
❑ July 1981–November 1982: 16 months;
❑ July 1990–March 1991: 8 months;
❑ March 2001–November 2001: 8 months; and
❑ December 2007–June 2009: 18 months.

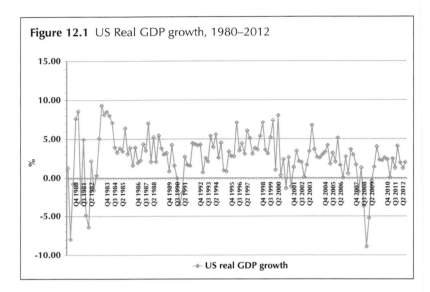

Figure 12.1 US Real GDP growth, 1980–2012

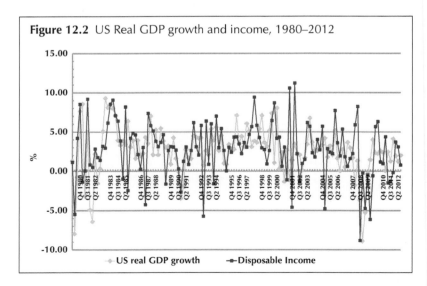

Figure 12.2 US Real GDP growth and income, 1980–2012

From Figure 12.2, we can see that a drop in GDP Growth Rate is usually associated with a drop in the Real Disposable Personal Income Growth Rate. Thus, we can state, in general, a stress economic condition is associated with a drop in Real Disposable Personal Income Growth.

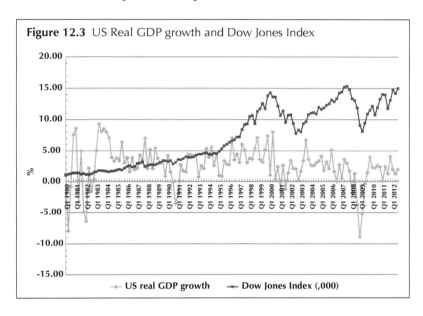

Figure 12.3 US Real GDP growth and Dow Jones Index

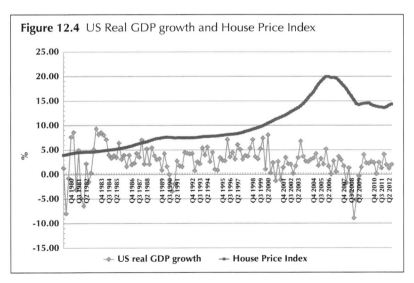

Figure 12.4 US Real GDP growth and House Price Index

From Figure 12.3, we can see that the last two recessions are associated with significant drops in the Dow Jones Index, and from Figure 12.4 we see that the most severe recession followed a huge drop in the House Price Index. Hence, we can also confidently claim that a stress economic condition is associated with a drop in Dow Jones Index or House Price Index.

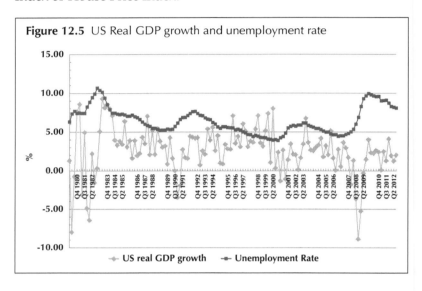

Figure 12.5 US Real GDP growth and unemployment rate

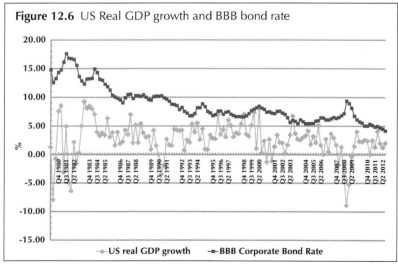

Figure 12.6 US Real GDP growth and BBB bond rate

Figure 12.5 clearly shows that each recession was associated with a rise in the unemployment rate. However, for BBB Corporate Bond Rate – although for the recessions in 1981 and 2008 we see a high increase in the BBB Rate – the rest of the data does not show a high association between GDP Growth Rate and BBB Bond Rate (Figure 12.6).

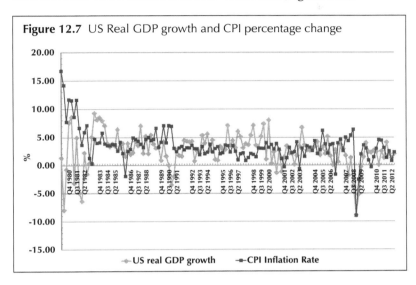

Figure 12.7 US Real GDP growth and CPI percentage change

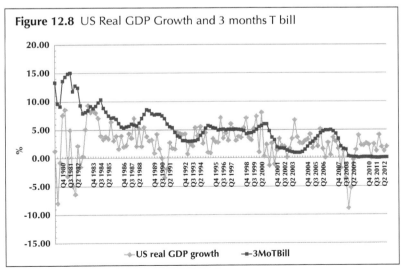

Figure 12.8 US Real GDP Growth and 3 months T bill

From Figure 12.7, we see only that a sharp drop in CPI is associated with the last recession, but, for the rest of the historical data, there is no obvious association between change in CPI and GDP Growth Rate.

As for the Three-Month Treasury Yield and the US 10-Year Treasury Yield, from Figures 12.8 and 12.9, there is no clear association between Real GDP Growth Rate and Treasury Yields. From examining the historical data, of the nine common macroeconomic variables defined in the stress scenarios we have seen that four of them – CPI, Three-Month Treasury Yield, 10-Year Treasury Yield and BBB Corporate Bond Rate – do not show any "directional" indication that either an increase or decrease in value is necessarily associated with a stress economic condition ("directional" means that, if a macroeconomic variable increases in value, then, historically, the economic condition always reacts the same way, either less or more severe in the same direction). Thus, these four variables will not be further considered in our discussion for measuring the severity of a stress scenario.

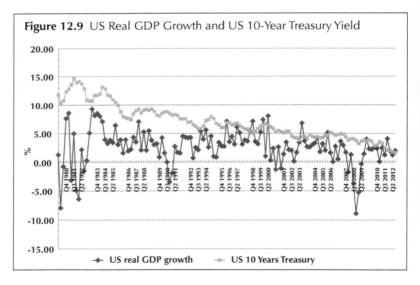

Figure 12.9 US Real GDP Growth and US 10-Year Treasury Yield

NINE-QUARTERS PROJECTIONS OF THE MACROECONOMIC VARIABLES

We will now examine the projections of the remaining five macro-economic variables in each of the four stress scenarios. From Figures 12.10 and 12.11, we can clearly see that the 2011 supervisory scenario is the least severe in terms of GDP and Real Disposable Personal Income. The 2013 scenario follows the same pattern as the 2012 scenario, but the drop at every quarter is only slightly less than that of 2012. As for the Hypothetical portfolio, it has the biggest drop in disposable income. However, the severity in Real GDP is not conclusive because the projected GDP in the Hypothetical are higher than scenarios 2012 and 2013 in some quarters, but lower in other quarters.

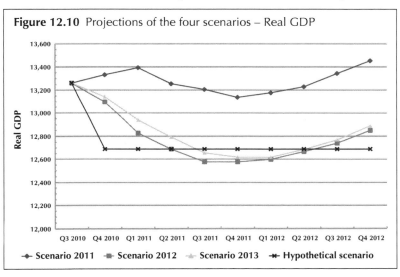

Figure 12.10 Projections of the four scenarios – Real GDP

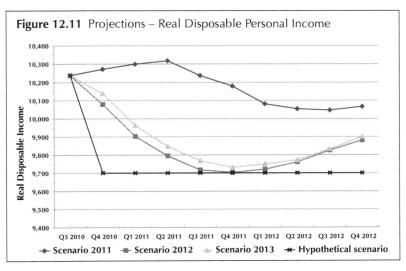

Figure 12.11 Projections – Real Disposable Personal Income

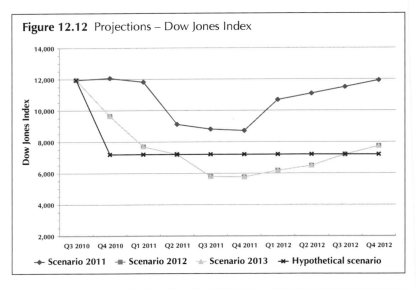

Figure 12.12 Projections – Dow Jones Index

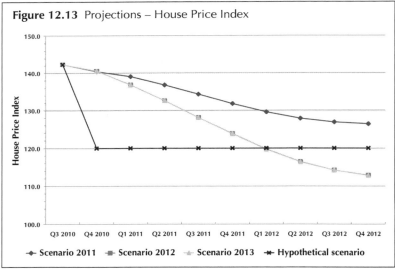

Figure 12.13 Projections – House Price Index

We now focus on the next two "directional" macroeconomic variables: Dow Jones Index and House Price Index. From Figures 12.12 and 12.13, we can see that scenarios 2012 and 2013 are exactly the same. The three supervisory scenarios follow similar patterns. On the Dow Jones Index, there is a sharp drop in the beginning, followed by an increase after the fourth quarter, and scenario 2011 shows that the drop is the mildest. As for the House Price Index, the projections are all declining quarter after quarter, and the decline in scenario 2011 is also the mildest. Since the Hypothetical cut across the curve of scenarios 2012 and 2013, by examining the charts, apart from scenario 2011, it is not conclusive which one is the most severe scenario.

Finally, on examining the Unemployment Rate (Figure 12.14), we see that the three supervisory scenarios all project that the unemployment rate will go up over the next six quarters, then plateau, and finally drop slightly at the end. It is also obvious that scenario 2011 is the mildest, and it is inconclusive between the Hypothetical scenario and scenarios 2012 and 2013. By now, we have established that for the three supervisory scenarios – since each of the variables we have seen follows the same pattern, on the whole – scenario 2011 is the mildest, and scenario 2012 and 2013 are almost the same except that scenario 2012 is slightly more severe.

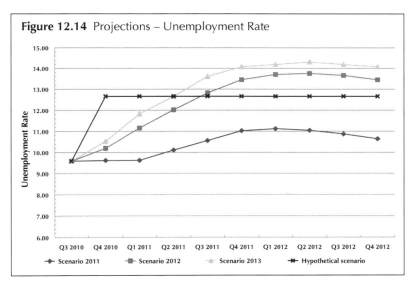

Figure 12.14 Projections – Unemployment Rate

When comparing the Hypothetical scenario with the 2012 and 2013 scenarios in Unemployment Rate, there are some quarters in which the hypothetical scenario has the higher Unemployment Rate, and some quarters in which the 2012 and 2013 scenarios have the higher Unemployment Rate. Therefore, in order to make an overall comparison, it is necessary to develop a statistic to summarise, measure and standardise the severity of each variable over the nine quarters.

Since we have aligned all the scenarios to the same starting point, the severity of each quarter is determined by the percentage change with respect to the starting quarter (Q3 2010). Thus, a probable summary statistic is the average of the percentage change with respect to the starting quarter. Another choice is the maximum change over the nine quarters, but the maximum value ignores the projections with recovery at the end of the nine quarters. The average of the percentage change is computed by Equation 12.3 below, where i is the index for the four scenarios, and j is the index for each of the projections.

$$Ave\ \%\ Change\ UR_i = \sum_{j=1}^{9} \frac{100}{9} \left(\frac{(UR_{i,j} - UR_{i,3Q2010})}{UR_{i,3Q2010}} \right) \quad (12.3)$$

This summary statistic can be computed for the five "directional" macroeconomic variables in each scenario. We now have a measure to compare the severity of the scenarios on each of the variables independently of the other variables. From Figure 12.15, we can see that the longer the vertical bar is away from zero, the more severity it indicates. Thus, for Unemployment Rate, the longest bar is in 2013, which means the most severe scenario is 2013. For GDP, Disposable Income, and HPI, the Hypothetical scenario is the most severe. For Dow Jones Index, the 2012, 2013 and Hypothetical scenarios are more or less the same. Viewing across the chart, we see that the 2011 scenario is the least severe in each of the five variables.

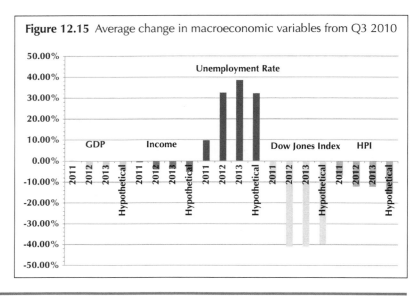

Figure 12.15 Average change in macroeconomic variables from Q3 2010

In terms of the magnitude of severity, we see that Unemployment Rate and Dow Jones Index have 30% to 40% average deterioration in scenarios 2012, 2013 and the Hypothetical, whereas the other variables are much less severe. Hence, we have a measurement of severity for each macroeconomic variable. In the next section, we will suggest some ways to combine all these measurement to give an overall view of the severity of a stress scenario.

AN OVERALL ASSESSMENT OF THE SEVERITY

At the start of our discussion, we mentioned that measuring severity is, in general, relative. However, some economists (Edge 2012) have tried to use historical recessions as anchors, and relate the stress scenarios to historical recessions to get some sense of magnitude as compared with past recessions. We will discuss other methodologies in more detail in the next section. For now, we will propose a simple methodology to summarise the severity of each scenario with reference to a historical recession.

For each macroeconomic variable, we have four scenarios. We will use an ordinal ranking to assign a rank to each of the scenario by using the Average % Change, giving rankings of 1–4 to indicate least to most severity. When the Average % Change shows that two scenarios are very similar (within 1% of each other), we assign the average of the two ranks to both scenarios. Since severity in Unemployment Rate is associated with increasing value, the lowest rank is given to the lowest Average % Change. Table 12.3 gives the ranking of each variable and the total ranking. By summing across the rank of each variable, we arrive at a statistic that gives an overall ranking (Total Rank) of the scenarios. With this simple methodology, we have determined the severity of the four macro stress scenarios. In order of severity, the most severe scenario is Hypothetical, followed by 2013, 2012 and 2011. However, on further examination, the differences in Total Rank between the Hypothetical, 2013 and 2012 scenarios are not that significant (<20%), hence these three scenarios are comparable in terms of severity.

Table 12.3 Ranking of each macroeconomic variable and the total rank of the scenario

Scenario	Real GDP		Disposable Income		Unemployment Rate		Dow Jones		HPI		Total Rank
	Ave % Change	RANK	Ave % Change	RANK	Ave % Change	RANK	Ave % Change	RANK	Ave % Change	RANK	
2011	0.2	1	-0.6	1	9.7	1	-11.0	1	-6.88	1	5.0
2012	-4.0	3	-4.1	2.5	32.4	2.5	-40.8	3	-12.2	2.5	13.5
2013	-3.5	3	-3.7	2.5	38.5	4	-40.8	3	-12.2	2.5	15.0
Hypothetical	-4.3	3	-5.2	4	32.2	2.5	-39.7	3	-15.7	4	16.5

Table 12.4 Nine-quarters values of changes for 2008 Recession[4]

Common Variables	Q3 2010	Q1 2008	Q2 2008	Q3 2008	Q4 2008	Q1 2009	Q2 2009	Q3 2009	Q4 2009	Q1 2010
Real GDP	13,261	13,202	13,245	13,122	12,820	12,649	12,639	12,684	12,810	12,884
Real Disposable Personal Income	10,237	10,385	10,592	10,350	10,344	10,220	10,208	10,048	10,033	10,172
Unemployment Rate	9.58	9.98	10.64	11.98	13.70	16.50	18.49	19.23	19.83	19.49
Dow Jones Index	11,947	10,748	10,540	9,574	7,326	6,541	7,598	8,797	9,269	9,804
House Price Index	142	137	131	126	120	114	112	113	114	115

Since all these four scenarios are hypothetical forward-looking scenarios, and we now have some understanding of the severity among them, the next logical question should be how they are related to our historical experience. Looking back at the past postwar recessions, we see that the most severe recession is the 2008 recession (December 2007 to June 2009), which lasted 18 months. In order to align with the nine projected quarters of our scenarios, we will use the NBER data and choose the consecutive nine quarters of Real GDP Growth Rate when the recession began in the first quarter of 2008. After aligning for Q3 2010 as the starting quarter and the conversion of the values as described in the last section on the remaining nine quarters, we have the similar values on the macroeconomic variables for comparison in Table 12.4. The first column has the actual values as in Q3 2010. This is used as the anchor to align all the scenarios that have the same starting values. The rest of the nine columns are from Q1 2008 to Q1 2010 (projections of nine quarters as in all supervisory scenarios). The values in these nine columns are scaled to the starting values of the first column, and so the 2008 Recession values start from the second column.

After we calculate the average percentage change of the five variables over the nine quarters, we find that the Average % Change on Real Disposable Personal Income is slightly positive (0.2%). Thus, during the 2008 Recession, the Real Disposable Personal Income is not "directional", as we once thought. We have come to realise that it is not necessarily true that Real Disposable Personal Income will decrease in a severe stress economic condition, especially when we are looking at the overall change in nine quarters. Therefore, including the Real Disposable Personal Income will taint our measurement of severity. Hence we will drop the Real Disposable Personal Income from our ranking on the overall severity. We can now put the Average % Change of the rest of the variables back into the ranking methodology and observe the ranking of the recession with other scenarios.

From Table 12.5, we observe that 2008 Recession is ranked as the most severe, followed by Hypothetical, 2013, 2012 and 2011. However, apart from the unemployment rate in 2008 Recession, the differences among the four most stressful scenarios are not so significant that they can be easily separated. In fact, for the Dow Jones Index, 2008 Recession is the second least severe of the five scenarios. Hence we conclude that the Hypothetical, 2013 and 2013 scenarios have similar severity to 2008 Recession.

Table 12.5 Ranking of each macroeconomic variable and the total rank of the scenario and recession

Scenario	Real GDP		Unemployment Rate		Dow Jones		HPI		Total Rank
	Ave % Change	RANK	Ave % Change	RANK	Ave % Change	RANK	Ave % Change	RANK	
2011	0.2	1	9.7	1	-11.0	1	-6.88	1	4.0
2012	-4.0	3.5	32.4	2.5	-40.8	4	-12.2	2.5	12.5
2013	-3.5	3.5	38.5	4	-40.8	4	-12.2	2.5	14.0
Hypothetical	-4.3	3.5	32.2	2.5	-39.7	4	-15.7	4.5	14.5
08 Recession	-2.8	3.5	62.2	5	-25.4	2	-15.5	4.5	15.0

In all our discussion so far, we have assumed that all the directional variables are of the same importance, hence we have not assigned different weights when aggregating the ranks of each variable. However, we know different macroeconomic variables will affect different banking institutions. For example, banks with large credit-card portfolios are more sensitive to the unemployment rate; banks with large mortgage portfolios are more sensitive to house prices; and banks with large corporate portfolios are more sensitive to real GDP and equity indexes. In addition, the severity of the loss is related to the credit quality of the portfolio. Thus, the severity of the stress scenario also depends on the risk profile and the businesses of a bank. Based on the bank's experience, different weights can be assigned to different variables to emphasise the importance of certain variables.

PANEL 12.1 CASE STUDY: BANCO DE ESPAÑA STRESS SCENARIO

In this chapter, we have demonstrated the use of a simple method to assess the relative severity of a stress macroeconomic scenario. To illustrate how simple that methodology is, let us try to assess the severity of the stress-test exercise (Wyman 2012) that was conducted by Oliver Wyman in 2012 on behalf of the Banco de España. Page 83 of the report describes the adverse scenario with eight macroeconomic variables, and four of them, Real GDP, Unemployment Rate, Housing Prices and Madrid Stock Exchange Index, are similar to the variables we have studied. After aligning the starting values, the average percentage change over the two-year periods for the four variables are, Real GDP −5.1%, Unemployment Rate 19.9%, Madrid Stock Exchange Index −52.5% and Housing Prices −21.7%. Compared with the scenarios in Table 12.5, except for the Unemployment Rate, the other three variables are the most extreme among all the scenarios examined. If we use the ranking assignment as above, this adverse scenario is the most severe among all the six scenarios.

However, comparing the severity of these scenarios this way is not without problems. First, there is no reason to assume that the macroeconomic variables will affect the economies of Spain and the US in the same way. In addition, Spain's unemployment rate is already at 21.6% to begin with, and 21.6% is double what we saw in the 2008 recession. We can say Spain is already under an economic stress that we have not seen in the US since the Great Depression. Thus, we face additional challenges when comparing scenarios across different countries with different starting values on the macroeconomic variables.

OTHER METHODOLOGIES OF MEASURING SEVERITY

Our approach to assessing severity is entirely ordinal and so the relative ranks do not reflect anything about the magnitudes of the average percentage change, or the degree of severities. Ranking the scenarios will necessarily give some scenarios high rankings even if all the scenarios are quite mild, and some scenarios low rankings even if all the scenarios are quite severe. As we saw earlier, our approach is to give relative ranking to the scenarios under consideration. By comparing the scenarios with 2008 Recession, we have attempted to give the four scenarios a reference point besides comparing them with each other.

There have been other attempts to quantify the severity of stress scenarios. One of them is to determine the probability of occurrence of a stress (or worst) scenario. The general belief is that the less likelihood there is of an occurrence of a stress scenario, the more severe the stress scenario will be. In the 2009 SCAP exercise, in Footnotes 3 and 4 of Federal Reserve (2009b), the supervisors attempted to assign a probability of occurrence to the adverse scenario by claiming that "the likelihood that the average unemployment rate in 2010 could be at least as high as in the alternative more adverse scenario is roughly 10 percent. In addition, the subjective probability assessments... imply a roughly 15 percent chance that real GDP growth could be at least as low, and unemployment at least as high... [and] there is roughly a 10 percent probability that house prices will be 10 percent lower than in the baseline by 2010". Another example appears in an article on Economy.com in which Ed Friedman (2012) assigned probabilities to the Fed's 2013 CCAR scenarios. He first put the probability for each baseline scenario at around 50%. Then he claimed, "The Fed's Severely Adverse scenario is comparable to one that Moody's Analytics terms S4. We currently see a 4% chance that this scenario will occur. The Fed's Adverse scenario is more puzzling... we believe [it] has about a 10% chance of occurring." It seems to us that most of this assigning of probabilities is based on judgement rather than any empirical derivation.

Table 12.6 Score of each macroeconomic variable and the average score of the scenario and recession

Scenario	Real GDP		Unemployment Rate		Dow Jones		HPI		Average SCORE
	Ave % Change	SCORE	Ave % Change	SCORE	Ave % Change	SCORE	Ave % Change	SCORE	
2011	0.2	0	9.7	16	-11.0	43	-6.88	44	26
2012	-4.0	100	32.4	52	-40.8	100	-12.2	78	83
2013	-3.5	100	38.5	62	-40.8	100	-12.2	78	85
Hypothetical	-4.3	100	32.2	52	-39.7	100	-15.7	100	88
08 Recession	-2.8	100	62.2	100	-25.4	100	-15.5	100	100

One of the more interesting approaches to quantifying severity is proposed by two Federal Reserve Board economists, Rochelle Edge and Sam Rosen. Their simple approach (2012) is for each scenario, they will score the Average % Change of the common variables by assigning a value of 100 to the variable if the deterioration in the variable equals what occurred in 2008 Recession (most severe), and by assigning a value of 0 to the variable if the deterioration equals what occurred on the average in the two recessions (mild recessions) before 2008 Recession. Below, we use a modified version of their approach to illustrate how severity can be quantified.

For each common variable in 2008 Recession, we assign a score of 100 for the Average % Change, and 0 if the Average % Change is 0. In addition, we cap the score of each variable at 100 and assign a floor of 0. We then use a simple linear interpolation to convert each variable of a scenario into a score. For example, the Average % Change in UR in 2008 Recession is 62.3%, and in Scenario 2013 is 38.5%. Thus the score for 2008 Recession in UR is 100, and for Scenario 2013 is given by the following equation:

$$Score\_2013_{UR} = 100\left(1 + \frac{(38.5 - 62.2)}{62.2}\right) = 62 \qquad (12.4)$$

Table 12.6 gives the results of the scoring approach. Using 2008 Recession as a reference point, Scenario Hypothetical, 2013 and 2012 are very similar to and a bit less severe than the 2008 recession. The 2011 scenario is the mildest and its average score is quite different from the rest. Although our choices in this approach are sometimes arbitrary, nonetheless the approach is intuitive and informative, and gives a good sense of how the scenarios are compared.

So far, the approaches we have discussed do not assume any correlations among the four common macroeconomic variables. The overall assessment is made by summing each variable independently. A statistical approach proposed by Debashish Sarkar (2012) attempted to solve the major problems of the aggregating of information across different variables and across time. He suggested using the Mahalanobis distance to solve these problems with a set of weights. The distance, D, is defined by the following equation:

$$D = \sqrt{(x - \mu)' W^{-1} (x - \mu)} \qquad (12.5)$$

In the formula, X is a vector that stacks different variables in a scenario through time. The vector μ stacks the same variables for a reference scenario. The matrix W collects the weights. This approach is to construct W based on the variance–covariance matrix of the out-of-sample forecast errors. While the main challenge of this approach is that the distance measure is not directional, it is also very sensitive to the choice of W and the reference scenario. Sarkar's results showed that this approach is best used in conjunction with some other methods and is more efficient for identifying outlier/problem scenarios. Similarly, in a somewhat related paper, Breuer *et al* (2009) also suggested using the Mahalanobis distance to quantify the plausibility of a severe stress scenario.

Lastly, we mention another approach that aggregates the information in different macroeconomic variables through a simple forecasting framework. In their 2012 paper, Guerrieri and Welch (2012) derived several forecasting models to predict some key metrics that measure the "health" of a bank holding company. The key metrics that they wanted to forecast were: net charge-offs on loans and leases, pre-provision net revenue (PPNR), net interest margin (NIM) and the Tier 1 regulatory capital ratio. The forecast is based on a set of macroeconomic variables: Real GDP Growth, Unemployment Rate, the growth rate of the national house price index, the term spread, the growth rate of the S&P 500 index, the implied volatility of the S&P 500 index options, and the real interest rate. For each macroeconomic variable V_i and for each key banking metric, C, they used a simple (lag) regression that takes the form:

$$C_t = \alpha + \beta C_{t-1} + \gamma_1 V_{t-1}^i + \gamma_2 V_{t-2}^i + \gamma_3 V_{t-3}^i + \gamma_4 V_{t-4}^i + u_t$$

(12.6)

They used the Consolidated Reports of Condition and Income (Call Report) of the Federal Deposit Insurance Corporation to develop their forecasting models. By applying the historical information from the Call Report data and the changes in the macroeconomic variables in the stress scenarios to the forecasting models, we can obtain the forecast estimates of the key metrics. Consequently, we can then use the results, eg, average forecast charge-offs, to quantify the severity of the scenarios. The usefulness of this approach depends highly on the accuracy of the forecasting models, especially on the later forecasting quarters. However, Guerrieri and Welch found large root-mean-square errors for the forecasts of all the metrics, and their best-performing model did not beat a random walk at all horizons for forecasting pre-provision net income.

CONCLUSION

Our approach is based on examining the extremities of each of the directional variables, and adding up the extremities without considering the correlation and the timing of the macroeconomic variables. We have avoided trying to quantify the severity and used ordinal ranking to smooth out the "noises" of the variations. There is no error estimate in our assessment, nor do we give any confidence levels on our assessment: there is a danger of pseudo-accuracy when we try to find precision, and precision is difficult to define. It is exceptionally difficult to validate a model to assess the severity of a stress scenario. In the previous section, we mention that economy. com states that the 2013 Fed Severely Adverse scenario has a 4% chance that it will occur. The interesting question is why it is 4% and not 10%? The figure seems arbitrary. No one will dispute that the 2008 recession is the most stressful economic period since the Great Depression. Using the 2008 recession as a severe stress scenario, someone might say it is a 1-in-80-year event because it is the most severe recession for 80 years. However, if another recession as severe as or more severe than the 2008 recession happens in the next 10 years after 2008, then it reduces the occurrence of such a severe event to a 1-in-45-year event. Thus, it is quite difficult to quantify such a rare event with certainty because any occurrence of a similar event in the future will render the estimate to be inaccurate.

One of the principles of stress testing listed in the 2009 BIS (BIS BCBS 2009) paper is, "Stress tests should feature a range of severities, including events capable of generating the most damage whether through size of loss or through loss of reputation." The challenge is how to define an event that will generate the most damage to a bank. In their paper, Borio, Drehmann and Tsatsaronis (2012) concluded that "stress tests failed spectacularly when they were needed most: none of them helped to detect the vulnerabilities in the financial system ahead of the recent financial crisis". To improve the performance of macro stress tests, they suggested increasing the severity of the scenarios. The financial crisis of 2008 can be used as a starting point to gauge the severity of a bank's stress scenario. According to the above 2009 BIS paper, "prior to the (2008) crisis, however, banks generally applied only moderate scenarios, either in terms of severity or the degree of interaction across portfolios or risk types... Scenarios that were considered extreme or innovative were often regarded as implausible by the board and senior management."

Have the banks learned their lessons? Are they designing severe stress scenarios that will result in estimates of losses that show their vulnerabilities? In this chapter, we have suggested a simple way to answer these questions, and discussed alternate methodologies to answer the same questions. In many countries, banking regulators are requiring banks to perform stress testing on an annual basis. As more data is gathered from these exercises, it will enhance further research on this topic, and hopefully the macro stress tests will become a valuable tool in the banks' risk-management arsenal.

REFERENCES

BCBS, 2009, "Principles for sound stress testing practices and supervision", Basel Committee on Banking Supervision, May, available at: http://www.bis.org/publ/bcbs155.pdf.

Borio, Claudio, Mathias Drehmann and Kostas Tsatsaronis, 2012, "Stress-testing macro stress testing: does it live up to expectations?", January, Monetary and Economic Department, BIS Working Papers No. 369, available at: http://www.bis.org/publ/work369.pdf.

Breuer, Thomas, *et al*, 2009, "How to Find Plausible, Severe and Useful Stress Scenarios", *International Journal of Central Banking* 5(3), pp. 205–24.

Edge, Rochelle, and Sam Rosen, 2012, "Assessing the Severity of Macro Scenarios in CCAR", February 3, Federal Reserve System internal document (availability by direct request to authors).

Federal Reserve, 2009a, "The Supervisory Capital Assessment Program: Overview of Results", Board of Governors of the Federal Reserve System, May 7, available at: http://www.federalreserve.gov/newsevents/press/bcreg/bcreg20090507a1.pdf.

Federal Reserve, 2009b, "The Supervisory Capital Assessment Program: Design and Implementation", Board of Governors of the Federal Reserve System, April 24, available at: http://www.federalreserve.gov/bankinforeg/bcreg20090424a1.pdf.

Federal Reserve, 2011a, "Comprehensive Capital Analysis and Review: Objectives and Overview", Board of Governors of the Federal Reserve System, March 18, available at: http://www.federalreserve.gov/newsevents/press/bcreg/bcreg20110318a1.pdf.

Federal Reserve, 2011b, "Federal Reserve System, Capital Plan Review, Summary Instructions and Guidance", Board of Governors of the Federal Reserve System, November 22, available at: http://www.federalreserve.gov/newsevents/press/bcreg/bcreg20111122e1.pdf.

Federal Reserve, 2012, "2013 Supervisory Scenarios for Annual Stress Tests Required under the Dodd–Frank Act Stress Testing Rules and the Capital Plan Rule", Board of Governors of the Federal Reserve System, November 15, available at: http://www.federalreserve.gov/bankinforeg/bcreg20121115a1.pdf.

Friedman, Ed, "2012, Bank Stress Scenarios Reflect Fed's Risk Views", November 26, available at: http://www.economy.com/dismal/article_free.asp?cid=235707.

Guerrieri, Luca, and Michelle Welch, 2012, "Can Macro Variables Used in Stress Testing Forecast the Performance of Banks?", July 23, Finance and Economics Discussion Series, Federal Reserve Board, available at: http://www.federalreserve.gov/pubs/feds/2012/201249/201249pap.pdf.

Peristian, Stavros, Donald P. Morgan and Vanessa Savino, 2010, "The Information Value of the Stress Test and Bank Opacity", July, Federal Reserve Bank of New York, Staff Report No. 460.

Sarkar, Debashish, 2012, "Severity Scoring Models for Assessment of BHC Stress Scenarios", February 10, Federal Reserve Bank of New York internal document (availability by direct request to author).

Wyman, Oliver, 2012, "Asset Quality Review and Bottom-up Stress Test Exercise", September 28, available at: http://www.bde.es/f/webbde/SSICOM/20120928/informe_ow280912e.pdf.

1 In 2013, six US BHCs were subject to estimate trading losses: Bank of America Corp, Citigroup, Goldman Sachs, JPMorgan Chase, Morgan Stanley and Wells Fargo & Co.

2 Historical Data: 1976 through Second Quarter 2012--October 9, 2012 (Excel) - available for download at http://www.federalreserve.gov/bankinforeg/ccar.htm

3 See http://www.nber.org/cycles.html

4 The nine quarters from Q1 2008 to Q1 2010 are converted to Q3 2010 as the starting values.

Index

(page numbers in italic type refer to figures and tables)

A

Advanced Internal Ratings Based (AIRB) approach 89, 96–7
Akaike Information Criterion (AIC) 158
Asian consumer portfolios 152–4
  Korea's credit-card crisis and structural changes in the consumer market 154

B

Banco de España stress scenario 217
bank-loan portfolios as diagnostic tool 71–87
  model estimation 82–4
  scenario design 79–82
  and stress-test goals, defining and achieving 73–8
  practical objectives 77–8
  and stress-test limitations 74–7
bank models for loan losses and reserves 91
see also loan losses and reserves, stress-test modelling for
banks' corporate credit portfolios, stress-testing 109–25, *111*, *114*, *115*, *116*, *117*, *123*
  framework 113–21
    and aggregate default rate, linking GDP to 118–20
    "conversion" function: mapping aggregate default rate into latent credit index to generate stressed transition matrix 120–1
    data: Prudential Common Reporting 113–14
    data: S&P Transition Matrices 114–17
    forecasting default rate 119–20
  model specification 110–12, *111*
    correlation factor, estimation of 112
    general 111–12
  numerical application 122–4

    calculation of risk-weighted assets and capital requirements for credit risk 122–4
    and French large banks' corporate credit portfolio and evolution over time of exposures at default 122
Basel Final Rule 58–9, 60, 64, 67
board of directors 2–3
Brazil *150*
  banking system 165–70, *168*, *169*
    discussed 165–70
    financial crisis's effects on 170–80
    and Fundo Garantidor de Créditos (FGC) 177
    and liquidity risk 161–91, *171*, *172*, *173*, *174*, *175*, *176*, *178*, *179*, *180*, *184*, *185*, *187*, *188*
    and liquidity stress tests 180–8
business disruption, and operational risk 60

C

challenges to modelling operational risk 61–3
  see also operational risk: modelling
charge-off rates across loan types 101–2, *102*
Committee of European Banking Supervisors (CEBS) 127–8
common pitfalls in stress-testing counterparty credit risk 52–3
  see also counterparty credit-risk exposures, stress-testing of
Comprehensive Capital Analysis and Review (CCAR) xxxiii, 30, 72, 75–6, 79, 85, 90, 93, 193–6 *passim*, 218
Consolidated Reports of Condition and Income 221
"conversion" function: mapping aggregate default rate into latent credit index to generate stressed transition matrix 120–1

corporate credit portfolios, stress-testing of 109–25, *111*, *114*, *115*, *116*, *117*, *123*
framework 113–21
and aggregate default rate, linking GDP to 118–20
"conversion" function: mapping aggregate default rate into latent credit index to generate stressed transition matrix 120–1
data: Prudential Common Reporting 113–14
data: S&P Transition Matrices 114–17
forecasting default rate 119–20
model specification 110–12, *111*
correlation factor, estimation of 112
general 111–12
numerical application 122–4
calculation of risk-weighted assets and capital requirements for credit risk 122–4
and French large banks' corporate credit portfolio and evolution over time of exposures at default 122
counterparty credit-risk exposures, stress-testing of 37–54, *47*, *48*
common pitfalls 52–3
and credit valuation adjustment (CVA) 49–52
current exposure 41–4, *42*
evolution of management of 37–40
implications of 40–1
loan equivalent 44–9
management of 37–40
evolution 37–40
Counterparty Risk Management Policy Group 38
credit risk, stress testing for 27–9

D
data diagnostics and model specification 157–8
Dodd–Frank Wall Street Reform and Consumer Protection Act (2010) xxi, xxx, 17, 30, 72, 80, 90, 95, 194

E
Edge, Rochelle 220
European Banking Authority 30, 109

capital exercise launched by 141
and EU-wide stress test 127–42, *138–40*
key characteristics of 128–33
lessons learned from 135–7
results and disclosure 133–4, *134*
European Systemic Risk Board (ESRB) 127
external fraud, and operational risk 59

F
Federal Deposit Insurance Corporation to develop their forecasting models. By applying the historical information 221
Final Rule 59, 60, 64, 67
Final Supervisory Guidance 64
financial crisis (2007–9) 15, 23, 25, 26, 71, 89, 129, 165, 180
and Brazilian banking system 170–80, 177, 189; *see also* Brazil
and dependence structure 67
and European Banking Authority, establishment of 127
to gauge severity of stress scenario 223
impacts of extreme illiquidity highlighted by 28
and liquidity, importance of 182
Fundo Garantidor de Créditos (FGC) 177

G
governance:
over stress testing 1–14
capital and liquidity 13
coverage 11
internal audit 10–11
other key aspects of 11–13
policies, procedures and documentation 5–7
types and approaches 12
validation and independent review 7–10
structure of 2–5
board of directors 2–3
senior management 3–5
Greece 144

I
Iceland 144
independent review and validation 7–10
see also stress testing: governance over
internal audit, and stress testing 10–11;

see also stress testing: governance over internal fraud, and operational risk 59
international exposures and activities: stress testing across 143–60, *145, 150, 153*
   Asian consumer portfolios 152–4
   data challenges concerning 146–8
   estimation results 158–9
   and foreign regulatory actions, factoring in 151–2
   and idiosyncratic world 143–6
   and Korean credit cards and unsecured loans, estimating losses on 155–6
   and Korean credit cards and unsecured loans, independent variables 156
   and model specification, data diagnostics may alter 157–8
   retail portfolios 148–9, *153*
   structural breaks and dummy variables 155
   structural and cyclical issues 149–51
Ireland 144

K
Korea 154, 155–6

L
Liquidity Coverage Ratio (LCR) 163, 181
liquidity risk:
   and Brazilian banking system 161–91, *171, 172, 173, 174, 175, 176, 178, 179, 180, 184, 185, 187, 188*
   stress tests: central bank's approach to 180–2
   stress tests: individual banks' approaches to 182–8
loan losses and reserves, stress-test modelling for 89–108, *92*
   allowance for loan and lease loss models 91–3, *92*
   bank models 91
   economic modelling issues 103–5
     estimation 104–5
     specification 103–4
   loan-level loss models 96–102
     charge-off rates across loan types 101–2, *102*
     credit and behavioural scoring models with macroeconomic factors 97

credit migration analyses 97–8
migration matrices, variant on use of 101
   stylised retail transition matrix *98*
pool-level loss models 93–5
Long-Term Capital Management 38
loss-distribution approach 58–61, 63, 67
   stress-testing frequency distribution within 63–4
   stress-testing severity distribution within 64

M
macroeconomic stress scenarios:
   determining severity of 193–223, *197–8, 200–2, 204, 205, 206, 207, 208, 209, 210, 211, 212, 214, 216, 219*
   historical trend of 203–8
   nine-quarters projections 208–13
   other methodologies for 218–22
   overall assessment 213–17
   US supervisory 194–203, *197–8*
     aligning 196–203
market risk, stress testing for 25–36
   aggregation of results 28–9
   choice of scenarios 29–30
   and credit risk, distinction between 27–9
   and stressed scenarios, revaluations and computation of P&L under 32–4
     mark-to-market versus market-to-model valuations 32–3
     model failures, cross-effects, approximations, specific risk and use of proxies 34
     revaluations: in practice 33–4
     revaluations: sensitivity-based, grid-based or full 33
   time horizon in 30–2
   see also stress testing
migration matrices, variant on use of 101
model risk 68, 75
model specification, data diagnostics may alter 157–8

N
Net Stable Funding Ratio 163

O
operational risk:

and business disruption and system
  failures 60
and clients, products and business
  practices 60
and damage to physical assets 60
and employment practices and
  workplace safety 59
and execution, delivery and process
  management 60
and external fraud 59
and internal fraud 59
modelling 58–63
  challenges to 61–3
  loss-distribution approach 59–61
stress-testing approaches 63–8
  1-in-N-year event, converting
    macroeconomic scenario into
    66–7
  dependence structure 67–8
  frequency distribution within
    LDA 63–4
  model risk 68
  severity distribution within 64
  using scenarios 64–6
stress-testing methodologies
  concerning 57–70
  approaches to 63–8
  modelling 58–63
and workplace safety and
  employment practices 59

P
physical assets, damage to, and
  operational risk 60
policies, procedures and
  documentation 5–7
  see also stress testing: governance over

R
risk-management tools 15–24, *17*, *18*,
  19, *22*
  enterprise-wide stress testing 16–20
  simple example 17–20
Rosen, Sam 220
Russia 147

S
S&P CreditPro 114–17
scenarios, stress testing using 64–6
  see also stress testing
senior management 3–5
Spain, and stress scenario: case study 217
stress test, EU-wide (2011) 127–42, *138–40*
  key characteristics 128–33

lessons learned from 135–7
results and disclosure 133–4, *134*
  see also European Banking Authority
stress testing:
  across international exposures and
    activities 143–60, *145*, *150*, *153*
  Asian consumer portfolios 152–4
  data challenges concerning 146–8
  estimation results 158–9
  and foreign regulatory actions,
    factoring in 151–2
  and idiosyncratic world 143–6
  and Korean credit cards and
    unsecured loans, estimating
    losses on 155–6
  and Korean credit cards and
    unsecured loans, independent
    variables 156
  and model specification, data
    diagnostics may alter 157–8
  retail portfolios 148–9, *153*
  structural breaks and dummy
    variables 155
  structural and cyclical issues
    149–51
aggregation of results from 28–9
of bank-loan portfolios, as
  diagnostic tool 71–87
  model estimation 82–4
  scenario design 79–82
  and stress-test goals, defining
    and achieving 73–8
of banks' corporate credit portfolios
  109–25, *111*, *114*, *115*, *116*, *117*, *123*
  framework 113–21
  model specification 110–12
  numerical application 122–4
as class of tools xi
of counterparty exposures 37–54, *47*,
  48, *53*
  common pitfalls 52–3
  and credit valuation adjustment
    (CVA) 49–52
  and current exposure 41–4, *42*
  evolution of 37–40
  implications 40–1
  and loan equivalent 44–9
  management of 37–40
  for credit risk 27–9
credit valuation adjustment (CVA)
  49–52
goals of, defining and achieving 73–8
  practical objectives 77–8
  and stress-test limitations 74–7

governance over 1–14; *see also* governance
  capital and liquidity 13
  coverage 11
  internal audit 10–11
  other key aspects of 11–13
  policies, procedures and documentation 5–7
  structure 2–5
  types and approaches 12
  validation and independent review 7–10
liquidity, Brazil 180–8
  central bank's approach 180–2
  individual banks' approaches 182–8
many approaches to xxvi
for market risk 25–36
  aggregation of results 28–9
  choice of scenarios 29–30
  and credit risk, distinction between 27–9
  and stressed scenarios, revaluations and computation of P&L under 32–4
  time horizon in 30–2
methodologies, for operational risk 57–70
  approaches to 63–8
  modelling 58–63
modelling for loan losses and reserves 89–108, *92*
  allowance for loan and lease loss models 91–3, *92*
  bank models 91
  economic modelling issues 103–5
  loan-level loss models 96–102
  pool-level loss models 93–5
need for effectiveness in xxvi
and other risk-management tools 15–24, *17, 18, 19, 22*
  enterprise-wide stress testing 16–20
practical objectives for 77–8
scenarios, macroeconomic 193–223, *197–8, 200–2, 204, 205, 206, 207, 208, 209, 210, 211, 212, 214, 216, 219*
  historical trend of 203–8
  nine-quarters projections 208–13
  severity, other methodologies for measuring 218–22
  severity, overall assessment of 213–17
  US supervisory 194–203, *197–8*

Supervisory Capital Assessment Program (SCAP) 71, 79, 90, 193, 195, 218
"Supervisory Guidance on Stress Testing for Banking Organizations with More Than $10 Billion in Total Consolidated Assets" 72
system failures, and operational risk 60

U
US supervisory stress scenarios 194–203
  aligning 196–203
  see also macroeconomic stress scenarios

V
validation and independent review 7–10
  see also stress testing: governance over
value-at-risk:
  measures, stressed calibration of 20–2, *22*
  models, in stress tests 20

irrot   onal lift of wrist

EIKO&KOMA

Published by the Walker Art Center,
Minneapolis, and edited by Joan Rothfuss
on the occasion of Eiko & Koma's
Retrospective Project.

The publication is made possible by
a grant from the Andrew W. Mellon
Foundation in support of Walker Art
Center publications.

Inquiries should be addressed to:
Publications Director
Walker Art Center
1750 Hennepin Avenue
Minneapolis, MN 55403

Every reasonable attempt has been
made to identify owners of copyright.
Errors or omissions will be corrected
in subsequent editions.

Available through D.A.P./
Distributed Art Publishers
155 Sixth Avenue
New York, NY 10013
www.artbook.com

ISBN 978-0-935640-97-7

Design Director: Emmet Byrne
Designer: Andrea Hyde
Publications Director: Lisa Middag
Editors: Pamela Johnson and
Kathleen McLean
Imaging Specialist: Greg Beckel

Printed in the USA at
Shapco Printing, Inc.
Minneapolis, Minnesota

Typefaces: Arnhem Fine,
F Grotesk, Romana BT

Cover: *Tree Song*, July 2004
Pages 1–2: Forrest Gander, "Schematic,"
   2010
Pages 3–4: Preparing for a performance
   of *Trilogy*, circa 1979
   Photo: Kazunobu Yanagi
Pages 10–11: Study for *Naked*, May 2010
   Photo: Anna Lee Campbell

Library of Congress Cataloging-in-
Publication Data

Eiko & Koma : time is not even, space is
not empty / published by the Walker Art
Center, Minneapolis, and edited by Joan
Rothfuss on the occasion of Eiko & Koma's
retrospective project.—1st ed.
      p. cm.
   Includes bibliographical references
and index.
   ISBN 978-0-935640-97-7 (pbk.)
1. Eiko and Koma—Criticism and
interpretation. 2. Eiko and Koma—
Catalogs. 3. Otake, Eiko. 4. Otake,
Takashi Koma. 5. Dancers—Japan.
6. Choreographers—Japan. 7. Artists—
Japan. 8. Performance artists—Japan.
I. Rothfuss, Joan. II. Walker Art Center.
III. Title: Eiko and Koma.
   GV1785.A1E535 2011
   792.80280922–dc22
   [B]
                              2011013530

Edited by Joan Rothfuss with texts
by Suzanne Carbonneau, André Lepecki,
Doryun Chong, Philip Bither, Sam Miller,
and Peter Taub

TIME IS
NOT
EVEN
SPACE IS
NOT
EMPTY

EIKO & KOMA

WALKER
ART
CENTER

TEXTS

14
FOREWORD
Olga Viso

18
NAKED: EIKO & KOMA IN ART & LIFE
Suzanne Carbonneau

48
RECIPROCAL TOPOGRAPHIES—EIKO & KOMA'S DANCESCULPTURES
André Lepecki

56
EVEN A DOG THAT WANDERS WILL FIND A BONE
Doryun Chong

72
WHERE TIME IS RELATIVE: EIKO & KOMA AT THE WALKER ART CENTER
Philip Bither

87
REVIEW: WHITE DANCE IN AMSTERDAM
Jan Willem Hofstra

88
REVIEW: WHITE DANCE: MOTH IN NEW YORK
Deborah Jowitt

105
EIKO & KOMA: THE STAGE AS A CUTTING BOARD
Irene Oppenheim

138
REVIEW: THIRST AND TREE IN TOKYO
Miyabi Ichikawa

145
LAMENT: FROM STAGE TO SCREEN
Dean Otto

208
BE WITH: COLLABORATION AS PROCESS
Anna Halprin

224
THE LIFE BEHIND DEATH POEM
Catharine R. Stimpson

233
REVIEW: CAMBODIAN STORIES IN LOS ANGELES
Daisuke Mutoh

255
EIKO + KOMA + KRONOS
David Harrington

260
DRIFTING ON MELODY SMOKE /A FLOWER OPENING TO THE MOON
Jan Henle

270
COLLABORATING WITH EIKO & KOMA
Philip Trager

282
THE LIMITS OF LANGUAGE
Sam Miller

290
AFTERWORD
Peter Taub

292
CONTRIBUTORS

292
SELECTED BIBLIOGRAPHY

293
APPENDIX A: FUNDERS AND COMMISSIONERS

296
APPENDIX B: OTHER PROJECTS

297
APPENDIX C: PERFORMANCE PRESENTERS

300
REPRODUCTION CREDITS

300
WALKER BOARD OF TRUSTEES

301
INDEX

1, 12, 16, 44, 54, 80, 256, 280, 288, 304
SCHEMATIC
Forrest Gander

WORKS

84
WHITE DANCE
ホワイトダンス

89
**WHITE DANCE:
MOTH**
ホワイトダンス　蛾

94
FUR SEAL
オットセイ

97
**BEFORE THE COCK
CROWS**
鶏が鳴く前に

100
**FLUTTERING
BLACK**
はためく黒

107
EVENT FISSION
分裂

110
TRILOGY
三部作

113
NURSE'S SONG
乳母の歌

116
GRAIN
穀物

119
BEAM
梁

122
TENTACLE
触手

125
NIGHT TIDE
夜の潮

128
WALLOW
這う

131
ELEGY
悲歌

134
BONE DREAM
骨の夢

139
THIRST
渇き

142
LAMENT
哀歌

147
BY THE RIVER
川辺で

150
SHADOW
影

151
HUSK
殻

154
UNDERTOW
引き波

157
TREE
樹

160
CANAL
水路

163
RUST
錆

166
MEMORY
記憶

169
PASSAGE
道

172
LAND
大地

175
WIND
風

178
DISTANT
遠い

178
ECHO
木魂

179
RIVER
川

184
RIVER (indoor version)
川（舞台作品）

187
PULSE
脈拍

190
BREATH
息

193
THE CARAVAN PROJECT
路上劇場

199
SNOW
雪

201
BREATH (video)
息

204
WHEN NIGHTS WERE DARK
夜が暗かった時

209
BE WITH
共に

212
OFFERING
供養

217
TREE SONG
樹の詩（うた）

220
DUET
二人で

225
DEATH POEM
死の歌

230
CAMBODIAN STORIES: AN OFFERING OF PAINTING AND DANCE
カンボジア物語：絵と踊りの供養

235
CAMBODIAN STORIES REVISITED
再びカンボジア物語

238
QUARTET
四人で

241
MOURNING
哀悼

244
HUNGER
飢え

247
RAVEN
大鴉

250
NAKED
裸

^{2} breathing through

skin, blow arms out

FOREWORD

Olga Viso

Over the course of their forty-year collaboration, Eiko & Koma have created a body of work that is like nothing else in contemporary art. Primal, intense, and powerfully moving, their pieces explore elemental themes such as birth, death, desire, struggle, and the profound connection between the human and natural realms. They have been acclaimed and embraced by the American dance community since their arrival in the United States in 1976. Yet Eiko & Koma do not consider themselves dancers in any traditional sense. Rather, they think of themselves as artists whose medium is movement and whose work resides in the spaces between dance, theater, performance art, and sculpture. This is why throughout their US careers they have frequently been invited to present their highly individual art form in arenas outside conventional dance venues and stages, often in the public areas of educational and cultural institutions, and in museums and multidisciplinary art centers such as the Walker Art Center.

The Walker has been fortunate to enjoy a long and fruitful history with the artists. Our thirty-year relationship has involved five successive performing arts curators and includes eleven different engagements and six commissions for new works, most recently *Naked*, a "living installation" in which the artists collaborated with the institution's curatorial departments of visual and performing arts to create a durational presentation in the museum galleries that lasted an entire month. The Walker's commission of *Naked* marks the second time that Eiko & Koma have presented their mesmerizing live installations within the context of galleries rather than in public communal and presentation spaces. The Walker is thus pleased to join the Whitney Museum of American Art (which presented the artists' first living installation, *Breath*, in 1998) in recognizing and affirming their significance beyond the world of dance and within the broader realm of contemporary visual arts.

Naked is but one component of the artists' extensive three-year Retrospective Project. Begun in 2009, it uses the visual arts model of the retrospective exhibition to both document their past and reveal ways for them to move and evolve into the future. Among the project's components are the creation of new work, revivals and reconstructions of previous pieces, exhibitions, a revamped website, and this volume. *Eiko & Koma: Time Is Not Even, Space Is Not Empty*, the first book devoted to the artists' work, is a comprehensive examination of their life and art. At the heart of the publication is a catalogue raisonné: a complete, illustrated listing of Eiko & Koma's movement and video works written by Joan Rothfuss. Several critical essays explore and analyze their opus. Suzanne Carbonneau provides an elegant and meticulously researched overview of the artists' careers. André Lepecki examines the sculptural qualities of Eiko & Koma's work; Philip Bither looks at the Walker's long history with the artists; Doryun Chong explores their early years in a hybrid interview/essay; and Peter Taub provides an afterword. Anna Halprin, David Harrington, Irene Oppenheim, Dean Otto, and Catharine R. Stimpson have written personal responses to specific pieces. Poet Forrest Gander and artists Jan Henle and Philip Trager all have made submissions to this volume that were inspired by their collaborative friendships with Eiko & Koma. The book is greatly enriched by all their contributions.

We are incredibly grateful to the Andrew W. Mellon Foundation for its generous support of this catalogue. It is also our great pleasure to acknowledge the many presenters and funding partners in the appendices of this book. As we mark this moment in Eiko & Koma's career, it is inspiring to reflect on the numerous individuals, foundations, government agencies, and institutions that have championed their work from the early 1970s to the present. Several foundations in particular have provided major support at critical junctures in that career. A John D. and Catherine T. MacArthur Foundation Fellowship (1996–2001) and awards from the Andrew W. Mellon Foundation (1998–2009, plus special Mellon support for the Retrospective Project, (2009–2012) have for the past fifteen years made it possible for the artists to make the works they envisioned. Most recently, a grant from the Andy Warhol Foundation for the Visual Arts has made it possible for Eiko & Koma to continue their exploration of museum and gallery spaces.

This catalogue—and the Retrospective Project as a whole—were the result of many conversations between Eiko & Koma and their longtime friend Sam Miller, a well-known figure in the dance world who is currently president of the Lower Manhattan Cultural Council in New York City. Miller is passionate about the need to creatively document and preserve the work of performing artists. As producer of the Retrospective Project and author of an essay written for this volume, Miller deserves our special thanks. We also must acknowledge the Retrospective Project's still-growing roster of institutional partners: the American Dance Festival, Asia Society, the Baryshnikov Arts Center, Brown University, Danspace Project, the Dublin Dance Festival, Japan Society, the Lincoln Center Out of Doors Festival, the Lower Manhattan Cultural Council, the Museum of Contemporary Art Chicago, the New York Public Library for the Performing Arts, Park Avenue Armory, the University of Maryland, Wesleyan University, and Yerba Buena Center for the Arts.

At the Walker, many people made essential contributions to *Time Is Not Even, Space Is Not Empty*. Chief curator Darsie Alexander's focus on advancing ambitious cross-disciplinary collaborations between artists, staff curators, and outside partners inspired the Walker's deep commitment to realizing this unprecedented project. Her desire to foster new scholarship on the relationship between dance and the visual arts continues a mission advanced by publications director Lisa Middag, chief of communications and audience engagement Andrew Blauvelt, and performing arts senior curator Philip Bither, all of whom led an equally inspired and enthusiastic charge to make this catalogue a reality. The Walker's publication project team included independent curator and educator Joan Rothfuss, who ably served as managing editor, researcher, and writer, bringing her distinct and graceful voice to the project and working closely with the artists and their staff; designer Andrea Hyde, who found an elegant way graphically to capture the dynamism and impermanence of dance; design director Emmet Byrne; editors Pamela Johnson and Kathleen McLean; senior imaging specialist Greg Beckel; performing arts coordinator Emily Taylor; special projects interns Jesse Leaneagh and Ella Reily-Stocker; and archivist Jill Vuchetich. Thanks also are due to Eiko & Koma's longtime manager, Ivan Sygoda, and their assistant, Lydia Bell, who did so much of the research for this volume.

Countless other Walker staff members participated in realizing *Naked*. Performing arts associate curator Doug Benidt and visual arts assistant curator Bartholomew Ryan adroitly, and with great humility and humor, modeled healthy cross-departmental discourse and understanding with each other and amid myriad collaborating departments across the institution. All labored collectively to support Eiko & Koma in realizing to their fullest potential their artistic aims and ideal engagement with our audiences.

At the center of everything were, of course, Eiko & Koma, whose immense integrity, clarity of purpose and vision, and staggering physical and emotional commitment inspired individual and communal support at every level within and outside the institution, leading to surprising discoveries and insights about the ways we work together internally and understand our relationships within our physical spaces and with our audiences. Their extreme generosity of spirit pervaded every aspect of their engagement, leaving an indelible mark at the Walker and in our community that will continue to reverberate and inspire us for many years to come.

^{3} arrow stage right,

sucking air

Study for *Naked*, Park Avenue Armory, New York City, September 2010   Photo: Anna Lee Campbell

NAKED: EIKO & KOMA IN ART & LIFE

Suzanne Carbonneau

1

John Berger, *Ways of Seeing* (London: Penguin, 1990), 54.

2

I am indebted to Theodore Bale for conversation on this subject.

3

When guiding improvisations in their Delicious Movement Workshops and discussing their work, Koma often says that "the body loves to move." Eiko's way of saying the same thing is "it is only a dead person who doesn't move." Eiko & Koma, interview with the author, New York City, July 18, 2010. For more information about these workshops, see http://www.eikoandkoma.org.

4

See Yuriko Saito, "The Japanese Aesthetics of Imperfection and Insufficiency," *Journal of Aesthetics and Art Criticism* 55 (autumn 1997): 377–385.

5

Eiko explains that she does not even "desire superb physicality, but I only wish to present a fragile, silent body that is also a landscape." Eiko Otake, *From Trinity to Trinity: Hayashi Kyoko Writes in Sustained Mourning* (MA thesis, Gallatin School of Individualized Study, New York University, 2007), 97.

In naming the Walker Art Center installation created for their three-year Retrospective Project, Eiko & Koma chose a single word: *Naked*. But the title is not meant to be provocative. Their nakedness is different in character from that usually seen on the stage in contemporary dance, where highly toned bodies invite a regard of what might be better termed "nudity." In contrast, Eiko & Koma's nakedness seems prelapsarian, unmindful of tempting devil or disapproving god. As in John Berger's famous formulation— "Nakedness reveals itself. Nudity is placed on display."[1]—they are indeed naked, without guile or shame, innocent of our observation.

Nakedness is also metaphor for unquenchable desire, the central conceit of Eiko & Koma's work.[2] In their choreography, all creatures want: food, water, shelter, sex, companionship, affection, knowledge. But the artists do not condemn desire. They embrace it as life force, as animal appetite, and as existential quest, expressed through the body.[3] This, they insist, is the engine of existence.

To embody this epic subject, they have developed a technique of prodigious duration. Time is both the content and form of their work, which is performed at a pace suggestive of geologic scale. Events seem to take place over lifetimes, eras, eons. In their choreography, time is at once undifferentiated (a stream of movements that stretch to infinitude) and precisely marked (each microsecond lucidly experienced). Always, their performances evoke a continuous act of becoming.

Nakedness indicates a raw aesthetic, and Eiko & Koma's dances leave the impression that nothing is too polished. As in traditional Japanese workmanship, however, this is a deliberately cultivated illusion. Their stagecraft is impeccable and arrived at arduously. A key element in their work is the concept of "insufficiency,"[4] the inverse of the Platonic perfection prized in the Western classical tradition. The aesthetic of insufficiency indicates the underlying nature of matter: everything is subject to age, wear, and decay.[5] And in this honest assessment of the world, Eiko & Koma find a bittersweet beauty.

They are the rarest of artists—inventors of a form that is virtually sui generis. Over a lifetime together, they have perfected a mode of art that is so singular as to be without direct ancestry or progeny. Fiercely independent by temperament and ideology, they have never been disciples, nor do they aspire to have disciples. Their inspiration has not come from the work or theories of other choreographers. Nor is their work allied with the zeitgeist. The hipster stance is unknown to them, conceptualism of no interest, the barrier between art and life firmly fixed, and the line between art and popular culture impregnable. In an artistic environment steeped in irony and cool, Eiko & Koma wear their sincerity with pride and are serious in their belief that art should strive for profundity. Theirs is a highly refined and cultivated sensibility, designed for the contemplation of the most profound existential questions. No matter where the art world has gone in search of novelty and relevance during their artistic life together, they have remained on their steady course, tacking against the winds of fashion.

Eiko & Koma's independence was nurtured in the countercultural uprisings of the 1960s and 1970s. They began their adult lives as radical political activists, and the values to which they pledged fealty as students have continued to guide their lives and their work as artists. They call their aesthetic "Poor Art,"[6] a variation on the late Polish director Jerzy Grotowski's Poor Theater, which rejected spectacle in favor of an intimate act of mental and physical openness. It has never been their goal to follow a career trajectory that defines success by the prestige of the venue in which they perform, and since 1995, Eiko & Koma have devised strategies for performing in public, free of charge, for anyone who happens upon them.

Out of their political convictions also came what they dub their aesthetic of "unreasonableness," a rejection of social conventions, orthodoxies, and rationalism in favor of the mindful cultivation of personal values. Their work invites audiences to make discoveries about their place in the universe, outside of the shibboleths offered by consumerism, corporate culture, organized religion, or conformist thinking. Resisting the conceptual trends in contemporary art, they have held fast to the lyrical and transcendental nature of the embodied art experience. Their dances are unabashedly centered in feelings. And while they are avowed atheists, Eiko & Koma create choreography of undeniable spiritual presence. As Eiko would have it, art is "a window through which you sense that another complete life ... exists right by you. That world extends both geographically and timewise, and it is there with you and without you.... Art is a corridor between the two worlds."[7]

While Eiko & Koma are singular artists, theirs is a conjoined singularity. When they began their partnership in 1971, they never intended it to be a lasting artistic association. But the alliance proved unexpectedly fecund, their joint exploration leading them ever more deeply into discoveries—aesthetic and philosophical— that seemed worth pursuing, and forty years on, they continue to find satisfaction in movement as an existential language. Theirs is a union of equals, rooted in a politics that rejects hierarchies. No other collaborative duo in the history of Western theatrical dance has worked together so constantly, so assiduously, so productively. Koma is the more visual person, Eiko the more conceptual. But they are remarkably like-minded, often finishing each other's sentences, and in the end, their work is created in consonance. Their admiration for each other is still unmistakable after all these years.

6
All biographical information was obtained from Eiko & Koma in interviews conducted by the author: Burlington, VT, May 29, 2009; New York City, March 21, 2010; Durham, NC, June 24 and 29, 2010; New York City, July 17 and 18, 2010. Artists' quotes throughout the essay are taken from the same sources.

7
Eiko Otake, *From Trinity to Trinity* (MA thesis), 71.

Koma (born Takashi Koma Yamada) grew up impoverished in Niigata on Japan's northwestern coast. In 1947, the year before Koma was born, Nobel laureate Yasunari Kawabata published his classic novel *Snow Country* (*Yukiguni*), which immortalized the isolation of Niigata Prefecture, the snowiest place on Earth at this latitude.[8] At times, the snow accumulated to such heights that Koma remembers having to exit the family home from a second-story window. Winters were dark and hushed, and life seemed "divorced from time through the long snowbound months."[9] Although it was a provincial capital, Niigata was not industrialized: the smells of the countryside permeated its low buildings and canals flowed through the city, with rice paddies hemming the outskirts. Koma's childhood spent outdoors in the harsh climate would instill in him the deep feeling for untamed nature that shaped his adult art, made in a foreign city halfway around the world.

In World War II, Koma's father was drafted into Japan's doomed cause. When the battleship on which he served was sunk, he was one of a handful of survivors who spent harrowing days in the ocean awaiting rescue. Koma believes that his father never recovered from the ordeal, sadly observing that "when he surfaced, he left most of his spirit under the water." When Koma was very young, his parents separated and they split their two children between them. Koma lived with his mother, and he remembers spending only a scant few days with his father and younger brother thereafter.

Niigata faces the Sea of Japan, the coastline the Japanese refer to as the "backside" of the country. When Koma was growing up there, the city was seven hours by steam train from Tokyo. But the distance was not only geographic. Eastern Japanese, who faced the open Pacific, considered Niigata to be hopelessly provincial and backward. Even those ambitious backsiders determined to escape to the "front side" realized upon reaching Tokyo that they were marked as rustics by their dialect, slow speech, and lack of cultural sophistication. Arriving at Waseda University in Tokyo in 1969 to study political science, this is exactly the position in which Koma found himself.

Eiko Otake could not have had a more different upbringing. Born in 1952 during the last year of the American occupation, she was a solidly middle-class Tokyo frontsider, the beloved only child of a banker and a homemaker. The family was extraordinarily cultured and Eiko was sent to modern dance classes in early childhood. She was not athletic and dance proved an awkward fit, so she took up piano study for nine years. But her real love was books. She read incessantly and intended to be a writer.

Eiko's parents aspired to the mainstream, settling for the "small happiness" of economic stability in postwar Japanese life. But beneath this veneer was a nonconformist family background. Her father's family were artists; her grandfather a well-known and politically inclined painter who associated with anarchists and early feminists. Both grandmothers were geishas, her maternal grandmother the proprietor of a geisha house; Eiko played with geishas

8
Yasunari Kawabata, *Snow Country*, trans. Edward G. Seidensticker (New York: Vintage International, 1996). See also Kawabata's exquisite 1972 distillation, "Gleanings from Snow Country," *Palm-of-the-Hand Stories*, trans. J. Martin Holman (New York: Farrar, Straus & Giroux, 1988), 247–259.

9
Edward G. Seidensticker, Introduction, Kawabata, *Snow Country*, vi.

Furumachi, Niigata, 1956

Trolley car station, Shibuya, Tokyo, circa 1955
Photo: Orlando/*Three Lions*
Courtesy Hulton Archive/Getty Images

and saw them dance from earliest childhood. And even though he worked in a bank, Eiko's father was also a committed communist and union organizer. The Otakes lived in a culturally vibrant area of downtown Tokyo, a good fit for their bohemianism.

As was Koma's father, Eiko's family also was scarred by the war. Her mother witnessed the incineration of her family home during the infamous American firebombing of Tokyo in March 1945. She and Eiko's father were married amid the ruins of central Tokyo that August, during the same week that atomic bombs destroyed Hiroshima and Nagasaki, and just five days before the Japanese surrendered. And while Eiko's father had been able to falsify his way out of foreign military service, her father's brother had spent much of the war fighting on the Chinese front and years thereafter as a prisoner in Siberia. Her uncle's heart-rending stories of his experiences as a P.O.W. seized Eiko's imagination.

Eiko's father was transferred frequently, and when she was seven, the family found itself in rural Tochigi Prefecture in central Japan, where they would live until she was a teenager. As the Otakes moved from town to town in Tochigi, Eiko attended six different grade schools in as many years. Though she would remain culturally urban, Eiko absorbed a feeling for the farms and fields of the countryside where she rambled until her father was posted back to Tokyo. As a child caught between two worlds, she felt a "stranger" both in Tochigi and Tokyo, an experience that prepared her for an adulthood as an immigrant who would never truly assimilate in her adopted country.

Despite their radically different childhoods, both Eiko and Koma were swept up in the political upheaval gripping Japan as they came of age in the 1960s. Although pacifism had been enshrined in the postwar Japanese constitution and ingrained in her citizens by the horror of the atomic bombings, postwar treaties secured Japanese soil as the staging area for America's Cold War incursions in Korea and Vietnam. Japan had erupted in demonstrations against renewing military compacts with the United States in 1960, and the protests continued through the decade as Japan regained its national self-confidence in the wake of historically unprecedented economic growth. But the boom engendered by Japan's embrace of Western-style capitalism was accompanied by industrial pollution, the manufacture of dangerously defective products, and runaway development. In concert with anti–Vietnam War and countercultural movements worldwide, Japanese students took to the streets in force in the late 1960s, their protests a stew of anti-Americanism, antimilitarism, and anti-industrialization.

When Koma entered Waseda University in 1967 to begin his studies, he was swept into the conflict as, he says, a committed "soldier in the people's army," and finally dropped out of university in his junior year in protest against the system. Living out his beliefs, he became a day laborer in the infamous slums of Kamagasaki and Sanya, hotbeds of sedition whose impoverished squalor rivaled the back alleys of Dickensian London.

Eiko on board a ship bound for the USSR, October 1972
Photo: Eiichi Otake

10
Novelist and essayist Ango Sakaguchi
was famous for his postwar essays on
"decadence" (*daraku*). He was critical of
the national illusions of samurai spirit
(*bushido*), on which Japanese militarism
and emperor worship had been based.
He was equally critical of the postwar
embrace of American values. Sakaguchi's
solution was to embrace *daraku*—that is,
to fall away from social and cultural norms
and instead develop a personal ethos.
Like Koma, Sakaguchi was a native of
Niigata, whose culture he deemed equally
worthy to the supposed sophistication
and refinement of Tokyo. See John W.
Dower, *Embracing Defeat: Japan in the
Wake of World War II* (New York: W. W.
Norton, 1999), 155–157.

11
Michiko Ishimure is known as the
"Rachel Carson of Japan." See Brian
Allen, Translator's Introduction, in
Michiko Ishimure, *Lake of Heaven: An
Original Translation of the Japanese
Novel* (Lanham, MD: Lexington Books,
2008), ix.

12
For information on butoh, see Kazuo
Ohno and Yoshito Ohno, *Kazuo Ohno's
World from Without and Within*, trans.
John Barrett (Middletown, CT: Wesleyan
University Press, 2004); Sondra
Fraleigh and Tamah Nakamura, *Hijikata
Tatsumi and Ohno Kazuo* (New York:
Routledge, 2006); and Sondra Horton
Fraleigh, *Dancing into Darkness: Butoh,
Zen, and Japan* (Pittsburgh: University
of Pittsburgh Press, 1999).

From a young age, Eiko was also deeply embedded in the movement, constructing barricades and leading the first strike by a high school in the nation. In 1970, she was accepted for study at Chuo University as one of the few women in its male-dominated law department. Like Koma, Eiko planned to study political science, but she too dropped out after only a single semester. In Japan, leaving school before graduation is an irrevocable step, but both felt keenly the hypocrisy of preparing to take part in the system they had committed to overturn. And these were heady times. In the exhilarating drama being played out in the streets of Tokyo, social revolution seemed tantalizingly possible. Even as Eiko and Koma were leaving university, however, the movement began to devolve. Rocked by ideological differences, it factionalized into splinter groups, which turned against each other with virulence. In despair, they both withdrew from the fray.

Set adrift, each of them turned to Tokyo's underground culture, haunting art venues and watching films by avant-garde directors such as Jean-Luc Godard, Sergei Eisenstein, and Nagisa Oshima. Both became enamored of the Japanese postwar "broken" writers, who suggested that it was luck rather than virtue that ensured survival. They shared Ango Sakaguchi's loss of faith in dogma and institutions, as well as his condemnation of postwar consumerism.[10] They also found inspiration in Nobel laureate Kenzaburo Oe's pacifism, existentialism, and nonconformism, and in novelist Kazumi Takahashi's *Ideology of Desolate Solitude* (*Koritsu muen no shisou*). As a conduit of victims' voices, environmental activist Michiko Ishimure profoundly influenced their political and artistic vision.[11]

Stumbling across a butoh performance by Tatsumi Hijikata's dance company, a sensation in the Tokyo artistic underground, Eiko was astounded, especially by the women who allowed themselves to look "strange and even ugly." Unable to shake this image, she decided to investigate Hijikata's classes. It was here that Eiko met Koma, a fellow refugee from the student movement who had arrived three months previously. At Hijikata's workshop, they decided to team as partners.

Butoh and German Expressionism

A potent form of Japanese expressionist dance, butoh emerged in concert with the burgeoning postwar Japanese avant-garde arts scene.[12] Its tenets mirrored the anarchism, antirationalism, anticonsumerism, and anti-industrialism of the political mobilization. In its early forms, butoh embraced as sources the Western artistic movements—Fluxus, surrealism, existentialism, Dadaism—then pervading the Tokyo underground.

Hijikata was a cofounder of butoh, which he would come to envision as a kind of backcountry kabuki. While he meant to create a self-consciously Japanese style of dance, he was deeply influenced by the Western avant-garde and the Theater of the Absurd, especially the work of writers Samuel Beckett and Jean Genet. Hijikata was also enamored of French playwright and director Antonin

Kazuo Ohno (left) and Tatsumi Hijikata, *Admiring La Argentina*, Dai-ichi Seimei Hall, Tokyo, 1977   Photo ©1977 Naoya Ikegami

Artaud, who embraced the grotesque as a stance against social conformity. He incorporated Artaud's theories in his *Rebellion of the Body* (1968), which defined his own voice as central to the Japanese avant-garde. In acknowledgment of the grim tenor of his work, Hijikata's butoh became known as *ankoku butoh* (dance of utter darkness).

He was joined in cofounding butoh by Kazuo Ohno, and the two men had a profound mutual impact. But where Hijikata was consumed with death, struggle, and sacrifice, Ohno emphasized memory of the womb and the female generative experience. Both artists had studied with Japanese teachers trained in German modern dance, known as Neue Tanz or Ausdruckstanz (sometimes called "Poison Dance" in Japan because of its grotesque gestures and expressive extremes).[13] Neue Tanz was integral to German Expressionism, an artistic movement engaged with emergent psychology and the violent distortion of form in order to achieve penetrating emotional effects. Developed by Rudolf Laban and Mary Wigman in the first quarter of the twentieth century, this style became the dominant form of modern dance in prewar Japan.

Western Europe

Steeped in the antiauthoritarianism of the student movement, neither Eiko nor Koma was looking to be Hijikata's disciple. Koma was increasingly at odds with Hijikata, and both he and Eiko chafed at the autocratic atmosphere of the studio. Just three months after her arrival, Koma suggested to Eiko that they quit Hijikata's workshop. Eiko agreed not only to leave the studio with Koma, but to leave Japan altogether.

At the time, Eiko and Koma were not set on establishing a creative partnership. They simply decided that their goal of seeing the world outside of Japan would be more easily accomplished together. The first order of business was to find work and save enough money to travel. They had danced in the nightclub shows that Hijikata organized to subsidize his studio, and they decided that they could devise their own cabaret act to raise funds. Under the name *Night Shockers*, Eiko and Koma performed their show dances throughout Japan, earning the money they needed for travel in less than a year. In their off hours, they also began to attend Ohno's classes. In Ohno, they found a teacher more consonant with their ideas. Hijikata had taught choreographed movement phrases, but Ohno encouraged them to develop their own voices through guided improvisation. After the violent implosion of the student movement, they found Ohno's tenderness and thoughtfulness a tonic. In a remembrance she wrote thirty-five years later, Eiko noted that Ohno was "most serious about being a playful artist." She called him "a beautiful, crazy flower."[14]

Upon leaving Japan in 1972, Eiko and Koma divested themselves of everything—even their family names—save for three books with particular conceptual and emotional resonance for the journey: Motokiyo Zeami's *Kadensho*, a fifteenth-century aesthetic treatise on Noh theater; Van Gogh's letters to his brother Theo,

13
Fraleigh and Nakamura, *Hijikata Tatsumi and Ohno Kazuo*, 2.

14
Eiko Otake, "A Crazy Flower: Kazuo Ohno (1906–2010)." An edited version of this remembrance appeared as "Kazuo Ohno (1906–2010)" in *Dance Magazine* 84 (September 2010): 67. Ohno had been inspired to begin dancing as a young man when he saw flamenco dancer La Argentina (Antonia Mercé y Luque) perform in Tokyo. In 1976, Eiko & Koma found photographs of La Argentina in the collection of the New York Performing Arts Library and sent them to Ohno. The resulting work by Ohno, *Admiring La Argentina* (1976), revived his career after a decade-long absence from the stage. It became his signature dance, sparking his international career, which flourished well into his nineties. See Ohno & Ohno, *Kazuo Ohno's World from Without and Within*, 143–169; and Fraleigh and Nakamura, *Hijikata Tatsumi and Ohno Kazuo*, 90–94.

First performance of original work, Waseda University, Tokyo, 1972

15
The use of an ampersand with Eiko and Koma's names indicates their artistic partnership, which began when they left Japan for Europe in 1972.

16
About this same time, Japanese choreographer Kei Takei was embarking on the cycle of dances she called simply *Light*.

Mary Wigman (left) and Manja Chmiel

which traced the artist's unlikely development into a creative genius; and the diary of Vaslav Nijinsky, which charted his Tolstoyan mysticism and descent into schizophrenia.

In homage to Nijinsky, Eiko & Koma[15] traveled by train from Siberia to Moscow, where they boarded a plane for western Europe. With the idea that they would support themselves by performing, they booked a theater in Munich for a month. They still were not thinking seriously about dance as a lifelong pursuit. Performing was, rather, a strategy for discovering the world. The dances they presented in Europe were loosely structured "events," concocted from what they had learned from Hijikata and Ohno, and from their own improvisational explorations—often with foodstuffs as props. In deliberate opposition to the "dance of utter darkness" they had studied in Japan, these events were all called *White Dance*.[16] In the style of traditional Japanese performers, they painted their faces and bodies with white rice powder. Embracing whiteness as an antidote to the black uniforms of anarchism they had worn in the student movement, they meant whiteness to signal their decision to leave their pasts behind in order to create anew. In *White Dance*, "feeling was everything."

Eiko & Koma had intended to study with Ohno's forebear, Mary Wigman, but she wrote to them that she was too ill to teach. Traveling to Hannover, they sought out Manja Chmiel, a distinguished solo performer who had served as Wigman's choreographic and teaching assistant for decades. Their first female teacher, Chmiel took the pair "into her arms." She found them a place to live and arranged for them to take ballet class every morning at the opera house in Hannover. (It was the only experience they would ever have with classical technique.) Chmiel recognized the value of Eiko & Koma's choreographic singularity and wisely left them to their own aesthetic and ethos, but she encouraged them to train their bodies for expansion and lift so that they could transmit movement on a larger scale. Always seekers rather than disciples, they found this an ideal training situation.

Without informing Eiko & Koma, Chmiel applied on their behalf for the 1973 Young Choreographers' Competition in Cologne, whose head juror was Kurt Jooss. Among the three finalists chosen to perform at the Cologne Opera, Eiko & Koma suddenly found themselves visible throughout the European choreographic scene. Other artists now sought them out. Hans van Manen, director of the Nederlands Dans Theater, came calling when they moved to Amsterdam, the de facto capital of dance experimentation in Europe. And Lucas Hoving, who had been a member of Ballets Jooss before performing in the United States with Martha Graham and José Limón, arranged a brief stint of teaching for them at the state school in Rotterdam he was then directing.

Even after two years of performing in Europe and the success in Cologne, Eiko & Koma still thought of their dancing not as a career, but as a temporary pursuit while they "researched [their] lives." Eiko was plagued with an ankle injury and, after travels in Tunisia and South Asia, she and Koma returned to

White Dance, Stedelijk Museum, Amsterdam, 1973 Photo © Ad Petersen, Amsterdam

White Dance, Hannover, Germany, 1973 Photo: Otto Umbehr

17

Beate Gordon's cousin had seen Eiko & Koma perform in Tunisia and recommended them to her. As a performance curator at both the Japan Society and the Asia Society, Gordon introduced many Asian artists—traditional and experimental—to New York. One of only two women assigned by the United States to help draft the Japanese constitution following World War II, Gordon is credited with the clause establishing gender equality. Hence, in an e-mail message to the author on January 27, 2011, Eiko asserts her indebtedness to Gordon in writing, "I owe her twice."

18

The Judson choreographers and those who follow are often labeled "postmodernists" by many American critics and scholars. Here, I will use the term "modern dance" in reference to nonclassical Western theatrical dance, so as not to confuse the generally accepted definition of postmodernism in the larger art scene with a particular historical moment in dance.

Koma in *White Dance: Moth*, Japan Society, New York, 1976 Photo: Osamu Honda

19

Deborah Jowitt, "Dancing in Tune with the Earth," *Dance Magazine* 80 (April 2006): 43.

Japan, thinking that it was the end of their performance careers. But Hoving had been adamant that they should not think of leaving dance before they had been to New York. He insisted that they would find the New York dance community of interest; he was just as sure that the New York dance community would be interested in them. With an invitation from Beate Gordon[17] to perform at the Japan Society in New York, Eiko & Koma set off for what they thought would be their last grand adventure in dance. After performances in San Francisco, arranged by Bay Area dance writer Irene Oppenheim, Eiko & Koma arrived in New York in spring 1976.

New York

In the late 1970s, stoked by an explosion of choreographic experimentation, the fabled American dance boom was in high gear. In New York, Eiko & Koma were delighted to find the host of colleagues in creative accord that Hoving had promised them. In the preceding decade, the artists affiliated with the movement that became known as Judson (after the Judson Dance Theater in Greenwich Village, where many of them had first performed) had dismantled the founding precepts of modern dance. Judson was allied with downtown visual artists, musicians, playwrights, and poets, and the choreographers embraced concepts from a wide range of artistic sources as they reinvented modern dance. From radically reductive high modernism to Fluxus to Experiments in Art and Technology (E.A.T.) and the beginnings of conceptualism, the Judson choreographers had a big tent in which to invent.[18] In the wake of Judson, the pluralism expanded even further, as each choreographer meant to create a new way of experiencing the world through movement.

While American choreographers emerged from radically different epistemic and aesthetic practices, the atmosphere encouraging individual experimentation among choreographers in downtown New York—not a guru in sight—encouraged Eiko & Koma to develop longer-term goals. During their first years in New York, they saw performances by Twyla Tharp, Trisha Brown, David Gordon, Lucinda Childs, Dana Reitz, Kei Takei, Daniel Nagrin, and Laura Dean. It was immediately clear to them that there was room on the New York scene for a vast range of voices and, for the first time since leaving the student movement, they began to think that they could be a part of something larger. But they were determined to do so on their own terms.

On their first New York visit, in addition to the Japan Society, Eiko & Koma danced at highly visible New York venues, including Dance Theater Workshop, Cubiculo, the Performing Garage, and the New York Public Library at both Lincoln Center and the Donnell Center. To critical enthusiasm, they performed a heavily revised version of *White Dance*, the choreography they had presented at the 1973 Cologne competition. Titled *White Dance: Moth*, it was a jolt to Americans—butoh had not yet made its way to the United States, and influential *Village Voice* critic Deborah Jowitt remembers seeing it as a "shocking, mesmerizing anomaly,"[19]

Eiko a
WHIT

the cubiculo

POETRY
FILM
DANCE
THEATRE

414 West 51st Street
New York, N. Y. 10019

d Koma
DANCE

Friday & Saturday
July 2 & 3, 1976
8:30 PM

Flyer for *White Dance: Moth*, Cubiculo, New York, 1976

Fluttering Black, San Francisco Museum of Modern Art, August 1979

Event Fission, Battery Park Landfill, New York City, September 1980   Photo © Johan Elbers

even within the context of the rich multiplicity of the experimental New York scene.

With their visas expiring, Eiko & Koma had to return to Japan. But they were determined to make their way back to New York with the intent—for the first time since they had begun dancing—to pursue serious careers as artists. In 1977, they reappeared in San Francisco and New York with a work that consciously distanced them from the influence of their teachers. This was *Fur Seal*, in which they crawled on their bellies in emulation of seals they had observed on a beach in California the previous year. They followed up with their first dance made solely in the United States, *Before the Cock Crows* (1978), which took as its theme the existential question of determinism versus free will.

In 1979, Eiko & Koma began work on a series of dances that attempted to come to grips with their political experiences in Japan, and to find a way to make their artistic and political selves meet. It was the end of a turbulent decade, when world liberation movements sank into torpor and democracies embraced conservative leaders. Eiko & Koma marked the historical moment with *Fluttering Black*. In reference to the anarchist flag, they swathed the stage and themselves in black fabric. They also used black cloth as blindfolds and plugged their ears tightly, as did their accompanying musicians, Glenn Branca's No Wave band, Static. As a metaphor for the end of an era of hope for radical political change, the dance was painfully potent.

That same year, they made *Fission*, a work with strong political overtones in its adoption of another flag—this time, the white flag of surrender—resonant of the battles among rebel factions that Eiko & Koma had experienced as student resisters in Tokyo. An expanded version, *Event Fission*, was a 1980 reworking on the Battery Park Landfill in the shadow of the World Trade Center in lower Manhattan. From the audience's perspective, Eiko appeared to be jousting with the mammoth buildings, a lone individual doing battle with the forces of wealth and corporate power— Don Quixote, tilting at windmills. But it is in light of the World Trade Center catastrophe two decades later that *Event: Fission* became retrospectively famous as an eerily precognizant event. Photographs and films of the event show Eiko & Koma, covered in cracked rice flour as though their skins are peeling away, marching below the towers, until Eiko impales Koma with the flagpole. They tumble down the dunes, where fires burn, before finally disappearing in a cloud of dust into a hole they had dug in the earth.

Eiko & Koma settled in as fixtures on the avant-garde scene, striking up acquaintances with artists and performers. They became close friends with Bob Carroll, the radical performance artist, who in turn introduced them to cellist Charlotte Moorman, founder of the New York Avant Garde Festival. While teaching at the Naropa Institute in 1980, they met Beat poet Allen Ginsberg and fell under the spell of his poetry and performance. Bob Carroll and his Dirt Band—an ensemble of their downtown friends constituted for the occasion—played Ginsberg's music for Eiko & Koma's *Nurse's Song* (1981). Eiko describes these early years in

Grain, 1983 (studio shot) Photo ©Johan Elbers

New York as their "bohemian time," and the hard living took its toll. Finding themselves in need of recuperation, Eiko & Koma decided to leave New York.

The Catskills: Nature

In 1982 Eiko and Koma moved to a ramshackle fifteen-acre farm in the Catskills, where they would live for the next two years. The move was a decisive moment for their art-making. Immersing themselves in nature for the first time as adults, they began to hone their observations of the properties and behavior of the highland flora and fauna, the rhythms of the days and the seasons, and the infinitely changing hues, textures, and scale of mountains and sky.

Inspired by these observations, Eiko & Koma created two seminal works. In *Grain* (1983), they enact a myth of the first arising of rice from the earth. With its larger metaphor concerning the appetites that drive creation, *Grain* incarnated the nucleus of all the work that would follow. Emphasizing the continuous struggle for survival, the dance considers the most elemental conditions of existence. In eschewing the Western pastoral tradition for more realistic depictions of nature, they embrace the grotesque—distorting their limbs, moving awkwardly, and punctuating their work with violence—in connection with a concept that they call the "wounded body."[20] For Eiko & Koma, the struggle for survival—the urge to live in the face of the inevitability of death—has its own kind of beauty.

A year later came *Night Tide*. Imbibing the stillness and majesty of the Catskills landscape, Eiko & Koma created a dance that hints at a mystical narrative: during the night, two mountains make their way to each other in infinitesimal increments, couple, and disappear with the dawn. The artists labored to design costumes for *Night Tide* but found nothing that satisfied the needs of the work. They finally decided that the solution was no costume at all—the anti-costume of nakedness. That is, they became the landscape itself. In *Night Tide*, Eiko & Koma first developed the concept of depicting their bodies *in* a landscape while simultaneously presenting their bodies *as* a landscape. It was an extraordinary feat of physical theater that left the viewer unsure how the performers were seemingly able to transmute from one state to the other, employing nothing other than unadorned moving flesh. It was a combination of technical accomplishments—distorted bodily positions, sustained time, and dexterous lighting—that produced this continuous image of metamorphosis. Often it is impossible to identify a single creature that is being depicted; rather, Eiko & Koma seem to be simultaneously all creatures, from single-celled organisms to humans. Somehow, in revealing themselves naked at their most elementally human—without props, masks, or costumes—they were best able to suggest other natural phenomena.

Grain and *Night Tide* manifest how deeply Eiko & Koma's art-making is rooted in an Asian worldview. These and the works that followed are situated in nature, where human beings are simply one of a limitless numbers of beings, sentient and non-sentient,

20
As a child, Eiko remembers seeing wounded veterans, with their "penetrating, assaulting eyes."

Platte Clove, Catskill Mountains, 2006
Photo: Daniel Case

Night Tide, 1984   Photo © Beatriz Schiller

that constitute the cosmos. They mine a collective consciousness that includes not only other animals, but also subatomic particles, amoebas, fish, trees, stars, geologic forms. The works examine ways that all creation is imbued with the same deeply instinctual urges: the will to live, the drive for companionship. Their dances are simultaneously microcosm (two creatures alone in the universe) and macrocosm (two creatures representing the universe). *Grain* and *Night Tide* are nothing less than the natural history of the world.

Land, with Robert Mirabal (left) and Ben Sandoval, 1991 (studio shot)   Photo © Johan Elbers

Eiko & Koma found that the decision to dance completely naked opened new areas of expressive possibility. Their movement became starker, quieter, more persistently sustained. And it would fundamentally change their staging and choreographic process. They realized that dancing naked necessitated that they reconceive the stage environment so that it became integral to their choreographic design. Neither of them had visual arts training, but they resolved, in Poor Art style, to create these environments themselves. They also adjusted their choreographic process so that they first created these environments before devising the movement to inhabit them. All materials for the décors were natural, chosen not only for visual suggestiveness, but also for sonic and kinetic possibilities. The first décors were relatively simple (leaves, pools of water, a chain-link fence, burned flour paste), but they gradually began to create more elaborate and painstakingly constructed three-dimensional environments.

Eiko & Koma with son Yuta on the set of *By the River*, Massachusetts College of Art, Boston, 1986   Photo: Richard M. Grabbert

The work Eiko & Koma produced in the Catskills also had a lasting effect on the artistic context in which they would be seen in the United States. During a self-produced monthlong run of *Grain* at a small downtown loft in New York, Charles and Stephanie Reinhart saw their work for the first time. Codirectors of the American Dance Festival (ADF), one of the most visible international dance venues, the Reinharts were so captivated by *Grain* that they commissioned a new work, *Beam*, which Eiko & Koma also created in the Catskills. This proved the beginning of an ongoing relationship between the artists and the festival; as of 2011, they have performed eighteen engagements. The ADF imprimatur had the effect of situating Eiko & Koma's work solidly within a dance context, an environment that perhaps seems obvious only in retrospect.

Eiko & Koma with son Shin onstage after a performance of *Wind*, Miami Dade Community College, 1996   Photo: Juan E. Cabrera

During their Catskills sojourn, Eiko & Koma had also begun to experiment with creating dances for the camera. In the series of videos they completed between 1983 and 1988, they developed a meticulous method to produce a dance-video from one long take, focusing on body parts in close-up so that they were abstracted into unrecognizability. In *Husk* (1987), for example, Koma filmed Eiko, moving the lens along with her body, which was embedded in leaves and raw silk, until she seemed to molt into a new creature.

When they received word in 1984 that their application for artist housing in Manhattan had been accepted, Eiko & Koma decided to return to the city. Their ties to New York deepened the following year when they became parents of an American child, their son Yuta. A second son, Shin, followed three years later.

Parenthood coincided with a series of commissions by the Brooklyn Academy of Music (BAM), the summit of American avant-garde performance. In *Shadow* (1986), Eiko seemed to be giving birth, and in 1991, six-year-old Yuta joined Eiko & Koma onstage at BAM for *Land* (1991), their first evening-length production with live music and commissioned score. *Land* was inspired by their visits to Taos, New Mexico, and the vast desert landscape—seemingly desolate yet teeming with life—ideally suited their aesthetic sensibility. Among its many themes, *Land* drew parallels between the American southwest—the site of the Manhattan Project—and Japan, where the United States dropped atomic bombs during World War II, prefiguring the work centered in mourning and remembrance that would occupy Eiko & Koma in the succeeding decade.[21]

As children, their sons were intimately involved in the family business, touring as performers in *Land* as well as in its successor, *Wind* (1993), two of Eiko & Koma's most frequently performed dances. In *Wind*, a child precedes his parents into death, and with the audience aware that they were watching these events enacted by a real family, the work was suffused with particular poignancy.

Outside the Theater

While Eiko & Koma had been simulating the natural environment in the theater, they were eager to extend their choreography into nature. In 1995, they performed in the Delaware River in a work they simply called *River*. With driftwood décor by sculptor Judd Weisberg, Eiko & Koma enacted a quiet ritual in the water, before floating downstream and out of sight. The metaphor of time as an inexorably moving river had been a theme of their dances for over a decade. "Time is immense and alive," Eiko writes. "Like a river, time suspends, flows, hesitates, gets stuck, accelerates.... Like a river, time is far longer than we can *remember*. A river has been flowing before I was born. It will continue to flow after I die."[22] With *River*, Eiko & Koma were able to physically realize the flow of life spans with remarkable directness.

In formulating ways to push forward the environmental direction in their work begun in *River*, Eiko & Koma were aided immeasurably by a five-year fellowship from the MacArthur Foundation, the first joint fellowship in its history. They began to push their art-making into entirely new modes of performance—what they call "theatrical work in untheatrical settings."[23] The first of these works was *Breath*, a "living installation" in a gallery space at the Whitney Museum of American Art in 1998. *Breath* was a monthlong marathon: Eiko & Koma performed seven hours a day, every day that the museum was open. With their audience free to come and go at any point during the performance, the artists reconceived their linear choreography as an open-ended form. Naked, they moved inside the environment at a pace that was even slower than that of their theatrical works. With the addition of a video of their bodies that seemed to float over the installation, *Breath* created what Eiko

21
In 2010, Eiko translated and edited Kyoko Hayashi's novella based on her experience as a survivor of the Nagasaki bombing and her pilgrimage to the Trinity test bomb site in New Mexico. See Kyoko Hayashi, *Torinichi kara Torinichi e (From Trinity to Trinity)*, trans. Eiko Otake (Barrytown, NY: Station Hill Press, 2010).

22
Eiko Otake, "Like a River, Time Is Naked," presented at 24 Hour Program on the Concept of Time, Solomon R. Guggenheim Museum, New York City, January 7, 2009.

23
Eiko & Koma, informational pamphlet for *The Caravan Project*, ed. Ivan Sygoda (New York: Inta, Inc., 1999).

Eiko & Koma with Lakshmi Aysola, *Offering*, Bryant Park, New York City,
July 2002   Photo: Tom Brazil

24
"Movement as Installation: Eiko & Koma in Conversation with Matthew Yokobosky," *PAJ: A Journal of Performance and Art* 64 (January 2000): 34–35.

25
Eiko, *Offering* (2001), http://eikoandkoma.org/offering.

26
Eiko & Koma, informational pamphlet for *The Caravan Project*.

The Caravan Project trailer at the future site of 171 Cedar Art Center, Boyceville, New York 1999 Photo: Terri Olson

27
Ibid.

Kamishabai, Otaru, Japan, 1950

28
Eiko, e-mail message to the author, October 15, 2010.

called an "ancestral body image." It conjured, as Whitney curator Matthew Yokobosky suggested, "a complete kinetic world."[24]

Committed to democratizing their performances, Eiko and Koma "wanted to radically enlarge the definition of the art audience"[25] and looked for ways "to encounter [the] kinds of people who are not conditioned to theatrical codes."[26] They wished to reverse the experience of theatergoing: seeking out audiences rather than having audiences come to them. The result was *The Caravan Project* (1999), a "living installation on wheels" conceived as a performance that would be more portable than *River* and *Breath*. In a small trailer, which opened on four sides, they installed an environment reminiscent of a cave filled with stalactites. Parked under a night sky, the trailer would open to reveal the jewel-box setting, with Eiko & Koma moving inside for up to three hours. Viewers were free to stay as long as they liked.

In conceiving *Caravan*, Eiko & Koma drew on the heritage of nineteenth- and early-twentieth-century Japanese street performers or traveling storytellers (*kamishabai*, or picture theater) that they both remembered from childhood. They created *Caravan* with as much technical care and conceptual rigor as any of their theatrical works. It was extraordinary that Eiko & Koma, whose choreography was regarded as among the most abstruse and challenging offered by the avant-garde, would adopt the *kamishabai* model for its presentation. But their instincts turned out to be right. Their "high art guerrilla ritual"[27] attracted crowds of people, some of whom lingered for just a couple of minutes and others who stayed riveted to the spot for as long as the performance lasted.

Offering

The year before the terrorist attacks on the World Trade Center, Eiko & Koma spent twelve months working on the ninety-first floor of the North Tower. As artists-in-residence with the Lower Manhattan Cultural Council, they created *When Nights Were Dark*, structured as a sequel to *Caravan*. Designed for the theater, the dance took place on a rotating sculpture suggestive of the cyclical nature of life, which turned so slowly over the course of the performance that its movement was almost imperceptible. *When Nights Were Dark* lamented the loss of darkness to artificial light, a metaphor for the eclipse of myth in contemporary culture.[28]

Concerned with the American refusal to face death squarely, Eiko & Koma were in the final stages of creating their next work, *Coffin Dance*, when terrorists took down the World Trade Center in 2001. Watching the smoking ruins from the windows of their apartment, they realized that another kind of dance of death was now called for. No longer oblivious to the realities of annihilation, Americans suddenly had been plunged into thinking of little else. In response, Eiko & Koma redesigned *Coffin Dance* as *Offering* (2002), a ritual intended to invite mourning and remembrance as well as to counter the impulse for revenge taken in the name of patriotism. *Offering* presented its viewers the opportunity to maintain a relationship with the dead and meditate on sorrow and violence. Presented outdoors in public settings with no admission—including parks near the World Trade Center—*Offering* was specifically constructed to engage the affected community.

In *Offering*, nakedness became important as a reminder of human commonality. Prohibited by law from performing naked in the public spaces of New York, Eiko & Koma devised the "metaphorical nakedness" of their two bodies—unmediated by complex theatrical or technological effects—enacting a simple ritual on and around a massive bier heaped with soil.[29] *Offering* was an attempt to become "intimate with the sadness and anger" of the victims. Citing the tradition of Noh theater, in which the dead appear to the living seeking commiseration as a means toward making peace with their condition, Eiko & Koma created *Offering* in the same spirit—as a channel for understanding and remembering the pain of the dead. The dance was also intended to elide past, present, and future, to serve as a "window" onto memories and expectations.[30] Much of the work the artists made through the next decade (*Tree Song, Death Poem, Quartet,* and *Mourning*) continued to be engaged with death, endurance, and prolonging remembrance of the deceased.[31]

Looking to the Future

As an art form that exists only in performance, dance is evanescent. Preserving work past its original interpretation is fragile at best, and seemingly impossible for artists such as Eiko & Koma, whose choreography and performance are indistinguishable. But friends urged them to think about how their work might be transmitted to succeeding generations. An opportunity to experiment arose in 2004 when Daravuth Ly, director of the Reyum Institute of Arts and Culture, invited them to work with young artists in Phnom Penh. Cambodia had experienced its own holocaust in the Khmer Rouge killing fields, where artists had been singled out for extinction. As had Eiko and Koma in postwar Japan, the Reyum students were coming of age in a culture in which older generations were both victims and victimizers on a mass scale. It seemed that dances of mourning and remembrance would particularly resonate in Cambodia. In 2006, Eiko & Koma's residencies in Reyum resulted in a remarkable work, *Cambodian Stories: An Offering of Painting and Dance,* a dance of intergenerational passage in which they worked with ten young Reyum artists. For the next two years, they continued to work with two of the students, Charian and Peace, a relationship that culminated in *Hunger.* A resonant work incorporating action from past choreography as well as foreshadowing their next dance, *Hunger* revisited Eiko & Koma's career-long interest in desire, here depicted as longing for sustenance of body, mind, and spirit.

Hunger's final image is a raven, a bird that has been both worshipped as a god and feared as an evil omen. Eiko & Koma employed this double-edged symbol as the central metaphor for their next dance, *Raven* (2010), whose décor includes a scorched backdrop and floor cloth, a visceral reminder of the acrid smell

29
Eiko, *Offering* (2001), http://eikoandkoma.org/offering.

30
Ibid.

31
In the introduction to her translation of Hayashi's book, Eiko elucidates the concept of what she calls "sustained mourning," the idea that art can be a means to maintain a relationship with the dead. See Kyoko Hayashi, *From Trinity to Trinity*, ix–xxxii.

Eiko & Koma with Reyum Painting Collective, Florida State University Campus, March 2006
Photo: Marc Ray

Koma with Reyum Painting Collective, Asia Society, New York City, May 2006
Photo: La Frances Hui

that permeated Tokyo after the bombings in 1945. At performances for their Retrospective Project, this latest dance shared programs with a revival of *White Dance*, their first professional choreography. While *White Dance* suggests an antic youthfulness in relation to the grave sensuality of *Raven*, seen together the works demonstrate that Eiko & Koma have hewn to a steady course over their careers: sympathetically embodying the kinds of creatures that cause humans unease, charting their evolutionary and life cycles, and mining their natures for suggestive metaphors and quasi-narratives. It might seem an irony that the dance of their youth finds them clothed, while that of their maturity exposes their bodies. But these choices chart the consistent path toward honest revelation that has characterized their art-making.

For Eiko & Koma, nakedness is more than a physical state—it is an ethical stance. Over the course of their working lives together, they have taken it as their charge to strip away gentility and politesse in order to gaze honestly at the nature of human existence: so are we born, so shall we die. And even as they age, they continue to perform with bodies exposed, fearlessly displaying the effects of time. In a culture bent on denying age and death, this is a courageous statement.

Eiko & Koma have extended the notion of nakedness to include time and space. In their performances, they have discovered the means to suggest the long view of experience, and therefore reveal its true nature: "Time is not even, space is not empty."[32] This distanced perspective allows the unveiling of what is usually too painful to say, too painful even to think. And once one is honest about the body—the essential self—other forms of honesty become second nature.

Four decades into a remarkable artistic and life partnership, Eiko & Koma persevere in the creation of art as a means toward insight into the nature of life. Their themes are the big ones: life and death, our place in the cosmos. In their numinous examinations of the interpenetration of all creation, they make the timely case for a rapprochement between human beings and a planet threatened by mindless consumption and arrogance. In response to violence and war, they teach us to mourn the dead and to refrain from retaliation. And in contrast to a culture that too often substitutes surface sheen for authentic aesthetic experience, Eiko & Koma demonstrate that a more profound beauty is to be had in searching out the naked truth of experience.

32
See note 22.

⁴ lingering six heart resisting

beats, splay thumbs, inertia

Wallow, Point Reyes National Seashore, Marin County, California, November 1983 (photo taken during videotaping)   Photo: Kazunobu Yanagi

RECIPROCAL TOPOGRAPHIES—EIKO & KOMA'S DANCESCULPTURES

André Lepecki

1. "The space and time continuum in which we move is not a white canvas that stands alone and empty."[1]

In the final sequence shot of Eiko & Koma's video work *Wallow* (1984; pages 46–47), the whole image is divided into two large horizontal bands. On the top half of the screen, an image of a platinum band of ocean is rhythmically traversed by other horizontal lines—crests of waves, moving down the frame, until the water's maximum reach on the sand. On the lower half of the image, a band of wet sand appears as a compact, solid plane. Cutting this balanced image vertically and disrupting it, two parallel lines, just barely curving, plow the sand and the field of vision: the tracks left by the crawling bodies of Eiko & Koma as they slowly, yet decisively, inch toward the water. Two incongruous black masses of flesh, wearing ragged pieces of some animal hide, arms under their torsos, legs inert, they progress, bound by an unbreakable alliance, in a difficult crawl. Stubbornly, painstakingly, and decisively they aim at the waves that will surely swallow them soon—and, with them, the whole frame. Ominous image? Hopeful image? A verdict is not possible. It is an image that refrains from proffering a judgment. Yet, its geometric composition does not remain abstract. The proximity of the two bodies that have purposefully relinquished verticality, bipedalism, manual ability (in short, the traits that mark the human as agent for action), and now face the forces of the earth as they share, side by side, a common, uncertain destiny, creates another image, this time not in our retina, but rather in our affective field. Eiko voiced this image in a poem printed in the program of *Fur Seal* (1977), the dance that would eventually originate *Wallow*, the dance in which Eiko & Koma fused, in six months of preparation, their lives with the lives of seals:

How mediocre, how banal you are
Your somber elastic shape
Your dolorous lumps of rubber
Bob and sink in the sea
In the sorrowful rays of the evening twilight[2]

Wallow is a silent film—neither its shots nor its editing ever convey a hint of narrative. Yet, sonority (whether music or poetry) blasts through its images in a silent resonance filled with rumors of the ocean, water crashing against rock and sand, wind whistling through crevices, sand crushing under the artists' breathing and panting bodies. The absence of sound in an image that remains so blatantly sonic reveals one of the principles in Eiko & Koma's

1
Eiko Otake, "Dancing through History," manuscript text, 2009, http://eikoandkoma.org/sites/ek/images/ek_2323_pdf.pdf. Accessed August 6, 2010.

2
The poem is loosely based on Mitsuharu Kaneko's poem "Seals." See Eiko Otake, program notes for *Fur Seal*, 1977, http://eikoandkoma.org/index.php?p=ek&id=3016. Accessed August 5, 2010.

mode of creating their art—each compositional element is always and constitutively linked to all others, and all constitutively linked to a fundamental, underlying movement, called vibration. Every image created by Eiko & Koma (on the stage, on video, on windy beaches, or in cold rivers) harnesses this fundamental or foundational sound-movement, which need not be heard, nor even seen, but simply sensed.

The creation of resoundingly silent images is explicitly discussed by Koma in an interview about their installation *Breath* (1998). Elements in this large environment included dry leaves, fabrics, lights, moving air, soil, their bodies—one of which was always present throughout the monthlong exhibition, seven hours a day, six days a week—and a silent video projection. According to Koma, the silent projection was there so that "the video *image* could *work as our sound*." Completing Koma's line of thought, Eiko similarly fused visuality and sonority: "We used these waving hills and breathing bodies as a *visual soundscape*. It's something that your ear doesn't pick up but your eye does."[3] The creation of a visual soundscape requires Eiko & Koma to produce *non-sonorous sonic sensations* aimed at being "picked up" by the eye. Naturally, by picking up sound visually, eyes become not only a kind of ear, but also a kind of hand. The artists' pieces work as much on their bodies as they do on their audience's.

The first condition for Eiko & Koma to scramble the organization of their audience's sensorial apparatus: to establish fundamentally non-hierarchical relations between objects, images, sounds, bodies. All are made to resonate with one another, thanks to that imperceptible element that binds them together—micromovement. Their understanding of movement is subtle. So that perception may be augmented to become sensation, movement must oscillate in a narrow band within which micro-events are distributed and take place. It has to be a very slow, occasionally spasmodic, almost still, and always intense movement. In this sense, movement is enacted in order to produce (a sense of) permanence. Whitney Museum of American Art curator Matthew Yokobosky referred to Eiko & Koma's particular mode of moving as "movement as installation."[4] Fusing a spatial and a kinetic dimension confirms Eiko & Koma's fundamental concern in leveling all compositional elements on a non-hierarchical, non-vertical distribution of the sensible. Like bands of silent waves crashing on the shore over two lumps of flesh, the works of Eiko & Koma pursue this kind of overflowing horizon of sensation.

2. "Being able to present ourselves as nameless creatures."[5]

Those who have followed Eiko & Koma's career know that the horizontal is a prevalent plane in their art. Their bodies are prone in *Wallow* and in many other works—on theater stages (*Land,* 1991; *Mourning,* 2007) or gallery floors (*Breath; Naked,* 2010), on a sandy beach (*Wallow*), on grass (*Offering,* 2004), in a graveyard (*Tree Song* at St Mark's Church in-the-Bowery, 2004). Whether lying down in dances of quasi-stillness or performing one of their non-spectacular crawlings, their spasmic or quivering

3
"Movement as Installation: Eiko & Koma in Conversation with Matthew Yokobosky," *PAJ: A Journal of Performance and Art* 64 (January 2000): 34. (Emphasis added by the author.)

4
Ibid., 26.

5
Eiko & Koma, "Our Ambitions," in http://eikoandkoma.org/index.php?p=ek&id=2885. Accessed October 3, 2010.

or smooth gestures reveal a surprising positivity, urgency, and force. Eiko & Koma's embrace of what only a hyper-agitated society would perceive as passivity is actually the very opposite of a lingering inertia, the opposite of a theatrics of failure, the reverse of any kind of wish to represent a theological fall. On the ground, their embrace of the horizontal is rather the activation of a necessary regime of quietness in which the body must become a conduit for micro-movements and align itself with a temporality that approximates it to a time-image; and with a horizontality that approximates it to the forces of the earth, turning a body into a kind of *thing*.

Several consequences at the level of composition ensue. Corporeal consequences: the privileging of micro-movements, the investment on intense motions rather than on movement as spectacle of displacement. Temporal consequences: stillness or slowness as kinetic activators of *duration*, a mode of endlessly stretching an instant into an intense, nonmeasurable temporality. Plastic or visual consequences: the creation of works that are veritable time-images, "movement as installation," or dancesculptures. Suturing it all is Eiko & Koma's mode of delineating a new horizon for being in the world—one where body and environment alloy, in conjoined thingliness, dance and sculpture.

The event of this fusion can be named a "becoming space" of the body—a fundamental compositional strategy where the dialectics of inside and outside, image and background, movement and rest, human and thing, organic and inorganic, as well as received notions of the body's presence in dance are pulverized. What I am calling "becoming space" (so instrumental in the composition of pieces such as *Husk* [1987], *Wallow* and *Hunger* [2008], *Mourning* and *Raven* [2010]) is a notion explored by Roger Caillois in his famous 1935 essay on animal mimicry[6] (the biological phenomenon of other animals acquiring perceived characteristics of other animals, plants, or the surrounding environment). It reveals, for Caillois, how bodies and space share "reciprocal topographies." He saw in mimicry a literal mix of sculpture and photography: "morphological mimicry ... could be an actual photography, but of the form and the relief, a photography on the level of the object and not on that of the image, a reproduction in space with solids and voids." This is what he called "teleplasty"[7]— a fusion between environment and corporeality that turned bodies into a new class of things situated somewhere between organism, sculpture, and image. This is precisely the crux of Eiko & Koma's work: a becoming space of the body, and a becoming body of space; a becoming thing of the organic, a becoming organic of things. For Caillois, there was some danger in this project. In this "real temptation by space," the body could dissolve into a mist, into a specter, thanks to a "depersonalization by assimilation to space."[8] But isn't this drive toward the depersonalized inorganic precisely what allows Eiko & Koma to create their dance as if it were a sculpture or even a mere thing? Isn't this drive toward the inorganic (so essential also to butoh, with which they were involved early in their artistic career and training) the specific force turning their art into a politics and an ethics?

6
Roger Caillois, "Mimicry and Legendary Psychasthenia," *October* 31 (winter 1984): 16–32.

7
Ibid., 23.

8
Ibid., 29.

This is the radical proposition made by Eiko & Koma's art: by synaesthetically leveling the perceptual field, by producing images that resound—installations that are movements, and movements that are installations—by siding with animals and plants and things to a point of (con)fusion, by producing dancesculptures, videodances, kineticpoems, and visual soundscapes as so many reciprocal topographies in which space and body, living and non-living, man and woman exchange positions, Eiko & Koma lead "the mind and the body to the extreme regions of the nonliving, where, perhaps, they were always already directed."[9] This is not a morbid project. It is rather the celebration of what Eiko calls a "sense of experimentation and adventure" where "sometimes it is not necessarily only about the human."[10] Sometimes it is about animals and plants—but many times it is also about inorganic things, about becoming space or becoming inorganic.

3. "… It is a relief for us not to be confined with humanity."[11]

What does it mean to make art in order to be relieved once in a while from humanity? It means to enter into what Italian philosopher Mario Perniola called the logic of *"things that feel."*[12] The call for dance to be "moved by a *thing* rather by oneself" was famously made in 1966 by Yvonne Rainer in her manifesto on minimalism in dance.[13] But in Eiko & Koma's work, we can see this call taking perhaps a more radical turn. Indeed, rather than being moved *by* a thing (thus surrendering part of authorial sovereignty to objects and devices), their project is to move *as* a thing (thus surrendering the human as emblem of absolute sovereignty).

What are the specifically corporeal steps Eiko & Koma devise in order to enter into this logic of things that feel and make it a mode for composing their work? First, they have to strike, between the world of humans and the world of things, an unbreakable alliance—a partnership so deep that it would deserve the name of symbiotic assemblage. Again: searching for inorganic and nonhuman modes of being is not equivalent to embrace diminished, impoverished, humiliated, or abject forms of living and of being in the world. As Eiko remarked, wishing not to be human all the time "is not to say I deny humanity, but to strengthen our sense of being."[14] One strengthens one's sense of being by embarking on an endless adventure of exploration without exploitation, an adventure that does not seek to colonize or dominate, but to openly yield to the call of beasts, plants, ghosts, elements, mere things. The trick is that one has to establish this alliance not vertically, as a representative of a species of conquerors (humanity), but horizontally, as just another *thing* amidst the many things of the earth—visible and invisible, physical or spectral. The creation of an aesthetics of horizontal permutations is exactly what Perniola sees as the "open horizon of installations"[15] in which a narrow band of micro-events allows for the artwork to overflow out of itself and fuse deeply with the world. While doing so, "it is the installation that feels the visitor, welcomes him, touches him, feels him up, stretches out to him, makes him enter into it, penetrates him, possesses him, overwhelms him."[16]

9
Mario Perniola, *The Sex Appeal of the Inorganic* (New York and London: Continuum, 2000), 16.

10
"Movement as Installation," 27.

11
Eiko, Ibid., 27.

12
Perniola, *The Sex Appeal of the Inorganic*, 1–40.

13
Yvonne Rainer, "A Quasi Survey of Some 'Minimalist' Tendencies in the Quantitatively Minimal Dance Activity Midst the Plethora, or an Analysis of *Trio A*," *Minimal Art: A Critical Anthology*, ed. Gregory Battcock (New York: E. P. Dutton, 1968), 269.

14
"Movement as Installation," 27.

15
Perniola, *The Sex Appeal of the Inorganic*, 103.

16
Ibid., 107.

4. "To be clear about what matters to us and to strengthen our insistence."[17]

It is rare to witness a true partnership—as symbiotic assemblage or reciprocal topography—that remains true to the individuating differences and singularities between its composing elements. Yet in 1999, after more than two decades of collaboration, Koma could still state the following about his work with Eiko: "I still have some trouble understanding where our interests over-lap—whether our motivations are the same or just related."[18] Koma makes clear that any surrender to the other (human, plant, animal, ghost, thing), any alliance or symbiosis, departs from preserving a difference. This mutual and ethical differentiation is exactly what allows for the creation of *reciprocal topographies* in their works—surveying and treating each other as mountain, as beast, as plant, as vapor, as image, as ghost, as human, as man, as woman, as cuts of wood, as chunks of mud, as pieces of cloth.

To treat your body and the body of your partner as bits of cloth is to carefully and attentively cut, fold, weave, and sew one to the other—so bodies may be assembled into movement-installations or dancesculptures. Again, Perniola says that "to give oneself as a *thing that feels* means asking that the clothes that make up the body of the partner are mixed with one's own, thus creating a single extension in which one can travel for hours, for days."[19] Clothing in Eiko & Koma's work means creating corporeal-thingly assemblages with fabrics, furs, white powder, cowhides, bare skin, sand, mud, water, tree branches, dry leaves, straw, wind, the sonic skin of a projected image, the percussive affects created by a drum or a prepared piano. Eiko: "We started to make our own costumes, and sometimes our costumes just got so large that they extended into the realm of setting—a blanket of leaves for example. So we literally started to wear nothing, but *the natural environment became our costume.*"[20] Once the environment is your costume, then the environment can finally be naked, but also it can finally be clothed by your naked body, "so the leaves, water, etc., are all a part of our body extension, which provokes us to move in a certain way. They become both our house and our costume,"[21] revealing a reversibility between bare bodies and bare nature, mutually clothing and undressing each other in reciprocal exchanges and alliances—so that one may dance on this sutured place for hours, days, perhaps even a lifetime.

5. "Time swallows time."[22]

Eiko & Koma's work sutures not only things, space, and bodies, but also temporality. This is the point of creating dancesculptures: to secrete in the quasi-stillness of the slow gesture a time that would otherwise never materialize. If Eiko & Koma's "movement as installation," or dancesculptures, offer us the possibility to realign our senses, they also give us something most precious and rare: the possibility to experience a time that extends itself end-lessly within the discrete contours of an instant. Eiko & Koma's pieces produce a temporality that is never at the service of measur-

17
Eiko & Koma. "Our Ambitions," http://eikoandkoma.org/index .php?p=ek&id=2885.

18
"Movement as Installation," 26.

19
Perniola, *The Sex Appeal of the Inorganic*, 10.

20
"Movement as Installation," 35. (Emphasis added by the author.)

21
Ibid.

22
Eiko Otake, "Like a River, Time Is Naked," presented at 24 Hour Program on the Concept of Time, Solomon R. Guggenheim Museum, New York City, January 7, 2009, http://eikoandkoma .org. Accessed August 5, 2010.

23
Vincent Mondillo and M. Munson,
Environmental Trilogy: An Introduction,
from a film produced by Elise Finger
(Easton, PA: Lafayette College, 1997).

ing motions so these can be *on time*. Instead, their art is one at the service of an intense movement that, by taking its time, *gives time to time*. As Eiko explains, the question for them is never "to have the audience feeling you want to finish this, you are rushing to an end."[23] Never rushing, and never aiming at an end: kinetic mode for intensifying a moment, for creating an affective time-image, or dancesculpture. By giving time to time, i.e., by moving as a thing that feels, Eiko & Koma give us everything.

^{5} monkey-pant Ai! buttock,

(愛), contract right going yellow

Daido Moriyama *Stray Dog, Misawa* 1971

EVEN A DOG THAT WANDERS WILL FIND A BONE[1]

Doryun Chong

1

This is a liberal translation of the Japanese saying *Inumo arukeba boni ataru.* Originally, it had the implied meaning that a dog that wanders might meet the fate of getting beaten with a stick. In recent years, it has acquired a more positive connotation and come to mean that if one works hard and perseveres, one will be rewarded with good fortune. The saying was invoked by Eiko during a conversation with the author at Wesleyan University, July 25, 2010.

My first encounter with Eiko & Koma took place in 2008, nearly forty years after their US debut. Since our first meeting, Eiko & Koma and I have had many conversations, and thanks to the artists' unfolding Retrospective Project, of which this publication is part, I have been able to see many of their older works through archival documentation. Even though I can count on one hand the number of their works I've been able to see restaged and performed in real time, our interaction during the past two years has been intense, cumulative, and instructive. The following hybrid—interview, reflection, and inquiry—results from that exchange.

Because Eiko & Koma are movement artists, it is perhaps natural that words such as "nakedness," "aging," "smell," and of course, "the body" are constants in their speech and writing. One interest I pursue here is to imagine the artists' bodies as they travel through locations, as they age, and as they interact with what is in the air, in the earth, and in their memories. Their own voices and words appear throughout, and I attempt to interweave my own thoughts and associations. At times, these are based on what the artists themselves have referred to; at other moments they originate from my own knowledge base, which is not necessarily shared with that of Eiko & Koma. This text is not meant to be comprehensive. It leans primarily toward their early years—the foundational period even before they were artists—and on recent years since I became acquainted with them. I am not taking this tack in order to draw some sort of logical, deterministic conclusion about how this early period may have shaped their four-decade-long body of work. Rather, it is to give credence to the fact that the central vehicle of their work—their bodies—is a traveling and evolving one; or, to be even more precise and to borrow the artists' words, a "devolving" one. In early 2009, I posed a few questions to Eiko & Koma about their early years in Japan.[2]

2

The interview in sections I and II is adapted from Doryun Chong, "Proliferating Chain Reaction," *ArtAsiaPacific* 62 (March/April 2009): 96–101.

I.

Let's start by talking about your memories of childhood in the 1950s.

Eiko: I was born in 1952, the year the US occupation of Japan ended. This was also during the Korean War, which helped Japan's economy grow out of the rubble of World War II. [During the Korean War (1950–1953), Japan served as a base and supply station for the US forces being deployed to Korea.] As a child, I remember the long hours people worked, the many empty lots there were to play in, the fear I felt looking at the many wounded war veterans begging in the streets, and the cooking smells that pervaded the small alleys of Tokyo.

Koma: I was born in 1948. My childhood home in Niigata, a provincial city on the coast of the Sea of Japan, was seven hours from Tokyo by train. I also remember those evocative smells: charcoal-broiled fish, soiled diapers, an old-style squat toilet full of wriggling maggots, as well as fig and persimmon trees. From the late 1950s to the early 1960s, I saw many Koreans who lived in Japan crying as they left their families and boarded special boats for North Korea. It was only later that I learned what a grave political issue this represented. Looking back, I feel these were striking visual images for a child.

Between these answers is an evocation of the destitution and confusion that befell Japan in the early postwar years as well as the origin of ideas of periphery and fringe for the artists. Tokyo was the target of fierce bombings and devastation during the final years of the war. Those living in the capital city, the seat of the Occupation Authority's headquarters after the war, must have felt an especially heightened sense of subjugation. Although Japan is not a particularly large country, it is a geographically diverse one—its precipitous mountain ranges separating and isolating many regions. Niigata is one such place—bordering on the Sea of Japan and facing the Korean peninsula. Koma's memory of the North Koreans (or those politically aligned to the Communist half of the country) waiting to head off to the socialist utopia not only speaks about the complex repercussions of the fallout from Japan's defeat, but also of its recent project of colonialism. Just as coming from the margins of Japanese society played a critical role in social and historical consciousness for Koma, Eiko also acknowledges that her childhood experiences in the countryside away from Tokyo were extremely formative.

Poverty and periphery, devastation and death, hope and reconstruction, and the human bodies beaten down, if not destroyed, yet still resilient: all of these coalesced to form the bedrock of Eiko & Koma's thinking about their own bodies. And those memories are intensely sensorial ones—in particular, olfactory. They say that they remember the smells of "death and illness, open sewage, human waste (used for fertilizer), outhouses, rain, tide, and seashore."[3] This is not the Japan that we know now—a cipher of technology, hypermodernity, and hygiene—but a place where life and death, the biological functions of humans and animals, are out in the open. A famous image titled *Stray Dog, Misawa*, by celebrated photographer Moriyama Daido,[4] was taken in 1971 in Misawa, Aomori Prefecture, where one of the US military bases is located. Though separated in time from the 1950s, when Eiko & Koma were growing up, as well as in space from either Tokyo or Niigata, the harshness and pathos encapsulated in that close-up image of an unwanted animal wandering the streets could very well stand for the environment described by the artists.

3
Eiko Otake, e-mail message to the author, September 13, 2010.

4
The Japanese names in this essay appear in the original order—the family name first, followed by the given name—unless the persons referred to are well known by the Western order of their names.

Following this period of reconstruction in the 1950s, what do you remember of the early 1960s?

5

The 1951 treaty was renewed in 1960 and 1970, and thereafter became permanent until revoked by both parties.

6

The casualty was Kanba Michiko, a twenty-two-year-old student at the University of Tokyo and a member of Zengakuren—shorthand for Zen-Nihon Gakusei Jichikai Sorengo (All-Japan Federation of Student Self-Government Associations)—the communist league of students that played an active role in organizing protests and demonstrations.

EIKO: The 1960s in Japan started with the tremendous movement against Anpo [a contraction for Nichibei anzenhosho joyaku (The US–Japan Mutual Cooperation and Security Treaty)].[5] Tens of thousands of people rallied and surrounded the parliament building in Tokyo. I remember how upset my mother was when a young female demonstrator was killed during a confrontation between demonstrators and the police,[6] and when the treaty was extended in spite of the strong opposition. The 1964 Tokyo Olympics changed the appearance of the city. Postwar houses and small alleys were razed and replaced with dull concrete buildings and highways. All the smells and atmosphere that I mentioned before gradually disappeared.

KOMA: In the early 1960s, I became aware of the difference between the haves and the have-nots. Some had wealth, beauty, education, happiness, ambitions, and dreams, while others did not. I decided early on that I would leave my hometown and conquer Tokyo.

EIKO: At that time, my friends and I were student activists. We were too busy with anti-government and anti–Vietnam War demonstrations to pursue art seriously. It was before and after those political protests that Japanese anti-establishment artists such as filmmaker Oshima Nagisa, playwright/theater director Kara Juro, artist Kudo Tetsumi, and designer/artist Yokoo Tadanori, as well as European filmmakers such as Jean-Luc Godard and Federico Fellini, meant something to us, and we learned about them by watching their films and through art magazines such as Bijutsu Techo [Art Handbook].

While numerous political theorists—none standing out any more than the others—presented us with logic, idealism, and tactical thinking, somehow these things led us to despair. By contrast, these artists showed us how they built their lives upon their confusion and frustration. In their works, we sensed that the means and the end are inseparable, that being revolutionary means being radical, and that the body is our vessel and foundation for exploration, experimentation, and expression. We liked the way they asked questions without restraint and how they pursued beauty in the grotesque. They did not adhere to the traditional Japanese virtues of silence, patience, and empty space. And after all, as aspiring but impatient youth, it was encouraging for us to see an older generation as aspiring and impatient as we were. It is important to note that Kudo, Oshima, Kara, and others were also talking to us and engaging with our ideas, incorporating them into their work—Kudo even said he specifically came back to Tokyo to see us student demonstrators "performing" in the streets.[7]

7

In 1970 Kudo stated: "I was deeply shocked by the May 1968 revolution. Since then, I have wandered from Paris to Venice, then Amsterdam, Düsseldorf, and Kassel. While on the road, I reflected on various things. Then, I thought, I want to go back to Japan and think again on these things in the streets of Tokyo. I felt like sharing and discussing my thoughts with the students, or rather, the young generation of Japan." Doryun Chong, "When the Body Changes into New Forms: Tracing Tetsumi Kudo," *Tetsumi Kudo: Garden of Metamorphosis*, exh. cat. (Minneapolis: Walker Art Center, 2008), 34. Translation by the author.

KOMA: I moved to Tokyo in 1966, and majored in political science in Waseda University in Tokyo. I became heavily involved in the student movement and New Left politics, but I found that even those areas were run according to old-fashioned hierarchies. The academic

Student Power, Kanda, Tokyo 1969   Photo: Hitomi Watanabe

Tetsumi Kudo *Philosophy of Impotence, or Distribution of Map of Impotence and the Appearance of Protective Domes at the Points of Saturation* 1961–1962

8
Eiko & Koma and I first met in October 2008 at the Walker Art Center when I was installing the exhibition *Tetsumi Kudo: Garden of Metamorphosis* and the dancers were presenting *Hunger*. Concurrently, the Walker presented In the Realm of Oshima: The Films of Japanese Master Nagisa Oshima, a touring film retrospective organized by Cinematheque Ontario. Our initial conversations unfolded through discussions of the work of the two older Japanese artists.

Nagisa Oshima *Still from Diary of a Shinjuku Thief* (*Shinjuku dorobo nikki*), 1968

9
Doryun Chong, "Proliferating Chain Reaction," 99.

world and even the avant-garde art movement had their masters and servants as well. These are not unrelated to the Japanese emperor system. The center of Tokyo is occupied by the emperor's palace and it is surrounded by the parliament, prestigious universities, the National Theatre, elite shopping districts, embassies, and investment centers. I thought people's faces lit up when they got closer to the palace. When I dropped out of college in 1971, I was also dropping out of that society. I was looking for something "real" to hang on to. It was out of pure luck that one day I met the dancer Ohno Kazuo—back when he was known only among artists, not at the national or international level. If I hadn't met him and studied with him, I can't imagine what path I might have taken.

The combination of growing economic prosperity and political turmoil supplied a fertile breeding ground for a whole range of avant-garde artistic experimentations, across media and genres, at this time. There are a number of ways to interpret this highly active and richly multidisciplinary period. One way I have viewed the era with Eiko & Koma was through particular artistic and cultural figures such as Kudo and Oshima.[8] Kudo, one of the enfants terribles of the time, made a powerful impression on the Tokyo art world in the late 1950s and early 1960s with a rapid-fire series of exhibitions and performances—the most notorious and celebrated being *Philosophy of Impotence* (1961–1962), a room-size installation of more than a hundred small, drooping, penis- or chrysalislike objects clustered around one large ejaculating phallus. Around the same time, Oshima, the Japanese New Wave director, was using his cinematic lens—and the industry itself—to look at the drastic transformations and growing inequities in his formally inventive films, such as *Town of Love and Hope* (1959), which depicts stark differences between rich and poor and the unbridgeable gaps between them. This was also a time when boundaries between creative disciplines were decisively blurred, and collaborations took place as the order of the day. Oshima's film *Diary of a Shinjuku Thief* (1968), for instance, features playwright and theater director Kara and his troupe, as well as renowned artist and graphic designer Yokoo playing the main character, Birdie Hilltop.

These artists were collectively thinking not only of the meaning of art, but also of the postwar years. It was in this kaleidoscopic landscape of experimentations that Eiko & Koma came of age intellectually, philosophically, and politically. As Eiko has acknowledged, these senior artists "inhabited the same world of explosive artistic ideas while also harboring the desire to transcend all the chaos taking place.... Their ideas and performances had a collective influence on us in the late 1960s."[9] Their entrée into the art world was through dance, specifically butoh, but it is as important to acknowledge this beginning as to stress their willing departure from it.

What influence did Ohno and Hijikata Tatsumi have on you at this time?

Eiko: I studied at Hijikata's studio from 1970 to 1971, after I saw his company's work. Koma had already been there for three months. When I saw his company perform, I was not so much moved as shocked. I wanted to find out how and why these dancers looked so out of this world. We took his dance classes at night, and all students ate and slept in his studio. They all seemed to follow his orders with utter devotion and together we performed in cabarets to make money for the studio or sometimes in a small, arty theater in the downtown Shinjuku area of Tokyo.

After only three months, Koma and I decided to leave and work on our own. Neither of us had gone to Hijikata's studio to become long-term disciples of his. His studio was a twenty-four-hour engagement, and we wanted to work on our own ideas and explore other worlds. We started to stage events and shows by ourselves. At the same time, we went to study with Ohno, whose classes were all about improvisation. He would show us books of paintings by Japanese avant-gardists and give us his thoughts on their work. That was another way in which we absorbed the work of artists who came before us. In speaking to us, Ohno was also able to construct and develop his own ideas.

Around then, however, Koma and I learned about a generation of amazing talents, including [conductor] Seiji Ozawa, whose long hair and intense sense of focus and performativity were attractive to us. Ozawa, Kudo, Yoko Ono, and other artists had left Japan at a young age to develop their artistic voices. That certainly influenced our decision to leave in 1972, to leave Ohno, political activities, and art publications behind. I didn't want to be a good student or an intellectual, but rather an independent and a rebel. That said, although we might have learned from the vigor of visual artists such as Kudo, we also wanted to live differently from them. Visual artists leave behind art objects and archives. As performing artists we leave fewer traces—except perhaps in people's memory, at least we thought then.

Eiko, first performance of original choreography, Waseda University, Tokyo, 1972

III.

In 1973, Eiko & Koma left for Europe. Living often in a car and constantly mobile for almost two years, they performed spontaneously and also at more formal venues by invitation. Each time they performed, a new element entered into their movement phrasings, such as Koma throwing an egg or Eiko cooking a fish, almost in a manner reminiscent of Fluxus. The accumulated result later gained the catchall title *White Dance*, but at this stage the artists understood it not so much as a "work" but as a potential for communication. They were also learning about a different, Western mode of communication—much more direct, in stark contrast to the more elusive and ambiguous Japanese way instilled in them. In their early to mid-twenties, Eiko & Koma were embarking on a journey, though "destiny" and "career" were possibly the last things they had in mind. Eiko recalls, "People started asking about our next work,

White Dance, Kunstverein, Hannover, Germany, 1973 Photo: Rolf Ostermeyer/Norbert Schittek

10
The conversation in section III is taken
from an interview with the artists in
New York City, April 24, 2010.

and we thought, 'What next work? Oh, we have to or can make a next piece?'"[10] By 1976, Eiko & Koma were in the United States. They found themselves in New York, after a quick stop in San Francisco.

You were in Europe, you returned to Japan briefly,
and then you came to the United States.
What was on your mind? Was this the logical next step
for you, or did you just want to try something new?

EIKO: We told many people we met in Europe that we might not continue to dance. Then they all said, "You can stop if you want to, but not before you go to New York."

KOMA: When we arrived here [in New York] in 1976, we had the feeling that somehow we missed a very important art movement. Already, Judson [Dance Theater] was over. We could see that Soho was developing into artists' lofts by then. We couldn't find Yayoi Kusama [she lived in New York from 1956 to 1973, when she returned to Japan] or Allen Ginsberg—though we did find Ginsberg later. And the city was bankrupt. Garbage was everywhere. People were lying down everywhere on the street. It was a weird time, but I thought, "Okay, now we have no time to mingle with other artists. We have to focus on our own dance." It was very clear.

And your time in the city didn't last that long. You retreated to
upstate New York after a few years.

EIKO: Yes, we moved upstate in 1981. After getting here in 1976, we created a new piece every year: Fur Seal *in 1977,* Before the Cock Crows *in 1978,* Fluttering Black *in 1979,* Event Fission *in 1980,* Nurse's Song *in 1981. The latter was a failure in many ways. We were so engrossed in trying new things, being new New Yorkers, and making friends.* Nurse's Song *was essentially about us with our friends Bob Carroll and Allen Ginsberg, but after our friendships grew older, the piece didn't hold the same meaning for us any more.*

We got to know New York rather quickly and became tired of it. I remember thinking it was time to go—as I said when we were in Europe, we were just exploring. Then [Ronald] Reagan had that landslide win [in the 1980 presidential election]. We had to wonder what to do philosophically, politically, culturally in the long run. That feeling kind of lingered all through the Reagan era. At the time, we wanted to be in a new place giving ourselves an experiment.

So the social climate as well as the way the dance field works—
the relentless production model in which you have to
make a new complete work and present it every season—
didn't make sense to you at this time.

Eiko: As for creating a dance, we never trained ourselves to make a finished piece. It still seems each performance is a process. One of the reasons why we were drawn to people like Ginsberg—he's one of those few people who managed to remain as a constant verb, being always in process and being goofy!

Living in the US brought us many excitements. The first few years, we got so excited about having this new way of communication, meeting interesting talented people who were all pretty much anti-authority. We went into punk rock, and this and that, but some of these excitements faded quickly. What remains important is what one really cares to explore over a long period of time. We had a very strong ambition to create art that was moving and to send our audiences home with something meaningful. We had to think about what to present that was valuable to our audiences. But it was not enough to be valuable to them; it had to be valuable to us. So, our focus shifted from youthful adventure to being professionals—a huge shift from being young artist wannabes.

IV.

Eiko & Koma's full-time return to New York City in 1984 coincided with the heightening of the AIDS crisis. A number of their friends, neighbors, and colleagues, especially those in the arts, were wasting away and dying. It was also a period when art and activism became—had to become—one. This is well exemplified by now iconic works by artist collectives such as ACT-UP's *Silence = Death*. Many of those whose bohemian lifestyle symbolized radical art in the destitute city would eventually become casualties. David Wojnarowicz is forever remembered by his angry protestation—sewing his lips shut in Rosa von Praunheim's film also titled *Silence = Death*.[11] One of the most iconic images of the period, for me, is Martin Wong's painting *Stanton near Forsyth* (1984), which shows the bleak urban landscape of the city's Lower East Side, flanked in the lower register of the picture by the artist's self-portrait with his lover, poet Miguel Piñero. Both artists would die from an AIDS-related illness.

Eiko & Koma recall that for them and many in their generation, this period of devastation reminded them of the anger and activism in the 1960s when they were growing up, as well as of another equation of silence with tacit support of the war. At the same time, the artists were no longer in their youthful, carefree prime. They were maturing. They became parents, which necessarily brought a change in their understanding of life, death, and the body. So here they were: the two people whose purpose for the voyage to the United States, to New York, was initially so open, even cavalier, were occupying an increasingly larger space and laying down deeper roots. That is not to say, however, that they blindly embraced their adopted home and everything it represented and severed their links to what gave rise to them in the first place.

ACT UP   *Silence = Death* poster, 1987

David Wojnarowicz   Untitled still from the film *Silence = Death*, 1990

11
In November 2010, David Wojnarowicz (1954–1992) was posthumously involved in a scandal when his film *Fire in My Belly* (1986–1987) was pulled from the group show *Hide and Seek: Difference and Desire in American Portraiture* at the Smithsonian National Portrait Gallery barely a few weeks into the exhibition. The video—shot in Super 8mm film during the artist's travels to Mexico, and existing in the original 13-minute version as well as in a 7-minute excerpt made by the artist—is a collage taken from various sources and pieces of footage and is a meditation on desire, faith, social inequality, and death.

The controversy was ignited when Bill Donohue, president of the Catholic League, called the 11-second segment showing a crucifix with ants crawling on it "hate speech," decrying it as "designed to insult and inflict injury and assault the sensibilities of Christians." (Blake Gopnik, "National Portrait Gallery Bows to Censors, Withdraws Wojnarowicz Video on Gay Love," *Washington Post*, November 30, 2010.) Several House Republicans also joined the fray and severely criticized the gallery for misusing taxpayers' money, resulting in the institution's decision to withdraw Wojnarowicz's work from the show.

In the opinion of this author and others, *Fire in My Belly* includes many images that are far more provocative and even shocking, including the image of a mouth being sewn shut. The mouth in the film, however, was not that of the artist's, but the image had been featured in many earlier paintings and drawings by him as early as 1983. The artist's own performance seems to have taken place sometime soon after *Fire in My Belly* and was included in Praunheim's film. I thank Cara Starke, assistant curator of media and performance at the Museum of Modern Art, and Jamie Sterns of P.P.O.W. Gallery, New York, for enlightening me on this matter.

12
The conversation in section IV is taken from an interview with the artists in New York City, April 24, 2010.

What does it mean for you now, as Asian Americans, to live and work in the United States? [12]

Eiko: America is an empire, and it's responsible for many wars. So it's a conflict for us to be here. If the US still had a mandatory draft and my kids were subjected to it, then I wouldn't be here. I probably would have made a different decision. But we came as individuals, with the knowledge that the government and individuals are different. We can be critical of US government policies, and this country allows that. In that sense, it's an interesting country to develop your own thinking, your own access, which I think is more available here.

Koma: For us as artists, like all artists, we needed that sense of being lost. You get that in America. Whenever we go to Queens or the Bronx, we don't know where we are. Where I came from in Japan, you know where you are supposed to go. If you go to an onsen [hot spring], a man goes to this side and a woman goes to that side. Everything has been set for a very long time. I don't get much inspiration. When I'm in Japan, I feel like I'm wasting my time because I feel we have fewer unknowns.

Eiko: This may be a little shameful after thirty-five years of being here, but to this day, I get the juiciest reading experience when I'm reading in Japanese. If I'm reading news or a novel in English, I can handle it. But when I'm reading a poem in English, even if I'm following the words, it doesn't physicalize itself to me. So there are certain limitations as first-generation immigrants. Maybe also because our work is nonverbal, we didn't need language to survive, so our language acquisition is minimal. We are still very much attached to the Japanese language when dealing with nuances, culture, and poetic images. I've always read a lot of postwar Japanese literature, because that's where we still confront history and the body and stories.

We still talk to each other in Japanese. We generate our pieces together, and to generate that kind of "smell," I often go to Japanese language—to poems. Also, the Japanese language uses Chinese ideograms, each of which visually embodies a meaning, practical and abstract. That sense of the double image of practical and abstract gives us a fertile ground for our imaginings beyond language's communication use.

Is there a kind of irreconcilable relationship between you being here, and your work here, and your attachment to Japan?

Eiko: No, I don't think I have too strong an attachment. It's something we carry within us. We're not bound, but rather critical about a lot of things about Japan. However, Japanese remains our learning and sensory language. Since visual art is not linguistic, we don't feel attached to art made in any one place. I really like [Jean-Michel] Basquiat's work, and we are crazy about [Mark] Rothko. There is no nationality. But there are certain things that involve fine nuances of language, such as literature and movies.

In October 2008, Eiko & Koma came to Minneapolis to premiere their new work, *Hunger*, commissioned by the Walker Art Center. The piece featured themselves as always, but also, unusually, two young Cambodian performers, Peace (Setpheap Sorn) and Charian (Chakreya So). *Hunger* was something of a palimpsest in which several of their past endeavors were revived and combined—a kind of regeneration. During a residency at the Reyum Institute of Art and Culture in Phnom Penh in 2006, Eiko & Koma had worked with local youths to create *Cambodian Stories*, a performance that included dance and action paintings created collectively onstage. Peace and Charian, respectively ages eighteen and seventeen at the time, rejoined Eiko & Koma in a quartet the following year for *Cambodian Stories Revisited*. Also in 2007, the two young dancers performed a revival of the older artists' 1983 piece *Grain*, and this led to *Hunger*.

I should interject that Eiko & Koma always produce their own sets; they consider those elements as more than backdrops and props, but almost as their cohabitants or even extensions of their own beings. These artistic creations are often organic in quality as well as in materials. In *Hunger*, a mound of raw and then cooked rice appears, which Eiko devours—in a way that reminded me of pathetic hungry ghosts in Buddhist hell. The physical installation consists of canvas draperies burned and punctured in places and encrusted with thick salt crystals, along with dark-colored soil and an "island" of raven feathers on the floor.

Absorbed in this environment, and minimally informed about this multiyear, cross-cultural, and cross-generational project at the time—not to mention the long trajectory of Eiko & Koma's work—I approached the piece with the unfiltered eye of a neophyte. Amazement at the moving body is perhaps too clichéd a way of appreciating dance, but that was my indisputable and pure response to *Hunger*—and most likely, that of most people in the audience. The Cambodian duo, barely twenty years of age, exuded the insouciant confidence of youth as well as a contradictory, distant quality that was probably was the result of nerves and vulnerability. And this was in a striking contrast with Eiko & Koma's stage presence on many levels: while their dance isn't known for any stereotypical mode of emoting, their expressions, both facial and corporeal, were dynamic, even turbulent, fitting for the title and theme of the piece. Their astonishingly flexible and powerful, yet visibly aging bodies—their skin not as taut as it once had been and their complexions made pale with makeup—created a counterpoint to the darker, suntanned tone of their younger Southeast Asian partners. Their bodies merged together like phantoms against the dark backdrop and hushed lighting of the theater. This pairing of pairs, I soon realized, may mean more than a mere convergence of two generations and two cultures.

Peace and Charian belong to the generation born after the atrocious tyranny of the Khmer Rouge's war upon its own people. It was during their parents' and grandparents' time that allegedly more than one million people were killed through executions and starvation. While I was absolutely enchanted by the young dancers' fluid movements and almost preternaturally pliant fingers, limbs, and joints, much the same as those figures one sees in the stunning relief sculptures at Angkor, I could not help but think of the evil and violence inflicted on so many of their forebears. And what must Eiko & Koma have felt in that land—which their home country had invaded and occupied in the final years of the Asia-Pacific War—and toward these youths? Did they feel affinity and solidarity, besides sympathy, with this "underdeveloped" country still tending the raw wounds of history? Were they reminded of the muddy roads of their childhood and of their once strong, youthful bodies and those of their comrades, and the pungent odor of the collective sweat emitted by those bodies protesting in the streets of Tokyo in the late 1960s?

Since then, through a number of conversations, some of which are documented here, I have been a fortunate observer of Eiko & Koma's journey with the Retrospective Project. One component of the project is the new movement piece, *Raven*. While the more conventional stage presentation of the piece—which I saw in different phases of development at Wesleyan University in November 2009 and at Danspace Project in New York in May 2010—was full of their signature slowness coupled with dramatic irruptions, the underlying tone was one of inert tension, also familiar in their work. It is the latter quality that seems to be extended and maximized in *Naked*, the living installation the artists developed for the Walker Art Center based on *Raven*. In this piece, the two dancers' unclothed bodies remained mostly parallel to an oblong island made primarily of black feathers, which they flanked like parentheses. Over the course of several hours each day—at any point during which viewers could enter the space and stay as long as they wanted—their bodies came together for brief moments but ultimately remained apart, separated by the mound, which was both fetal and funerary.[13]

Koma uses the Japanese expression *kawa no youni neru* to describe this movement. Literally, the phrase means "sleeping like a river," but more precisely it refers to the morphology of the *kanji*, a Sino-Japanese ideogram for "river," which consists of three parallel vertical lines. For Koma, this expression not only describes the way in which a family has to sleep in a house too small for the number of its members, but also suggests the manner in which "everything happens in a small theater" of a house. At the same time, for Eiko & Koma, this paralleling of bodies evokes *shinju*, the "double suicide" of lovers who believe they will be united in the afterlife, a subject that has long been portrayed and immortalized in Japanese literature and theater.[14] Although *shinju* has been artistically romanticized, Eiko reminded me that often the reason lovers ended their lives together was because their bond was illegitimate—such as an extramarital relation or unbridgeable social classes. The bodies of these dead lovers were denied the dignity of rite and burial, left out in the open to rot or to be consumed by animal scavengers as a warning to all against disrupting the social order.

13
Eiko & Koma developed *Naked* during a residency at the Park Avenue Armory in New York City in summer 2010. This description is based on my observation of an excerpt of the work-in-progress and a subsequent conversation at the armory on October 8, 2010.

14
One well-known example is Shinoda Masahiro's 1969 film *Double Suicide*, also known under the original Japanese title *Shinju: Ten no amijima* (*The Love Suicides at Amijima*), which is based on an early eighteenth-century play and often performed as a Bunraku puppet play.

爆心地の話をつたえてくれる人は、いません.

Iri and Toshi Maruki
Illustration from *Pika don*, 1950

VI.

It is not my intention to simply suggest the romanticism of love and anti-authoritarianism by invoking the image of a convention-defying amorous couple committing a double suicide. But bodies abandoned and decaying, and the souls or ghosts of the departed are things that have been evoked by Eiko & Koma's work. That is why, in closing this text, I want to allude to another important aspect of the artists' thinking and Eiko's academic research, in particular. Both artists are longtime avid readers of postwar Japanese literature, and Eiko has translated and written on that which deals with the experience of atomic bombings. There have been, of course, notable cultural figures and works that address the topic, from Nobel laureate Oe Kenzaburo, especially in his 1965 book *Hiroshima Notes*, to photographers Domon Ken in *Hiroshima-Nagasaki Document 1961* and Tomatsu Shomei in *Time Stopped at 11:02, 1945, Nagasaki, 1961*. But it is on the work of Hayashi Kyoko, a survivor of the Nagasaki bombing and a celebrated writer, that Eiko has focused a considerable amount of attention and thinking. In an essay on Hayashi's work, Eiko writes, "Every *hibakusha* [atomic-bomb survivor] knows their survival carries within it the wailing and silence of the dead."[15] She also observes, "Many people died screaming while many people vanished without a scream. Looking back on those deaths, Hayashi says that the atomic bomb deprived the victims not only of their lives, but also of their 'own personal deaths,' which, as humans, they were entitled to experience."[16]

Eiko, and also Koma, seem to believe that every Japanese person, especially of the generation that lived through the war or came of age in the wake of it, cannot but be a survivor and must carry the guilt of living on. The fact that Eiko & Koma settled in the US and are now long-time immigrants in this country does not distance them from that fate, but rather sharpens the memory, consciousness, and conscience that are becoming increasingly more faint in Japan with every year that passes. Discussing Hayashi's American sojourn in the 1990s and her visit to the Trinity site in New Mexico, where the first atomic bomb test was conducted, Eiko writes, "Living in the United States also gave Hayashi time and distance away from Japan, making her work more *naked* as a *hibakusha* writer." And here we find the important key word and defining characteristic—the courageous, matter-of-fact realness—of Eiko & Koma's singular body of work. I would not imagine that they would ever claim to "represent," "depict," or "embody" *hibakusha* bodies in their work. "Sympathy" and "resonance" are words almost as inadequate, but these were on Eiko's mind when she quoted Hayashi's writing: "The white flash burned *hibakusha*'s bodies, making them live *nakedly*."[17]

What does it mean to live nakedly? Giorgio Agamben, in his famous formulation, argues that law, since the antiquity, has functioned to define and to have power over "bare life," that which is excluded from but thus should be transformed and included into the political body by the sovereignty of the state.[18] This also means that there is always part of bare life that remains or falls

15
Eiko Otake, Introduction, Kyoko Hayashi, *From Trinity to Trinity*, trans. Eiko Otake (Barrytown, NY: Station Hill Press, 2010), xi.
16
Ibid., xv.

17
Ibid., xxvii.

18
Giorgio Agamben, *Homo Sacer: Sovereign Power and Bare Life*, trans. Daniel Heller-Roazen (Stanford, CA: Stanford University Press, 1998).

Tomatsu Shomei *Time Stopped at 11:02, 1945, Nagasaki, 1961* 1961

outside of the political body, utterly vulnerable and unprotected, unsocialized and unpoliticized, and thus totally liberated—or rather that there is no need for liberation, as it was never shackled down in the first place. This is perhaps the question one could bear in mind when in the space of the wilderness, the scorched earth and sky of *Naked*, and faced with the stupendously writhing bodies of Eiko & Koma.

Nagasaki, August 10, 1945 Photo: Yosuke Yamahata

White Dance: Moth, Anwatin Middle School, Minneapolis, Minnesota, October 1981

WHERE TIME IS RELATIVE: EIKO & KOMA AT THE WALKER ART CENTER

Philip Bither

What we do through artistic expression is to share with people our desire to affirm life in the context of the flow of time.[1]

1
Eiko Otake, e-mail message to the author, February 21, 2010.

Eiko & Koma's indelible body of work has always held a special relationship with time. Temporal notions—how time is perceived or altered in the experience of a performance, its relationship to a full review of an artist's lifework, and its role as connective tissue between certain artists and their most supportive institutions—are embedded within their three-year Retrospective Project (2009–2012), which includes the 2010 gallery installation *Naked* at the Walker as well as dozens of other projects and performances spread across the country.

Central to the experience of an Eiko & Koma work is an almost visceral sense of time's elasticity. Their intensely focused performances—simultaneously ancient and modern, shamanistic and deeply organic, intimate and existential, gorgeous and grueling—unfold at a pace that seems to challenge linear perceptions of time itself. Primordial in its expression, their work allows one to live in something ambient music pioneer Brian Eno has termed the "Long Now—the recognition that the precise moment you are in now grows out of the past and is a seed for the future." His elaboration is an apt description of Eiko & Koma's core philosophy. "The longer your sense of Now," writes Eno, "the more past and future it includes." The sense of dislocation and altered time often felt when watching the artists perform stands in sharp contrast to the pressure of our culture's accelerating speed. Their work offers an alternative to what Eno calls the "Short Now—where everything is exciting, fast, current and temporary."[2]

2
Brian Eno, "The Long Now," *Small Acts: Performance, the Millennium and the Marking of Time*, ed. Adrian Heathfield (London: Black Dog Publishing, 2000), 92–95.

The pace and immersive qualities of Eiko & Koma's staged work, which involves striking visual designs of organic materials conceived and constructed by the artists, have long placed it somewhere between choreographed dance and kinetic, conceptual installation. It is, however, their own remarkably expressive bodies that have always anchored their works, making profoundly manifest the pain, stillness, desire, violence, hunger and thirst, and ultimately, the peace found in our humanness.

3
The Walker has organized several Eiko & Koma film programs over the years. These include Video Choreography in 1993, which featured five of the artists' early films; and in fall 2010, Dance for Camera: Selected Works, organized by associate film curator Dean Otto, screened continuously at the Walker for two months, providing added context for the artists' installation *Naked*.

Since Eiko & Koma's first appearance at the Walker in 1981, the institution has supported a full range of their creative expression—new live performance commissions, stage presentations, site-based productions, dance videos,[3] community residencies, gallery installation works, and now the publication of this catalogue. For three decades, Twin Cities audiences have had the opportunity literally to watch these artists age, to witness the weight of their life experiences continuing to inform their movement and installation choices. Contemplating the passage of time in their lives was a central motivation in making *Naked*, which was conceived twelve years after their first gallery-based performance installation.[4] "We are inviting a close look at another one-month period of time in our bodies," Eiko wrote about *Naked*. "In the collapsed time, we have lingered as much as we have aged." She challenged gallery-goers to "stay here with your eyes, live, and kinetically observe how our bodies move toward the unknown."[5]

The Walker first presented Eiko & Koma in October 1981, just five years after their arrival in the United States. Nigel Redden, Walker director of performing arts, invited the duo to perform in Minneapolis as part of his ambitious New Dance USA Festival, a ten-day survey of innovative movement art that featured David Gordon, Karole Armitage, Trisha Brown, Lucinda Childs, Laura Dean, Douglas Dunn, Molissa Fenley, Deborah Hay, Margaret Jenkins, Bill T. Jones, Dana Reitz, Kei Takei, and many others performing at venues across the city. Even within this diverse mix of American dance pioneers, Eiko & Koma stood out as singular. They performed *White Dance: Moth*—the piece they had composed for their US debut in 1976—on the humble stage of Anwatin Middle School in Minneapolis. "Eiko & Koma ... seemed to magnetize the audience, perhaps because the performers immediately prepare you for extreme slowness and decondition you for 'dancing,' and because their intensity is so great," wrote Deborah Jowitt, who traveled to Minneapolis to review the entire festival for the *Village Voice*.[6]

In 1984, Eiko & Koma returned at the invitation of the Walker's new performing arts director, Robert Stearns. In Studio 6A at the Hennepin Center for the Arts in downtown Minneapolis, they presented *Grain*, a powerful, even violent seminal work that integrated their video piece *Tentacle*. And in 1985, Walker media director Melinda Ward commissioned a collaboration between Eiko & Koma and Minnesota-based video artist James Byrne. The result, *Lament* (1986), was later shown nationwide on *Alive from Off Center*, a PBS television showcase for new music, theater, dance, and video work.[7]

Although very different works, these first three Walker presentations—*White Dance: Moth, Grain*, and *Lament*—represent two important modalities in Eiko & Koma's work: mixed media and collaboration with other artists. Both *White Dance: Moth* and *Grain* included projected imagery; the collaborative *Lament* is an example of their "media dances," works made for and by the camera that are simultaneously dance and video art. Across the three decades the artists have been performing at the Walker, they have continued to develop and deepen these processes.

For example, in 1989 Eiko & Koma were invited by performing arts director John Killacky to conduct a five-week artist residency in Minnesota, during which they conceived, rehearsed, and presented *Canal*, their first Walker-commissioned work. This early experiment in choreographing for performers in addition to

4
Eiko & Koma's first gallery-based installation, *Breath*, also a month in duration, was presented in 1998 at the Whitney Museum of American Art, New York.

5
Eiko Otake, e-mail message to the author, February 21, 2010. The "collapsed time" that Eiko refers to here is between 1998 and 2010, an intense twelve-year period between the two installation works during which their collaborations multiplied and their lived experience brought new perspectives to their work.

6
Deborah Jowitt, "What if the Package Betrays Its Contents?" *Village Voice*, October 21–27, 1981.

7
Alive from Off Center was initially launched and coproduced in 1985 by the Walker Art Center and KCTA-TV.

For a complete roster of collaborating performers, see page 162.

9

Among the partner organizations were Intermedia Arts, the University of Minnesota Dance Department, the American Indian Center, and the Minnesota (now American) Composer's Forum.

10

Eiko Otake, excerpt from her narrative in the documentary film *Dancing in Water: The Making of "River" (2009),"* directed by Eiko & Koma and coedited by Shoko Letton, which follows the artists from rehearsals in the Catskills to performances in the Delaware River and at the American Dance Festival.

11

Days before the event, Eiko & Koma realized how loud and busy the lake is at sunset, the time scheduled for a work dependent on a sense of stillness and quiet. The artists, along with Walker staff and volunteers, spent days leafleting the docks and shores of Medicine Lake, asking for boaters' restraint and cooperation, and inviting them to attend. There was near full compliance with the request, with many community members coming over to witness the performance.

12

The Walker's presentation of *River* was the central event of Waterways, a community-wide exploration of environmental and clean-water issues produced by the Walker in association with Hennepin Parks and the Metropolitan Council Environmental Services Division. The weekend also included panel discussions, art labs, workshops, and an Eco Info Fair.

themselves included four additional movement artists (three from Minnesota) as well as several area technicians and designers.[8] After extended negotiations between Killacky and the Southern Theater, which copresented the work, the artists were able to realize their vision for the piece's unique staging—a scenic environment in which water flowed down the theater's beautifully distressed back wall and dripped from multiple outlets hidden in the ceiling's lighting grid. Eiko & Koma and their collaborators performed naked on the flooded stage floor.

In 1993, Killacky invited the artists back for a two-week residency for which they presented *Land* and premiered *Wind* at the Hennepin Center for the Arts. The residency involved Taos Pueblo composer and musician Robert Mirabal, their musical collaborator for both works, and also included workshops, presentations, panels, and film screenings across the Twin Cities.[9] Since that time, fostering a deep connection with the communities in which they perform has become increasingly important for Eiko & Koma.

This commitment to community was further amplified in 1996, when the Walker presented Eiko & Koma's landmark site work *River* at Medicine Lake in Plymouth, Minnesota. Several hundred people gathered to watch from the shore as the piece unfolded. The artists stood chest-high in the water, holding aloft a driftwood structure draped with muslin that served as a screen for their film *Lament*, which glowed on the horizon like a cinematic sunset. As darkness fell and the film faded out, the pair slowly moved together and over one another, fading and then emerging seemingly weightless on the water's surface. They gradually drifted farther out into the lake and down the shore, ultimately disappearing, "swallowed by the river of time."[10]

Performed free of charge in a popular recreational area,[11] *River* was offered by its creators with a sense of humility and inclusiveness, and it pulled together a diverse group of viewers to celebrate the deep bonds between art and the environment.[12] *River* also opened up their work to a broader range of Minnesotans, some of whom simply happened upon the performance. According to Eiko, their desire to connect directly and deeply with non-arts community members without altering the purity or sometimes brutal intensity of their work emanates from a specifically American, democratic influence, one that actively resists art serving as a form of class division. Their years in the United States, combined with their lifelong populist beliefs, have continued to this day to inform their choices about how and where to show their work.

My personal commitment to Eiko & Koma began in 1986. At that time, I was associate director of the Brooklyn Academy of Music's Next Wave Festival, where the artists premiered the tetralogy *New Moon Stories*. During the *Night Tide* section, I watched with stunned fascination as two ghostly, enigmatic figures, seemingly part human and part animal, crept toward one another at an almost imperceptible pace from opposite corners of BAM's vast Lepercq Space stage. Time stood still. When their bodies finally came together, the emotional and metaphysical impact of that collision of souls felt both agonizing and sublime. I was sure I would never forget the experience, a response I later found to be common for viewers encountering Eiko & Koma's work for the first time. During the 1990s, while I was director of programming at the Flynn Theater in Burlington, Vermont, I invited them to come several times to develop and present work, and subsequently to mount *River* in Vermont's Winooski River.

When I took the position of performing arts curator at the Walker in 1997, it felt both natural and essential to continue the institution's commitment to Eiko & Koma. In early 2002, with the national trauma of the September 11 attacks the previous year still raw and palpable, the Walker co-commissioned *Offering*. With their expansive sense of time and their deep understanding of psychic and physical trauma, the duo seemed to me uniquely positioned to create a meaningful response to the destruction unleashed upon their adopted city and country. The work premiered in New York in a Battery Park City plaza overlooking the Hudson River, just blocks from the gaping holes where the Twin Towers had once stood. *Offering* sanctified that desecrated place and sought to heal a damaged society. Six months later, with the drumbeats for war in Iraq growing louder—the stated US response to 9/11—the Walker presented the first indoor performances of *Offering* at the Southern Theater, the opening event of the Walker's 2003 Out There festival. The performers entered through the Southern's decaying proscenium arch and proceeded toward a roughhewn sculptural icon not unlike a large funeral pyre. With exquisite grace, their bodies seemed to channel the collective sadness of tragedies past. The piece clearly sprang from the philosophy outlined in a manifesto Eiko & Koma use in teaching their Delicious Movement workshops: "Move to create a sustainable culture of peace" and "move to forget and remember."[13] Paired with clarinetist David Krakauer's yearning score, performed live, *Offering* was a lament but also a plea, and a particularly poignant one at a moment when the country was in a rush to war.

While the Walker had presented Eiko & Koma's work at locales across the Twin Cities, it was not until 2005, with the opening of its building expansion and state-of-the-art McGuire Theater, that the institution possessed the theatrical tools to showcase their staged work on-site. When the Walker commissioned *Hunger*, the commitment included a two-week production residency in the McGuire that allowed the artists to technically mount this new work. I put the artists in touch with St. Paul–based Joko Sutrisno, a master Javanese gamelan musician and composer, who eventually created and performed the score. Choreographed for a quartet that included Eiko & Koma and two young Cambodian artists, Charian and Peace, *Hunger* was a powerful melding of music, movement, and visual elements that bridged both cultures and generations.[14]

Hunger marked the beginning of a process by the duo of stepping back and assessing the full history their work together. Nudged along by dance activist and visionary Sam Miller, a longtime friend and supporter, Eiko & Koma decided to attempt the ultimate

13
Rosemary Candelario, "A Manifesto for Moving: Eiko & Koma's Delicious Movement Workshops," *Theatre, Dance and Performance Training* 1, (2010): 1, 88–100.

14
For a complete listing of collaborating performers, see page 246.

River, Medicine Lake at French Regional Park, Plymouth, Minnesota, July 1996

Raven, Walker Art Center, Minneapolis, Minnesota, October 2010   Photo: Gene Pittman

quantification of time: a three-year, multiplatformed Retrospective Project that would allow them to simultaneously look backward and forward, something that performing artists, particularly living dance artists, are rarely able to do. The idea synched perfectly with the Walker's increasing interdisciplinary practice and the intellectual and physical resources it has at its disposal as a visual arts center and an experienced commissioner and presenter of contemporary dance, so the institution committed much of its fall 2010 season to Eiko & Koma's Retrospective Project. Activities included the presentation to a family audience of their newest stage work, the deeply organic and earthbound Raven; a three-month screening of their media dance videos; a series of talks, classes, and community interactions; and, at the center, the commissioning and mounting of Naked, a living installation that took place in a specially designed space in the heart of the Walker's permanent collection galleries.

What Eiko & and Koma achieved with Naked is easy to quantify in factual terms. They performed for a total of one hundred forty-four hours: six hours per day, six days per week for the entire month of November. Nearly 7,800 people saw the work. The eight weeks that Eiko & Koma spent in the Twin Cities to install, rehearse, and perform Naked was the longest single artistic residency in the Walker's performing arts history. Minneapolis' daily newspaper, the Star Tribune, ran an article about Naked on its front page—rare placement for a cultural story. Journalists, presenters, funders, and scholars flew in from around the country; the mayor of Minneapolis came for a private viewing. The in-depth collaboration between the Walker's visual arts and performing arts departments set a new standard—not just internally, but for multidisciplinary art centers nationwide.

More important than all of this, Naked was a stunning artistic achievement. After decades of stripping their work to its bare essentials, Eiko & Koma found a way to pare back even further. Walking into the environment—a floor cloth and three backdrops of scorched canvas stiffened with rice paste and embedded with salt and feathers—one felt an immediate sense of hushed, intense reverence. Just a few feet away from the viewers, on a nest of feathers, dirt, and canvas, two bodies lay naked under slowly shifting lights that mirrored the nearly imperceptible tonal variations of daylight. The sound of dripping water, the smell of salt and dirt, and the feel of a light breeze filled the air. At first glance the figures seemed motionless, but soon their slight movements, executed with focused precision and minute nuance, riveted one's attention. Every ripple of a muscle, turn of a finger, and extension of a toe felt acutely amplified in the space.

Naked was a moving, hypnotic, and intimate experience that invited viewers into Eiko & Koma's internal universe and resonated with themes that have long suffused their work: death, decay, struggle, essential human bonds. But more than any previous work they have made, it offered a fresh temporal experience. While watching the piece, time seemed to stop, as if one had stepped into Brian Eno's Long Now. In Naked, Eiko & Koma once again allowed audiences to connect deeply with their own humanity and to frame time's flow in new ways.

Philip Bither (left) with Eiko & Koma on the McGuire Theater stage, Walker Art Center, Minneapolis, Minnesota, October 2010
Photo: Cameron Wittig

⁶ reversing shoulder limpfalling

forward, cleaving,
away

Study for *Trilogy*, Leatherdale Studio, New York City   Photo: Marcus Leatherdale

CATALOGUE OF WORKS

Editor's Note

Performance is an inherently variable medium that in some ways resists cataloguing efforts such as this one. Changes in venue, audience, weather, resources, and the performer's body ensure that no two presentations of any given work are exactly alike. Eiko & Koma have embraced this mutability. When conditions warrant, they do not hesitate to adjust their movement, music, props, costumes, setting, lights, and collaborators. Since they consider the part to be more significant than the whole, they often reuse elements from their past projects in new ones. It is not unusual for them refine, reshape, and retitle pieces after their official premieres. Eiko & Koma have even made works that purposely assume different shapes in different situations. These might be described as concepts attached to a flexible framework—living, ongoing projects rather than finished, immutable "pieces." They have found that this engagement with change helps them discover what is most essential about each work. It also catalyzes the ongoing engagement of their audience. In short, their works are never truly finished but continue to evolve over time and space.

What follows, then, is a catalogue of Eiko & Koma's major works as they existed at one point in time: the date of their premiere. (This does not apply to their dance videos, which have been "fixed" by virtue of being released.) Entries are arranged chronologically by date of premiere. Both English and Japanese titles are given for each piece, since Japanese characters carry both linguistic and visual meaning that might shed additional light on their projects. In order to facilitate further study of the artists' work, each entry includes selected reviews, a few of which have been reprinted in full.

The length of any given piece varies from one performance to another. The lengths given here are approximate. Eiko & Koma design and handcraft all aspects of their sets and costumes. They either develop their own lighting or work closely with a lighting designer. Some entries do not include photographs because none were available.

Eiko & Koma have occasionally choreographed dances for other performers. These comprise a different category of work, so they are listed in Appendix B along with a handful of thematic programs. Funders, commissioners, and presenters are listed in Appendices A and C.

Readers are encouraged to consult the artists' website, http://www.eikoandkoma.org, a rich, dynamic resource and an important counterpart to this book. The extensive video documentation posted there provides information about their work that cannot be conveyed in text and photographs.

—Joan Rothfuss

White Dance, Young Choreographers' Competition, Cologne Opera, Germany, 1973 Photo: A. Loffler

WHITE DANCE
ホワイトダンス 1972–1974

Length: 60 minutes

Costumes: Various, by Eiko & Koma

Sound: Japanese and Western pop and big band music

Selected reviews: Wolfgang Stache, "Antriebe aus Religiosität," *Göttinger Allgemeine* (Kassel, Germany), September 8, 1973.

1

Eiko & Koma, e-mail message to the editor, February 2, 2011.

From 1972 to 1974, Eiko & Koma created performance events in Germany, the Netherlands, France, and elsewhere in Europe. Each event was unique; venues ranged from art galleries to churches to student centers. The pieces were not formally choreographed, although the artists did decide in advance roughly what they might do and in what order. The events combined moves they had learned from their various dance teachers—Kazuo Ohno, Tatsumi Hijikata, and others—with such Dadaesque actions as cutting their hair, throwing raw eggs, cooking fish, dragging a bundle of carrots, and painting their bodies with dough.

All of these performances were collectively titled *White Dance*. For Eiko & Koma, the name evoked associations with the color white—surrender, rituals, beginning anew—and differentiated their work from butoh, which was known among its practitioners as "the dance of utter darkness."

In 1973 Eiko & Koma were one of three finalists in the prestigious Young Choreographers' Competition in Cologne, Germany. Their entry, a condensed version of *White Dance*, became the seed from which they developed *White Dance: Moth* for the United States in 1976.

During our first museum performance, we cooked a large fish on a burner. Curators and viewers disliked the smell and the smoke.[1]

FINE JAPANESE DANCES

In the very pleasant, intimate, and hip theatre-in-the-round De Melkweg, at Lijnbaansgracht 234 A in Amsterdam, Eiko and Koma danced their Japanese dances yesterday evening.

When I arrived, a hip young man with headphones was onstage. He was listening with obvious delight to music from his tape recorder, which was placed near him on the floor. When the theatre's excellent sound system began to play American hit songs, he started to dance by himself.

After a short time he was asked to leave so that the audience could see the dancers. The four-sided stage was surrounded by spectators, who lay about on the more-or-less attractive and more-or-less luxurious carpets that had been placed around its perimeter. Here and there a few not-so-young persons, dressed predictably in colorful dresses or blue jeans and smocks, were smoking a joint. Aside from their giggles it was deadly quiet, as people relaxed and waited to see what would happen.

Not much did. A young Japanese couple wearing loose kimonos began to move in a way that is

familiar from slow-motion films. They danced to terribly ordinary big band tunes, the kind of banal Japanese-American music that can be heard in every Japanese department store and TV show. Their expressionless faces were powdered matte, as were their bodies. After a while their movement clarified what they had written (in very clumsy English) in what seemed to be the program: "We are dancers who have decided to devote ourselves to God. He doesn't want us to be commercial, but to dedicate all our time to our own insanity. Everyone should be insane." Etc. etc.

Virtuoso

The female dancer, in particular, achieved an amazing virtuosity in imitating the catatonic postures of the mentally ill. Her movements were performed with great intensity, and her facial expressivity was especially skillful. Although her mask-like face remained a mask, it changed rapidly; each new expression registered another emotion, and one mood followed another. Tenderness, grief, anger, rage—almost all human emotions, in short—were mirrored on her small face and in her very controlled, technically precise movements.

I have no idea if these "dances" are different every time, or if Eiko and Koma follow a fixed scheme. The man was the perfect complement for the girl, although his contribution was far less accomplished. In one exquisite scene near the beginning, the man stood behind the girl and bent towards her, placing his head on her neck as if he were about to kiss her. It was an exceptionally tender moment.

This couple would be very handsome artist's models. The girl, especially, seems to have been cut out of a Japanese print. As to the spiritual foundations on which this art of movement seems to be built, I cannot remark. I can only say that the result is often beautiful and sometimes impressive. It is movement that shows us the gestures and expressions of people who are trapped in some paroxysm of desire.

You can see them at De Melkweg tonight and Saturday evening at around nine-thirty.

—Jan Willem Hofstra. Originally published in *De Tijd* (Amsterdam), July 13, 1973. Translation by Mark Luyten.

IN THEIR DANCE NO WIND BLOWS

Both their faces are white. The man in his short red kimono stares straight ahead of him with unblinking intensity; strong, but infinitesimal shudders seize his body, causing subtle changes in the way his legs turn in his hip sockets. His hands are as stiff as paws. A short distance from him, a woman sits; she seems to be trying to lower part of her weight back onto her elbows, trying to recline by increments. Meanwhile, a tape recorder is playing "The Agincourt Carol." I think it's been recorded by non-English singers, which gives the bellicose male voices a strange and barbaric edge. This goes on for what seems a very long time. I wonder what terror, what ineluctable force is causing the tremors in the people. My sense of their isolation deepens. The man shuffles away.

This is the beginning of "White Dance," by Eiko and Koma, two young dancers who describe their work as "an avant-garde dance in the Japanese manner." They appeared suddenly on the New York scene, danced at Japan House, the Cubiculo, the Performing Garage, and departed. You can see in the sparseness and fastidious precision of "White Dance" the influence of Japanese tradition. It's also possible to detect slight hints of an influence from German and American modern dance (Eiko and Koma studied in Berlin with Manja Chmiel, a Wigman disciple, and with Lucas Hoving in Rotterdam). Very occasionally, Eiko, who is slim, beautiful, fragile, jars me by extending one leg high to the side, a strikingly Grahamesque pose. Yet "White Dance" seems to come principally from sources deep inside both performers.

I cannot say what it is "about." A stylized projection of a moth appears from time to time on the back wall. A poem about a moth is printed in the program. The climate the dance creates is like that of the poem: "No moon was seen/But moonlight flooded everywhere./The sky like a layer of salt./The earth so dim and quiet/That even dewdrops could be heard dropping/Onto the bed of grass from the twigs above." In this hushed and eerie world, the dancers seem as delicate, as febrile, as fated as moths.

But their work isn't pretty or sentimental; it's pervaded with horror, studded with moments of violence. You watch with fascination their quaking toes, their eyes that seem to be crossing as the gaze folds inward. Eiko, sitting on the floor, lets her legs swim upward, and for a long time stays there, her toes separating and stretching as if they had individual sensibilities. Later, she dances with her mouth wide open, but the rest of her face unmoved; you sense some horror which she—like an animal—feels, but can't comprehend. Both performers change clothes during the dance, she reappearing in a beautiful wide-sleeved dress, dark with big patterns. But both of them are naked under their robes except for white cotton strips that pass between their legs and along the cleft of their buttocks. When their robes swing open in back, the effect is shocking in some way I can't articulate; they look bandaged. Once, Koma springs into the air and falls all in one piece to a sit—his knees and ankles making a great clatter against the floor. Once, one of them leans a head against the other's hand, but that is their only contact except for a combat in which they cross heads and push against each other with their shoulders. Leaning together, they quiver with the strain. A fight that deadlocks them into immobility.

"White Dance" didn't end; it just stopped going on. Although it often, without my willing it, resumes in my head.

—Deborah Jowitt. Originally published in the *Village Voice*, August 9, 1976.

Premiere: May 6, 1976, Japan Society, New York City

Length: 60 minutes

Visual design: Eiko & Koma

Costumes: Eiko & Koma

Sound: Anonymous, "Agincourt Carol"; J. S. Bach, Concerto for Harpsichord, and Sarabande from Suite for Solo Cello no. 5 in C Minor; Tibetan horn and cymbal

Selected reviews: Mona Sulzman, "*Moth Comes to Life as Eiko and Koma White Dance*," *SoHo Weekly News*, July 29, 1976; Irene Oppenheim, "A Mix of Pleasure and Pain," *The Independent and Gazette* (Oakland, CA), October 20, 1977; Janice Ross, "Tension in the Cocoon," *San Francisco Bay Guardian*, October 27, 1977.

1
Press release for *White Dance: Moth*, 1976

WHITE DANCE: MOTH
ホワイトダンス　蛾 1976

The premiere of *White Dance: Moth* was Eiko & Koma's US debut. Constructed between 1974 and 1976 while the artists were in Japan studying with Kazuo Ohno, the piece was inspired by twentieth-century Japanese poet Mitsuharu Kaneko's "A Moth." Eiko's free adaptation of the text appeared in the program.

The structure of *White Dance: Moth* was episodic. Each section was defined by costumes, lighting, music, and projections of hugely magnified moths. The choreography included extended periods of stasis and floor work for Eiko, necessary because of an ankle injury she had sustained in Europe. Koma's movements were more angular and forceful. In the final section he dashed across the stage several times to spill sacks of unwashed potatoes onto the floor; the clouds of dust this produced were an important visual component of the piece. Both artists wore white makeup and kimono-inspired costumes of their own design. *White Dance: Moth* was a staple in Eiko & Koma's repertoire for several years, with lighting by Blu. It was revived in 2010 as part of their Retrospective Project.

Metaphorically explores the moth and its febrile, short-lived existence.[1]

White Dance: Moth, Japan Society, New York City, May 1976 (dress rehearsal)　Photo: Osamu Honda

A MOTH

No moon was seen
But moonlight flooded everywhere,
The sky like a layer of salt,
The earth too dim and quiet
That even dewdrops could be heard dropping
Onto the bed of grass from the twigs above.

Just like a fan with broken vanes,
There appeared, flapping,
A nocturnal moth swimming through the foggy sea of moonlight
In the broad sleeves of his crested gown,
Heavy with a layer of dew.
He moved his wings as if in a dream,
Showing by his course that changed continuously
His determination not to drown.

To live is to be fragile,
So is it a fault to nurture a dream?
Oh moth! what is life to you?
You've been exhausted ever since you lost your cosy pupa,
You've carried the weight of time upon your back
And gasped for breathe
While taking a rest
After such a short journey,
Then started on another voyage
Into an unknown future.

Pages from the program for a performance of *White Dance: Moth*, Theater of Man, San Francisco, November 18–20, 1977

While most of human kind are in the sleep of slaves
The earth runs on at full tilt, like a frightened thief,
With every burden on its shoulders
Looking for the chance to cast them off.
Only the few who cannot sleep so easily
Know and await the coming punishment-
The magnificent shipwreck on the promised land.

The moth flies on with silent eloquence,
Flapping his fragile wings in clamorous
Desperation.
On each wing there appears some scales
Like the layers of powder on a lady's mirror.
Each scale means death.

The moth is overburdened.

As I wander along the beach around the lake,
I sense under every step I make
The softness of fallen corpses,
O dead moths,
And so I know that I am nothing more
Than a tiny shadow in the moonlight night.

Fur Seal, Riverside Church, New York City, June 1977 (dress rehearsal)   Photo: Nathaniel Tileston

FUR SEAL
オットセイ 1977

In this dance Eiko & Koma meshed human and animal movements as they enacted a mating ritual. The work was inspired by the seals the artists had seen in California during their 1976 visit as well as "Seals" by twentieth-century Japanese poet Mitsuharu Kaneko. The set included a tree trunk without branches or roots, which hung from the ceiling. During the dance it functioned as a toy for the seals; it also made clear the connections between tree trunks, human and animal torsos, and the choreography of this piece, which deemphasized ornamental and everyday hand movements.

Eiko's free adaptation (below) of Kaneko's poem was printed in a 1977 program for *Fur Seal*.

Premiere: June 2, 1977, Riverside Church, New York City

Length: 65 minutes

Set: Eiko & Koma

Lighting: Blu

Costumes: Eiko & Koma

Sound: The Beatles, "I Am the Walrus"; Bob Dylan, "One More Cup of Coffee"; Franz Schubert, Andante con molto from Piano Trio no. 2; recorded songs of the humpback whale

Selected reviews: Janice Ross, "Eiko and Koma in 'Fur Seal,'" *Artweek* 8 (December 3, 1977); Anna Kisselgoff, "Two Dancers from Japan in 'Fur Seal,'" *New York Times*, February 25, 1978; Leslie Friedman, "Dance: Eiko and Koma," *Saint Louis Literary Supplement* 2 (January–February 1978).

1 Eiko & Koma, e-mail message to the editor, February 2, 2011.

```
FUR SEAL


The sunlight beats down like sleet
Today is their wedding feast
Today is their big holiday

All day long they wallow in the mud
Ceaselessly bowing and curtseying
Rubbing their fins together
And rolling their bodies like barrels

Fur seal
How foul-smelling is your breath
How slimy is your back
Clammy as the abysmal depth of an open grave
Your body is ponderous as sand-bags
How mediocre, how banal you are

Your somber elastic shape
Your dolorous lumps of rubber
Bob and sink in the sea
In the sorrowful rays of the evening twilight
```

To Bob Dylan's "One More Cup of Coffee," we danced our encore jumping around, blowing whistles.[1]

Premiere: July 8, 1978,
Santa Barbara Museum of Art,
Santa Barbara, California

Length: 60 minutes

Set: Eiko & Koma

Lighting: Eiko & Koma
(with Blu in later performances)

Costumes: Eiko & Koma

Sound: George Abdo, "Raks Leyla";
Romanian folk song, "Doina from
Gorj"; recorded rooster noises

Selected reviews: Julie McLeod, "Eiko,
Koma Impressive," *Santa Barbara
News-Press*, July 10, 1978; Deborah
Jowitt, "Dance," *Village Voice*,
November 20, 1978; Tobi Tobias,
"Eiko and Koma," *Dance Magazine*
53 (January 1979).

   1
Matthew 26:34

BEFORE THE COCK CROWS
鶏が鳴く前に 1978

Truly I say to you that this very night, before the cock crows, you shall deny me three times.[1]

This dance, the first that Eiko & Koma created entirely in the United States, explores the dynamic between fate and human will through movements that convey the tension of anticipation. In a performance space marked out by birch limbs, the artists both danced seductively; Eiko's movement evoked belly dance, which she had studied in preparation for this piece. In the final sequence, she divided the stage in half with a log as Koma entered, balancing an enormous lattice of branches on his back.

THEIR DANCE HAS FASCINATING POWER OF THE LEGENDARY COBRA.
THEY HYPNOTIZE YOU, THEN STRIKE. —VILLAGE VOICE

Eiko +Koma

AUG. 3, 4, 10, 11, 17, 18, FRI. & SAT. **2 PROGRAMS EACH NIGHT**

8 P.M. PROGRAM A "BEFORE THE COCK CROWS"
10 P.M. PROGRAM B "FUR SEAL" & STATIC
"FLUTTERING BLACK" (PREMIERE)
ALONG WITH NO WAVE ROCK ON STAGE

THE PERFORMING GARAGE
33 WOOSTER ST. SOHO, N.Y.C.

$4. or T.D.F. & $1.50
RESERVATION 966-3651

Flyer for 1979 concert at the Performing Garage, New York City

Before the Cock Crows, 1978 (rehearsal) Photo: David A. Fullard

Fluttering Black, Performing Garage, New York City, August 1979

Fluttering Black, San Francisco Museum of Modern Art, August 1979 Photo ©1979 Marion Gray All rights reserved.

FLUTTERING BLACK
はためく黒 1979

Premiere: August 3, 1979,
Performing Garage, New York City

Length: 20 minutes

Set: Eiko & Koma

Lighting: Blu

Costumes: Eiko & Koma

Sound: Commissioned score
by Glenn Branca

Musicians: Glenn Branca and Static

Selected reviews: Tobi Tobias,
"Flagging," *SoHo Weekly News*,
August 16, 1979; Burt Supree,
"Only Disconnect," *Village Voice*,
August 27, 1979.

Fluttering Black was first performed in collaboration with musician Glenn Branca and his band Static. The piece explored one's natural tendency to synchronize movement with sound (that is, to "dance") by eliminating all visual and sonic connections between the two. Eiko & Koma and the musicians wore blindfolds and plugged their ears with cotton and adhesive tape or wore high-quality headphones to block out sounds. Audience members also were offered cotton balls to protect their ears. Each performer worked alone within the loud soundscape of electric music; since the musicians could not hear one another, the sound became increasingly chaotic.[2] To ensure that they stayed within the performance area, Eiko & Koma marked its perimeter with water.

On August 23 and 26, 1979, the artists performed a sixty-minute version of *Fluttering Black* at the San Francisco Museum of Modern Art, where the exhibition *Isamu Noguchi: Imaginary Landscapes* was on view. As an integral part of the installation, Noguchi had created a performance setting of moveable sculptures titled *Variable Landscapes*. Eiko & Koma, finding this setting "too Japanese," covered most of it with a huge banner bearing the hand-painted phrase "NO WAVE."[3] During the performance, a huge black cloth was unfolded from the ceiling and hung fluttering in the air. Blindfolded, Eiko & Koma moved slowly, as if they were in search of something. Blasts of recorded electronic music punctuated the performance.

1

Eiko & Koma, e-mail message to the editor, February 2, 2011.

2

Branca included the music for *Fluttering Black* on his second album, *The Ascension* (1981), under the title "The Spectacular Commodity (for Eiko and Koma)."

3

Eiko & Koma, e-mail message to the editor, April 5, 2011.

Black is the color of anarchism.[1]

EIKO & KOMA: THE STAGE AS A CUTTING BOARD

When we perform we like to imagine that each of us is a fresh fish which was just caught and is on the cutting board. The fish intuits that somebody will eat it. No room to be coquettish. The fish's body is tight, shining blue, eyes wide open. No way to escape.

The audience sits on cushions and chairs that line three sides of the marble-floored, white-walled rotunda of the San Francisco Museum of Art. As they wait, a young woman appears with a bag of flour that she sprinkles close to the first row of sitters, making a powdery demarcation of the performing area.

At the rear of the room, suspended from wires attached to the high vaulted ceiling, is a huge screen with white cloth stretched across its thirty-foot width on which the words "NO WAVE" have been painted in large, brush-stroked black lettering. Two performers, a man and a woman, walk across the designated stage area and stand at either side of the sign. They are dressed in black; street-worn pants and shirts. Each is blindfolded, their eyes covered by a strip of black cloth.

Our choreography is nothing more than patchwork and we are sneak thieves. But as we keep wearing them, even patched clothes become suitable to our bodies. We love the illusion that we wear our patches so well that nobody can see the cloth separating from us. Inevitably clothes become tired and miserable white, at the same time, our bodies become old at a different speed. When the cloth gets to be disturbing we throw it away. Patching the next piece, we also have to gather some tricks as performers. With one action, or one smile, the choreography must, momentarily, disappear.

The word-painted screen forming a background, the two performers stand in a way that is both limp and expectant. They look like the newspaper pictures of Iranian firing squad victims frozen by the camera in a final posture of resigned passivity. Over the loudspeakers come the electronically mixed sounds of thunder and carnival music, which repeats itself in short cycles briefly interrupting the silence like an ominous litany.

Our work is not choreography borrowed from others, or that we can lend to others to perform. It is, instead, simply the dance which exists on stage and we, as well as the audience, are witnesses to what takes place. The form is just a recipe, as if we were cooks. It is there to be adjusted. For what we want is to create a dish of a kind people have never yet tasted. We try to avoid fancy recipes or over-cooking as we absolutely don't want those who have come to see our performance only to admire our hard kitchen work. We would like to present our bodies as raw and spontaneous.

Separately the pair begins to move slowly forward; their hands like quivering fish explore the space before them. Then, released from a skylight, an enormous piece of black material unfolds downward. Partially obscuring the screen, the cloth begins to slowly undulate, moved by the warm air. Simultaneously, the performers, still blindfolded, reach the perimeter of the performing space. Feeling the flour barrier with their bare feet, they bend down to touch the flour and then their blindfolds, leaving a white streak on the black binding that looks like a caste marking or a smear of Christian ash.

We hate symmetrical movements. We cannot stand it when two steps are measured against two steps. There won't be much pleasure if both legs weigh the same. When we move forward it is as if somebody was grabbing us from the back, as if our right sides were landsliding—the heart must be quiet to listen to that sound. Our bodies are most unreasonable toys which often betray us; which laugh at the pretension that we stand at the edge of a cliff.

The statements are by performers Eiko Otake and Takashi Koma Otake. Using material from *Fluttering Black*, there with the accompaniment, the work takes its initial visual inspiration from the black flag of anarchism and its artistic impulse from an "acknowledgement," say Eiko & Koma, "of the last summer of the 1970s."

From Japan, but for the past two years residents of the United States, Eiko & Koma call themselves dancers. However, their work, all of their own conception, is not traditionally choreographic but falls, instead, into an idiomatic, hybrid theater/dance genre. Although their pieces are almost entirely non-verbal, Eiko and Koma's primary focus is not, as is most dance, the exploration or extension of physicality. What interests them, and what they try to portray, is that dark area that separates what can be said with language and the kinetic expressions and abstractions of movement.

Eluding both simile and allegory, it's the area of visceral recognition evoked by the German philosopher Ludwig Wittgenstein when he, in his *Philosophical Investigations*, challenges his readers to "describe the aroma of coffee." Wittgenstein's example may seem trivial, but by projection it affirms the existence of a realm of experiential or intuitive knowledge, a realm including that for which there are no adequate symbolic substitutions such as, for instance, our awareness of the "feel" of breathing.

It's this existential endeavor—giving form to the inexpressible—that threads through Eiko and Koma's "dances," and along the way, some intriguing conceptual hurdles are created for both performers and audience. Eiko & Koma's work can, for example, have disarmingly literal aspects as in *Fur Seal* (1977) where Eiko, costumed in the seal lining of an old coat, and Koma, bare chested, in a waist-to-thigh strip of seal skin, seem, as they grunt, slither, and hiss their way around the stage, to be attempting little more than imitation. But at some indefinable point in the work it becomes clear that their humanness has never been relinquished; that we are being drawn into the company of weighted blubber on bone, of stinking fish breath, to be told an ineffable but human something about the pleasurable and painful compulsions of instinct; that we are being told something about a world without mind.

Neither Eiko nor Koma has studied traditional Japanese theater or dance forms. Indeed, their teacher in Japan, Hijikata, had in the post–World War I years of Euro/Japanese cultural cross-fertilization been strongly influenced by the romantic aura surrounding the divinely mad Nijinsky as well as by the intellectual clarity of German Expressionist dance as epitomized by Mary Wigman. Nijinsky left little room for emulation, but the roots of German dramatic dance could be explored, and on first leaving Japan, Eiko & Koma traveled to Hannover where they studied with Wigman disciple Manja Chmiel before setting out on their own to perform in Europe, North Africa, and finally America.

Eiko & Koma use kimonos in only one of their early pieces, *White Dance: Moth*, given its American premiere in 1976, but, of course, the Japanese elements of their work extend beyond the choice of costume. These elements might include their pacing, which, for some, seems abusively slow; a fondness for contorted limbs and features as well as for self-directed violence such as demonstrations of hair-flailing dementia, whopping fist to chest, or slamming their bodies to the floor. In addition, having spent most of their careers performing for Western audiences, they occasionally lean on their exoticness for effect.

The balance, however, is on the debit side. For in their intense performances, in which they generally perform one hourlong piece, Eiko & Koma carry their audiences through breathtakingly precarious shifts of mood and juxtapositions of style

that can lead to an equally breathtaking stew of pathos, absurdity, and beauty. Take, for example, a moment late in *White Dance: Moth* when, after firmly establishing a somber aura of fragility and death, a kimonoed Koma hoists a burlap bag to his shoulder and proceeds to fill the stage with the thud of a hundred pounds of ordinary, very genuine, potatoes. As the audience reacts with nervous laughter, Eiko proceeds to wade her way through the brown lumps with a poignant eloquence and this, despite the incongruity of the scenery, quietly pulls those watching back into the piece.

In a different guise, this same device appears in *Before the Cock Crows* (1978). Making thematic use of the biblical parable of betrayal, Eiko & Koma perform in Near Eastern costumes to Near Eastern music evoking some remote time and place as they explore the gestural textures of self-absorption, decadence, and deception. But just as everything seems firmly shrouded in lulling obscurity, Eiko forms her fingers into the shape of a very contemporary gun and, aiming her digits at the already prostrate Koma, she commits the coup de grace with the loud shout of "bang, bang, bang."

—Irene Oppenheim. Previously unpublished essay written in 1979.

Premiere: September 7, 1980,
Battery Park Landfill, New York City

Length: 50 minutes

Site preparation: Eiko & Koma

Costumes: Eiko & Koma

Sound: Ambient; Chilean folk music

Selected review: Cate Miodini,
"Placing the Breath within the Body,"
Downtown Review 3 (spring 1981):
34–35.

1
Eiko & Koma, e-mail message to the
editor, February 2, 2011.

EVENT FISSION
分裂 1980

Event Fission took place at sunset on Battery Park Landfill in
Manhattan, which was created from sand dredged from New
York Harbor and earth excavated during the construction of
the World Trade Center. With the then new Twin Towers as
a backdrop, Eiko suggestively attacked the lower Manhattan
landscape with a white flag. She and Koma jousted with
the flag atop a sand dune, their bodies wrapped in rags and
coated with a paste made of rice flour and water. After slowly
rolling down the dune, they moved about in a performance
area marked out on the sand and flanked by two open fires.
Then they crawled toward a deep hole—dug before the performance and hidden from view—and fell in, disappearing
in a cloud of dust.

Event Fission was a site-specific version of *Fission* (1979). It
was made and performed once for Art on the Beach 2, a three-
month-long series of environmental sculptures, music, dance,
and conceptual art performances organized by Creative Time
that ran from June 14 through September 14, 1980.

We offered a white flag, not a national flag.[1]

Studies for *Event Fission*, Battery Park Landfill, New York City, September 1980   Photos ©Johan Elbers

Fission (part two of *Trilogy*), Zellerbach Auditorium, University of California, Berkeley, June 1980   Photo: Kazunobu Yanagi

TRILOGY (*Cell, Fission, Entropy*)
三部作 ——
細胞、分裂、エントロピー 1980

Premiere: September 18, 1980,
Oberlin College, Oberlin, Ohio

Length: 60 minutes

Set: Eiko & Koma

Lighting: Blu

Costumes: Eiko & Koma

Sound: Andean folk music

Selected reviews: Wilma Salisbury,
"'Shogun' Outmystified at Oberlin,"
Cleveland Plain Dealer, September
20, 1980; Jennifer Dunning, "Dance:
Eiko and Koma Experiment," *New
York Times*, April 19, 1981; Deborah
Jowitt, "Dance," *Village Voice*, May
6–12, 1981.

1
Eiko & Koma, program notes for
Trilogy, 1980.

Trilogy was a study in mediation between infinitely large and infinitesimally small energies. It comprised three short works that Eiko & Koma combined to make an evening-length program. Part one was *Cell*, a piece constructed of Eiko's small movements performed partly on a rolling floor dolly (pushed by Koma) and on the flour-covered stage floor. Part two, *Fission*, took place mostly on a fifteen-by-twelve-foot floor mat painted with white dough, and included more combative and blunt movements. In both *Cell* and *Fission*, Eiko & Koma wore tattered white garments and covered their skin with strips of silk gauze and a paste made from flour and water.

The third and final part, *Entropy*, was performed both on and off the mat. Eiko & Koma, having added red bibs and red shoes to their costumes, shuffled with effort through the space, alternately welcoming and resisting each other's assistance. In subsequent performances, *Entropy* was significantly changed: the artists sang a children's song while dancing an odd pas de deux.

Of *Trilogy*'s three parts, *Fission* was created first, in 1979. *Cell* and *Entropy* both were made in 1980. Although all three were conceived as independent works, only *Fission* was performed outside the context of *Trilogy*.

Their calm is illusionary.[1]

Premiere: November 27, 1981,
The Kitchen, New York City

Length: 20 minutes

Set: Eiko & Koma

Lighting: Blu

Costumes: Eiko & Koma

Sound: Music by Allen Ginsberg

Musicians: Bob Carroll and the
Dirt Band

Selected reviews: Jennifer Dunning,
"Dance: 'Nurse's Song' at the Kitchen,"
New York Times, November 30,
1981; Deborah Jowitt, "Caught in the
Cross-Cultural Riptide," *Village Voice*,
December 9–15, 1981.

1
William Blake, "Nurse's Song,"
Songs of Innocence and of Experience
(New York: Avon Books), 1971. First
published 1789.

NURSE'S SONG
乳母の歌 1981

Eiko & Koma made *Nurse's Song* after their summer residency at Naropa Institute in Boulder, Colorado. The dance, inspired by American Beat poet Allen Ginsberg and his musical performances, was described in the press release as "an acknowledgment of the childhood joy in all of us." Dressed in approximations of South Sea Islands garb, Eiko & Koma romped through games such as leapfrog and tag before curling up drowsily together on the stage floor. The music—Ginsberg's setting for William Blake's poem "Nurse's Song" from *Songs of Innocence*—was performed live by Bob Carroll and the Dirt Band.

**The little ones leaped & shouted & laugh'd
And all the hills echoed.**[1]

Nurse's Song, 1981 (studio shot)   Photo: Steven Mark Needham

Grain, 1984 (studio shot)   Photo: David A. Fullard

GRAIN
穀物 1983

Premiere: January 28, 1983,
Kampo Cultural Center, New York City

Length: 60 minutes

Set: Eiko & Koma

Lighting: Blu

Costumes: Eiko & Koma

Sound: Japanese and Tibetan folk
music played at half speed;
Indonesian gamelan music

Selected reviews: Deborah Jowitt,
"Crawling into a Womb of Rice," *Village
Voice*, February 22, 1983; Tobi Tobias,
"Food for the Eye," *New York* 16,
(March 14, 1983); Hedwig Rhode,
"Ein Reiskorn wird geboren," *Der
Tagesspiegel* (Berlin), June 3, 1984.

Grain was danced on a white platform eight feet wide, twenty-eight feet deep, and six inches high, on which a futon had been placed. Consisting of eight distinct scenes separated by blackouts, it began with a screening of raw footage from the video *Tentacle* and included several solos by each dancer that culminated in a violent coupling. In the final scene, Koma entered carrying a tray of cooked rice and lit candles; Eiko stuffed handfuls of the rice into her mouth and Koma snuffed out the candles with his hands.

In one myth, beans and grains grow visibly and magically from different parts of the corpse. In another, juicy wild rice grows on an unmarked grave.[1]

1
Eiko & Koma, press release for *Grain*,
1983.

Premiere: July 20, 1983,
American Dance Festival/
Reynolds Theater,
Durham, North Carolina

Length: 20 minutes

Set: Eiko & Koma

Lighting: Blu

Costumes: Eiko & Koma

Recorded and layered sound: Asian
folk music performed by Eiko on the
harmonium

Selected reviews: Jack Anderson,
"Dance: Eiko and Koma Control Time,"
New York Times, July 24, 1983;
Deborah Jowitt, "Fecundity and Death,"
Village Voice, December 7, 1986.

1
Eiko & Koma, press release for *Beam*,
1983.

BEAM
梁 1983

Beam was performed center stage on a large pile of dirt whose summit Eiko & Koma struggled to reach. Under a strong, vertical beam of light that seemed to bind their bodies together, Koma carried Eiko on his shoulder to the top of the six-foot mound, which was built up on a wood and canvas structure created by the artists. The piece was inspired by an ancient Japanese practice known as "human pole," in which the construction of an important bridge or castle was marked by the sacrifice of one or more persons as a prayer to the gods.

Beam was the first piece commissioned from Eiko & Koma by the American Dance Festival. It also was part of the tetralogy *New Moon Stories* (see Appendix B, page 296).

**A dirt mountain holds in it a man
and a woman who endure(d), reach(ed) out, and
collapse(d) into the mountain.**[1]

Beam, Brooklyn Academy of Music, New York City, November 1986 (dress rehearsal)   Photo: Johan Elbers

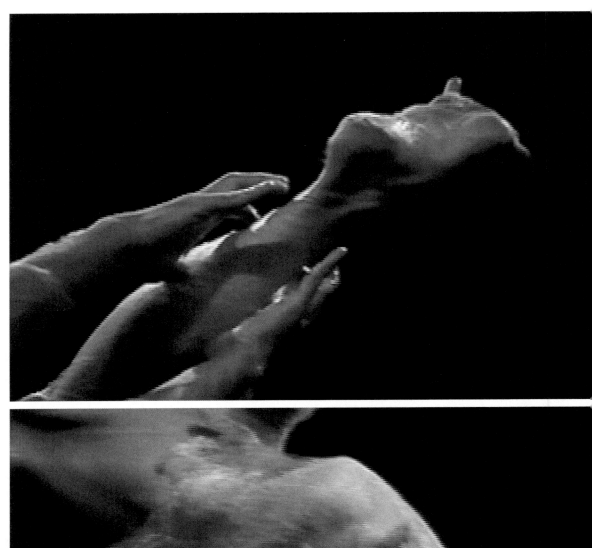

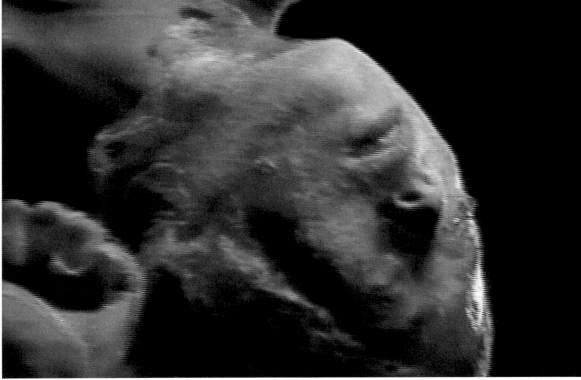

Stills from *Tentacle*, 1983

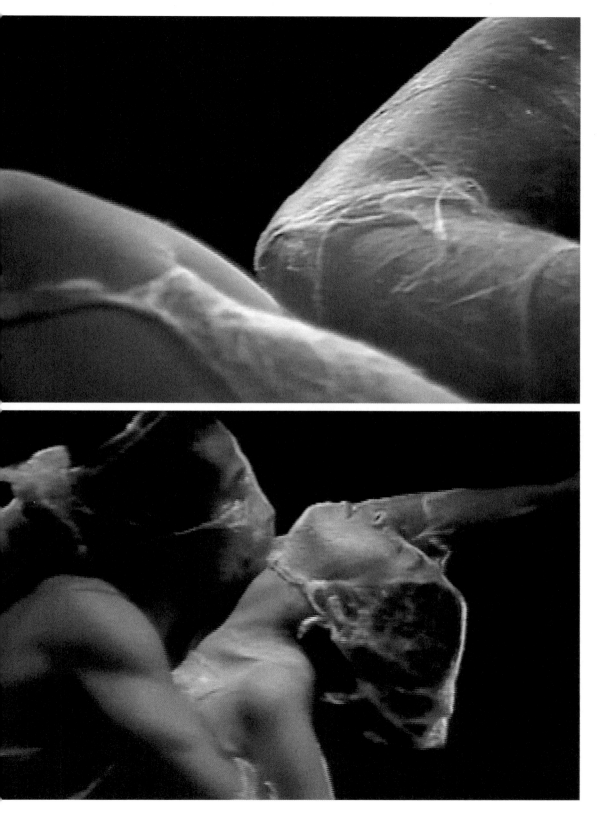

TENTACLE (video)
触手 1983

Video (color, sound)

Running time 7:11 minutes

Lighting: Eiko & Koma, with Jeff Bush and Celia Ipiotis

Costumes: Eiko & Koma

Sound: Eiko & Koma, with Phil Lee; Japanese Gagaku music at slow speed

Camera: Celia Ipiotis

Tentacle was taped in summer 1983 at the studio of Art Resources in Collaboration, New York City.

Tentacle, a collaboration with dance video artists Jeff Bush and Celia Ipiotis, was the first work Eiko & Koma choreographed specifically for the camera. Their bodies, sticky with silkworm cotton, are seen in close-up as they move slowly in tandem, intertwining their limbs and violently colliding at the end.

To make *Tentacle,* the collaborators created a process in which both the editing and choreography occurred during the taping. Eiko & Koma first improvised movement phrases for the camera. Then the collaborators watched the replay of the footage, Eiko & Koma selected and refined some of the passages and performed them again, and the videographers adjusted the camera as needed for subsequent takes. The team continued to work this way until all movement of bodies and cameras was negotiated. Finally, the videographers shot a series of final takes, from which one piece was selected by consensus, and the result is a dance video that is one continuous shot without cuts or edits.

Premiere: January 25, 1984,
Dance Theater Workshop,
New York City

Length: 17 minutes

Lighting: Dave Feldman

Sound: Eiko & Koma, collage of
sea animal sounds

Selected reviews: Jack Anderson,
"Dance: Eiko and Koma Portray
Nature," *New York Times*, January
28, 1984; Burt Supree, "The Sex
Life of the Polyp," *Village Voice*,
February 21, 1984; Allan Ullrich,
"Japanese Primal Pioneers Put on
a Sinewy Display," *San Francisco
Examiner*, March 20, 1987.

1
Poem by Eiko, included in press
release for *Night Tide*, 1984.

NIGHT TIDE
夜の潮 1984

Night Tide explored the body as landscape and was the first
dance during which Eiko & Koma were nude during the entire
piece. As it opened, the artists were hunched face down on
the stage in separate pools of light. They slowly swayed, raised
their buttocks very high, then fell to the stage floor. Their bodies seemed to vacillate among human, animal, and landscape
forms, from mountain peaks to bleached bones; at one point
Eiko's back and raised buttocks suggested an erect penis. The
piece was inspired by their solitary life in the Catskills, where,
Eiko has written, they felt "the movement of the mountains."

Night Tide was part of two tetralogies: *New Moon Stories* and
Memory (see Appendix B, page 296).

The tide's marking…
Moon draws silent howl
Blood dances its sweet

The tide's ebbing…
Eye glare the night
the hillock loses its shadow
crumbling away [1]

Night Tide, Dance Theater Workshop, New York City, January 1984 (studio shot)　Photo ©Beatriz Schiller

Wallow, Point Reyes, California, November 1983 (photos taken during the videotaping) Photos: Kazunobu Yanagi

WALLOW (video)
這う 1984

Video (color, silent)
Running time 19:21 minutes
Costumes: Eiko & Koma
Camera: Peter Yaple
Eiko & Koma edited *Wallow* with Jeff Bush at Arts Resources in Collaboration, New York City.

A media work based on their performance piece *Fur Seal*, *Wallow* was an experiment in making a work that went beyond the theatrical. It was shot in November 1983 at Point Reyes National Seashore in Marin County, California, where Eiko & Koma physically and emotionally inhabited the realm of harbor seals. In the video, we see the dancers crawl on their bellies in the wet sand, bask in the sun, and endure the wind. After a rough coupling, they crawl separately toward the surf, where they are nearly swallowed by a big wave.

We watched the seals and the seals watched us. [1]

1

Eiko & Koma, e-mail message to the editor, February 2, 2011.

Premiere: June 19, 1984,
American Dance Festival/
Reynolds Theater,
Durham, North Carolina

Length: 17 minutes

Set: Eiko & Koma

Lighting: Blu

Sound collage: Eiko & Koma

Selected reviews: Anna Kisselgoff,
"Dance: Eiko and Koma in a Durham
Premiere," *New York Times*, June 24,
1984; Debra Cash, "Eiko and Koma
Move with Exquisite Detail," *Boston
Globe*, December 14, 1985; Deborah
Jowitt, "Fecundity and Death," *Village
Voice*, December 7, 1986.

1
Eiko & Koma, press release for
Elegy, 1984.

ELEGY
悲歌 1984

Shadows of death dwell in every living fold.[1]

Elegy, which was performed in the nude, opened with each dancer standing in a separate, kidney-shaped pool of water. Dramatic lighting created reflections and stark shadows as the dancers slowly sank into their respective pools and moved in the water. Although their movements suggested that they were aware of one another, they remained isolated in their own pools, never touching or moving closer together. Thus, they were simultaneously alone and not alone.

Elegy was part of two tetralogies: *New Moon Stories* and *Memory* (see Appendix B, page 296).

Elegy, Dance Theater Workshop, New York City, November 1985 (studio shot)   Photo ©Beatriz Schiller

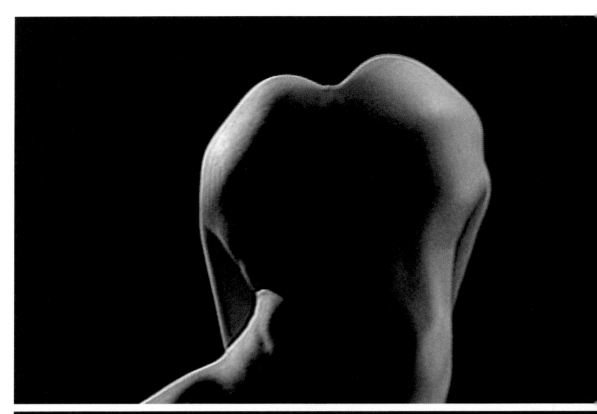

Stills from *Bone Dream*, 1985

BONE DREAM (video)
骨の夢 1985

A collaboration with dance video artists Jeff Bush and Celia Ipiotis, *Bone Dream* was performed in the nude against a black background with lighting that emphasized the outline of the artists' body shapes. This work, loosely based on the material from *Night Tide*, begins with near-abstract shots of undulating muscles, bones, tendons, and hair. As Eiko & Koma reach for one another and briefly connect, the camera pulls back to reveal their entire bodies, then returns to another close-up of gently rolling forms. One continuous take, this video was made in the same manner as *Tentacle*.

Video (sound, color)
Running time 7:12 minutes
Lighting: Eiko & Koma, with Celia Ipiotis and Jeff Bush
Sound mix: Eiko & Koma, with Phil Lee
Camera: Jeff Bush
Bone Dream was taped in August 1985 at the studio of Arts Resources in Collaboration, New York City.

THE LURE OF DEATH AND THE THIRST FOR LIFE...EXPRESSED IN DANCE

Eiko & Koma, a Japanese performance duo active on the American contemporary dance scene, have arrived in Japan. They performed two works, *Thirst* and *Tree*, back to back.

In *Thirst*, a man and woman, their clothes stained the color of earth, stand a short distance apart in front of a huge earth-colored canvas. The man raises his right hand to his face and gives the appearance of being about to flee. The woman opens her eyes wide in blank surprise, indicating that she is at a loss what to do. One can sense from this the man's lust for life, but the woman seems somehow enticed by death. The two are bathed in light so bright it almost resembles a heat ray, sucking the moisture out of their bodies.

The distance between them is such that they cannot extend their arms and touch one another. At such a distance, each is alone as he or she experiences the fear of thirst. This scene, which opens one's eyes to the possibility that death may strike at any moment, is a scene of extraordinary beauty.

This beauty is all the more striking given the distance between the performers and the audience—around 20 meters....If viewed close up the perspiration and agonized emotions of the dancers would come to the fore, but it seems the artists are averse to this, preferring to keep their distance in the hope of attracting a more dispassionate gaze.

The work is around forty minutes long and consists of four scenes each around ten minutes long. These four scenes, which are connected by blackouts, depict four days over which the protagonists grow increasingly thirsty. The dance movements of Eiko & Koma consist almost entirely of what could best be described as sluggish actions. Because these sluggish actions lack phrasing and posing, the audience is unable to avert their eyes and is required to study the movements carefully.

Moreover, perhaps because the work is performed in silence, it is as if the audience is calling on their sense of hearing as well as their sense of sight as they concentrate on the pair. However, the events that unfold over these four days are not presented in a linear fashion. Proceedings are interrupted by the sudden blackouts and when they resume the audience finds itself watching action from the following day after a time lapse. What has happened and what is about to happen? Perhaps unsettled by the interval of darkness, the audience...experiences the fascination and anxiety of trying to figure out if there is any continuity between each new scene with the one that preceded it.

In fact, the "thirst" depicted in the sequence of scenes in which the woman suffers alone, in which the man still has the desire to live while the woman is doubled over, having abandoned all hope, and in which the man and woman drain all their remaining energy in approaching each other and appear about to touch, only to pass each other, has nothing to do with water; rather it is a metaphor for love.

Why are Eiko & Koma so pitiful? Is it that they are trying to imprison their bodies in suffering? It seems as if they are suffering from something, as a result of which they are forced to lie flat on the ground, as if the weight of the heavens is bearing down on them.

The second work, *Tree*, also features a naked woman lying on the ground. I seem to recall that *Fur Seal* and *Trilogy*, two other works by Eiko & Koma that I saw previously, also featured pitiful characters crawling around on the floor. Eiko & Koma belong to the generation of the 1970s that "dropped out" and sought not only to radically change society but also to deconstruct their bodies, which they felt had been eaten away by the system.

Their bodily memories of this time have settled into their dance style and become inextricably linked to it. This is clearly visible in *Tree*, but at that same time I was able to sense in the approximation to nature of their naked bodies a determination to transcend their pitiful bodies and rise up.

Eiko & Koma are certainly very popular in Europe and North America, and I think the reason for this may lie in these pitiful bodies. In the sense that their work is a theatre of imagery, it is akin to that of Robert Wilson, although Wilson's work does not have these pitiful bodies. Furthermore, concentration and quietness are hallmarks of Eiko & Koma's work, giving it texture that is absent from American contemporary dance.

—Miyabi Ichikawa. Originally published in *Asahigurafu* (Tokyo), January 27, 1989. Translation by Pamela Miki.

Premiere: November 14, 1985, Dance Theater Workshop, New York City

Length: 35 minutes

Set: Eiko & Koma

Lighting: Blu

Costumes: Eiko & Koma

Sound: Ambient

Selected reviews: Tobi Tobias, "Going to Extremes," *New York Magazine*, December 2, 1985; Deborah Jowitt, "Feast and Famine," *Village Voice*, December 10, 1985; Rita Henss-Wottawa, "Kampf gegen das Ende," *Frankfurter Allgemeine*, August 30, 1988.

1
Eiko & Koma, e-mail message to the editor, February 2, 2011.

THIRST

渇き 1985

In *Thirst*, Eiko & Koma moved together and apart as they searched for moisture on the ground, in the air, and from one another's bodies. Wearing rustic garments of starched, tea-dyed silk and cotton, they seemed to merge with the backdrop and floor covering, which they had slathered with a paste made of flour burned in a frying pan and then mixed with water. As the dancers' bodies touched and moved against the backdrop, chunks of dried paste fell to the floor and were moved about by their feet, producing a muffled, staccato soundscape. When *Thirst* was performed in larger spaces, the stage floor was amplified, creating an eloquent contrast between the sounds of movement and the silence of stasis.

Although this piece was inspired by news stories about the famine in Ethiopia, it considers thirst more broadly as a fundamental longing for both water and intimacy.

Cradling our thirst within, we see our longing to live.[1]

Thirst, Dance Theater Workshop, New York City, November 1985   Photo ©Jack Vartoogian/FrontRowPhotos

Stills from Lament, *1986*

LAMENT (video)
哀歌 1986

In this dance video, commissioned by the Walker Art Center and created in collaboration with media artist James Byrne, Eiko & Koma danced naked in a large pool of water on the stage of the Triplex Theater in New York City. It is based on *Elegy*, and both works treat the theme of death and dying through similar movement phrases. The chief difference between the two was that *Lament* was performed in one large pool of water rather than the two used in *Elegy*. In addition, the dancers are seen from the side rather than the front—a new perspective used to better accommodate the shape of the video screen. The atonal sound collage is an otherworldly mix of ringing, reverberating tones and abstract vocalizations.

Video (black and white, sound)
Running time 8:56 minutes
Lighting: Eiko & Koma, with James Byrne
Sound collage: Eiko & Koma
Camera: James Byrne
Lament was taped in July 1985 and edited by James Byrne, with Eiko & Koma, at New Jersey City University, New Jersey, in 1986.

1
Eiko Otake, e-mail message to the editor, in reference to many friends and performing artists lost to AIDS, February 2, 2011.

For friends who died, wanting to live.[1]

LAMENT: FROM STAGE TO SCREEN

Lament (1986), a collaboration between Minneapolis-based video artist James Byrne and Eiko & Koma, was adapted from the dancers' 1984 stage work *Elegy*. More than just documentation for the historical record or a type of notation for the work to be replicated or interpreted by others in the future, this short video serves as an extension of *Elegy* that builds on that work's mood, production, and theme.

Eiko & Koma began making "media dance" in 1983, in part because they considered their performance works ill-suited to video documentation. During the presentation *Video Choreography* at the Walker Art Center on March 23, 1993, Eiko said, "The video pieces gave us a different position to work with. It's difficult to document our work. We don't move in a normal structured way ... however, we realize that there is some way to use the medium." To date they have made seven media dances, all of which, like *Lament*, reference the themes of their performances but remain distinct pieces.

Walker media curator Melinda Ward, who commissioned *Lament*, suggested Byrne as a collaborator. Although he had some experience filming dance (*Reel 5 Take 2 Set and Reset* [1984] with choreographer Trisha Brown), Eiko & Koma were drawn to his early work, such as *Meditations on the Northern Shore* (1982), which demonstrated a sensitivity to *Lament's* primary imagery, water. Together, the three created *Lament* during the process of filming. With instant access to the video footage during production, Eiko & Koma were able to choreograph their movement and the placement of Byrne's camera to execute the work as they had envisioned it. Eiko stressed that the action needed to be shot from a low vantage point. With the camera at this level, the viewer is brought into a space of intimacy with the dancers. The technique also conveyed their experience of Japanese daily life, much of which is lived close to the floor.

Lament puts the viewer off guard immediately. The establishing shot shows the backs of two headless, naked human torsos curled up atop one another, in perfect symmetry. Several seconds pass before one of them begins to move, and only when this motion causes the lower torso to shimmer does it become apparent that we are looking at one body and its reflection in a pool of water.

The tension between the performer and the mirror image begins to drive the piece and negotiate the body's relationship to the water.

Soon a second figure, whose skin glistens with droplets of water, appears closer in the frame and in sharp focus, disturbing one's perception of distance from the first torso, which is now in the background. This second person is often shown in slow motion; sometimes, due to the stark lighting, only an outline is visible. Both bodies writhe about in the water and then seem to morph into three figures superimposed over each other in a complex layering of images. The piece ends with a shot of one arm retracting and another outstretched as if requesting assistance.

Lament expands on the themes of death and dying that were so important in *Elegy*, which was mounted during the early years of the AIDS crisis. Like many others, the artists lost friends and colleagues to the pandemic, but *Lament* is not a direct reference to AIDS. Instead, its more generalized approach to the theme of mourning gives the piece universal relevance.

—Dean Otto

BY THE RIVER

川辺で 1986

Premiere: June 18, 1986, Boston Dance Umbrella/Massachusetts College of Art, Boston

Length: 55 minutes

Set: Clayton Campbell, with Eiko & Koma

Lighting: Blu

Costumes: Eiko & Koma

Sound: Eiko & Koma

Selected reviews: Christine Temin, "New Eiko and Koma Work Tedious Yet Enthralling," *Boston Globe*, June 14, 1986; Lisa F. Hillyer, "Eye of the Storm," *Boston Phoenix*, June 24, 1986; Joan Acocella, "Eiko and Koma," *Dance Magazine*, February 1988.

1
Eiko & Koma, in collaboration with Irene Oppenheim, program notes for *Eye Below*, 1986.

2
At the premiere, the piece was titled *Eye Below*.

By the River[2] was an intermedia work created during a month-long residency in Boston. Its grisaille environment, conceived by Eiko & Koma and executed in tandem with others, included David Geary's video of flickering candles; a "river" of pale light on the floor by Blu; and two drops painted by Clayton Campbell that covered the back wall, ceiling, and stage floor, creating a cavelike environment. At the conclusion of the performance, audience members were given a leaflet of poems written by Eiko (with translation assistance from Irene Oppenheim).

The setting represented the river that must be crossed by the dying. On both banks were stones that could be seen as either graves or human remains. Eiko was nude throughout the dance; Koma, in gray shift and black shawl, was guardian or keeper of the waterway. Early in the piece, Eiko moved like a spider as she wandered the bank; later she seemed to drift toward Koma in the stream of light. When she reached Koma, he lifted her onto his shoulders but failed to get her to shore. In the final scene, he covered her prone body with a black cloth and she rolled toward the river as he thrust his fist into the air.

**In the night
Weeds grow
Tree roots dangle**

**Maggots eat
Fossils sigh**

**Here pain is not feared.
Memory is lost.**[1]

By the River, Dance Umbrella/Massachusetts College of Art, Boston, June 1986 Photo: Richard M. Grabbert

SHADOW (Not Pictured)

影 1986

A solo is a duet waiting for a shadow.
A duet is a solo remembering a shadow.[1]

As this piece began, backlighting framed the outline of Eiko's body, which could be seen clearly through her wet, clinging kimono. She squatted, stretched, and bent her body as if she were giving birth or negotiating with unseen forces. A naked Koma emerged from the shadows upstage and moved toward Eiko. The final vignette was an embrace.

Shadow was created to complete the tetralogy *New Moon Stories* (see Appendix B, page 296).

Premiere: November 18, 1986, Brooklyn Academy of Music Next Wave Festival/Lepercq Space, New York City

Length: 15 minutes

Lighting: Blu

Costume: Eiko

Sound: Recording of insects and frogs

Selected reviews: Jack Anderson, "Eiko and Koma in Brooklyn," *New York Times*, November 20, 1986; Camille Hardy, "Eiko & Koma," *Dance Magazine* 61 (April 1987): 26–28.

1
Eiko & Koma, Delicious Movement Workshop Manifesto, n.d., http://eikoandkoma.org/deliciousmanifesto. Accessed February 7, 2011.

Video (color, sound)

Running time 9:33 minutes

Set: Eiko & Koma

Lighting: Eiko & Koma

Costume: Eiko

Sound: Eiko & Koma

Camera: Koma

Selected reviews: Jack Anderson, "Trees, Fallen Leaves, Growth and Decay," *New York Times*, November 21, 1995.

Husk was taped at the Kampo Cultural Center, New York City, in May 1987.

1
Eiko & Koma, e-mail message to the editor, February 2, 2011.

HUSK (video)

殻 1987

Husk is a media work through which Eiko & Koma explored an alternate way to collaborate: Koma as cameraman and Eiko as solo performer. It was filmed in a dimly lit studio on a bed of dry leaves, which were blown gently by fans concealed from view. A long close-up follows Eiko's unhurried emergence from a husklike costume of thick raw silk and leaves. In the final sequence, she manages to push herself out of her casing, leaving it empty on the ground as she moves off camera.

In order to achieve a continuous, steady shot with his handheld camera and to film from the lowest vantage point possible, Koma replaced the tripod with a tennis ball and worked on the floor on his belly. Choreography for both the movement and camerawork was created during the process—by watching the monitor to see how she was framed by the camera, Eiko was able to adjust her movements accordingly. The video required no postproduction edit except the addition of sound.

Husk was screened as part of the tetralogy *Autumn Passage* (see Appendix B, page 296).

This is as low as the camera could possibly be.¹

Stills from *Husk*, 1987

Stills from *Undertow*, 1988

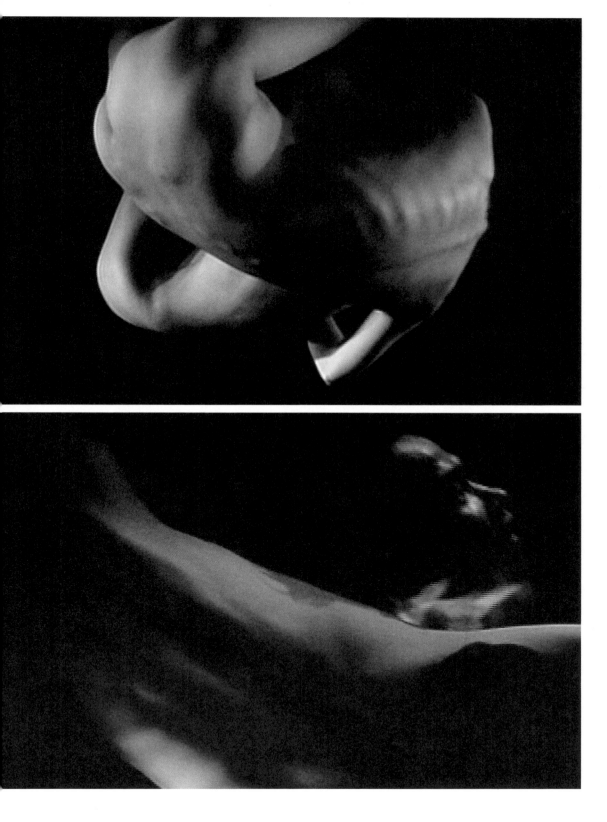

UNDERTOW (video)
引き波 1988

Video (black and white, sound)

Running time 7:34 minutes

Lighting: Eiko & Koma, with James Byrne

Sound: Music by Ushio Torikai

Camera: James Byrne

Undertow was taped at New Jersey City University, New Jersey, in August 1988 and edited by James Byrne, with Eiko & Koma

In this video, their second collaboration with James Byrne, Eiko & Koma's nude bodies seem to tumble weightlessly within a black void that suggests deep water or deep space. They achieved this disorienting effect by having Byrne shoot the entire video with a hand-held camera from atop a ladder, looking directly down on the performers; the lighting was cut at knee height so that their lower bodies are never visible.

Premiere: November 29, 1988,
Brooklyn Academy of Music Next Wave
Festival/Lepercq Space, New York City

Length: 30 minutes

Set: Eiko & Koma

Lighting: Blu

Costume: Koma

Sound: Recorded insect noise and
night sounds

Selected reviews: Jack Anderson, "The
Forces of Nature Unleashed, but
Slowly," *New York Times*, December 1,
1988; Joan Acocella, "Pretzel Logic,"
7 Days, December 21, 1988.

1
Eiko & Koma, press release for *Tree*,
1988.

TREE
樹 1988

The centerpiece of this dance was an ancient, scarred tree trunk, represented by a narrow vertical backdrop of hand-sewn, tea-dyed silk and leaves created by Eiko & Koma. Most of the time, both artists were nude, streaked with terra-cotta and brown paint, and much of the dance was performed on the floor amid a profusion of dry leaves. But at times they seemed to merge with the tree, allowing parts of their bodies to become lost in the soft folds of silk. Their controlled, slow movements suggested the long lives of trees.

Tree was part of the tetralogy *Autumn Passage* (see Appendix B, page 296).

A tree is wounded with its own memory.[1]

Tree, 1988 (studio shot) Photo ©Beatriz Schiller

Tree, 1988 (studio shot)　Photo © Johan Elbers

Canal, Southern Theater, Minneapolis, Minnesota, May 1989

CANAL

水路 1989

Developed during a monthlong residency in Minneapolis, *Canal* featured Eiko & Koma and four local performers who were chosen from the workshop participants. Water coursed down a red backdrop and drizzled from the ceiling onto the stage floor, which was also a deep red hue. The cast performed nude, rolling and crawling in the shallow pool of water onstage.

The work's title alludes to the subterranean atmosphere of the interior of the Southern Theater, with its peeling proscenium arch and brick walls. It also evokes the water lines that course through both human bodies and human-built cities.

At the 1989 American Dance Festival, Eiko & Koma performed *Canal* with only one additional performer, Jeffrey Black. Later, the piece was reworked as *Passage*.

Premiere: May 3, 1989, Walker Art Center/Southern Theater, Minneapolis, Minnesota

Length: 35 minutes

Set: Eiko & Koma

Lighting: Jeff Fontaine

Sound: "Alturas de Macchu Picchu," by Los Jaivas; sound of breaking iceberg

Other performers: Jeffrey Black, Marcela Kingman, Sharon Varosh, Laurie van Wieren

Selected reviews: Mike Steele, "Dance: Eiko and Koma Perform at Dreamlike Pace," *Minneapolis Star Tribune*, May 5, 1989; Jack Anderson, "Dance, Like Life Itself, Emerging from Water," *New York Times*, June 22, 1989.

1
Eiko & Koma, e-mail message to the editor, February 2, 2011.

Three naked women in red water. Koma did not leave the side wall.[1]

Premiere: June 19, 1989,
American Dance Festival/
Reynolds Theater,
Durham, North Carolina

Length: 15 minutes

Set: Eiko & Koma

Lighting: Blu

Sound: Ambient

Selected reviews: Susan Broili, "Eiko
and Koma Work Spell in Watery World
Onstage at the ADF," *Durham Sun*,
June 20, 1989; Anna Kisselgoff,
"Japanese Distillation in 3 Works at the
Joyce," *New York Times*, April 5, 1990;
Deborah Jowitt, "Ordeals We Crave,"
Village Voice, April 18–24, 1990.

1
Eiko & Koma, rehearsal notes for *Rust*
1989.

RUST

錆 1989

In *Rust*, which was performed in the nude, Eiko & Koma clung upside down to two suspended sections of chain-link fence. Their attachment to the fence suggested the adhesion of rust to metal, or the way that garbage sometimes gets caught in sewer grilles. During the dance they slowly inched toward one another, eventually changing places without ever making meaningful contact. For later performances in larger spaces, the sound of their movements on the fence was subtly amplified.

**We are being rusted
and we are rusting the chain link
fences.**[1]

Rust, American Dance Festival/Reynolds Theater, Durham, North Carolina, June 1989 Photo: Jay Anderson

Memory, Joyce Theater, New York City, April 1990 Photo ©Beatriz Schiller

MEMORY
記憶 1989

Premiere: July 29, 1989, Art Awareness/New Lex Theater, Lexington, New York

Length: 15 minutes

Set: Eiko & Koma

Lighting: Blu

Sound: Georg Deuter, "Haleakala"

Selected reviews: Alan M. Kriegsman, "The Clinging Creations of Eiko & Koma," *Washington Post*, November 20, 1989; Anna Kisselgoff, "Japanese Distillation in 3 Works at the Joyce," *New York Times*, April 5, 1990; Deborah Jowitt, "Ordeals We Crave," *Village Voice*, April 18–24, 1990.

1
Eiko & Koma, rehearsal notes for *Memory*, 1989.

Created as a complement to *Rust*, this dance was also performed in the nude against suspended sections of chain-link fence. Eiko & Koma were seen on opposite sides of the fence, which both united and separated them. The almost magical lighting changes made it seem that Koma appeared and disappeared as Eiko reached out to him.

Memory was part of a tetralogy with the same title (see Appendix B, page 296).

Where is he?
He is in her dream.[1]

Premiere: November 10, 1989,
Painted Bride Art Center,
Philadelphia, Pennsylvania

Length: 40 minutes

Set: Eiko & Koma, drops painted
by Vaughn Patterson

Lighting: Jeff Fontaine

Sound: Dripping water

Selected reviews: Alan M. Kriegsman,
"The Clinging Creations of Eiko &
Koma," *Washington Post*, November
20, 1989; John Howell, "The Slow
Beauty of Eiko and Koma," *Newsday*,
April 5, 1990.

1
Eiko & Koma, e-mail message to the
editor, February 2, 2011.

PASSAGE
道 1989

Passage was developed out of *Canal* as a duet for Eiko & Koma. Both dancers performed nude. The set comprised a pool of water that covered the entire stage and was contained by a blood-red floor cloth. On top of the cloth, a loose pile of red fabric added texture to the floor surface, and also became a prop for Koma during his solos. Upstage was a red backdrop and a mock proscenium arch, a re-creation of the Southern Theater's, where *Canal* premiered. Intermittently, water ran down the backdrop and drizzled from hidden ceiling spouts onto the floor. This created a soundscape that alternated between silence and the sounds of running and dripping water.

As a prelude to the dance, a video by David Geary was projected on the water that oozed down the red backdrop. Its abstract images evoked bodies and shadows, an effect that was emphasized by the use of candlelight. The intense red in the set, the color of both blood and lava, suggested a link between human bodies and the earth.

Twenty-eight water faucets.[1]

Passage, Jacob's Pillow, Becket, New York, 1989

Land, 1991 (studio shot) Photo ©1991 Blanche Mackey Photography

LAND
大地 1991

Land is a reflection on the inseparability of the earth from the life it supports. Its scenic landscape included a backdrop and floor cloth, painted by visual artist Sandra Lerner. The sand, dried plants, and other organic materials that had been added to the set were scattered as Eiko & Koma moved.

The movement, structured in five sections, drew from such themes and activities as the struggle of living, remorse, prayer, and acceptance. In one scene Koma pushed a buffalo head and hide across the floor. In another, Eiko & Koma's six-year-old son Yuta walked slowly upstage, a child venturing alone into a seemingly vast, empty space. The journey was suggestive of the future—both its unlimited possibilities and its inescapable solitude.

The music, scored for flute, drum, rattles, and vocals, was commissioned from Taos Pueblo musician Robert Mirabal and composed after he spent a few months in Japan with the artists.[2]

Eiko & Koma's initial inspiration for the piece was the landscape, history, and culture of Taos, New Mexico, which they visited for the first time in 1990. But their intention was never to make a work only about New Mexico. *Land* was previewed at the Hiroshima Contemporary Art Museum so that the artists and their collaborators could reflect on the history of the atomic bomb, which had profoundly affected the land and people of both New Mexico and Japan, not to mention the world at large.

A ceremony begins to develop inside the audience.[1]

Premiere: November 5, 1991, Brooklyn Academy of Music Next Wave Festival/Lepercq Space, New York City

Length: 70 minutes

Set: Eiko & Koma, drops painted by Sandra Lerner

Lighting: Jeff Fontaine

Costumes: Eiko & Koma, with Robert Mirabal

Sound: Commissioned score by Robert Mirabal

Musicians: Robert Mirabal and Ben Sandoval (in later performances, Mirabal and Reynaldo Lujan)

Other performers: Yuta Otake (in later performances, Shin Otake)

Selected reviews: Deborah Jowitt, "Terrain," *Village Voice*, November 26, 1991; Alan M. Kriegsman, "Primal Layers of 'Land,'" *Washington Post*, March 10, 1992; Mary Grace Butler, "Elemental 'Land' Comes to Pillow," *Berkshire Eagle*, July 23, 1995.

1
Robert Mirabal, post-performance discussion, Danspace Project, New York City, May 29, 2010.

2
The score received a Bessie Award in 1992 and was included on Mirabal's CD *Land* (1995).

Premiere: March 26, 1993,
Walker Art Center/Hennepin
Center for the Performing Arts,
Minneapolis, Minnesota

Length: 70 minutes

Set: Eiko & Koma, floor cloth painted
by Vaughn Patterson

Lighting: Jeff Fontaine

Costumes: Eiko & Koma

Sound: Commissioned score by Robert
Mirabal; Francisco Guerrero, "Virgen
Sancta," arranged by Joseph Jennings
and performed by male vocal ensemble
Chanticleer; Eiko & Koma's sound
mix of Irish uilleann pipe music and
Japanese gagaku played at half speed

Musicians: Chanticleer and Bill Ochs
(Irish uilleann pipe)

Other performers: Yuta Otake (in later
performances, Shin Otake)

Selected reviews: Deborah Jowitt,
"Day's Catch," *Village Voice*, September
21, 1993; Allan Ullrich, "A Pair
of Natural Dancers," *San Francisco
Examiner*, January 20, 1995.

1
Eiko & Koma, e-mail message to the
editor, February 2, 2011.

2
After the premiere, the pool of water
was eliminated in favor of a floor
cloth, painted by Vaughn Patterson
to resemble a galaxy.

WIND
風 1993

In the opening scene of *Wind*, Koma shot an arrow into the empty space as feathers drifted down from the ceiling toward a thin pool of water on the stage.[2] A breeze from offstage set them swirling—an evocation of wind. In this otherworldly scene, Eiko & Koma and their son Yuta danced a series of solos and duets that explored the ethereal power of air, the passage of time, and the inevitable passing of lives. The performers always entered from stage right and exited stage left, with one exception: a scene in which the child entered from the left, as if he were a visitor from another world.

A child could easily die before parents. Our assumed order is fragile.[1]

top, bottom, and bottom right: Eiko & Koma with son Shin, *Wind*, Colony Theater, Miami Dade College, Florida, 1996
Photos: Juan E. Cabrera

top: *Wind*, Joyce Theater, New York City, 1993   Photo: Tom Brazil

DISTANT (not pictured)
遠い 1994

Her whereabouts are unknown.[1]

This work was a solo for Koma, performed in a cavelike space in which mossy vegetation hung above a bed of dry leaves. The action was simple: Koma rose from the leaves very slowly until he could suckle the hanging fronds. Near the end of the piece he was joined by Eiko, who until then had been hidden within the leaves.

Distant was part of the tetralogy *Autumn Passage* (see Appendix B, page 296).

Premiere: August 27, 1994, Art Awareness/New Lex Theater, Lexington, New York

Length: 12 minutes

Set: Eiko & Koma

Lighting: Jeff Fontaine

Sound: Ushio Torikai, "Shomyo"

Selected reviews: Jack Anderson, "Trees, Fallen Leaves, Growth and Decay," *New York Times*, November 21, 1995; Deborah Jowitt, "Whose Story Is This?" *Village Voice*, December 5, 1995.

1
Eiko & Koma, *Distant* rehearsal conversation, 1994.

ECHO (not pictured)
木魂 1995

In *Echo*, Eiko & Koma worked on a floor covered with dry leaves. Much of the dance involved Eiko slowly rising from the leaves and then sinking back down, as if she were attempting to burrow into the earth. Koma seemed to disappear into the landscape of Sandra Lerner's drawings, slides of which were projected on the back wall.

Echo was created to complete the tetralogy *Autumn Passage* (see Appendix B, page 296).

Premiere: November 16, 1995, Japan Society, New York City

Length: 20 minutes

Set: Eiko & Koma

Lighting: Jeff Fontaine

Costumes: Eiko & Koma

Sound: Traditional Japanese music

Selected reviews: Jack Anderson, "Trees, Fallen Leaves, Growth and Decay," *New York Times*, November 21, 1995; Deborah Jowitt, "Whose Story Is This?" *Village Voice*, December 5, 1995.

1
Eiko & Koma, e-mail message to the editor, February 2, 2011.

Trees and a mountain god answer a human voice. That is an echo.[1]

Premiere: September 8, 1995,
Lafayette College/Delaware River,
Easton, Pennsylvania

Length: 60 minutes

Visual design: Eiko & Koma, with
sculpture by Judd Weisberg

Lighting: Eiko & Koma

Costumes: Eiko & Koma

Sound: Traditional Japanese music
and ambient sound

Performances: Chattahoochie River,
Atlanta, Georgia; Cherry Creek, Denver,
Colorado; Huron River, Ann Arbor,
Michigan; Medicine Lake, Plymouth,
Minnesota; Monongahela River,
Pittsburgh, Pennsylvania; Nakatsugawa,
Tanzawa Mountains, Japan; Schoharie
Creek, Catskill Mountains, New York;
Teien-oike Garden Pond, Sarah P. Duke
Gardens, Duke University, Durham,
North Carolina; Winooski River,
Burlington, Vermont

Selected reviews: Jennifer Dunning,
"A Nuanced Production with Nature
as Co-Star," *New York Times*,
September 11, 1995; Robert
Greskovic, "riverrun, past Adam and
Eve's," *Native Dance*, October 9,
1995; Jane Vranish, "Eiko & Koma
Became Force of Nature in 'River,'"
Pittsburgh Post-Gazette, June 14,
1999.

Eiko & Koma's video about the process
of creating this work, *Dancing in
Water: The Making of "River"* (2009),
can be viewed on their website at http://
www.eikoandkoma.org/videos.

1
Eiko & Koma, press release for *River*,
1995.

RIVER

JII 1995

Created and previewed in Schoharie Creek, a mountain stream in the Catskills, *River* was an outdoor work performed in bodies of water—mainly rivers, but occasionally ponds and lakes. Audiences gathered on one shore to view the piece. Shortly after twilight, a 16mm film version of *Lament* was projected on a screen of canvas stretched between tree limbs that they held erect in the water. As darkness fell, the film ended and Eiko & Koma dropped the screen and let it float away. They then began to move, emphasizing the flow of the river by floating downstream, their only prop a large driftwood sculpture commissioned from visual artist Judd Weisberg. As darkness deepened, sculpture and dancers alike were illuminated by stage lights that had been placed along the shore. Quiet music, which emanated from several pairs of small speakers also concealed along the shoreline, began upstream of the dancers and slowly moved downstream and away, as if a couple of musicians had floated by in a boat. Ambient sounds and sights, which would have been a distraction inside a theater, here became part of the production.

River provided an opportunity for extended interdisciplinary collaboration with presenting organizations. Venues were asked to help locate a body of water with optimal accessibility, depth, current, cleanliness, sightlines, and quietude, a process that led to heightened awareness of the community's water resources. Many presenters also offered workshops and seminars on river history, ecology, and environmental issues.

We are no more than driftwood and leaves flowing down the river of time.[1]

River, Schoharie Creek, Catskill Mountains, New York, August 1995 (rehearsal) Photos: Harper Blanchet

River, Medicine Lake at French Regional Park, Plymouth, Minnesota, July 1996

River (indoor version) with the Kronos Quartet, Williams Center for the Arts, Lafayette College, Easton, Pennsylvania, November 1997   Photo: Elizabeth Keegin Colley

RIVER (indoor version)
川（舞台作品）　1997

After performing *River* at outdoor sites, Eiko & Koma developed the idea to adapt it for indoor presentation. This goal was realized during a summer residency at Lafayette College, where the new work also premiered. Both versions used the river as a metaphor for the flow of time, but the indoor *River* was a highly theatrical, collaborative piece performed partly in the nude.

It opened with several minutes of complete darkness and quiet. When the lights gradually came up, Eiko & Koma could be seen huddled in a diagonal swath of water whose banks were formed of blackened Spanish moss. The choreography included Eiko's slow drift toward Koma, who stood on the river's bank, and his futile attempt to push a large driftwood sculpture, created by Judd Weisberg, into an upright position. Acceptance of death, and continuous mourning, were the themes of this piece.

The artists commissioned Japanese composer Somei Satoh to create a river of sound, which was performed live by the Kronos Quartet at the premiere and at three later engagements.

Premiere: August 29, 1997, Lafayette College/Delaware River, Easton, Pennsylvania

Length: 75 minutes

Set: Eiko & Koma, with sculpture by with Judd Weisberg

Lighting: Jeff Fontaine

Costumes: Eiko & Koma

Sound: Commissioned score by Somei Satoh

Musicians: Kronos Quartet (David Harrington and John Sherb, violin; Hank Dutt, viola; and Joan Jeanrenaud, cello)

Selected reviews: Kathryn Williams, "Eiko and Koma Take an Hour's Journey from Silence to an Emotional Charge," *The Morning Call* (Allentown, PA), September 2, 1997; Jack Anderson, "At the Creation, a Tender Adam as Eve's Rescuer," *New York Times*, December 5, 1997; Deborah Jowitt, "Without a Net," *Village Voice*, December 23, 1997.

1
Eiko & Koma, e-mail message to the editor, March 2011.

Somei's music filled the theater as a river. Kronos played on a "riverbank," their figures reflected fully in black water. There we remembered many water sites where we danced *River*.[1]

Premiere: April 7, 1998, John F. Kennedy Center for the Performing Arts, Washington, DC

Length: 30 minutes

Set: Eiko & Koma

Lighting: Jeff Fontaine

Costumes: Eiko & Koma

Sound: Ambient

Selected reviews: Susan Brioli, "Husband and Wife Duo Mesmerize," *Herald-Sun* (Durham, NC), June 30, 1999; Jack Anderson, "In Summer, They Speak the Language of Snow," *New York Times*, July 2, 1999.

1
Eiko & Koma, e-mail message to the editor, February 2, 2011.

PULSE
脈拍 1998

Meditation in dried flowers.[1]

The setting for this piece was a snowy bank strewn with dried brown weeds. Eiko & Koma began the piece burrowed into the snow, camouflaged from view by their sheer white garments. They struggled separately and together to escape from the drifts, but the piece ended as it had begun.

Pulse, American Dance Festival/Reynolds Theater, Durham, North Carolina, June 1999

Breath, Whitney Museum of American Art, New York City, June 1998   Photo: David Allison

BREATH

息 1998

Premiere: May 28, 1998,
Whitney Museum of American Art,
New York City

Set: Eiko & Koma

Lighting: Eiko & Koma, with Scott Poitras

Sound: Ambient

Selected reviews: Valerie Gladstone, "Like
a Painting in Slow Motion," *New York
Times*, May 24, 1998; Jennifer Dunning,
"A Landscape's Darkness Illuminated by a
Nude," *New York Times*, June 8, 1998.

1
Eiko & Koma, "Breath," Whitney
Museum of American Art member
magazine 2 (summer 1998): 20.

Eiko & Koma created their first "living installation" at the invitation of Matthew Yokobosky, associate curator of film and video at the Whitney Museum of American Art, New York City. He offered the artists the second-floor film and video gallery for one month, and asked them to make an installation that included their bodies.

Breath was performed in a dark, cavelike environment of tea-stained, hand-sewn silk and dried leaves in autumnal colors, which the artists had constructed in a rented loft over a six-month period and then installed in the gallery. Electric fans, concealed from view, blew the leaves gently within the space and moved thin metallic strips hanging in front of the lighting fixtures. The lighting itself was programmed to shift subtly in a ninety-minute loop that included many cues. All of these effects together evoked nature: earth, trees, breeze, light shimmering through a forest canopy, the movement of the sun.

On the curved black walls of the space, Eiko & Koma's naked, moving bodies were shown on three video projections in which they shifted and sometimes disappeared, more like clouds than human forms. Through their choices in lighting, wall color, projection surface, and projection quality (purposely low), they had found a way to eliminate the rectangle that usually frames video images. This made the projections puzzling; some people even mistook them for holograms.

Breath was on view from May 28 through June 21, 1998, whenever the museum was open to the public. For seven hours a day, one of the artists—rarely both—lay in the leaves and moved slowly, sometimes imperceptibly. The piece was performed in the nude.

Fish and stones are all naked. So are we![1]

Premiere: May 25, 1999,
future site of 171 Cedar Arts Center,
Corning, New York

Length: one to three hours

Custom-designed trailer and interior:
Eiko & Koma

Lighting: Eiko & Koma

Costumes: Eiko & Koma

Sound: Variable

Selected reviews: Susan Barnard,
"Eiko and Koma Draw Rapt Crowd
in Hanover," *Valley News* (White
River Junction, VT), July 15, 2000;
Julia Bookman, "Dancers' Slow
Pace Reveals Artistic Power," *Atlanta
Journal-Constitution*, September
23, 2000.

1
Eiko & Koma, choreographers' notes
for *The Caravan Project*, 1999.

THE CARAVAN PROJECT
路上劇場 1999

In the late 1990s, inspired and invigorated by their experiences with *River* and *Breath*, Eiko & Koma began to imagine other ways to make their work available to a broad audience in an open-ended format. *The Caravan Project*, an installation on wheels, came out of this urge. It was also inspired by *kamishibai* or "paper theater." In this pre-television–era form of entertainment, a storyteller traveled from town to town on a bicycle rigged with a box with removable sides. The performer would park on a street corner and open the box, which magically became a theatrical frame for large, painted cards depicting popular stories. An audience of neighborhood children would gather to buy the candies he sold and listen to his dramatic tale.

In *The Caravan Project*, Eiko & Koma performed inside a trailer they pulled behind their Jeep and parked at a site. The customized trailer had doors on all four sides; at dusk an assistant opened them to reveal an environment of vines, twigs, and shredded, dyed cheesecloth in which Eiko & Koma were nestled. All lighting instruments were placed within the set, hidden from the audience's view. For the next one to three hours, they moved and slowly shifted within the space. The work could be viewed from any side, and audience members were free to come and go. When an assistant closed the doors, the performance was over.

**When the second door opened, the
wind blew through.**[1]

The Caravan Project, Lexington, New York, May 1999 (rehearsal)   Photo: Koma Otake

The Caravan Project, Wesleyan University, Middletown, Connecticut, November 2009   Photo: George Ruhe/ENELYSION®

Snow, American Dance Festival/Reynolds Theater, Durham, North Carolina, June 1999   Photo: Bruce R. Feeley

SNOW

雪 1999

In this duet, performed in falling snow, Eiko & Koma made their way laboriously across a vast, snowy field. Their stage design suggested space as a lonely place that is full of longing, but their movement, along with the periodic snowfall, implied that space is far from empty.

A visitor arrives and leaves quietly on a snowy night.[1]

Premiere: June 28, 1999, American Dance Festival/ Reynolds Theater, Durham, North Carolina

Length: 30 minutes

Set: Eiko & Koma

Lighting: Jeff Fontaine

Costumes: Eiko & Koma

Sound: Rentaro Taki, "Kojo no tsuki" ("The Moon Over the Ruined Castle")

Selected reviews: Susan Brioli, "Husband and Wife Duo Mesmerize," *Herald-Sun* (Durham, NC), June 30, 1999; Jack Anderson, "In Summer, They Speak the Language of Snow," *New York Times*, July 2, 1999.

1
Eiko & Koma, e-mail message to the editor, February 2, 2011.

Video (color, sound)
Running time 14:57 minutes
Set: Eiko & Koma
Lighting: Eiko & Koma, with Scott Poitras
Sound: Jerry Pantzer
Camera and direction: Jerry Pantzer
Editing: Eiko & Koma with Jerry Pantzer

BREATH (video)
息 1999

This video was shot at the Whitney Museum of American Art, New York City, in June 1998, during Eiko & Koma's living installation of the same name. A collaboration with video artist Jerry Pantzer and conceived as both creative archive and independent media work, the video captures and condenses the visual and kinetic experience of the artists' marathon performance. While the living installation in the gallery was composed mostly of solos, for this video Eiko & Koma created a duet more suited to the camera. For the filming and editing, they collaborated with videographer Jerry Pantzer. However, the process of editing the footage revealed different sensitivities between movement artists and filmmaker. With respect for each other's visions, Pantzer and the artists agreed to the release of two different versions of *Breath*. This description refers to Eiko & Koma's version.

Stills from *Breath*, 1999

When Nights Were Dark, Novel Hall, Taipei, Taiwan, May 26, 2000 (dress rehearsal)   Photo: Hui-En Teng

WHEN NIGHTS
WERE DARK
夜が暗かった時 2000

Eiko & Koma conceived this work as the indoor sequel to *The Caravan Project*. Viewers of that work had been free to choose their own vantage point(s) as they moved around the trailer, which was parked at various outdoor sites. To create a similar multidirectional viewing experience in a theater setting, where audiences must remain in assigned seats, the artists built a sculptural set that they mounted on a large-scale turntable that was turned manually (by onstage assistants not visible to the audience). It moved almost imperceptibly, making one nearly complete revolution during the seventy-five-minute program.

Through a grant from the Lower Manhattan Cultural Council, the set was constructed in their ninety-first-floor studio in the World Trade Center. There, Eiko & Koma made a nest of sticks and painted cheesecloth under primeval tree limbs hung with strips of fabric. Each of the four sides of the set evoked a different landscape: a cave, a plain, and two hills, one cool white and the other fiery red. The set glowed from within, and hidden fans caused the fabric strips to move gently. The artists began the dance in thin robes—white for Eiko, red for Koma—but as it progressed, they shed their clothing, ending the piece in the nude.

When Nights Were Dark was performed to a vocal composition commissioned from Joseph Jennings (then Chanticleer's music director) and performed live by the Praise Choir Singers, an a cappella group assembled by Jennings for this production.

Premiere: June 20, 2000, American Dance Festival/ Reynolds Theater, Durham, North Carolina

Length: 75 minutes

Set: Eiko & Koma

Lighting: Scott Poitras, from a design by Jeff Fontaine

Costumes: Eiko & Koma

Sound: Commissioned score by Joseph Jennings

Musicians: Praise Choir Singers (Tunesha Crispell, alto; Corey Durham, bass-baritone; Clifton Hill, tenor; and Michelle Hutcherson, soprano)

Selected reviews: Susan Brioli, "Dancing Duo Stage 'Delicious' Performance in the 'Dark,'" *Herald-Sun* (Durham, NC), June 22, 2000; Anna Kisselgoff, "An Eerie Beauty Darkly Smolders," *New York Times*, December 1, 2000; Deborah Jowitt, "The Other Virtuosity," *Village Voice*, December 26, 2000.

1
Eiko & Koma, e-mail message to the editor regarding the American Dance Festival premiere of *When Nights Were Dark*, June 2000.

Darker nights
harbored
stories and
awe.[1]

BE WITH: COLLABORATION AS PROCESS

The first day we met at my studio in California, Eiko & Koma sat down in a viewing area and asked me to imagine I'm an egg—yes, that is right, imagine that I am an egg, and develop that idea into a dance. I was amazed, excited, challenged, and curious.

During our collaboration over four visits during the year, I continued to be amazed, excited, challenged, and curious as I gradually evolved out of an egg. Amazed because I was always surprised by what would happen at each improvisational session. Excited because there would always be a series of new possibilities. Challenged because our style of movement was so different. And I was curious because the shape of the dance was taking on a life of its own. It seemed to become a series of images that evoked its own mysterious mythology. We

explored, improvised, and allowed the piece to evolve. And also curious because, rather then working from any fixed idea, it came about intuitively. Joan Jeanrenaud added a musical support that became a unifying element and a bridge between myself and the team of Eiko & Koma.

An interesting situation arose when it became apparent that Eiko & Koma were such a strong duo that when they interacted with each other, I felt left out. Over the years they had developed a personal style, and when they danced together they blended as one. I just didn't fit in. I struggled with the situation. Then I had an idea: "You two cannot dance together as a duet. I will relate to Eiko & Koma separately, or all three of us together."

They were obliging, and because of that limitation a particular image of our relationship evolved. Nothing literal; rather, something that

had its own life and fueled our interactions. When I danced with Eiko, our interactions were soft, tender, and flowing, whereas with Koma, the movements were aggressive, sharp, and tense. A polarity in our relationship just happened. We had not preconceived it, but it set the course for what would follow.

The closure of the dance was an integration of all three of us, which Koma supported with a wonderful stage set. The collaboration began with a blank canvas, started out with an egg, went through a journey of uncertainty, and when the curtain went up our journey had reached some level of Peace. Eiko called it *Be With*, which described our process.

—Anna Halprin

Premiere: October 16, 2001,
John F. Kennedy Center for the
Performing Arts, Washington, DC

Length: 40 minutes

Set: Eiko & Koma

Lighting: Patti-Ann Farrell

Costumes: Eiko & Koma, with Anna
Halprin

Sound: Commissioned score
by Joan Jeanrenaud

Musician: Joan Jeanrenaud

Other performer: Anna Halprin

Selected reviews: Sarah Kaufman,
"Anna Halprin, Dancing around
Death," *Washington Post*, October
18, 2001; Janice Ross, "At 81,
Dancing with Partners," *New York
Times*, January 27, 2002; Anna
Kisselgoff, "Travel Companions on
Life's Inevitable Journey," *New York
Times*, January 31, 2002.

BE WITH
共に 2001

Be With, a meditation on caring, nurturing, aging, and friend-ship, was made in collaboration with Eiko & Koma's long-time friends, choreographer Anna Halprin and cellist Joan Jeanrenaud. It comprised one trio and a series of duets between Halprin and either Eiko or Koma. The work was developed in Halprin's studio in Marin County, California. Her hus-band, Lawrence, attended rehearsals, offered feedback, and made several drawings of the process. The music, composed by former Kronos Quartet cellist Jeanrenaud, was created dur-ing the rehearsal process and played live at all performances.

After its premiere, *Be With* was performed in only two other cities, New York and San Francisco.

Lawrence Halprin, sketch made during rehearsals for *Be With*, 2001

Eiko & Koma with Anna Halprin, *Be With*, Joyce Theater, New York City, January 29, 2002 Photo: Terri Olson

Offering, Boulder, Colorado, July 2006   Photo: Takahiro Haneda

Offering, Warsaw, Poland, July 2002 Photo: Jaroslaw Brzezinski, Poland

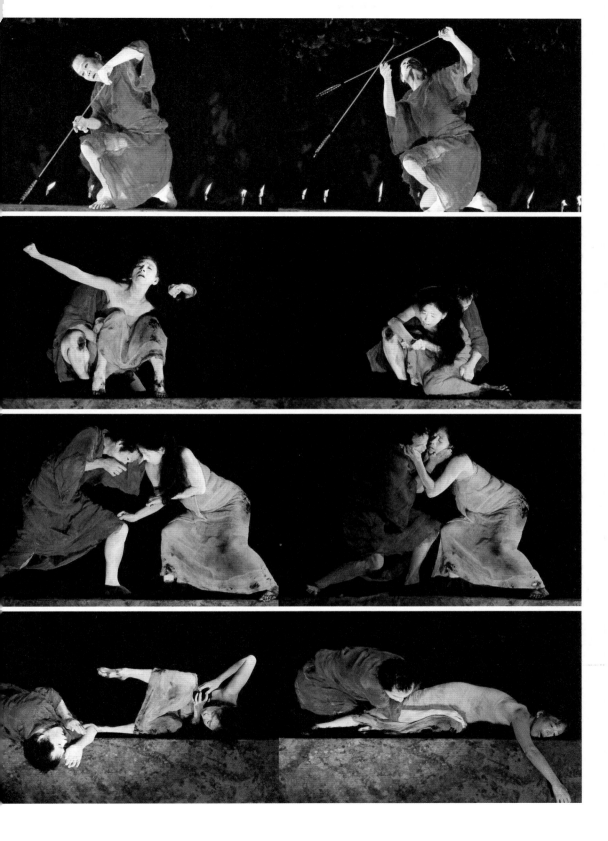

OFFERING

供養 2002

Dirt absorbed blood, tears, and bodies.[1]

Eiko & Koma have called *Offering* "a portable dance installation"—a variable project whose every aspect can be adapted to most any site and context. They have performed it indoors and out, in daytime and evening, with or without a set, with live or recorded sound, and using a range of costumes, props, and collaborators. Linking all versions is the theme of mourning and an interaction with the earth in the form of soil.

This work's original title was *Coffin Dance*, but in the wake of the September 11 attacks on New York City in 2001, the artists renamed it *Offering*. To address their own and their community's need to mourn, they gave a series of free outdoor performances in six public parks in Manhattan in July 2002, beginning at the Belvedere, near the former World Trade Center site. For that program, which started an hour before sunset, Eiko & Koma, with dancer Lakshmi Aysola, performed on a dirt-covered structure that suggested an altar, coffin, or pyre. Composer David Krakauer played his score live on the clarinet.

Premiere: July 16, 2002, Dancing in the Streets/Belvedere Park, Battery Park City, New York City

Length: 60 minutes

Set: Eiko & Koma

Lighting: Eiko & Koma

Costumes: Eiko & Koma

Sound: Commissioned score by David Krakauer

Musician: David Krakauer

Other performer: Lakshmi Aysola (New York only)

Performances: Tucson, Arizona; Phnom Penh, Cambodia; Vancouver, British Columbia, Canada; Los Angeles and Riverside, California; Boulder, Colorado; Middletown, Connecticut; Rakvere, Estonia; Vilnius, Lithuania; Bangor and Lewiston, Maine; Plainfield, North Adams, and Boston, Massachusetts; Minneapolis, Minnesota; Hanover, New Hampshire; Rhinebeck, Tivoli, and New York City, New York; Raleigh and Durham, North Carolina; Portland, Oregon; Lublin, Sonok, Bytom, Jeleniogory, and Warsaw, Poland; Burlington, Vermont; Seattle, Washington

1
Eiko & Koma, choreographers' notes for *Offering*, 2002.

TREE SONG
樹の詩（うた） 2003–2004

Premiere: July 5, 2003, American Dance Festival/Reynolds Theater, Durham, North Carolina

Length: 50 minutes

Set: Eiko & Koma

Lighting: Eiko & Koma

Costumes: Eiko & Koma

Sound: Music by Rentaro Taki; ambient night sounds

Selected reviews: Jennifer Dunning, "For Primal Duo, the Memories of Trees Hold No Terror," *New York Times*, July 14, 2003; Eva Yaa Asantewaa, "Eiko and Koma," *Dance Magazine* 78 (2004): 92, 94.

1
Eiko & Koma, e-mail message to the editor, February 2, 2011.

Tree Song was always performed as a free, outdoor event. Eiko & Koma usually began the evening lying prostrate and motionless on the ground as the audience slowly gathered around them. Then they began to stir; their movements, they have written, were of "roots digging further down and trunks remembering their cut branches, enduring." They wore loose fur shifts and white makeup over their dirt-smeared skin.

During its premiere engagement, this work was performed in two locations, once before a towering pine and the following night in front of a mature magnolia tree. A pile of cut green boughs and white flowers burned near the audience throughout the dance.

A revised version of *Tree Song* was presented May 27 through 29, 2004, in the graveyard at St. Mark's Church in-the-Bowery in New York City. It featured a commissioned score by Georgia Wyeth, performed live by Wyeth (piano) and her mother, Sharon Dennis Wyeth (vocalizations and text).

We celebrated trees, their memories, and their endurance.[1]

Tree Song, Bytom, Poland, July 2004

DUET
二人で 2004

Premiere: June 27, 2004,
American Dance Festival/Reynolds
Theater, Durham, North Carolina

Length: 20 minutes

Lighting: David Ferri

Costumes: Eiko & Koma

Sound: Music by Rentaro Taki

Selected reviews: Jack Anderson,
"Eiko and Koma Win Scripps Award,"
New York Times, June 29, 2004.

A demonstration piece meant to give a sense of their style, *Duet* was created on the occasion of Eiko & Koma's Samuel H. Scripps American Dance Festival Award for Lifetime Achievement in Modern Dance. It was later performed in various settings when a short, concise work was required, for example at senior citizens' residences, hospitals, and private homes; or when the artists shared a program with others. Its simple sequence begins with the two dancers slowly approaching one another from opposite sides of the space, until Koma sticks an arrow into Eiko's chest. The movement, which varied with each iteration, ranged from helping one another to animalistic courting.

This is a love song.[1]

1
Eiko & Koma, choreographers' notes for *Duet*, 2004.

THE LIFE BEHIND *DEATH POEM*

In 1996 Eiko and Koma received a MacArthur Fellowship, or so-called "genius grant." They were the first collaborative couple to do so. I was then the director of the program, and their selection led me yet again to reflect on the designation conferred by this award.

"Genius" is a battered word, the victim of two different sets of abusers.

The first set, the Romantics, decree that the genius is a godlike individual, flinging lightning bolts of art and thought from a Mount Olympus. The second set, the Democratizers, find genius everywhere, from a pop star's self-designed navel ring to a child's first homemade cupcake. The Romantics escalate the genius until he or she escapes history. The Democratizers de-escalate genius into a sweet moment in the swill of everyday.

Eiko & Koma are the real thing. They are geniuses. When I say why, I can also recuperate that battered word and restore its meaning.

As all geniuses must, they have original powers of thought, imagination, and action. They have had teachers. They will have imitators. Nevertheless, on the grand, intricate transmission belts of culture, they are establishing their own big, singular mark. A banal statement: to have such powers is the base line of genius.

They have cultivated their powers. These two Japanese university students have become "Eiko & Koma" because they have worked. They have exhibited a persistent, even inexorable will to create and to perform—whether the venue is a hallowed concert hall or a street. The Democratizers forget that genius is not the ability to bake one cake, but to redefine "cakeness" itself through ardent, arduous, disciplined labor.

They are, of course, collaborators, linked together as vitally as veins, arteries, and capillaries. They rebuke the Romantic belief in the genius as the towering, isolated individual. Yet, even in their most stringent effacements of the self through stagecraft (setting, costume, makeup), and even in the most passionate fusions of their bodies on stage or whatever is approximating a stage, and even in their most deliberate dissolutions of themselves into nature or an evocation of death, they are still discernibly "Eiko" or "Koma." The self, the core of humanism, remains. Part of their originality is to show the constant transmutation of the self into the couple and the couple into the self.

Genius never plays it safe. Famously, Eiko & Koma take multiple risks. They put themselves in danger—be it the danger of losing their audience through the lengthy duration of their movements; or the danger of their nakedness (not being seen because only the shockingly naked body seems visible); or the danger of floating in a polluted river; or the danger of living as experimental, immigrant artists in the United States; or the danger, as experimental artists, of using the deepest, most mysterious narratives of life and death to structure their performances. In person, they have great charm and generosity. In their work, they have an elemental intensity.

Grace or the approximation of grace is the consequence for an audience that is the beneficiary of their genius—the originality and force of their powers, the indefatigability, the staring down of danger and the possibility of failure and injury. I believe that I first saw *Death Poem* in a historic fieldstone church whose worshippers have been a part of Colonial American and United States history. Like others, I could play the serious game of find that theme. Is this, I could ask, their adaptation of the myth of Orpheus and Eurydice? Yet, the genius of Eiko and Koma was to lead me into a far more serious game, the imagining and re-imagining of my very existence. At the end of the game, I was not in Hades, though I might have been there, but beyond Hades in that place of exalted light and shadow that is the grace of art. The gifts of genius, those who are greatly gifted, become gifts to us.

—Catharine R. Stimpson

DEATH POEM

死の歌 2004-2005[1]

One can only learn about death by attending the deaths of others.[2]

Premiere: November 18, 2004, Dance Center, Columbia College, Chicago, Illinois

Length: 35 minutes

Set: Eiko & Koma

Lighting: David Ferri

Costumes: Eiko & Koma

Sound: John Dowland, "Lachrymae Antiquae" (1604), and Hildegard von Bingen, "O Virtus Sapientiae" (12th century), both from the album *Early Music* by the Kronos Quartet; sounds of insects

Selected reviews: Jack Anderson, "Evoking the Delicacy of Life, in a Subtle Dance of Death," *New York Times*, June 25, 2005; Deborah Jowitt, "Shape-Shifting," *Village Voice*, July 5, 2005.

1
The date spans two years because a partial version of *Death Poem* was premiered in Chicago in 2004 and the full version at Danspace Project/St. Mark's Church in-the-Bowery in New York City in 2005.

2
Eiko & Koma, choreographers' notes for *Death Poem*, 2004.

Death Poem was titled for the Japanese tradition of composing a poem when one is on the verge of death; the choreography came out of Eiko's experience tending to a dying friend during the summer of 2004. The piece centers around a forty-minute solo for Eiko, much of which she performed on a futon. With small, slow, and delicate movements she sat up, lay down, rolled, and eventually crawled upstage. Koma appeared at both the beginning and end of the piece to witness, assist, or welcome Eiko's passage. *Death Poem* ends with the stage in darkness but for a single flickering candle.

The set featured a painting of a pale, prone woman half-submerged in water and surrounded by pink lotus blossoms. Made by the Reyum Painting Collective in Phnom Penh, Cambodia, the work was lowered to the floor near the end of the dance and became the field on which the artists attempted to reach one another.

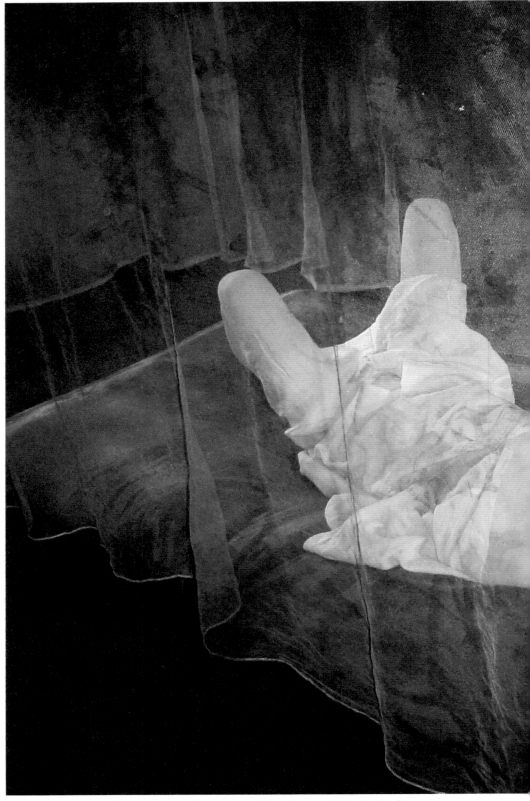

Death Poem, Dance Center, Columbia College, Chicago, November 2004 Photo: David Ferri

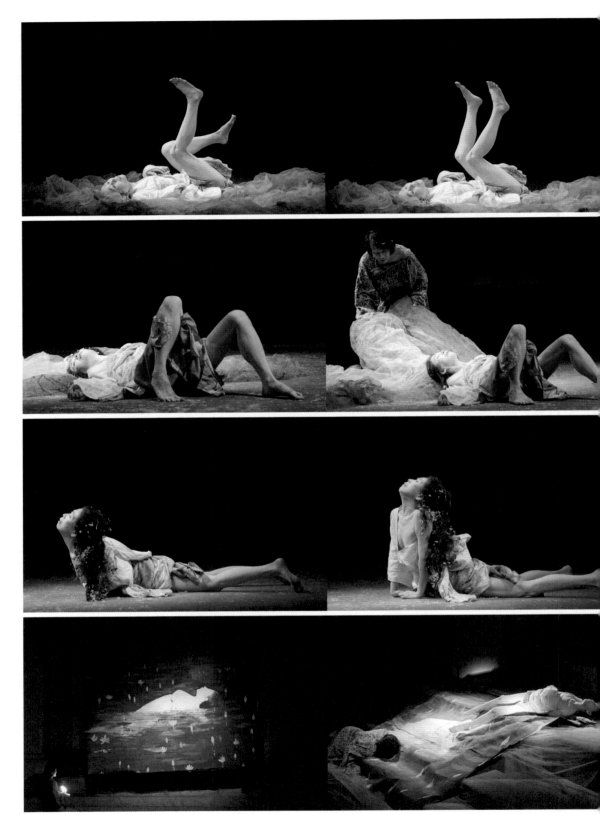

Death Poem, Danspace Project/St. Mark's Church in-the-Bowery, New York City, June 2005   Photos: Steven Schreiber

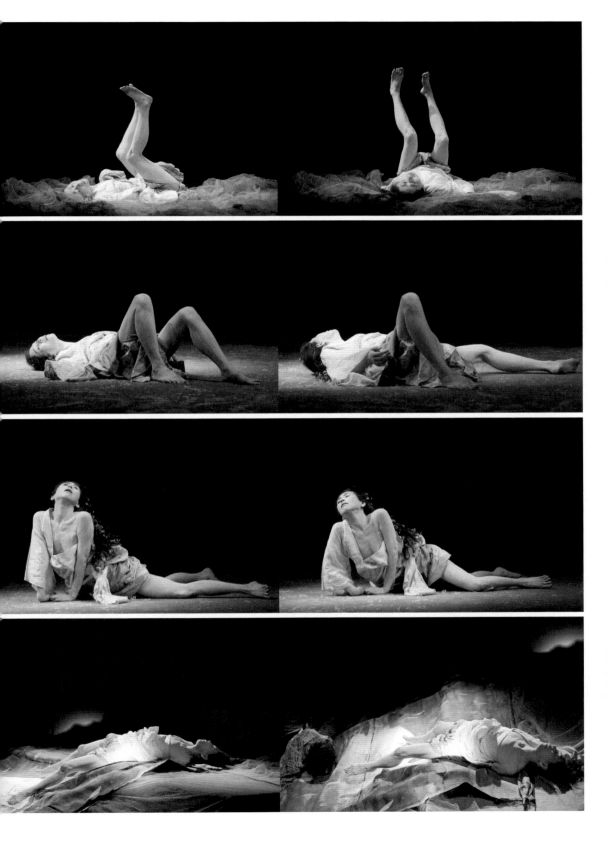

Cambodian Stories: An Offering of Painting and Dance, Asia Society, New York City, May 2006 Photo: La Frances Hui

CAMBODIAN STORIES: AN OFFERING OF PAINTING AND DANCE
カンボジア物語：絵と踊りの供養

2006

Cross-disciplinary, cross-cultural, and intergenerational, *Cambodian Stories: An Offering of Painting and Dance* came out of Eiko & Koma's 2004 residency at the Reyum Institute of Arts and Culture in Phnom Penh, Cambodia. After they returned home, they had the idea to collaborate with some of the young artists they had met, and invited students who were interested to take part. Nine boys and one girl, ages sixteen to twenty-two, became their collaborators. During the next two years, Eiko & Koma returned to the Reyum School several times, offering a series of works-in-progress showings as training for the cast. Dancing in front of their friends, neighbors, and families was the quickest way for the young painters to become performers.

Cambodian Stories began with the students introducing themselves, each stating his or her name and dreams for the future (most of them wanted to become famous artists). As an integral part of the choreography, the boys painted and hung two backdrops, both stylized images of women. The youngest two students, Chakreya "Charian" So and Setpheap "Peace" Sorn, performed the central duets, while the rest of the cast also danced and painted. Eiko & Koma functioned primarily as elder guiding spirits. In the finale, the company knelt and faced the audience in a posture of prayer. Cambodian ethnomusicologist Sam-Ang Sam provided the music, some of which he composed himself.

After its premiere, *Cambodian Stories* toured to twelve cities across the United States and also was performed in Taiwan. At each stop, an exhibition of paintings by the Reyum Collective appeared concurrently. These works as well as those created during the performance were sold to benefit the Reyum Institute of Arts and Culture.

Premiere: March 30, 2006, University of Maryland, College Park

Length: 80 minutes

Set: Eiko & Koma, with cast

Lighting: David Ferri

Costumes: Eiko & Koma

Sound: Cambodian pop and traditional music, arranged by Sam-Ang Sam

Other performers: Thorn Chan, Vannak Huoth, Sotha Kun, Sokchanthorn Ngin, Nimit Ouen, Sopon Phe, Chakreya "Charian" So, Setpheap "Peace" Sorn, Sok Than, Chivalry Yok

Selected reviews: Pamela Squires, "A Moving Portrait of Cambodia," *Washington Post*, April 1, 2006; Lewis Segal, "'Cambodian Stories' Affirms a Lust for Life," *Los Angeles Times*, April 7, 2006; Jennifer Dunning, "Grand Themes, Conveyed in Movement and in Paint, in 'Cambodian Stories,'" *New York Times*, May 22, 2006.

Eiko & Koma's video about the process of creating this work, *The Making of Cambodian Stories* (2006), can be viewed on their website at http://www.eikoandkoma.org/videos.

EIKO & KOMA, *CAMBODIAN STORIES*

I saw this new work by the New York–based performance duo Eiko & Koma at CalArts Theater in Los Angeles. It was created during a visit to Cambodia by the duo with a group of students in their late teens and early twenties who study painting and work at the Reyum Institute of Arts and Culture in Phnom Penh. Eiko & Koma themselves appear in only a handful of scenes, the leading roles filled by the nine young male performers and one young female performer who have no dance experience whatsoever. Having said that, their bodies were surprisingly raw and fresh, and also gave the impression that they had a strong inner core. In fact, their almost uncanny strength made me tremble at the realization that people can "speak" so eloquently using nothing but their bodies.

The show opens with the performers introducing themselves briefly in English, giving their names, ages, family composition, and dreams for the future. Nearly all have lost one or both parents and have several siblings. All mention that they want to become famous artists (in some kind of traditional craft, it seems). To the left and right of the stage, which is covered in yellow sand, hang large paintings of female figures depicted in unpretentious lines and colors. During the show, the audience also witnesses the spectacle of the male performers using a wooden scaffold to paint before their very eyes an enormous female

figure. One thing that did weigh on my mind was the naiveté with which the combination of the young female performer and Eiko emphasized the image of the "mother" representing the female as the source of life, thereby sentimentally reiterating the ideology of a reproductive system centered on the modern family. However, I appreciated the staging, which was straightforward and honest to the point that no attempt was made to hide such weaknesses. In fact, although the theater was occasionally filled with the strains of what I took to be Cambodian popular songs, there were no dramatic effects whatsoever; the lighting by David Ferri shining uniformly across the stage from start to finish. This lighting, which enveloped everything in a warm glow while at the same time laying bare even the slightest details of the events unfolding on stage, ensured the entire audience could appreciate every aspect of the performance, from Eiko & Koma's choreographic vocabulary of slow and simple movements and flowing gait to the stirring of the bodies of the young men and woman who seemed to savor their every movement.

Such beauty probably has a profound effect on everyone. However, there is certainly a lot more to it than that, by which I mean that if one were to describe it as merely beautiful while ignoring the microscopic drama that contributes to this strong sense of beauty, then even this beauty would likely lose its substance. This is because such a view fails to recognize the fragility of those who are on the stage.

More than anything else, the young performers appear before the audience as people deprived of language. Of course, I don't mean this in the sense that they are performing in front of an American audience unable to understand Khmer. I mean that when people whose bodies are accustomed to painting are deprived of painting and try to speak using nothing but their bodies, they must rely on a language that is unfamiliar to them, which is nothing less than taking a risk on the possibilities of communication. As they repeat over and over again movements such as slightly lowering their center of gravity, extending their long, thin arms diagonally to the front and back, and slowly crossing the stage, or repeating rhythmically to the left and right organic curves described with twisted upper bodies, their bodies are constantly pulsating due to their slight hesitation. Unlike expert dancers who are completely confident in their technical abilities, these young performers exhibit a delicacy of sensibility as if straining to corroborate every single movement, producing vibrations so subtle they are almost invisible to the naked eye and adding texture to their performance. It stems not from inability but from the sheer intensity of the risk their own bodies have taken.

Unable to draw on their skills as painters, the bodies of the performers are rendered naked. One could say that depriving them of their language or artistic medium also deprives the audience of the same. I have no doubt that this relationship in which both sides are deprived of a medium for communication is precisely what Eiko & Koma aimed for. And yet these disarmed performers still manage to communicate something. Their slow movements, as if negotiating a treacherous tightrope, cause the bodies of us, the viewers, to quiver. What is happening here? Just what are they trying to tell us in this fragile language? Is it the story of Cambodia scarred by bloody civil war and genocide under the Pol Pot regime, or the (multiple) stories of the mothers of sixteen-year-old Chakreya and twenty-one-year-old Vannak? No, rather I think that words were forsaken and communication was at stake in an effort to avoid

at all costs the violent intervention of such stereo-typical symbols or representations. Rather than telling a story, perhaps the young performers are simply speaking of the truth that there is a story that cannot be told. Perhaps the simple truth that the actuality of people who live in far-off lands is undeniably real, albeit separated from us by a very real distance, is able to cross the threshold of meaning and send quivers through the bodies of viewers.

It may well be that dance is always rooted like this in the distance between bodies standing op-posite to each other, making us aware of distance

through proximity and of the fact that others are in fact others. But at the same time it is also show-ing us that it is possible to share this unbridge-able distance. *Cambodian Stories* rejects symbols or representations of the reality of Cambodia, and in doing so transforms the reality of distance into something palpable. What is at work here is noth-ing less than the ethical and critical power that the dancing body alone can possess.

—Daisuke Mutoh. Originally published in *CUT IN 52* (July 2006). Translation by Pamela Miki.

Premiere: May 24, 2007,
Danspace Project/St. Mark's Church
in-the-Bowery, New York City

Length: 60 minutes

Set: Eiko & Koma, with Charian
and Peace

Lighting: David Ferri

Costumes: Eiko & Koma

Sound: Cambodian pop and
traditional music

Other Performers: Chakreya "Charian"
So and Setpheap "Peace" Sorn

Selected reviews: Alistair Macaulay, "A
World of Glacial Movements, Tense
with Emotions," *New York Times*, May
26, 2007; Jack Anderson, "Eiko and
Koma: Cambodia Again," *New York
Theatre Wire*, May 27, 2007, http://
www.nytheatre-wire.com/ja07053t
-eiko-and-koma-cambodian-stories
-revisited.htm.

1
Eiko & Koma, e-mail message to the
editor, February 16, 2011

CAMBODIAN STORIES REVISITED

再びカンボジア物語 2007

The large colorful paintings and Cambodian pop music traveled down Second Avenue.[1]

Cambodian Stories Revisited was a restructuring of the original as a quartet for Eiko & Koma, Charian, and Peace. Performed outdoors at night and free of charge in the graveyard of historic St. Mark's Church in-the-Bowery, the dance presented images of grief, dreams, and prayer by pairing dancers of different generations. The performance area was hung with paintings by the Reyum Collective; during the presentation, Eiko & Koma joined Charian and Peace in creating an additional large, colorful painting.

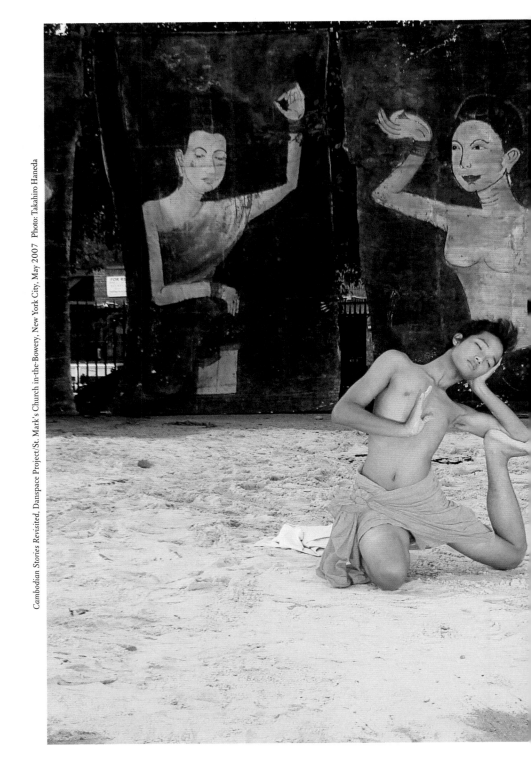

Cambodian Stories Revisited, Danspace Project/St. Mark's Church in-the-Bowery, New York City, May 2007 Photo: Takahiro Haneda

Eiko & Koma with Chakreya So and Setpheap Sorn, *Quartet*, American Dance Festival/Reynolds Theater, Durham, North Carolina, June 2007 Photo: Gregory Georges

QUARTET
四人で 2007

After several of their longtime friends, including American Dance Festival director Charles Reinhart, encouraged them to teach their unique style of dance movement to a younger generation of performers, Eiko & Koma invited *Cambodian Stories* soloists Charian and Peace to the United States for an extended stay during the spring and summer of 2007.

Quartet opened with Charian and Peace lying prostrate on the floor as Eiko & Koma bent in mourning over their bodies. This image became less sorrowful as the piece progressed and unexpected lust by the older couple was revealed. But ultimately *Quartet* explored the complex exchange of nurturing, loss, and survival that complicates the bonds between one generation and another.

Grain (2007), a duet set on Charian and Peace, was premiered on the same program as *Quartet* (see Appendix B, page 296).

Premiere: June 25, 2007, American Dance Festival/Reynolds Theater, Durham, North Carolina

Length: 30 minutes

Set: Eiko & Koma

Lighting: David Ferri

Costumes: Eiko & Koma

Sound: Cambodian song for the dead; insect sounds

Other performers: Chakreya "Charian" So and Setpheap "Peace" Sorn

Selected reviews: Linda Belans, "How Times Have Changed," *News and Observer* (Raleigh, NC), June 27, 2007; Alistair Macaulay, "The Slowness of Motion, and What It May Reveal," *New York Times*, June 29, 2007; Byron Woods, "Accept No Substitutes," *Independent Weekly* (Durham, NC), July 4, 2007.

1
Eiko & Koma, e-mail message to the editor, February 2, 2011.

Charian and Peace brought us funeral music from Cambodia.[1]

Premiere: October 18, 2007, Japan Society, New York City

Length: 60 minutes

Set: Eiko & Koma

Lighting: David Ferri

Costumes: Eiko & Koma

Sound: John Cage, "In the Name of the Holocaust"; Bunita Marcus, "Merry Christmas, Mrs. Whiting"; two works by Somei Satoh, "Litania" and "A Gate into the Stars"

Musician: Margaret Leng Tan

Selected reviews: Gia Kourlas, "Human Predators at Large, Butoh Style," *New York Times*, October 20, 2007; Deborah Jowitt, "Eiko and Koma Pity the Earth," *Village Voice*, October 30, 2007; Thea Singer, "A Primal 'Mourning' and Hope for Rebirth," *Boston Globe*, July 19, 2008.

1
Margaret Leng Tan, post-performance discussion with Eiko & Koma, Danspace Project, New York City, May 27, 2010.

MOURNING
哀悼 2007

Mourning was performed on a dirt-covered stage dominated by a massive tree trunk constructed of the same material used in *Tree* and *Breath*. The movement was intensely sexual, visceral, and even violent, blurring the boundaries between animal and human, life and death.

Mourning was a collaboration with pianist Margaret Leng Tan, whose highly visual live performance, which included one of her toy pianos, was an integral part of the piece—in fact, it is never performed without her. Leng Tan played three works from her repertoire with which she had an especially deep familiarity. Eiko & Koma wanted to have a comparable level of ease with their material; thus the choreography for *Mourning* intentionally quoted two of their earlier works, *Fur Seal* and *Tree Song*.

We don't synchronize; that's not the point of collaboration.[1]

Eiko & Koma with Margaret Leng Tan, *Mourning*, Summer Stages Dance/Concord Academy, Massachusetts, July 2008   Photo: Jaye R. Phillips

とちゅう*Hunger*, McGuire Theater, Walker Art Center, Minneapolis, Minnesota, October 2008 Photo: Cameron Wittig

HUNGER

飢え 2008

Hunger was the culmination of Eiko & Koma's four-year collaboration with the Cambodian dancers Chakreya "Charian" So and Setpheap "Peace" Sorn. In the opening scene, adapted from their 1989 piece *Rust*, Eiko & Koma clung upside down to a chain-link fence; the fence was left onstage for the rest of the evening so that the audience would recall the dancers' naked bodies. In subsequent scenes taken from *Grain* (2007), the dancers fed on and with one another, with much of the action taking place on a floor mat strewn with rice. The raven, a bird associated with an appetite for carrion, was a leitmotif: during the performance Charian and Peace painted an image of ravens on a backdrop, and the bird's raucous calls were part of the sound score. The theme of hunger—for food, but also for knowledge, intimacy, and life—was particularly present during a marathon duet between Eiko & Koma that was developed specifically for this work. The premiere, as well as later performances in New York, featured vocal and gamelan music, some of it prerecorded and some performed live by Joko Sutrisno.

Premiere: October 9, 2008, Walker Art Center, Minneapolis, Minnesota

Length: 70 minutes

Set: Eiko & Koma, with Charian and Peace

Lighting: David Ferri

Costumes: Eiko & Koma

Sound: Gamelan music; vocals; raven song

Musician: Joko Sutrisno

Other performers: Chakreya "Charian" So and Setpheap "Peace" Sorn

Selected reviews: Rohan Preston, "Eiko & Koma's Non-Narrative of Loss and Love," *Star Tribune* (Minneapolis), October 10, 2008; Tom Strini, "'Hunger' Feeds on Themes of Decay," *Milwaukee Journal-Sentinel*, October 19, 2008; Camille LeFevre, "Eiko & Koma," *Dance Magazine* 82 (November 2008), http://www.dancemagazine.com/reviews/November-2008/Eiko-and-Koma.

1
Eiko & Koma, choreographers' notes for *Hunger*, 2008.

In Cambodia people throw rice balls on graves on festival days. People understand that the dead also become hungry and need to be tended to.[1]

Premiere: May 27, 2010,
Danspace Project/St. Mark's Church
in-the-Bowery, New York City

Length: 30 minutes

Set: Eiko & Koma

Lighting: Kathy F. Kaufmann

Costumes: Eiko & Koma

Sound: Music by Robert Mirabal

Musician: Robert Mirabal

Selected reviews: Deborah Jowitt,
"Retrospective Project I: Regeneration,"
Village Voice, June 1, 2010;
Wendy Perron, "Eiko and Koma at
Dancespace," *Dance Magazine* 84
(June 1, 2010).

1
Eiko & Koma, choreographers' notes
for *Raven*, 2009.

RAVEN

大鴉 2010

We have black hair, like a raven. Ravens are scavengers.[1]

Raven was conceived as a flexible piece that could vary in length and be adapted for theater, gallery, or outdoor performance. As the centerpiece of Eiko & Koma's Retrospective Project, the dance gestured toward the past by incorporating movement and music from *Land* (1991) and thematic material from *Hunger* (2008). But it also included new elements, such as the image of a burned landscape: a floor cloth and backdrop made of scorched canvas and a mass of black feathers that evoked nonhuman species. *Raven* began with Eiko alone on the floor, which was strewn with feathers, straw, and salt. After a slow, searching solo, she was joined by Koma; the two confronted one another in their search for sustenance.

Raven, American Dance Festival/Reynolds Theater, Durham, North Carolina, June 2010   Photo: Anna Lee Campbell

Naked, Walker Art Center, Minneapolis, Minnesota, November 2010   Photo: Cameron Wittig

Naked, Walker Art Center, Minneapolis, Minnesota, November 2010   Photo: Cameron Wittig

NAKED

裸 2010

Premiere: November 2, 2010
Walker Art Center, Minneapolis, Minnesota
Set: Eiko & Koma
Lighting: Eiko & Koma
Sound: Dripping water
Selected reviews: Mary Abbe, "Getting 'Naked' at the Walker—For Art," *Star Tribune* November 18, 2010; Eva Yoa Asantewaa, "Dance Matters: Taking It Slow," *Dance Magazine* (November 2010), http://www.dancemagazine .com/issues/November–2010/Dance-Matters-The-Art-of-Taking-It-Slow; Roslyn Sulcas, "Poetry of Stillness, in a Moment Stretched to Infinity," *New York Times*, March 30, 2011.

1
Eiko & Koma, choreographers' notes for *Naked*, February 2, 2011.

For six hours each day, six days a week from November 2 through 30, Eiko & Koma's nude, mud-streaked bodies were on view in *Naked*, their second "living installation." The piece took place in a specially designed environment within the Walker Art Center's permanent collection exhibition *Event Horizon*. The performance space was defined by three large canvas drops encrusted with a mixture of sweet rice paste, sea salt, feathers, and dried grasses and dotted with large burn holes through which viewers could see into the space. If they chose to enter, they were free to come and go as they pleased.

Inside, only a few feet from the audience, Eiko & Koma lay on either side of an oblong nest of canvas, feathers, and grasses. They gently shifted and rolled, stretching hands and feet toward one another but never fully breaching the mound between them. Hidden fans moved the feathers gently, and lighting changes suggested the passage of time. Water dripped sporadically from the ceiling onto the bed of soil that surrounded them. The smell of scorched canvas and damp earth pervaded the space. Because they were so close to the audience, Eiko & Koma's relationship with their viewers was more intimate than it had ever been.

Naked drew on themes and imagery explored in *Raven* (2010). But its more direct predecessor was *Breath* (1998), Eiko & Koma's first living installation. In both *Naked* and *Breath*, museum visitors confronted the artists' living bodies in the midst of static art objects, raising issues of materiality, time, and mortality—core aspects of the artists' work.

Linger, stay here with your eyes, and kinetically observe how our bodies move toward the unknown.[1]

EIKO+KOMA+KRONOS

There is something about the work of Eiko & Koma that makes me feel I've known it for much longer than I actually have. It was not long after a terrible tragedy struck my family—there is no way to recover—I could only take one breath at a time and try not to fall off the world—then, almost magically I remember seeing Eiko & Koma for the first time on a video. This would have been late 1995 or early 1996. The slow motion of their dance and their bare bodies became a close friend to the iceberg of my grief. Shortly after this video encounter I remember visiting them in Japan: a beautiful walk up a forested hill, wonderful food, and then a performance where they were just a few feet away with their painted nakedness. I don't remember if there was music in this dance. Somehow Eiko & Koma seemed to be making intimate physical and tactile connections to the sounds I have carried inside of me since I first heard string quartet music when I was twelve years old. I immediately

realized that the friction of rosined horsehair against taut strings had parallels in their dance and that an astonishing experience could happen when and if we made something together. And so *River* came into the work and lives of the Kronos Quartet in 1997.

We have remained close since then. I remember one fantastic evening at Eiko & Koma's home several years ago. They both give me so much energy. And I get more ideas per square second when I'm with them than at any other time. And for people who move so slowly and deeply on stage, I'm always amazed at how much fun it is to be with them. They have attended a few of our concerts over the years and are very appreciative of our work. I always hoped that we might find a way to work together again.

Then in the summer of 2010, I visited Eiko & Koma at the Park Avenue Armory in New York City to see their most recent piece, which was in development. I was totally unprepared for what I saw. I've never wept at a dance performance before. But there we were together, in a darkened

space, their glacial nakedness a deeper expression than I remembered, much deeper and somehow more exposed. Their scope of expression had found more revealing forms. I realized that I was witnessing an absolute center of life, where all layers of protection are removed, where time is irrelevant. Their performance had led me back once again to being a naked infant. The image I was left with was that we are all naked, aging infants in the face of the universe. Eiko & Koma's bodies had become metaphors for the universal, fragile nakedness we try to hide, their bare skin and awesome, slow movements had become a story of communal privacy. To me this is the precise area where music is most alive.

Later Eiko said something that was perfect in her inimitable light and offhanded way, "Of course we don't really need music for our work." What greater challenge can be issued to a group of musicians? Kronos is greatly looking forward to exploring together with Eiko & Koma.

—David Harrington

⁷ Koma mirroring

Eiko mirroring

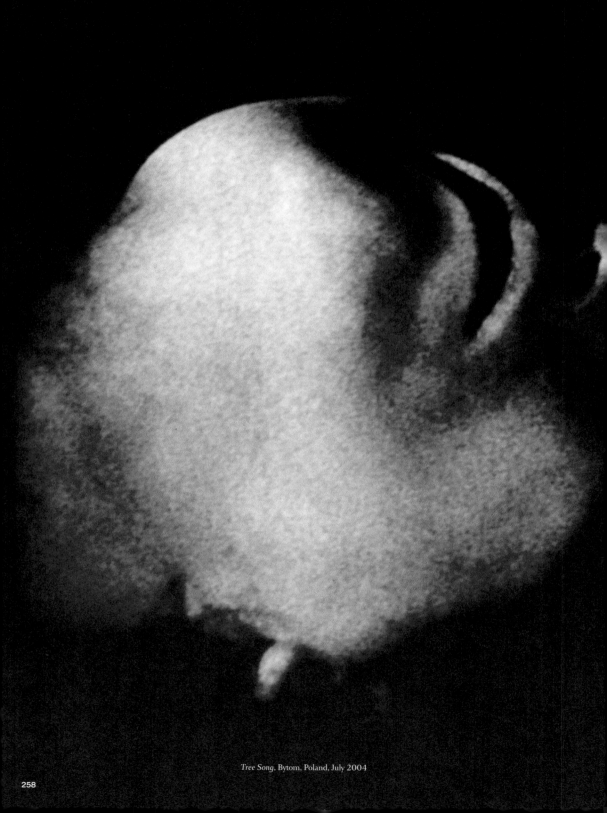

Tree Song, Bytom, Poland, July 2004

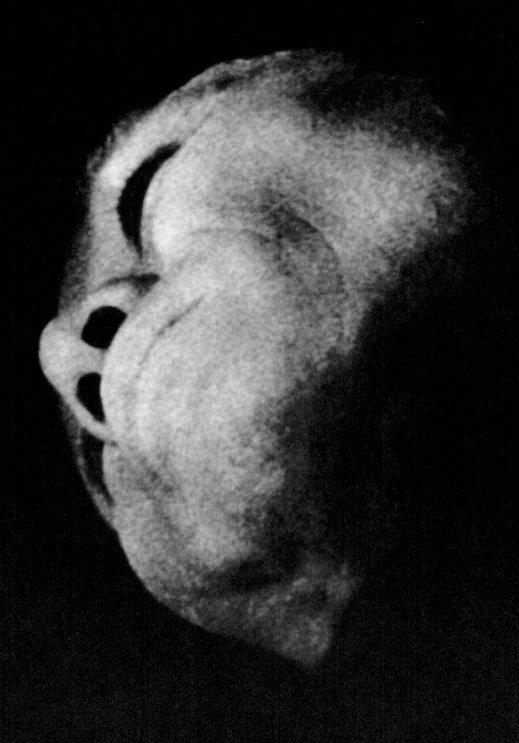

Selections from

DRIFTING ON MELODY SMOKE/A FLOWER OPENING TO THE MOON

A collaboration with Jan Henle

In 1976, Eiko & Koma traveled to St. Croix, US Virgin Islands, to visit artist Jan Henle, who had seen them dance in the Netherlands and whom they had met in New York when they first came to the city and performed at Japan Society. For a few months Eiko & Koma stayed with him in St. Croix and spent much of their time walking the beach, swimming, hiking, and sharing meals and conversation with Jan. A chronic pain Eiko had developed in her ankle, which had threatened to end their dance career, magically disappeared as a result of this new routine.

Henle was the first artist of their own generation, from a different culture, with whom Eiko & Koma developed a leisurely, personal relationship. Their friendship evolved into a four-year-long collaboration during which they worked in St. Croix, New York, Mexico, and Massachusetts. Working outdoors with Henle and his camera but without the human audience to which they were accustomed led Eiko & Koma to experiment with ways to interact with what was at hand—landscape, rocks, waves, trees, cows. These images capture that process of exploration. As Henle has put it, the photographs are "an attempt to get beyond 'you' and 'I,' an attempt to create a hybrid through life shared together, a fusion of art forms, a oneness with nature."[1] Eiko & Koma today consider Henle their first serious collaborator, and recognize the work they did with him as the basis for their future exploration of outdoor settings for their dance.

—Joan Rothfuss

1
Jan Henle, e-mail message to the author, June 13, 2010.

COLLABORATING WITH
EIKO & KOMA

I first photographed Eiko & Koma at Omega Institute in 1988 for my book *Dancers*. When photographing dancers my habit was to arrive early, select two or three sites in the landscape, choose costumes with the dancers, and then select segments of dances.

Photographing Eiko & Koma was different. I arrived to find that Eiko had already made a costume that would meld with a site they had chosen a few days earlier.

Although this was a different process, our collaboration was easy: slow, sure movements laden with emotion. The three of us, totally focused, exchanged ideas quietly. We did not discuss concepts; instead, we responded to our visceral feelings.

We came together again at Jacob's Pillow in the winter of 1993. Having been commissioned to engage in a true collaboration, the three of us endeavored to create something unique and new.

It was freezing. I photographed Eiko & Koma, half-clad, on ice and snow. There was no heat or water. Aborting the project was out of the question. Alert and attentive to one another, we shared a single-minded resolve. Our work together was totally open, often informing each other without words. This was shared creative impetus at its best.

But this should have come as no surprise. Even before I started photographing them, I knew that we were totally attuned to one another, that everything would work out beautifully. The day before I arrived, Eiko & Koma chose locations for our session. I then chose some myself. From the myriad possibilities at Jacob's Pillow, we had selected exactly the same sites.

—Philip Trager

^{8} release weight up constellate

ward, offering throat,
center stage

Retrospective Project banner by Megamu Tagami, 2009   Photo: Anna Lee Campbell

Eiko & Koma with Sam Miller, American Dance Festival/Reynolds Theater, Durham, North Carolina, June 2010
Photo: Anna Lee Campbell

THE LIMITS OF LANGUAGE

Sam Miller

You go to the theater and see an artist you've cared deeply about for twenty-five years. Each image on stage animates others from past productions. You realize you are old. You look around and understand that for the younger people sitting in front of you, it might be their first time seeing this work. They too are moved, immersed in the same moments you are, and yet for them, the moments are memory-free. The young people can't go back in time. They can flip through CD racks or library shelves—or more likely they go online—looking for earlier work by the artist who has moved them so, searching in vain for some trace of the depth they glimpsed.

The idea of a retrospective is not new. Recently in New York you could have seen a forty-year survey of Gerhard Richter drawings on Wooster Street or twenty years of Olivier Assayas films at the Brooklyn Academy of Music. Over the past few years, you could see a season of Jerome Robbins dances at City Ballet, or concerts all over the city celebrating the one hundredth birthday of composer Olivier Messiaen.

None of these revived works, however, originate in the artists' own bodies. Eiko & Koma are their own clay. It has been forty years since they started working together, so you could say it has not been fired but aged. We need to look back with them, for them, and for others—to recover or reimagine what we can, in hopes that the remaking will take on its own shape, though still from the same clay. And so I suggested the idea of the Retrospective Project to the artists.[1] Eiko & Koma first ran it by their sons, Shin and Yuta, and luckily it met with their approval.

Now we needed partners. Wesleyan University served as convener, incubator, host, midwife, and a source of renewable human energy thanks to Pam Tatge's embrace of Eiko and the Center for Creative Research (CCR).[2] It was at Wesleyan where we gathered for a day at the Freeman Center for East Asian Studies in April 2009. There were thirty-nine individuals from more than a dozen organizations, rehearsing for a role in a play we would write together over the next three years.

As we talked that day, it was clear that replication was not the goal for this retrospective. Eiko & Koma are living and working artists, their art based in their bodies but not confined to flesh or its past perfect. We would work across disciplines and into the future declension.

Nor would this be a simple generic program transported from one place to the next. We decided to address communities according to their particular history, opportunities, and topography. This Retrospective Project would be an accumulation of elements made over time from what had gone before, serving as both reflec-

1

Why Eiko & Koma? When I was at Jacob's Pillow (from 1986–1995), we worked together with Philip Trager on an experiment in art documenting art. We came up with a series of images that stopped time in an inhabited landscape (some of these images are in this catalogue), and a journey began. You carry from one century to another the work that matters and that you want others to know and care about, but your caring cannot be carried, it will not come with you. The artists also cross over, and what's been left behind matters both to them and to you, and so the experiment in recovery and renewal is accepted in its delicious futility.

2

The Center for Creative Research (CCR) was originally launched in 2005 at the New England Foundation for the Arts (NEFA) as a pilot project designed to reimagine the relationship between mature, individual movement-based artists and research institutions. Now a research program in the Graduate School of Arts & Science at New York University, CCR seeks to complement existing models for artists and university engagement by highlighting and facilitating the rigorous inter- and transdisciplinary contributions that artists and universities can make to each other. Eiko is one of the eleven founding artists of CCR, and Wesleyan is one of the pilot institutions.

tion and prophecy—new work made from old, old work emerging from new. The project is not a culmination, it is an assemblage extracted from a body of work that becomes both the prologue and the foundation for the next journey.

Eiko & Koma have lived and worked together for four decades. Living and working, working and living—as artists, in self-imposed exile, raising American sons, making work on their bodies. They are their own country, their own cause, their own disciples.[3] And so a process began, a series of journeys by two artists between home—which also functions as studio, laboratory, social center, think tank, and guesthouse—and places new and old across the United States and beyond.

First we confirmed parts and partners—a virtual world in a website (designed by Brian Lemond and the Brooklyn Digital Foundry), this catalogue (published by the Walker Art Center), films (some old, some new), photos, installations, and bodies in made theater and gallery spaces, movement made from movement, movement made with music, silence, feathers, rice, salt, sand, and burnt canvas.

Collaborators were called. They came, shared, remembered, made new things from old ... drummer Robert Mirabal, violinist David Harrington, dancer Anna Halprin, pianist Margaret Leng Tan, video artist James Byrne, visual artist Sandra Lerner. Curators who had convened at Wesleyan began, with Eiko & Koma, to shape time and space that mattered, a sequence, a necklace of years and places, a path prepared for images, objects, environments—the making of something that knows better than time what time knows.

2 bodies / 3 threads
(like Fates spinning, like waters woven together)

From 2009 to 2010, Eiko & Koma made *Raven*, a new piece for the stage. They worked on it at home, with feathers plucked from Indonesian dusters hand-carried to the United States by co-conspirators (you know who you are). They drew on themes from *Land* and *Hunger*, collaborated with Mirabal, incubated the piece at MANCC[4] and at Wesleyan, performed it at Danspace Project[5] and the American Dance Festival, paired it with *White Dance*, *Night Tide*, and a video work inspired by the making of *River*.

White Dance! Here was a revelation that almost broke our rules, a revival of Eiko & Koma's first dance that might also be their last, a miracle of remembrances and solos that tells you (almost) everything you need to know about Eiko & Koma.

Then there was *Naked*, commissioned by and first performed at the Walker Art Center, born from *Breath* and *Raven*, built at the Park Avenue Armory, shared and refined by and for the friends who visited their studio. Soon it will be translated for the Baryshnikov Arts Center (New York City), the Yerba Buena Center for the Arts (San Francisco), REDCAT (Roy and Edna Disney/CalArts Theater, Los Angeles), Clarice Smith Performing Arts Center at the University of Maryland, Dublin Dance Festival, and other places yet unseen.[6]

3
How does a couple collaborate closely for so long? What role does each play? First the idea, then movement from one, and terrain from the other—and then an exchange, a shared stage for woman, man, earth, light. Eiko & Koma are left behind at home sleeping, dreaming the next page. These are not the characters they play; this is not a manuscript that they both sign. This is subordinating alchemy.

4
MANCC stands for the Maggie Allesee National Center for Choreography, a dance and choreographic research center housed on the Florida State University campus. Director Jennifer Calienes has been very supportive of Eiko & Koma's work through technical and creative residencies.

5
Each presenter and collaborator is partner in this process and each space offers its own history. Judy Hussie-Taylor and Eiko & Koma talked of their history at St. Mark's Church and how to situate their performances in May 2010. Twenty years after collaborating on *Land* together, Robert Mirabal flew to New York from Taos, New Mexico, to record music for the planned performances. After he saw what was unfolding in the apartment/studio, he decided to stay for two weeks instead of two days and played live for every performance.

6
In addition to presenters, the funders on this project have been creative in responding to the retrospective's multiple goals. The Mellon Foundation has, from the beginning, been supportive of its scope and its importance to the field. The American Express Foundation, the National Endowment for the Arts, and the Japan Foundation have also been key supporters—in particular, Isao Tsujimoto, the president of the Japan Foundation, whose long history with Eiko & Koma has made him sensitive to the notion that new work can be made from old. The Andy Warhol Foundation will fund the exhibition aspect of this project at the Museum of Contemporary Art in Chicago and beyond.

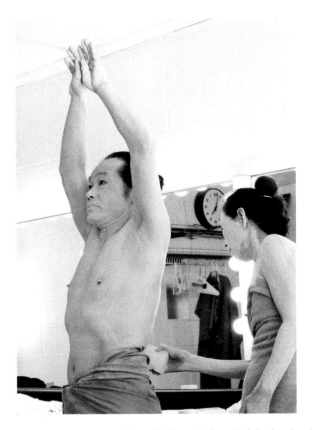

Dressing room, American Dance Festival/Reynolds Theater, Durham, North Carolina, June 2010
Photos: Anna Lee Campbell

Koma at home in New York City, 2010   Photo: Eiko Otake

Setting the stage for a performance of *Raven*, Danspace Project/St. Mark's Church in-the-Bowery, New York City, May 2009
Photo: Anna Lee Campbell

Peter Taub sees Eiko & Koma's art as extending beyond performance. He relates to them as visual artists and in turn has offered them several galleries for installation, meant to exist without their bodies. Koma, in particular, responds to this—the power of the space they make and abandon will be fully examined. Here the visitor will be the living body in places where others once were.

8
Charles L. Reinhart is director of the American Dance Festival (ADF) at Duke University. He and his late wife, Stephanie, first saw Eiko & Koma perform in an East Village loft in 1983. Since then, he has brought Eiko & Koma to ADF seventeen times.

Naked presents two bodies in a dark space (are they breathing?), two bodies as a landscape, whispering, as water falls. The visitors in the Walker's permanent collection galleries are caught between Rauschenberg and Oldenburg and the refuge of the museum café. Sitting, eating my lunch, I think: they are still there. Always, the bodies.

But not in Chicago. At the Museum of Contemporary Art, Chicago, Eiko & Koma will work with curator Peter Taub to create spaces based on the body's presence, an experiment in absence.[7]

And finally (almost), a return to *River*, performed originally from 1995 to 1999, in bodies of water from Delaware to Japan—now to be restored in a rectangle of still water haunted by Henry Moore at Lincoln Center and in the gardens at Duke University one last time for Charles L. Reinhart.[8]

So here we are, you and Eiko & Koma along with their family of friends/collaborators. You are holding this book in your hands—it is what you can take away from your visit to this experiment in time and motion.

It's a small trove you can visit when you miss the meaning found in the rooms and spaces we've left behind. Your memories and your retrospective, carrying you into the future.

And in this future, relationships will have changed. Eiko & Koma are now recognizable as artists, not simply dancers who make hours erode, but sculptors of time and space who are still working, making stories of loss and recovery that challenge the static narratives hanging on gallery walls.

Eiko & Koma know how much of what they make is lost. We now know what might be saved. By saving a little, we are in fact saving a lot. Onstage, in the gallery, outdoors—and within this catalogue—images, voices, histories, words of gratitude and remembrance.

Thanks to Eiko & Koma. Thanks to the Walker Art Center and its inspired team for fully understanding and embracing this project's potential. Thanks to every single individual who participated in this project with such incredible generosity and amazing faith.

Now what shall we do next?

[9] orthogonal eyebeams, radiate

stoppering breath,
stillness

AFTERWORD
Peter Taub

How we survive has always been important. Almost every project has to be sustainable.[1]

1
Eiko Otake in conversation with the author, October 2010.

Often when I think about a life, a trajectory of living over time, I imagine a pattern emerging from the dense web of the world. It's almost as if I need that pattern as evidence of the human effort to create meaning. And at the same time I know, and can't help but enjoy knowing, that the map is not the terrain.

What do we want from a legacy? Is it a sense of continuity? Is it a resolution and closure? Is it the gift of perspective about what's come before, providing a clear place to stand for what comes next? I feel moved by Eiko & Koma's willingness, some forty years into their public career, to take it upon themselves to face this issue, and by characteristically developing a way to do this that is inherently revealing about the questions at hand.

Their Retrospective Project, rather than being completed by the time we see it publicly, gains shape through multiple iterations over three years, its features evolving until it becomes whole. Instead of working with a specific curator, Eiko & Koma are involving multiple arts organizers and curators, mining and folding in their long-term relationships with colleagues and audiences. Their history unfurls along a spiraling path, letting us take the measure of their work and ideas as they themselves come full cycle.

A term such as "legacy" is, naturally enough, foreign to the voices of Eiko & Koma. Their interests are grounded by what they build and how they connect with people through their art. From the time they first committed themselves to being artists in 1971, they have maintained a practice that insists on the simplicity of what is. Their scale is what they have, each other. Their materials are their bodies, in this world. They balance what they can hold, and no more.

Sometimes I'm surprised to realize how good the artists are at seeming normal. I catch myself then, against the broader sweep that pushes me to gain by getting, and to grow by becoming bigger. The quiet urgency of Eiko & Koma tells me to think again. The urgency, as they say, is not a matter of time but a matter of necessity.

> We move through the world as life moves through us:
> we all have bodies, and this is the dance.

Eiko & Koma apply their material bodies, as they were then, as they are today, to make the meaning of their movement. At times they claim not to be trained dancers, and that they instead use physical limitations to define their movement. In an early piece such as *White Dance*, when Eiko lies on her back and dances with her feet in the air, she is learning to dance before she stands. This is how we dream, sleeping, rising from the floor. Works such as *River* harness patterns of nature to shape their movements. Current creations such as *Raven* no longer have space for the speed of youth, and seek a reconciliation between their bodies and mortality.

Art starts with people.

From early on Eiko & Koma chose to accept any invitation to perform, turning each into an opportunity. *The Caravan Project* and other nomadic works take it further by creating a mobile platform. Is this a principle of inclusiveness? A strategy of economy? For me it's stirring, a positive act that preemptively moves the art world closer to people. And it doesn't end with accepting the invitation: with a work such as *Naked*, with the audience a few short feet away, we all gain a clear sense of the importance, and impact, of proximity.

Take what is available, and make it useful.

When they established their company, Eiko & Koma chose a less conventional path, sidestepping the organizational structures that support a company of dancers and the related administrative yoke. Their commitment was to make work as wife and husband, not as a singular project but for a lifetime. They speak of this work together as being no different from that of farmers or fishermen with a daily practice of cycles and schedules, hope and harvest. Taken as a whole, this is sustainable art-making. In the day to day, it's a matter of balancing the intensity of what they delve into with the deepest integrity of the how. It's a practice grounded in being resourceful, determinedly shaping the entirety of what they explore—not only as choreographers and performers, but also as designers and builders.

When Eiko & Koma do involve collaborators—whether musicians Margaret Leng Tan or Robert Mirabal, or performers Anna Halprin or the young Cambodians Charian and Peace—it's a different kind of research. Without knowing what will come, they try to motivate problems that may emerge, and use these to discover the essential knowledge to express.

Their approach to collaborating with artists is extended to organizations. As decidedly independent artists, they maintain direct personal communications with curators and performing arts presenters, establishing close working alliances over extended periods of time. Eiko & Koma embrace these individuals as peers and challenge them as vested partners to jointly reach the best realization of the projects. Through this modest yet committed personal approach, the artists have shaped a curatorial enterprise, consciously animating relations with key organizations and their audiences.

So then, through Eiko & Koma I arrive at a place of example, a place of motivation and possibility. Their clearing of this path, natural as it may seem, is a distinctly political act. Deliberately, embracing the consequences, they move toward art that is focused, strong, available, and ongoing. Eiko & Koma's gift is in showing us the elemental connection between the powerful forces they explore and their insistence on its accessibility. How do we reach it? Through the life around us. How do we sustain it? Their passion is contagious.

2
Koma Otake in conversation with the author, October 2010.

Do it all ourselves. And share everything![2]

CONTRIBUTORS

Philip Bither is the William and Nadine McGuire Senior Curator of Performing Arts at the Walker Art Center.

Suzanne Carbonneau is professor of performance at George Mason University, Washington, DC, and director of the Institute of Dance Criticism at the American Dance Festival, Durham, NC.

Doryun Chong is associate curator of painting and sculpture at the Museum of Modern Art, New York.

Forrest Gander is a writer and translator and the Adele Kellenberg Seaver Professor at Brown University.

Anna Halprin, a dancer, choreographer, and educator, is founder of the San Francisco Dancer's Workshop (1955), co-founder of the Tamalpa Institute (1978), and an early pioneer in the expressive arts healing movement.

David Harrington is the founder, artistic director, and first violinist of the Kronos Quartet.

Jan Henle is an artist known primarily for film drawings related to his large-scale land sculptures.

Jan Willem Hofstra (1907–1991) was an actor, novelist, and journalist known as one of the most influential theater critics of his day.

Miyabi Ichikawa, PhD (1937–1997) was an influential dance critic and scholar who introduced Japanese dance artists to international audiences, and international artists to Japan.

Deborah Jowitt has been a dance critic for the *Village Voice* since 1967.

André Lepecki is associate professor of performance studies at the Tisch School of the Arts, New York University.

Sam Miller, Retrospective Project producer, is the president of the Lower Manhattan Cultural Council, New York City.

Daisuke Mutoh is a dance critic and assistant professor at Gunma Prefectural Women's University, Tamamura, Gunma, Japan.

Irene Oppenheim was a dance/theater critic in San Francisco from 1970–1985. She now writes cultural essays for the *Threepenny Review.*

Dean Otto is associate curator of film and video at the Walker Art Center.

Joan Rothfuss is an independent curator, writer, and educator based in Minneapolis.

Catharine R. Stimpson is a professor and dean emerita of the Graduate School of Arts and Science, New York University.

Peter Taub is director of performance programs at the Museum of Contemporary Art, Chicago.

Philip Trager has been a photographer of dance and architecture since 1966.

SELECTED BIBLIOGRAPHY

Acocella, Joan. "Bare Truths: Eiko & Koma in *Naked.*" *New Yorker* LXXXVII (April 11, 2011): 78–79.

Aloff, Mindy. "Black Milk, Iron Paths, Tree." *The Threepenny Review* 37 (spring 1989): 23–25.

_____. "Dance: Eiko and Koma." *The Nation* (June 14, 1986): 835–836.

Barnes, Fabian, Heidi Ducker, and Eiko Otake. "Leading Off the Beaten Path." *Dance USA* 21 (fall 2005): 22–27.

Bither, Philip. "Eiko and Koma," Joan Rothfuss and Elizabeth Carpenter, eds., *Bits & Pieces Put Together to Present a Semblance of a Whole: Walker Art Center Collections.* Minneapolis: Walker Art Center, 2005.

_____. "Eiko & Koma: *Naked*: Time Is Not Even, Space Is Not Empty." *Walker* magazine (November/December 2010): 14–16.

Bremser, Martha, and Lorna Sanders, eds. *Fifty Contemporary Choreographers.* New York: Routledge, 1999.

Brown, Alan. "Two Striking Dancers Want to Be Understood." *Independent and Gazette* (Oakland, CA), June 6, 1980.

Candelario, Rosemary. "A Manifesto for Moving: Eiko & Koma's Delicious Movement Workshops." *Theatre, Dance and Performance Training* 1 (2010): 1, 88–100.

Chong, Doryun. "Tetsumi Kudo: Proliferating Chain Reaction." *ArtAsiaPacific* 62 (March/April 2009): 96–101.

Chung, Mingder. "Expulse God from the Eden of Dance: A Discourse on Eiko & Koma, the Sacred and the Secular," in *The Art of Sacredness: Tell It Forward with Jerzy Grotowski.* Taipei: Yangzhi Publisher, 2001. (Text in Mandarin)

Eichenbaum, Rose, and Aron Hirt-Manheimer, eds. *The Dancer Within: Intimate Conversations with Great Dancers.* Middletown, CT: Wesleyan University Press, 2008.

Eiko & Koma website, http://www.eikoandkoma.org/.

Huaimin, Lin. "Eiko & Koma." *China Times*, May 26, 1990. (Text in Mandarin)

Josa-Jones, Paula. "Delicious Moving." *Contact Quarterly* 11 (winter 1986): 11–15.

Jowitt, Deborah. "Dancing in Tune with the Earth." *Dance Magazine* 80 (April 2006): 43–44, 46.

Kendall, Elizabeth. "Dance of the Elements." *Elle* 5 (April 1990): 118.

Kloetzel, Melanie, and Carolyn Pavlik, eds. *Site Dance: Choreographers and the Lure of Alternative Spaces*. Gainesville, FL: University of Florida Press, 2009.

Kocache, Moukhtar, and Erin Shirreff, eds. *Site Matters: The Lower Manhattan Cultural Council's World Trade Center Artists Residency, 1997–2001*. New York: Lower Manhattan Cultural Council, 2004.

Kourlas, Gia. "Dance: Strip Down." *Time Out New York*, March 18, 2011.

Kurihara, Nanako. "Eiko and Koma: Movement Approach and Works." Master's thesis. New York University, 1988.

Letton, Shoko Yamahata. "Eiko and Koma: Dance Philosophy and Aesthetic." Master's thesis. Florida State University, 2007.

Misaki, Eri. "Eiko & Koma: 'We Are Even More Confused About Dancing.'" *The Arts Cure* 12 (June 2003): 7–8.

Morgenroth, Joyce. *Speaking of Dance: Twelve Contemporary Choreographers on Their Craft*. New York: Routledge, 2004.

"Movement as Installation: Eiko & Koma in Conversation with Matthew Yokobosky." *PAJ* 64 (January 2000): 26–35.

Otake, Eiko. "A Dancer Behind the Lens," in Judy Mitoma, Elizabeth Zimmer, and Dale Ann Stieber, eds. *Envisioning Dance on Film and Video*. New York: Routledge, 2003.

_____ and Koma, and Deborah Jowitt. Interview with Eiko & Koma. New York Public Library audio archive, 1998. Transcript and 2 audio cassettes.

Perron, Wendy. "Dance Magazine Awards 2006." *Dance Magazine* 80 (November 2006): 32–33.

_____. "East (Coast) Meets West (Coast): Eiko & Koma Meld Styles with Anna Halprin." *Dancemagazine* 75 (October 2001): 69–71, 109.

Peters, Kurt. "Siebzehnter Akademie-Bericht aus Köln." *Das Tanzarchiv: Deutsche Zeitschrift für Tanzkunst und Folklore* 4 (September 1973): 101–125.

Rosloff, Kate. "To See Us Dance Is to See Us Naked." *Dance West* 1 (July 1980): 21.

Trager, Philip. *Faces*. Göttingen, Germany: Steidl, 2005.

_____. *Dancers*. New York: Little, Brown, 1992.

_____. *Retrospective*. Essays by Barbara L. Michaels, Norton Owen, Andrew Szegedy-Maszak, and John Wood. Interview by Stephanie Wiles. Göttingen, Germany: Steidl, 2006.

Windham, Leslie. "A Conversation with Eiko and Koma." *Ballet Review* 16 (summer 1988): 47–59.

Yokobosky, Matthew. "Eiko & Koma: Breath." Exhibition brochure. New York: Whitney Museum of American Art, 1998.

APPENDIX A
Funders and Commissioners

This information was compiled over the years by Eiko & Koma's longtime manager, Ivan Sygoda. Works not listed here were produced and funded by Eiko & Koma.

Be With 2001
Commissioned by the John F. Kennedy Center for the Performing Arts, made possible by a National Dance Project Production Grant and support from the Japan Foundation's Performing Arts Japan program, the National Endowment for the Arts, the Chase Manhattan Foundation, and the Zellerbach Family Fund.

Beam 1983
Commissioned by the 1983 American Dance Festival.

Bone Dream 1985
Made possible with funds from the National Endowment for the Arts. Produced and distributed by ARC Videodance. ©1985 Eiko & Koma, Jeff Bush, and Celia Ipiotis

Breath 1998
Commissioned by the Whitney Museum of American Art (New York). Made possible with support from the Japan Foundation's Performing Arts Japan program and by the Lila Acheson Wallace Theater Fund at New York Community Trust.

Breath (video) 1999
Produced by and included in the Jerome Robbins Archive of the Recorded Moving Image Dance Collection, New York Public Library. Underwritten by the Pew Charitable Trusts and administered at the John F. Kennedy Center for the Performing Arts as well as the National Initiative to Preserve America's Dance. Assisted by the New York State Council on the Arts and the National Endowment for the Arts.

Broken Pieces 1986
Commissioned by CoDanceCo (Nancy Duncan, artistic director) under the auspices of the National Choreography Project.

By the River 1986
Commissioned by Dance Umbrella (Boston), with funds from the Massachusetts Council on the Arts New Works Program. Additional funding provided by the National Endowment for the Arts Inter-Arts Program.

Cambodian Stories 2006
Developed during residencies at Reyum Art School (Phnom Penh, Cambodia) and the Maggie Allesee National Center for Choreography (MANCC) at Florida State University (Tallahassee). Made possible by a National Dance Project Production Grant and support from the Japan Foundation's Performing Arts Japan program, the National Endowment for the Arts Dance Program, the Rockefeller Foundation's Multi-Arts Production Fund, the Andrew W. Mellon Foundation, Asian Cultural Council, and Altria Group, Inc.

Cambodian Stories Revisited 2007
Coproduced by Inta, Inc., Danspace Project (New York), and Asia Society (New York) and made possible in part by the Asian Cultural Council and the National Endowment for the Arts.

Canal 1989
Commissioned by the Walker Art Center (Minneapolis, MN) in collaboration with the Southern Theater and the Minnesota Dance Alliance. Created during a five-week McKnight residency and made possible with funds from the National Endowment for the Arts Inter-Arts Program and the McKnight Foundation.

The Caravan Project 1999
Co-commissioned by Art Awareness (Lexington, NY) and Dancing in the Streets (New York). Developed at Art Awareness during a long-term upstate residency made possible by the New York State Council on the Arts Dance Program. Support was provided by: the Japan Foundation's Performing Arts Japan program, administered by the Japan-United States Partnership for the Performing Arts; Meet the Composer's Composer/Choreographer Project, a national program funded by the Pew Charitable Trusts, Philip Morris Companies Inc. and the Irene Diamond Fund; the Rockefeller Foundation's Multi-Arts Production Fund; a National Dance Project Production Grant, administered by the New England Foundation for the Arts with funding from the National Endowment for the Arts, the Doris Duke Charitable Trust, the Andrew W. Mellon Foundation, and Philip Morris Companies Inc.; and also the National Endowment for the Arts Presentation & Creation Program, the New York State Council on the Arts Dance Program, and the Chase Manhattan Foundation.

Death Poem 2004–2005
Commissioned by the Dance Center of Columbia College (Chicago) and Danspace Project (New York). Also made possible with funding from the National Endowment for the Arts and Altria Group, Inc.

Distant 1994
Developed at Art Awareness (Lexington, NY) during an August 1994 creative residency made possible by the National Endowment for the Arts Dance Program.

Dream 1994
Commissioned by Dance Alloy (Pittsburgh) under the auspices of the National Dance Repertory Enrichment Program.

Duet 2002
Created on the occasion of the presentation to Eiko & Koma of the 2004 Samuel H. Scripps/American Dance Festival Award for lifetime achievement in modern dance, and called on that occasion *Duet for Tonight*.

Echo 1995
Developed at Art Awareness (Lexington, NY) during creative residencies made possible by the National Endowment for the Arts Dance Program. Commissioned by Japan Society. Additional funding from the New York State Council on the Arts and the Harkness Foundations for Dance.

Elegy 1984
Commissioned by the 1984 American Dance Festival in celebration of its 50th anniversary season. Also made possible by the National Endowment for the Arts Dance Program.

Grain 1983
Made possible with funding from the Foundation for Contemporary Performance Art.

Grain 2007
Commissioned by the 2007 American Dance Festival with support from the Asian Cultural Council and the National Endowment for the Arts.

Hunger 2008
Developed during residencies at Vassar College (Poughkeepsie, NY) and the Maggie Allesee National Center for Choreography at Florida State University (Tallahassee). Co-commissioned by the Joyce Theater's Stephen and Cathy Weinroth Fund for New Work and by the Walker Art Center (Minneapolis, MN) with support provided by the William and Nadine McGuire Commissioning Fund. Additional funding provided by the National Endowment for the Arts, the New York State Council on the Arts, and the Andrew W. Mellon Foundation.

Husk 1987
Made possible by a Dance/Film/Video grant from the National Endowment for the Arts. Produced by the Foundation for Independent Artists. ©1987 Eiko & Koma

Lament 1985
Commissioned by the Walker Art Center (Minneapolis, MN) and made possible with funds from the National Endowment for the Arts and the Jerome Foundation (St. Paul, MN). ©1986 Eiko & Koma, James Byrne, Walker Art Center

Land 1991
Co-commissioned by the 1991 Next Wave Festival, the 1991 American Dance Festival, and the Lied Center at the University of Nebraska, Lincoln. Major funding provided by the Rockefeller Foundation's Multi-Arts Production Fund and Meet the Composer's Composer/Choreographer Project.

Memory 1989
Developed at Art Awareness (Lexington, NY) during a July 1989 creative residency made possible by a commissions grant from the Presenting Organizations Program of the New York State Council on the Arts.

Mourning 2007
Commissioned by Japan Society in celebration of its centennial. Funded in part by the National Dance Project of the New England Foundation for the Arts, with lead funding from the Doris Duke Charitable Foundation. Additional funding provided by the Andrew W. Mellon Foundation, the Ford Foundation, and JP Morgan Chase. Support for the creation of *Mourning* was provided by the Japan Foundation's Performing Arts Japan program; the National Endowment for the Arts Dance Program; the New York State Council on the Arts Dance Program; the New York State Music Fund; the American Music Center's Live Music for Dance program; the Andrew W. Mellon Foundation; United States Artists; and Altria Group, Inc.

Naked 2010
Commissioned by the Walker Art Center (Minneapolis, MN) with funding from the William and Nadine McGuire Commissioning Fund, the Andrew W. Mellon Foundation, and the National Endowment for the Arts. Additional support provided by the Andrew W. Mellon Foundation and the National Endowment for the Arts awards to Eiko & Koma. It was developed, in part, during a three-month creative residency at the Park Avenue Armory (New York).

Night Tide 1984
Commissioned by Dance Theater Workshop (New York) under a grant from the Jerome Foundation (St. Paul, MN). Also made possible by National Endowment for the Arts Grants to Dance Companies funding.

Offering 2002
Co-commissioned by Dancing in the Streets (New York), the Walker Art Center (Minneapolis, MN), and the University of Arizona (Tucson). Also made possible with funding from the Japan Foundation's Performing Arts Japan program and the National Endowment for the Arts. The world premiere at the Festival Baltoscandal (Rakvere, Estonia) was made possible with funding from the Trust for Mutual Understanding and Arts International.

Passage 1989
Co-commissioned by the Painted Bride Art Center (Philadelphia), the Dance Place (Washington, DC), and Dance Umbrella (Boston) under the auspices of the National Performance Network Creation Fund, administered by Dance Theater Workshop of New York.

Pulse 1998
Commissioned by the John F. Kennedy Center for the Performing Arts (Washington, DC) with funds from the Doris Duke Charitable Foundation.

Quartet 2007
Commissioned by the 2007 American Dance Festival with support from the Asian Cultural Council and the National Endowment for the Arts.

Raven 2010
Created during a fall 2009 residency at Wesleyan University (Middletown, CT). Commissioned by Danspace Project (New York) with funds from the 2009–2010 Danspace Project Commissioning Initiative. Additional funding was provided by the Andrew W. Mellon Foundation, the New England Foundation for the Arts' National Dance Project, the National Endowment for the Arts, and the Japan Foundation's Performing Arts Japan program.

River (outdoor version) 1995
Supported by the Japan Foundation's Performing Arts Japan program and the Rockefeller Foundation's Multi-Arts Production Fund. Commissioned jointly by Art Awareness (Lexington, NY), the Williams Center for the Arts at Lafayette College (Easton, PA), the Atlantic Center for the Arts (New Smyrna Beach, FL), the American Dance Festival (Durham, NC), the Walker Art Center (Minneapolis, MN), the Jacob's Pillow Dance Festival (Becket, MA), and the Environmental Performance Network, a project of Dancing in the Streets (New York). This commission was made possible, in part, with funds from the National Endowment for the Arts Presenting and Commissioning Program.

River (indoor version) 1997
Made possible with funding support from the Japan Foundation's Performing Arts Japan program, the newly inaugurated Meet the Composer/International Creative Collaborations program funded by the Ford Foundation, the National Dance Project, the National Endowment for the Arts Creation & Presentation Program, and a Lila Wallace-Reader's Digest Arts Partners Project Grant to the Williams Center for the Arts at Lafayette College.

Rust 1989
Commissioned by the 1989 American Dance Festival with funds from the Lila Wallace-Reader's Digest Fund.

Shadow 1986
Commissioned by the 1986 Brooklyn Academy of Music Next Wave Festival.

Snow 1999
Commissioned by the 1999 American Dance Festival with funds from the Doris Duke Charitable Foundation.

Tentacle 1983
Made possible with funds from the National Endowment for the Arts and the Beard's Fund. Produced and distributed by ARC Videodance. ©1983 Eiko & Koma, Jeff Bush, and Celia Ipiotis

Thirst 1985
Made possible by a grant from the Jerome Foundation (St. Paul, MN) and a Guggenheim Fellowship to Eiko & Koma. Additional funding provided by the National Endowment for the Arts Dance Program.

Tree 1988
Commissioned by and premiered at the 1988 Brooklyn Academy of Music Next Wave Festival. Made possible with funding from Art Matters, Inc. and the National Endowment for the Arts Dance Program.

Tree Song 2003–2004
Commissioned by the 2003 American Dance Festival with support from the Doris Duke Awards for New Work and Altria Group, Inc. The work was developed during a residency at the Kaatsbaan International Dance Center (Tivoli, NY) that was made possible with funds from the New York State Council on the Arts. The work's creation was also made possible with funds from the Japan Foundation's Performing Arts Japan program, the Rockefeller Foundation's Multi-Arts Production Fund, and the National Endowment for the Arts.

Undertow 1998
Made possible by a Dance/Film/Video grant from the National Endowment for the Arts. Produced by the Foundation for Independent Artists, Inc. ©1988 Eiko & Koma and James Byrne

Wallow 1984
Made possible with funds from the National Endowment for the Arts. Produced by the Foundation for Independent Artists, Inc. ©1984 Eiko & Koma

When Nights Were Dark 2000
Commissioned by the 2000 American Dance Festival with funds from the Doris Duke Charitable Foundation. The creation of the work was made possible by support from the Doris Duke Fund for Dance of the National Dance Project, a program administered by the New England Foundation for the Arts with lead funding from the National Endowment for the Arts and the Andrew W. Mellon Foundation; Meet the Composer's Composer/Choreographer Project, a national program funded by the Pew Charitable Trusts, Philip Morris Companies, Inc., and the Irene Diamond Fund; the Japan Foundation's Performing Arts Japan program; the Rockefeller Foundation's Multi-Arts Production Fund; the National Endowment for the Arts Presentation and Creation Program; and the New York State Council on the Arts Dance Program. Other support was provided by the Charles and Catherine MacArthur Foundation, the Andrew W. Mellon Foundation, the Lila Acheson Wallace Theater Fund, and the Chase Manhattan Foundation. The 2000–2001 tour of *When Nights Were Dark* was made possible in part with fee support from the National Dance Project.

White Dance (re-creation) 2008
A re-creation of the 1976 work commissioned by the Flynn Center for the Performing Arts (Burlington, VT) with support from the National Endowment for the Arts.

Wind 1993

Created in part during creative residencies at Jacob's Pillow and Art Awareness. Commissioned jointly by the Walker Art Center (Minneapolis, MN), the Jacob's Pillow Dance Festival (Becket, MA), Art Awareness (Lexington, NY), the Krannert Center for the Performing Arts/University of Illinois (Urbana), the Wexner Center for the Arts/Ohio State University (Columbus), the American Dance Festival (Durham, NC, and Salt Lake City, UT), the University of California (Los Angeles), and the Japanese American Cultural and Community Center (Los Angeles). This commission was made possible in part with funds from the National Endowment for the Arts. The composer and choreographer commission fees were made possible by a grant from Meet the Composer's Composer/Choreographer Project, a national program funded by the Ford Foundation and the Pew Charitable Trusts. Additional funding was provided by the Nathan Cummings Foundation, the Greenwall Foundation, the Harkness Foundations for Dance, and the Joyce Mertz-Gilmore Foundation.

APPENDIX B
Other Projects

Choreography for others

Broken Pieces 1986
Premiere: October 23, 1986,
Dance Theater Workshop/
Schönberg Theater, New York City
Length: 30 minutes
Set: Eiko & Koma
Lighting: Eiko & Koma
Costumes: Eiko & Koma
Sound: Indian sarangai music

Created for three members of
CoDanceCo, New York City

Dream 1994
Premiere: February 9, 1994,
City Theater, Pittsburgh
Length: 20 minutes
Set: Eiko & Koma
Lighting: Eiko & Koma
Costumes: Eiko & Koma
Sound: Music by Jon Gibson

Created for five members of the
Dance Alloy Theater, Pittsburgh

Grain 2007
Premiere: June 25, 2007,
American Dance Festival/Reynolds
Theater, Durham, North Carolina
Length: 35 minutes
Set: Eiko & Koma
Lighting: David Ferri
Costumes: Eiko & Koma
Sound: Japanese and Tibetan folk
music played half-speed; Indonesian
gamelan music

A reworking of *Grain* (1983) as a duet for Chakreya "Charian" So and Setpheap "Peace" Sorn

Tetralogies
Evening-length programs of four linked works

New Moon Stories 1986
Premiere: November 18, 1986,
Brooklyn Academy of Music,
New York City
Length: 75 minutes

Eiko & Koma created *New Moon Stories* for their first season at the Brooklyn Academy of Music. The program included *Night Tide*, *Beam*, *Shadow*, and *Elegy*, in that order. *Shadow* was created especially for *New Moon Stories* and was not performed on its own.

Autumn Passage 1995
Premiere: November 16, 1995,
Japan Society, New York City
Length: 70 minutes

This program was commissioned by the Japan Society to celebrate the twentieth anniversary of Eiko & Koma's arrival in the United States. It included the dance video *Husk* as well as *Distant*, *Tree*, and *Echo*. *Echo* was created especially for *Autumn Passage* and was not performed on its own.

Memory 1990
Premiere: January 11, 1990, Playhouse,
University of California, Berkeley
Length: 60 minutes

This program included *Night Tide*, *Memory*, *Rust*, and *Elegy*, in that order.

APPENDIX C
Performance Presenters 1972–2011

Argentina
Primer Festival Internacional de Teatro y
Danza, Buenos Aires (1997)

Austria
Wiener Internationalen Festival Tanz,
Vienna (1982, 1984)

Brazil
Japao–Brasil 100 Anjos: Tokyogaqui/
SESC, São Paulo (2008)
SESC Fortaleza (2008)

Cambodia
Reyum Institute for Arts and Culture,
Phnom Penh (2005, 2006)

Canada
College d'Alma (1981)
College de Chicoutimi (1981)
East West Cultural Center, Vancouver
(1982)
Harbourfront Centre, Toronto
(1989, 1993)
National Arts Center, Ottawa
(1996)
Musée d'art contemporain de Montréal
(1981)
Simon Fraser University, Vancouver
(1982)
Vancouver International Dance Festival
(2003)

China
Guangdong International Theater
Festival, Guangzhou (1995)

Columbia
Teatro Amira de la Rosa, Medellín
(2004)
Teatro Jorge Eliecer Gaitán, Bogotá
(2004)
Teatro Metropolitano, Barranquilla
(2004)

Estonia
7th Baltoscandale Festival, Rakvere
(2002)
Finland
Helsinki Festival (1983)

France
American Center, Paris (1981)
Apartment Festival, Paris (1982)
Avignon Festival (1984)
Millie Club, St. Tropez (1973)

Germany
Akademie der Künste, Berlin
(1984, 1989)
Bayersiche Staatsoper, Munich (1984)
Forum, Leverkusen (1984, 1990, 1994)
International Theater Festival, Munich
(1982)
Jüngen Theater, Göttingen (1973)

Kassel Art Council (1974)
Kulturzirkus, Nuremberg (1984)
Kunstverein, Darmstadt (1982)
Kunstverein, Hannover (1973)
Ludwig-Maximilians-Universität,
Munich (1972)
MAMU Festival, Göttingen (1993)
Mittwoch Theater, Munich (1973)
Munich Dance Festival (1984)
Musikhochschule, Hannover (1988)
Schauspielhaus, Düsseldorf
(1984, 1990)
Schauspielhaus, Wuppertal
(1984, 1990, 1994)
Stadt Theater, Krefeld (1974)
Stadthalle, Neuss (1994)
Summer Dance Academy Young
Choreographers' Competition,
Cologne (1973)
Tanz-forum, Cologne (1984)
Tanzmesse, Düsseldorf (2006)
Theater am Turm, Frankfurt
(1974, 1982, 1983, 1988)
Theater Pro T, Munich (1972)
Theater Scheustrasse, Dortmund (1990)

Great Britain
Cambridge Arts Theatre (1981, 1991)
Chapter Art Center, Cardiff (1987, 1991)
Dance Umbrella (1987)
ICA, London (1981)
Mayfest, Glasgow (1990)
The Place Theatre, London (1981, 1991)
Queen Elizabeth Hall, London
(1981, 1998)
University of Warwick (1981)

Hungary
Arcus Temporum Festival of Pannonhalma
(2006)

Indonesia
Festival Salihara, Jakarta (2009)

Ireland
Dublin Dance Festival (2011)

Israel
Israel Festival, Jerusalem (1989)

Japan
First Intermedia Arts Festival, Tanzawa
(1996)
Hiroshima City Museum of Contemporary
Art (1991, 1996)
JADE International Dance Festival, Tokyo
(2002)
Kirin Plaza, Osaka (1990)
Shirayuri Yochien, Sagamiharashi (1976)
Spiral Hall, Tokyo (1989)
Waseda University, Tokyo (1972)

Korea
Juksan International Arts Festival, Seoul
(1996)
Suwon Hwasung Fortress International
Festival (2000)

Lithuania
Printing House Dance Festival, Vilnius
(2002)

Mexico
City Theater, Enchilada (1979)
Festival del Centro Histórico,
Mexico City (1991)
University of Tijuana (1979)

The Netherlands
De Blauwe Zaal, Utrecht (1984)
Holland Festival: Amsterdam, Den Haag,
Utrecht, Nijmegen, Groningen (1983)
Kosmos, Amsterdam (1973)
Lak Theate, Leiden (1984)
Lantaren, Rotterdam
(1974, 1981, 1983, 1984)
Melkweg, Amsterdam (1973, 1974)
Paradiso, Amsterdam (1973)
Shaffy Theater, Amsterdam (1974)
Stedelijk Museum, Amsterdam (1973)
Toneelschuur, Haarlem (1984)

Poland
Festiwal Teatrów Ulicznych, Jelenia
Góra (2002)
International Contemporary Dance
Festival, Bytom (2001, 2002, 2004)
Manggha Cultural Centre, Krakow (2004)
Plac Litewski, Lublin (2002)
Rynek Nowego Miasta, Warsaw (2002)
Sanocki Dom Kultury, Sanok (2002)

Portugal
Gulbenkian Foundation, Lisbon (1987)

Switzerland
Basel Tanzt (1990)
Berner Tanztage (1991)
International Theater Festival,
Bern (1974)
Performance-Festival, Biel-Bienne
(2004)
Zürcher Theater Spektakel (1982)

Taiwan
National Institute of the Arts, Taipei
(1996)
Novel Hall, Taipei (2000, 2009)

Tunisia
Tabarka Art Festival (1974)

United States
Alabama
University of Alabama, Tuscaloosa
(1995)

Alaska
Alaska Dance Theater, Anchorage
(2007, 2009)
Camai Dance Festival, Bethel (2009)

Arizona
Arizona State University, Tempe
(2001, 2006)
University of Arizona/Pima College,
Tucson (1996, 2003)

California
Cabrillo College, Aptos (1978)
CalArts/REDCAT, Los Angeles
(2006, 2011)

California State University/Carpenter
  Center, Long Beach (2006)
College of Marin, Kentfield (1978)
George Coates Performance Works,
  San Francisco (1991)
Humboldt State University, Arcata (1981)
Japan America Cultural and Community
  Center, Los Angeles (1995, 1997,
  2001)
Joseph Krysiak Production, Mill Valley
  (1978)
Los Angeles Area Dance Alliance (1985)
Los Angeles Institute of Contemporary Art
  (1981)
Monterey Peninsula College (1981)
Oberlin Dance Gallery, San Francisco
  (1977)
San Diego State University (1981)
San Francisco Art Institute (1977)
San Francisco International Theater
  Festival (1982)
San Francisco Museum of Modern Art
  (1978, 1979)
San Francisco Performances
  (1995, 1997)
San Francisco State University (1979)
San Jose State University (1983)
Santa Barbara Museum of Art
  (1978, 1983)
Skirball Cultural Center, Los Angeles
  (2003, 2006, 2011)
Some Serious Business, Los Angeles
  (1977)
Sunset Cultural Center, Carmel (1981)
Sushi Gallery, San Diego (1987)
Theater Artaud, San Francisco (1987)
Theater Gumption, San Francisco (1976)
Theater of Man, San Francisco (1977)
University of California, Berkeley
  (1980, 1990)
University of California, Davis (1978)
University of California, Los Angeles
  (1980, 1995, 1997, 2001, 2007)
University of California, Riverside (2003)
University of California, San Francisco
  (1977, 1980)
University of California, Santa Barbara
  (2008)
University of California, Santa Cruz
  (1979)
University of San Francisco (1978)
Yerba Buena Center for the Arts,
  San Francisco (2002, 2006)

Connecticut
Aldrich Museum, Ridgefield
  (2000, 2009)
Nuclear Freeze Campaign: The Planet
  Hartford (1981)
Trinity College, Hartford (1987)
Wesleyan University, Middletown
  (2002, 2006, 2007, 2009, 2010)

Colorado
Ballet Aspen/Aspen Art Museum (1987)
Colorado College, Colorado Springs
  (1992)
Colorado Dance Festival, Boulder
  (1985, 1987, 1993)
Dance Aspen (1993)

Denver Art Museum (2006)
EcoArts, Boulder (2006)
Naropa Institute, Boulder (1981)
Telluride Dance Festival (1982)
Telluride Institute (1993)

Florida
Atlantic Center for the Arts, New Smyrna
  Beach (1995, 1996)
Dance Umbrella, Miami (1986)
Kravis Center, West Palm Beach (1998)
Florida Dance Festival, Tampa (1990)
Florida State University/Maggie Allesee
  Center for Choreography, Tallahassee
  (2006, 2008, 2009)
Inroads: The Americas/MDCC, Miami
  (1998)
Miami Contemporary Performance Series
  (1990)
Miami-Dade Community College (1996)
Ringling Museum of Art/Historic Asolo
  Theater, Sarasota (2011)
Tigertail Productions/Colony Theater,
  Miami (2011)

Georgia
Arts Festival of Atlanta (1996)
Dancer's Collective, Atlanta (1995, 2000)
Emory University, Atlanta (1982, 2000)
More Productions, Atlanta (1987, 1989)

Hawaii
University of Hawaii, Honolulu (1980)

Illinois
Dance Center of Columbia College,
  Chicago (1997, 2004)
Krannert Center, Urbana (1993)
MoMing, Chicago (1980, 1981, 1986)
Museum of Contemporary Art, Chicago
  (2006, 2011)
Performing Arts Chicago (1999, 2001)

Kentucky
Artwatch, Louisville (1995)
University of Kentucky, Lexington (1996)

Maine
Bates Dance Festival, Lewiston
  (1989, 2002)
Colby College, Waterville (1987)
Maine Festival, Bangor (2002)

Maryland
Theater Project, Baltimore (1981)
Towson State University, Towson (1992)
University of Maryland/Clarice Smith
  Center, College Park (2006, 2011)

Massachusetts
Amherst College (1993)
Boston Dance Umbrella
  (1985, 1986, 1990, 1992, 1997)
Children's Museum, Boston (1979)
Crash Arts, Boston (2003)
Earthdance, Plainfield (2002)
East Street Contemporary Dance, Hadley
  (1985)
Jacob's Pillow Dance Festival, Becket
  (1992, 1993, 1994, 1995, 1997)

MASS MoCA, North Adams (2002)
Museum of Fine Arts, Boston (1979)
Summer Stages Dance, Concord (2008)

Michigan
University of Michigan/Arts on Earth,
  Ann Arbor (2007)
University Musical Society, Ann Arbor
  (1998)

Minnesota
Walker Art Center, Minneapolis
  (1981, 1984, 1989, 1993, 1996,
  2003, 2008, 2010)

Missouri
Dance St. Louis (1990)

Montana
Myrna Loy Center, Helena (2008)
University of Montana, Missoula (1980)

Nebraska
University of Nebraska, Lincoln (1992)

New Hampshire
Dartmouth College, Hanover
  (1991, 2000, 2002, 2006)

New Jersey
Drew University, Union (2005)
Kean College, Elizabeth (1982)
Princeton University (1984)

New Mexico
Armory for the Arts, Santa Fe (1987)
Center for Contemporary Arts, Santa Fe
  (1993)
KiMo Theater, Albuquerque
  (1990, 1996)
Taos Art Association (1990, 1993)
VSA North Fourth Art Center, Albuquerque
  (2005, 2006)

New York
171 Cedar Arts Center, Corning (1999)
Art Awareness, Lexington (1985, 1989,
  1991, 1992, 1993, 1994, 1995,
  1999)
Asia Society, New York City
  (1986, 2004, 2006)
BAM/Harvey: Sam Scripps
  Commemoration, Brooklyn (2007)
BAM/Next Wave Festival, Brooklyn
  (1986, 1988, 1991, 1997, 2000)
Baryshnikov Arts Center, New York City
  (2011)
City Center/Fall for Dance Festival,
  New York City (2004)
Celebrate Brooklyn Festival (1987)
Columbia University/Donald Keene
  Center, New York City (2011)
Cornell University, Ithaca (1984)
Creative Time/Art on the Beach,
  New York City (1980)
Cubiculo, New York City (1976, 1977)
Dance Theater Workshop, New York City
  (1977, 1978, 1984, 1985)
Dance Umbrella Festival, New York City
  (1979)

Dancing in the Streets, New York City
(1999, 2002, 2005)
Danspace Project, New York City
(1997, 2003, 2004, 2005, 2007,
2010)
Donnell Library, New York City (1976)
Dutchess Community College,
Poughkeepsie (1980)
Greene Space, New York City (1981)
Japan Society, New York City
(1976, 1977, 1995, 2007)
Jefferson Community College, Watertown
(1980)
Joyce Theater, New York City
(1990, 1993, 2002, 2008)
June Kelly Gallery, New York City (1999)
Kaatsbaan International Dance Center,
Tivoli (2003)
Kampo Cultural Center, New York City
(1983)
The Kitchen, New York City
(1981, 1987)
Lincoln Center/Library for the
Performing Arts, New York City (1976)
Lincoln Center Outdoor Festival,
New York City (2011)
National Conference on Site Work,
Pocantico Hills (2000)
New York State Council on the Arts/New
Works New Audiences, Syracuse (1989)
Ohio Theater, New York City (1981)
Open Stage Production, New York City
(1980)
Pace University/Movement Research,
New York City (1991)
Park Avenue Armory, New York City
(2011)
Performing Arts in Rhinebeck
(1995, 2003)
Performing Garage, New York City
(1976, 1979)
Riverside Dance Festival, New York City
(1977)
State University of New York, Binghamton
(1991)
State University of New York, Brockport
(1980)
State University of New York, Buffalo
(1983, 1986)
Stony Brook University/Wang Center
(2007, 2008)
Stubblefield's, Boyceville (1999)
Upper Catskill Community Council on the
Arts, Oneonta (1986)
Vassar College, Poughkeepsie (2008)
Whitney Museum of American Art,
New York City (1998)

North Carolina
American Dance Festival, Durham
(1983, 1984, 1985, 1986, 1989,
1990, 1991, 1992, 1994, 1996,
1999, 2000, 2003, 2004, 2007,
2008, 2010, 2011)
Duke University, Durham
(1999, 2003, 2005)
Durham Central Park (2003)
GlaxoSmithKline Auditorium, Durham
(2003)
North Carolina Museum of Art, Raleigh
(2003)

Southeastern Center for Contemporary
Art, Winston-Salem (1986, 1987)
University of North Carolina, Asheville
(2008)
University of North Carolina, Chapel Hill
(2003)
University of North Carolina, Greensboro
(1985)

Ohio
Dance Cleveland (1991)
Heritage Village, Columbus (1987)
Oberlin College (1980, 2003)
Wexner Center for the Arts, Columbus
(1991, 1993)

Oregon
Portland Center for the Visual Arts
(1981, 2003)
Portland State University (1992)
Reed College, Portland (2003, 2007)
University of Oregon, Eugene (1981)

Pennsylvania
Bucknell University, Lewisburg (2001)
Lafayette College, Easton
(1995, 1997, 2000, 2008)
Little Pond Arts Retreat, Nazareth (2000)
The Mattress Factory, Pittsburgh (1988)
Muhlenberg College, Allentown (1979)
Painted Bride Art Center, Philadelphia
(1982, 1989, 1994)
Pennsylvania State University,
Philadelphia (1978)
Philadelphia Museum of Art (1986)
Pittsburgh Center for the Arts (2001)
Pittsburgh Dance Council
(1994, 1997, 1999, 2000)
Swarthmore College (1988, 1997)

South Carolina
Byrne Miller Dance Theater, Beaufort
(1995)
Spoleto Festival USA, Charleston (1986)

Texas
Arts Resources Department, El Paso
(1998)
Carver Community Cultural Center,
San Antonio (1990, 1998)
International Festival of the Arts, Houston
(1991)
Sharir Dance Company, Austin (1989)

Utah
American Dance Festival West, Salt Lake
City (1992)
University of Utah, Salt Lake City (2011)

Vermont
Bennington College (2000, 2005)
Flynn Theater, Burlington
(1992, 1997, 2000, 2002, 2009)
Middlebury College (1997)

Virginia
Virginia Museum of Fine Arts, Richmond
(1985)

Washington
Bumbershoot Festival, Seattle (1980)
Centrum Foundation, Port Townsend
(1986)
Evergreen State College, Olympia (1982)
On the Boards, Seattle
(1982, 1986, 1993, 2003)
Western Washington University,
Bellingham (1980)

Washington, DC
The Dance Place (1985, 1987, 1988,
1989)
Kennedy Center for the Performing Arts
(1998, 2001)
Washington Performing Arts Society
(1992)

Wisconsin
Alverno Presents, Milwaukee (2008,
2011)
Lynden Sculpture Garden (2011)
Wisconsin Union Theater, Madison
(1994)

US Virgin Islands
Island Center, St. Croix (1979)
Reinhold Theater, St. Thomas (1979)
Virgin Islands Council of the Arts,
St. Croix (1976)

REPRODUCTION CREDITS

Images

26 (top and bottom), 27, 32–33, 62, 34, 35, 102–103 www.mariongray.com 92–93, 100–101, 218–219, 32–33 Courtesy Eiko & Koma

41 (top) theimagephoto.com; (bottom) Courtesy Takashima Folk Museum, Otaru, Japan

42 (top) Courtesy the Maggie Allesee National Center for Choreography

56 Gelatin silver print, 18 7/8 x 28 in. (48.0 x 71.2 cm). Gift of the photographer. The Museum of Modern Art, New York, NY, US. Digital Image © The Museum of Modern Art/ Licensed by SCALA/ Art Resource, NY

61 (top) *Impo tetsugaku—impo bunbuzu to sono howa bubun ni okeru hogo domuno hassei*. Plastic bowls, paper, cotton, plastic, polyester, duct tape, lightbulbs, string, magazine pages. Dimensions variable. Collection Walker Art Center, Minneapolis, T. B. Walker Acquisition Fund, 2009; (bottom) Courtesy Oshima Productions Ltd.

64 (top) Courtesy ACT UP, New York; (bottom) Courtesy the estate of David Wojnarowicz and P.P.O.W Gallery, New York

68 Courtesy the Maruki Gallery, Saitama, Japan (Tokyo: Potsdam Shoten, 1950)

69 (Printed 1991). Gelatin silver print, 19 15/16 x 16 in. (50.6 x 40.6 cm). San Francisco Museum of Modern Art Accessions Committee Fund

70–71 © Shogo Yamahata/Courtesy IDG Films

72, 77 (top and bottom), 79, 160–161, 182–183, 244–245, 250–251, 252–253 Courtesy Walker Art Center

82–83 www.marcusleatherdale.com

164–165 Courtesy Jay Anderson and the American Dance Festival

170–171 Courtesy Jacob's Pillow Video Archive

180–181 Courtesy Twilight Studios, New York

199 Courtesy Bruce R. Feeley and the American Dance Festival

202–203 Produced by the New York Public Library for the Performing Arts, Jerome Robbins Dance Division

209 Courtesy Anna Halprin

228–229 www.numberedcopy11.com

261–269 Courtesy Jan Henle

271–279 Courtesy Philip Trager

Unless otherwise noted, all photographs are courtesy Eiko & Koma.

Texts

1, 12, 16, 44, 54, 80, 258, 280, 288, 304 Excerpts from Forrest Gander's poem "Schematic" are published with permission from the author.

88 "In Their Dance No Wind Blows" is reprinted with permission from the *Village Voice*, February 2, 2011.

105 "Eiko and Koma: The Stage as a Cutting Board" is published with permission from the author.

138 "The Lure of Death and the Thirst for Life…Expressed in Dance" is reprinted with permission from the author's estate.

209 "*Be With*: Collaboration as Process" is published with permission from the author.

224 "The Life Behind *Death Poem*" is published with permission from the author.

233 "Eiko & Koma, *Cambodian Stories*" is reprinted with permission from the author.

255 "Eiko+Koma+Kronos" is published with permission of the author.

282 "The Limits of Language" is published with permission from the author.

290 "Afterword" is published with permission from the author.

INDEX

Boldface page references refer to illustrations. Footnotes are indicated with "n" followed by the footnote number. All works are by Eiko & Koma unless otherwise attributed.

A

Admiring La Argentina
  (Ohno and Hijikata), **24**, 25n14
Agamben, Giorgio, 68
AIDS crisis, 64, 145
Alive from Off Center
  (television show), 74
American Dance Festival, 38, 119,
  162, 222, **282**
ankoku butoh, 25
Anpo, 59
Artaud, Antonin, 23
Art on the Beach, 107
The Ascension (Branca), 104n2
Asian American experiences, 65
atomic bombings, 39, 68, **70–71**, 174
Ausdruckstanz, 25
Autumn Passage, 151, 157, 178, 296
Aysola, Lakshmi, **40**, 216

B

Basquiat, Jean-Michel, 65
Beam, 38, 119, **120–121**, 293
Before the Cock Crows
  creation and description, 35, 63, 97
  essay, 105
  promotional flyer, **98**
  rehearsal photo, **99**
Bessie Award, 174n2
Be With (with A. Halprin and
  Jeanrenaud), 208, **209**, **210–211**,
  293
Be With sketches (L. Halprin), **209**
Bijutsu Techo (magazine), 59
Black, Jeffrey, 162
Blake, William, 113
Blu, 147
Bone Dream (with Bush and Ipiotis),
  134–135, 136, 293
Branca, Glenn, 35, 104
  See also *Fluttering Black*
Breath (living installation)
  commission and funding, 293
  creation and description, 39, 49,
    74n4, 192
  performances, **190–191**
  as predecessor to other works, 254
Breath (video, with Pantzer), 201, **202**,
  203, 293
Broken Pieces, 293, 296
Bush, Jeff, 124.
  See also *Bone Dream*; *Tentacle*
butoh, 23, 86
Byrne, James, 74, 144, 145, 156.
  See also *Lament*; *Undertow*
By the River (formerly *Eye Below*), **38**,
  147, **148–149**, 293

C

Caillois, Roger, 50
Calienes, Jennifer, 284n4

Cambodian Stories (with Charian
  and Peace), 42, 66, **230–231**,
  232–234, 294
Cambodian Stories Revisited
  (with Charian and Peace), 66, 235,
  236–237, 294
Campbell, Clayton, 147
Canal
  commission and funding, 294
  creation and description, 74–75, 162
  performances, **160–161**
  performances developed from, 169
The Caravan Project
  commission and funding, 294
  creation and description, 41, 193, 291
  installation-performances, **41**,
    194–195, **196–197**
  sequels to, 206
Carroll, Bob, 35, 63, 113
Catskill Mountains, **37**, 37–38,
  125, 179
Cell, 112
Center for Creative Research (CCR), 283
Charian (Chakreya So). See also *Hunger*
  background, 66–67
  Cambodian Stories, with Peace, Eiko
    and Koma, 42, 66, **230–231**,
    232–234, 294
  Cambodian Stories Revisited, with
    Peace, Eiko and Koma, 66, 235,
    236–237, 294
  Grain (2007), with Peace, 240,
    294, 296
  Quartet, with Peace, Eiko and Koma,
    42, **238–239**, 240, 295
Chmiel, Manja, 27, **27**, 106
Coffin Dance. See *Offering*
collaboration, 52, 241, 284n3,
costume development, 37, 42, 52.
  See also specific titles
Collaborating with Eiko & Koma (Trager),
  270, 283n1, **271–279**

D

Dance for Camera: Selected Works
  (film program), 73n3
dancesculptures, 49, 51, 52–53
Dancing in Water (documentary film),
  75n10
daraku, 23n10
death, as theme
  AIDS crisis, 145
  atomic bomb experiences, 39, 68
  generational bonds, 240
  nakedness and, 43
  process and experience of, 131, 147,
    175, 225
  suicide and afterlife, 67–68
  World Trade Center attacks, 41–42,
    76, 216
Death Poem
  commission and funding, 293
  creation and description, 42, 225
  performances, **226–227**, **228**, **229**
  reviews, 224
Delicious Movement Workshop, 19n3,
  76, 150–1
Diary of a Shinjuku Thief (Oshima), 61, **61**
Dirt Band, 113
Distant, 178, 293, 295
Domon, Ken, 68
Donohue, Bill, 64–65n11

Double Suicide (Shinoda), 67–15
Dream, 293, 295
*Drifting on Melody Smoke/A Flower
  Opening to the Moon* (Henle)
  260, **261–269**
Duet, **220–221**, 222, 293

E

Echo, 178, 293, 294
Eiko (Eiko Otake)
  on art, 20
  awards, 222
  background and early years, 21–23,
    23, 57–65
  on body physicality, 19n5
  on dance as process, 63–64, 105
  dance training, 23, 25, 27, 62, 106
  as first-generation Asian Americans, 65
  with Koma, American Dance Festival
    dressing room, **285**
  with Koma, early performances, **26**, **62**
  with Koma and Bither, McGuire
    Theater stage, **79**
  with Koma and Miller, American
    Dance Festival, **282**
  legacy, 290–291
  on movement, 19n3, 76
  partnership with Koma, description,
    20, 52
  on time, 73
Eisenstein, Sergei, 23
Elegy, 131, **132–133**, 144, 294, 296
Eno, Brian, 73, 78
Entropy, 112
environments, stage, 38, 39, 52, 66
Event Fission
  creation and description, 35, 63, 107
  performances, **34**
  photos, **108**, **109**
Eye Below. See *By the River*

F

Fellini, Federico, 59
Fire in My Belly (Wojnarowicz),
  64–65n11
Fission, 35, 107, **110–111**, 112
Fluttering Black (with Branca)
  creation and description, 35, 63, 104
  music recordings, 104n2
  performances, **34**, **100**, **101**,
    102–103
  promotional flyers, **98**
  reviews, 105–106
Freeman Center for East Asian Studies,
  283
From Trinity to Trinity (Hayashi),
  39n21, 42n31, 68
Fur Seal
  creation and description, 35, 63, 96
  other performances using
    choreography from, 241
  performances, **94–95**
  programs, 48
  promotional flyers, **98**
  reviews, 106
  videos inspired by, 130
"Fur Seal" (Eiko Otake), 96

G

Gander, Forrest, **304**
Geary, David, 147, 169
German Expressionism, 25, 105

Ginsberg, Allen, 35, 63, 64, 113
Godard, Jean-Luc, 23, 59
Gogh, Vincent van, 25
Gordon, Beate, 31
Grain (1983)
    commission and funding, 294
    creation and description,
        37–38, 118
    performances, 66, 74
    studio photos, **36**, **116–117**
Grain (2007), 240, 294, 296
Grotowski, Jerzy, 20

H
Halprin, Anna, 208, 209.
    See also *Be With*
Halprin, Lawrence: *Be With* sketches,
    209, **209**
Harrington, David, 255
Hayashi, Kyoko, 39n21, 42n31, 68
Henle, Jan, *Drifting on Melody Smoke/
    A Flower Opening to the Moon*, 260,
    261–269.
hibakusha, 68.
    See also atomic bombings
Hide and Seek (exhibition), 64–65n11
Hijikata, Tatsumi
    Admiring La Argentina, with Ohno,
        24, 25n14
    dance forms cofounded by, 23, 25
    Rebellion of the Body, 23
    as teacher and influence, 25, 62
Hiroshima-Nagasaki Document 1961
    (Domon), 68
Hiroshima Notes (Oe), 68
Hofstra, Jan Willem, 87
horizonality, 49–50, 51–52
Hoving, Lucas, 27, 31
human pole, 119
Hunger (with Charian and Peace)
    commission and funding, 294
    creation and description, 42, 50, 66,
        76, 246
    performances, 76, **244–245**
Husk
    commission and funding, 294
    creation and description, 38, 50
    tetralogy programs including, 296
    video stills from, **152–153**
Hussie-Taylor, Judy, 284n5

I
Ichikawa, Miyabi, 138
Ideology of Desolate Solitude
    (Takahashi), 23
insufficiency, 19
Inumo arukeba boni ataru (saying),
    57n1
Ipiotis, Celia, 124. See also *Bone
    Dream*; *Tentacle*
Isamu Noguchi (exhibition), 104
Ishimure, Michiko, 23

J
Japan, postwar, **21**, 22, 57–59, **60**, 68
Jeanrenaud, Joan, 209. See also *Be With*
Jennings, Joseph, 206
Jooss, Kurt, 27
Jowitt, Deborah, 31, 88
Judson dance movement, 31

K
Kadensho (Motokiyo), 25
kamishabai, 41, 193
Kanba, Michiko, 59n6
Kaneko, Mitsuharu, 48n2, 89,
    92–93, 96
kanji, 67
Kara, Juro, 59, 61
kawa no youni neru, 67
Killacky, John, 74–75
Koma (Takashi Koma Yamada)
    awards, 222
    background and early years, 21, **21**,
        22, 58–65
    dance training, 23, 25, 27, 62, 106
    with Eiko, early performances, **26**, **62**
    with Eiko and Bither at McGuire
        Theater stage, **79**
    with Eiko and Miller at American
        Dance Festival, **282**
    with Eiko at American Dance Festival
        dressing room, **285**
    as first-generation Asian Americans, 65
    at home in New York City, **286**
    legacy, 290–291
    on movement, 19n3
    partnership with Eiko, description,
        20, 52
    with Reyum Painting Collective, 42, **42**
Krakauer, David, 76, 216
Kronos Quartet, **184**, 186, 255
Kudo, Tetsumi
    as influence, 59, 61, 62
    Philosophy of Impotence, 61, **61**
Kusuma, Yayoi, 63

L
La Argentina, 25n14
Laban, Rudolf, 25
Lament (with Byrne)
    commission and funding, 293
    creation and description, 74, 144
    other performances using, 75, 179
    reviews, 145
    video stills from, **142**, **143**
Land (Mirabal CD), 174n2
Land (with Mirabal)
    commission and funding, 293
    creation and description, 39, 49, 174
    performances, with Mirabal and
        Sandoval, 38, 75
    publicity photos, **172–173**
Leng Tan, Margaret, 241, **243**.
    See also *Mourning*
Lerner, Sandra, 174, 178
Light (Takei), 27n16
Long Now, 73, 78
Lower Manhattan Cultural Council, 41
Ly, Daravuth, 42

M
MacArthur Foundation Fellowship,
    39, 224
The Making of Cambodian Stories (film),
    232
MANCC (Maggie Allesee National Center
    for Choreography), 284
Manen, Hans van, 27
Maruki, Iri and Toshi, *Pika don*, **68**
Memory (1989), **166–167**, 168,
    294, 295
Memory (tetralogy), 131, 168, 296

Mercé y Luque, Antonia, 25n14
Mirabal, Robert, **38**, 75, 174, 284.
    See also *Land*; *Wind*
Moorman, Charlotte, 35
Moriyama, Daido: *Stray Dog, Misawa*,
    56, 58
"A Moth" (Kaneko, Eiko adaptation), 89,
    92–93
Motokiyo, Zeami, 25
Mourning (with Leng Tan)
    commission and funding, 293
    creation and description, 42, 49,
        50, 241
    performances, **242–243**
movement
    as installation (dancesculptures), 49,
        51, 52–53
    philosophies of, 19n3, 67, 76, 105
    as sound, 48–49, 104
    stage environment and, 38, 39
    workshops and manifestos on,
        76, 150n1
Mutoh, Daisuke, 233–234

N
Naked
    commission and funding, 294
    creation and description, 19, 49, 67,
        74, 254
    installation-performances, 73, 78,
        250–251, **252–253**
    as Retrospective Project program,
        284, 287
    studies for, **10–11**, **18**
nakedness
    as art theme, 19, 42, 43
    and costume development, 37
    as life philosophy, 68–69
Naropa Institute, 113
nature, as theme, 37–38, 39
Neue Tanz, 25
New Dance USA Festival, 74
New Moon Stories, 75, 119, 131,
    150, 295
Next Wave Festival, 75–76
Night Shockers, 25
Night Tide
    commission and funding, 294
    creation and description, 37–38,
        125, 295
    performances, **37**, 75–76, **126–127**
    videos inspired by, 136
Niigata, Japan, 21, **21**, 58
Nijinsky, Vaslav, 27, 105
9/11 attacks, 41–42, 76, 216
Nurse's Song, 35, 63, 113, **114–115**

O
Oe, Kenzaburo, 23, 68
Offering (formerly *Coffin Dance*)
    commission and funding, 294
    creation and description, 41–42,
        49, 216
    performances, **40**, 76, **212–213**,
        214, **215**
Ohno, Kazuo
    Admiring La Argentina, with Hijikata,
        24, 25n14
    dance forms cofounded by, 25
    as teacher and influence, 25, 61, 62
Ono, Yoko, 62
Oppenheim, Irene, 31, 105–106, 147

Oshima, Nagisa, 23, 59, 61, **61**
Otake, Shin, **38**, 38–39
Otake, Yuta, **38**, 38–39, 174, 175, **176, 177**
Otto, Dean, 73n3, 145
Out There festival, 76
Ozawa, Seiji, 62

P
Pantzer, Jerry, 201.
    See also *Breath* (video)
Park Avenue Armory residency, 67n13, 284
Passage, 162, 169, **170, 171**, 295
Peace (Setpheap Sorn). See also *Hunger*
    background, 66–67
    Cambodian Stories, with Charian,
        Eiko & Koma, 42, 66, **230–231**, 232–234, 293
    Cambodian Stories Revisited, with
        Charian, Eiko & Koma, 66, 235, **236–237**, 293
    Grain (2007), with Charian, 240, 293, 295
    Quartet, with Charian, Eiko &
        Koma, 42, **238–239**, 240, 295
Perniola, Mario, 51, 52
Philosophy of Impotence (Kudo), 59, 61, **61**
Pika don, Marucki and Marucki, **68**
Piñero, Miguel, 64
Poison Dance, 25
political activism, 20, 22, 59, **60**, 61
Poor Art, 20, 38
Praise Choir Singers, 206
Pulse, 187, **188, 189**, 295

Q
Quartet (with Charian and Peace), 42, **238–239**, 240, 294

R
Rainer, Yvonne, 51
Raven
    commission and funding, 295
    creation and description, 42–43, 50, 67, 247, 284, 291
    performances, **77, 248–249**
    stage setting, 286
Rebellion of the Body (Hijikata), 25
reciprocal topographies, 52
Reinhart, Charles, 38, 240, 287
Reinhart, Stephanie, 38, 287n8
Retrospective Project
    banners for, **282**
    concept and development, 73, 76, 78, 283–284, 290
    funding for, 284n6
    performances, 19, 42–43, 73, 89, 284, 287
Reyum Institute of Arts and Culture, 42, 66, 232, 233
Reyum Painting Collective, **42**, 225, 232, 235
River (indoor version), **184–185**, 186, 287, 295
River (outdoor version)
    commission and funding, 295
    creation and description, 39, 179, 290
    performances, 75, 76, **77, 180, 181, 182–183**
Rothko, Mark, 65
Rust, 163, **164–165**, 295, 296

S
Sakaguchi, Ango, 23
Sam, Sam-Ang, 232
Sandoval, Ben, **38**
Satoh, Somei, 186
"Schematic" (Gander), **304**
Scripps American Dance Festival Award
    for Lifetime Achievement in Modern
    Dance, 222
"Seals" (Kaneko), 48n2, 96
set development and environments, 38, 39, 52, 66.
    See also specific titles
Shadow, 38–39, 150, 295, 296
shinju, 67
Shinoda, Masahiro, 67n15
Short Now, 73
Silence = Death (ACT UP poster), 64, **64**
Silence = Death (Praunheim film), 64, **64**
Snow, **199**, 200, 294
So, Chakreya. See Charian
Songs of Innocence (Blake), 113
Sorn, Setpheap. See Peace
soundscapes, 48–49, 51, 104, 139, 169
space, as theme, 43, 48, 50–51, 52
Stanton near Forsyth (Wong), 64
Static, 36, 104
Stearns, Robert, 74
Stimpson, Catharine R., 224
Stray Dog, Misawa (Moriyama), **56**, 58
suicide, double, 67–68
sustainability, 76, 290
sustained mourning, 42n31
Sutrisno, Joko, 76

T
Takahashi, Kazumi, 23
Takei, Kei: *Light*, 27n16, 74
teleplasty, 50
Tentacle (with Bush and Ipiotis)
    commission and funding, 295
    creation and description, 124
    other performances using, 74, 118
    video stills from, **122, 123**
Thirst, 138, 139, **140–141**, 294
time
    elasticity and, 73
    horizontality and, 49–50
    movement and, 52–53
    nakedness and effects of, 43
    philosophies of, 19, 39, 43, 73–78
Tokyo, Japan, **21**, 21–23
Tomatsu, Shomei: *Time Stopped at
    11:02*, 68, **69**
Town of Love and Hope (Oshima), 61
Trager, Philip, 270, **271–279**
Tree
    commission and funding, 295
    creation and description, 157
    performances, **157, 158**
    reviews, 138
    tetralogy programs including, 296
Tree Song
    commission and funding, 294
    creation and description, 42, 49, 217
    other performances using choreography
        from, 241
    performances, **218, 219, 258–259**
Trilogy, 2–3, 35, 82–83, 110–111, 112

U
Undertow (with Byrne), **154, 155**, 156, 295
unreasonableness, 20
The US–Japan Mutual Cooperation and
    Security Treaty, 59

V
Video Choreography (film program), 73n3, 145
visual soundscapes, 48–49

W
Wallow
    commission and funding, 294
    creation and description, 48–49, 50, 130
    performances, **46–47, 128–129**
Waterways, 75n12
website, 83
Weisberg, Judd, 39
When Nights Were Dark, 41, **204–205**, 206, 295
White Dance
    commission and funding, 295
    creation and description, 27, 62, 74, 86, 290
    performances, **28–29, 30**, 31, 42–43, **84–85**
    as Retrospective Project program, 284
    reviews, 87–88
White Dance: Moth
    creation and description, 86, 89
    performances, 31, **31, 72**, 74, **90–91**
    program pages, **32–33, 92**, 92–93, **93**
    reviews, 106
Wigman, Mary, 25, 27, **27**, 106
Wind (with Mirabal)
    commission and funding, 296
    creation and description, 75, 175
    performances, **38, 39, 176, 177**
Wojnarowicz, David, 64, **64**
Wong, Martin: *Stanton near Forsyth*, 64
World Trade Center
    9/11 attacks and national trauma
        themes, 41–42, 76, 216
    performances using images of, 34, 107, **108, 109**
wounded body, 37
Wyeth, Georgia, 217
Wyeth, Sharon Dennis, 217

Y
Yokobosky, Matthew, 39, 49, 192
Yokoo, Tadanori, 59, 61
Young Choreographers' Competition, 27, **84–8**5, 86

Z
Zengakuren Tokyo Student Protests, 59n6

SCHEMATIC

Forrest Gander

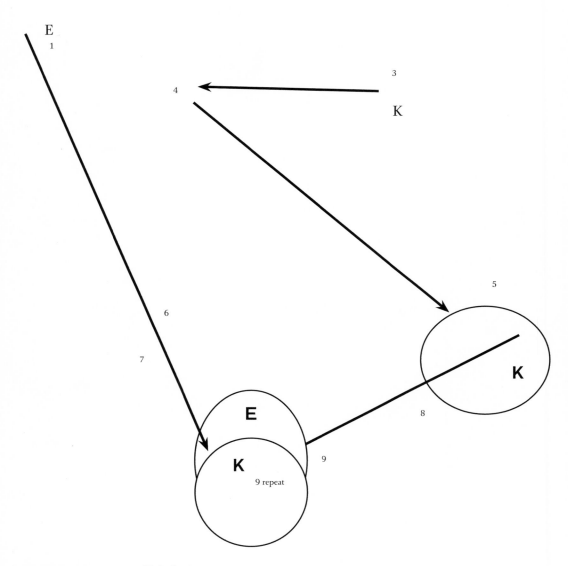

[1] forestalling step, irrotational lift of wrist
[2] breathing through skin, blow arms out
[3] arrow stage right, sucking air
[4] lingering six heartbeats, splay thumbs, resisting inertia
[5] monkey-pant Ai! (愛), contract right buttock, going yellow
[6] reversing shoulder forward, cleaving, limpfalling away
[7] Koma mirroring Eiko mirroring
[8] release weight upward, offering throat, constellate center stage
[9] orthogonal eyebeams, stoppering breath, radiate stillness